A CENTURY OF
GRAND PRIX
MOTOR RACING

A CENTURY OF
GRAND PRIX
MOTOR RACING

Compiled by Anthony Pritchard

Foreword by Stirling Moss

MOTOR RACING PUBLICATIONS

Dedication

Motor racing tends to concentrate on the drivers and the cars. The designers and engineers tend to be forgotten. One of the names mentioned here would be far less well known to the general public if he had not allegedly been involved in a major financial scandal.

A major technical innovation can be conceived by the chief engineer and implemented by his assistants. Or it can be conceived by an assistant and authorized and encouraged by the chief engineer – as in the case of Lotus and 'ground effect'. Accordingly, in the two tributes below I have chosen to use the word 'creator', as I think it is a more appropriate general term.

This book is dedicated to the memory of two of the greatest automobile engineers whose intellects did much to advance motor racing design and technology:

Vittorio Jano, of Fiat, Alfa Romeo, Lancia and Ferrari; creator of the Alfa Romeo P2 and Monoposto, the Lancia DSO and the Ferrari Dino; perfecter of the V6 engine.

Colin Chapman, of Lotus, consultant to Vanwall and BRM; creator of the Lotus 18, 33, 49, 70 and 79 Formula 1 cars amongst many others; creator of the original Lotus Elite, one of the finest road cars ever raced.

Two men of different nationalities, intellects, tastes and ambition, but with the common purpose of advancing Grand Prix racing.

British Library Cataloguing in Publication Data

Pritchard, Anthony
A century of Grand Prix motor racing. – New, rev., expanded ed.
1. Grand Prix racing – History – 20th Century
1. Title II. Grand Prix Racing
796.7'2'0904

ISBN 1899870385

Published in 1998 by
Motor Racing Publications Ltd
Unit 6 The Pilton Estate, 46 Pitlake, Croydon CR0 3RY
© Motor Racing Publications Ltd and Anthony Pritchard 1991 and 1998

Designed by Chris Hand

Printed in England by
The Amadeus Press,
Huddersfield, West Yorkshire

CONTENTS

FOREWORD

Motor racing has been my life – my consuming passion and my professional career. And my life inevitably has become part of motor racing history. Although I drove a pre-war BMW '328' in a number of events, my serious career started in 1948 with a Cooper 500 and lasted until my crash at Goodwood in 1962.

This anthology of Grand Prix racing spans a period of over 100 years, with many classic pieces of motor racing journalism, but I found especially nostalgic those sections that cover the rise of Great Britain from a motor racing nonentity to becoming the leading motor racing nation. This was the era when I was racing and nothing gave me greater satisfaction than to win at the wheel of a British car.

In 1950-1 I drove for John Heath's HWM team which was such a successful British pioneer in Formula 2 and so I enjoyed the extract from Alf Francis' book on how we ran the cars in the 1950 Bari Grand Prix and Alf later became my own mechanic. I tested (but did not race) the Vl6 BRM

and David Hodges' and Harry Mundy's profile of this disastrous design brings back to me the full horrors of the BRM's many shortcomings. Much space is properly devoted to the efforts of Tony Vandervell who finally defeated the might of Italy with his Vanwalls and I drove for Vanwall in 1957-58 . And Mike Hawthorn's description of the 1958 Moroccan Grand Prix reminds me only too well how I was so narrowly defeated in that year's World Championship.

These are just a few of the over forty extracts and articles republished in *Grand Prix Racing: The Enthusiast's Companion*. Most of these will be new to readers who will find that they provide a fine insight into motor racing and motor racing personalities of the past. I wish the book every success.

Stirling Moss
London
1991

AUTHOR'S NOTE

A Century of Grand Prix Motor Racing, which is an updated edition of my earlier book *Grand Prix Racing: The Enthusiast's Companion*, is intended as a motor racing book that is very different from any of its predecessors: the evolution and history of Grand Prix racing is told in words and photographs with a broad selection of classic motor racing writing of the past to enliven and enrich the story.

Many of the articles and extracts are from magazines that will not have been seen by most enthusiasts or from books that have long been out of print. Researching these parts of the book brought back many happy memories and reminded me of the very high standards of so many motor racing writers. I enjoyed reading these again and hope that they will give as much enjoyment to the reader.

I am very grateful to all the writers and publishers who have given consent for the reproduction here of articles and extracts and I owe an especial debt of thanks to the late Cyril Posthumus, who was so helpful in making available difficult to find photographs of the early days of motor racing.

In every case consent was sought for the reproduction of the articles and extracts, but there is little doubt, in certain cases, that there is confusion as to who is the copyright holder. If any extract has been reproduced without the correct consent, we can only apologize and endeavour to make amends.

Anthony Pritchard
Ruislip, Middlesex
1991 and 1998

Grand Prix Milestones

It is interesting to speculate on the cars that have proved the real milestones, not necessarily technically, in Grand Prix history. This is a personal list of the top 20 (with reasons), but I have not extended my list back to the very earliest days.

Peugeot 7.6-litre, 1912
Small engine, four valves per cylinder, twin overhead camshaft, designed by Ernest Henry.

Mercedes 4.5-litre, 1914
Superb overall, but conventional design, and superb race organization, winner of the 1914 French Grand Prix.

Duesenberg, 1921
Winner of the 1921 French Grand Prix that pioneered hydraulic brakes in racing.

Fiat Tipo 804, 1923
Introduced superchargers to Grand Prix racing.

Alfa Romeo P2, 1924
Its successes gave the first clear demonstration of the genius of designer Vittorio Jano.

Bugatti Type 35, 1924
It and its successors won more races than any other Grand Prix car, despite its reactionary design.

Alfa Romeo Monoposto, 1932
The ultimate in traditional racing cars, superbly engineered, winner of many races and another tribute to the genius of Jano.

Mercedes-Benz W25, 1934
(together with Auto Union Type A) pioneered light stiff tubular chassis construction with independent suspension and very powerful engine to exploit to the limit the 750 kg regulations.

Alfa Romeo 158, 1938
First appearance of the car that was to dominate early post-war Grand Prix racing.

Ferrari Tipo 500, 1952
Strictly a Formula 2 car, but Grand Prix racing was held to Formula 2 rules in 1952-53. Probably the most successful Grand Prix car ever, as it won 15 races in succession during two years.

Mercedes-Benz W196, 1954
A triumph of development and organization over design, it dominated racing in 1954-55.

Lancia D50, 1954
Jano's design was well in advance of its time and showed other designers what they should be doing.

Vanwall, 1956
The scientific application of aerodynamics (by Frank Costin).

Cooper-Climax, 1959
The first rear-engined car to win the World Championship (Jack Brabham).

Lotus 25-Climax, 1962
First successful monocoque Grand Prix car (but certainly not the first). Driven by Jim Clark to maximum points World Championship victory in 1963 and repeated by him in 1965 with its successor, the 33.

Lotus 49-Cosworth, 1967
First car to use the Cosworth-Ford V8 engine that was to dominate Formula 1 for 15 years. Used engine as a stressed member (but did not pioneer this feature).

Lotus 72-Cosworth, 1970
Superbly designed, 'long-lived' Formula 1 car raced by Lotus for six seasons and won two World Championships.

Lotus 78-Cosworth, 1977
The birth of the 'wing' car.

Renault RS01, 1977
The first turbocharged Formula 1 car.

McLaren MP4/1, 1980
John Barnard design that pioneered carbon-fibre construction.

Part 1: PIONEERING DAYS, 1895-1914

Controversy still reigns as to who was responsible for the birth of the motor car, but certainly the technical pioneers were Germans Benz and Daimler. It was in France, however, that the concept of motor racing was evolved and French manufacturers were the greatest supporters of the sport in its early years. The first event was not a race, but would perhaps more accurately be described as a 'regularity trial' and was held in 1894 between Paris and Rouen. The results were decided by a panel of judges on a somewhat arbitrary basis and was awarded jointly to a total of 12 Peugeots and Panhard-Levassors, all Daimler-powered and all of which reached Rouen within the time schedule.

1895-1900

A year later a race was held from Paris to Bordeaux and back to Paris and this is regarded as the first motor race proper. The winner was Émile Levassor with his Panhard et Levassor who covered the 1200 km in 48 hours – less than half the expected time. Races followed in Italy a little later in 1895, in New York in 1896 and there were further events in France. Mayade and Markel (with Panhards) took the first two places in the 1897 Paris-Marseilles-Paris race and Panhard again took the first two places in the 1898 Paris-Amsterdam-Paris, first four places in the 1899 Tour de France and first five places in the 1899 Paris-Bordeaux. From 1896 onwards the Panhards were powered by 4-cylinder engines, as were most of the opposition.

In 1900 there was held the first Gordon Bennett race, a series sponsored by American newspaper magnate James Gordon Bennett and to a formula that specified a weight of between 400 and 1000 kg (without driver, co-driver, fuel, oil, water, battery, tools, spares, luggage, etc.) and driver and co-driver had each to weigh at least 60 kg (any shortfall was made up by ballast). It was organized by the Automobile Club de France between Paris and Lyon and it was perhaps the first truly international race as teams were attracted from Belgium, Germany and the United States, as well as France. Almost inevitably the winner was a Panhard, driven by Charron. A Mors driven by Levegh, however, won that year's Paris-Toulouse race.

1901-06

For 1901 and the next five years three classes of racing were established:

Unlimited:	Over 650 kg
Voitures Légères:	250-400 kg
Voiturettes	Less than 250 kg

Although the French Mors and Panhard were the most successful makes in 1901, there appeared a major new development from Germany, the Mercedes. The late Cecil Clutton described the new car – and compared it with its contemporaries in *The Racing Car, Development & Design* (B.T. Batsford Ltd, 1956).

The 1901 Mercedes

'If racing car design during the nineteenth century had little to show by way of progress except increasing size, 1901 was in general a year of great performance.

'To begin with, it saw the effective end of Panhard supremacy, for although they could continue to hold their heads high in the racing field until the end of

One of the most successful drivers of the Veteran era was Fernand Charron who drove for the French Panhard et Levassor company. Here he is seen at the wheel of the 12 hp Panhard which he drove to victory in the 1899 Paris-Bordeaux race at an average of 29.9 mph. *(Cyril Posthumus)*

1904, Mors was clearly the marque of the year in 1901. But although we are told by Charles Jarrott that the 40 hp Panhard of 1901 was a most responsive and charming creature, both it and the Mors remained essentially products of the nineteenth century, with their flimsy wooden frames, quadrant-change gears, constant-speed engines and generally crude and clumsy appearance. They were, in every sense of the word as it is now understood, "Veteran Cars".

Another photograph of Charron, this time with his Panhard et Levassor in the 1900 Gordon Bennett race held between Paris and Lyons, a distance of 353¾ miles; this was yet another race won by Charron. As the car arrives at Lyons, the mechanic is holding the broken water pump against the flywheel to keep it working. *(Cyril Posthumus)*

'By contrast, the 1901 Mercedes was clearly the first "Edwardian", and in many ways, the first modern car.

'The name "Mercedes" itself was new to motoring, for the car should, by all rights, have been a German Daimler. But Daimler had a wealthy and perceptive client in Émile Jellinek, who not only suggested many features of the car which Wilhelm Maybach designed for him at the Daimler works, but suggested that the name "Daimler" provoked a great deal of sales-resistance in France. The new model was accordingly called a "Mercedes", after Jellinek's daughter; and the Daimler was no more heard of.

'The new model was epoch-making in almost every way. The wooden chassis frame gave way to one of pressed steel, and all the wheels were of equal size. It also looked much lower built than its short high contemporaries.

'Gear selection hitherto had been by means of a lever working in a quadrant (or a segment of a circle) whereupon were cut notches representing, successively, reverse, neutral, 1st, 2nd, 3rd and top. Between each pair of gears there was an undefined neutral position, and coupled with the fixed speed engines, silent gear changing was a very difficult achievement, which few, if any, attempted at that time. It is, in fact, possible to change down silently on a quadrant change by using the normal double-declutching technique. That is to say, by waiting until speed on a hill had brought the engine down to, say, 500 rpm; when neutral is selected as the first stage of double-declutching the engine will regain its governed 800 rpm, whereupon the next gear may be silently engaged – provided the vehicle has not by then come entirely to rest. Nor is the process made easier by the somewhat evasive neutral position. When changing upwards, the entire disengagement of the clutch must either be relied upon or the engine slowed down by the decelerator, when fitted, or by neutralising the ignition. It is by no means certain when double-declutching was first thought of, perhaps as early as 1900, and S. F. Edge said that he used it in the Gordon Bennett race of 1902, which he won with a 3-speed Napier with a missing middle gear.

'The Mercedes, by contrast, had the "gate" change which has survived into modern times.

'The Mercedes engine was also much quieter and

flexible than its contemporaries. But Maybach did not yet feel able to control engine-speed by a throttled carburettor, and arranged instead for a variable-lift to the inlet valves, which decided the amount of gas to be sucked into the engine. This, in turn, involved mechanical operation of the inlet valves by a camshaft where other designers were content to have the inlet valve opened atmospherically by the vacuum created in the cylinder by the descending piston . . . Ignition was by low-tension magneto, which, again, was a noteworthy advance in reliability (although not for ease of starting from cold) over the earlier battery and trembler coil . . .

'The old style of radiator consisted of a long pipe bent backwards and forwards into a stack, and fitted with cooling fins. The Mercedes had the much tidier and more sightly honeycomb radiator which remained in use in high quality cars throughout the thirties.'

Clutton also points out that one of the major problems suffered by racing motorists at the time was perpetual tyre trouble, especially on the heavy cars, and that as there were no detachable wheels or rims, punctures had to be repaired by the driver and mechanic in *situ*. The first use of pneumatic tyres in racing had been on André Michelin's Peugeot in the 1895 Paris-Bordeaux-Paris race. Although Michelin failed to finish within the prescribed time because he had so many punctures, initial ridicule of the pneumatic tyre was soon overcome and their use became universal.

The Mercedes was built primarily as a fast tourer, but its influence on racing car design was immense. Panhard was still dominant in 1902, but with one notable exception, the Gordon Bennett, held from Paris to Innsbruck in conjunction with the Paris-Vienna. Only three entries from each country could compete in the Gordon Bennett and S. F. Edge with the Napier was the winner, scoring Britain's first important motor racing success.

The last of the town-to-town races, the Paris-Madrid was held in 1903, but it was stopped short at Bordeaux after a series of fatal accidents including Marcel Renault at the wheel of a car bearing his own name. His brother, Louis Renault, finished second to Gabriel (Mors). Following Edge's 1902 win the Gordon Bennett was scheduled to be held in Great

S.F. Edge, the great British entrepreneur, at the wheel of the British Napier with which he won the 1902 Gordon Bennett race held in Germany over a circuit in the Taunus Mountains. It was Britain's first important international motor racing success. *(Cyril Posthumus)*

Britain and was staged in Ireland over a racing circuit for the first time. Jenatzy won with a Mercedes, from the Panhards of de Knyff and Farman. It was the first major success for the German Daimler company.

This resulted in the 1904 Gordon Bennett being held in Germany, over a circuit in the Taunus mountains and was won by the French Richard-Brasier driven by Théry with Jenatzy's Mercedes in second place. More races were being added to the calendar, the Coppa Florio in Italy, Brescia-Cremona-Montina-Brescia, was won by Vincenzo Lancia with a 14-litre Fiat and victory in the Vanderbilt Cup, promoted by multi-millionaire William K. Vanderbilt on Long Island, New York, went to Heath (Panhard). The final Gordon Bennett race in 1905 was staged in the Auvergne mountains and won again by Théry, although his car was now known simply as a Brasier. In Britain the Tourist Trophy was held for the first time on the Isle of Man, but it was strictly for touring cars, did not attract strong Continental entries, and was won by J. S. Napier with a Scottish Arrol-Johnston from Northey's Rolls-Royce.

1906-11

As France had won the Gordon Bennett Cup outright that was the end of the series, a new race was organized in 1906 in France, the Grand Prix of the Automobile Club de France at Le Mans over two days (it was only later that the term 'Grand Prix' became attributed to all major races) and the winner was Ferencz Szisz with a Renault 90 cv with a 12,986 cc engine and which like the entries from Clément-Bayard and Fiat, featured detachable rims. Renault was also the persistent adherent of shaft drive which eventually became universal. The winner's average for the total of 770 miles was 63.00 mph. This is the account of the race by Gerald Rose from *Record of Motor Racing from 1894 to 1908.*

The 1906 French Grand Prix

The arrangements for the Grand Prix had been early taken in hand, and were by now rapidly approaching completion. It had been decided to make the race a two days' affair, with no neutralisations or stops of any kind whatever; it was to be a continuous race from start to finish on each day, and, moreover, no outside help was to be allowed to the competitors, who had hitherto been accustomed to do nothing but drive, leaving the tyre changes and repairs whenever possible to outside assistance. But the ACF determined to make the new race the finest test of men and motors that had ever been held, and the Commission Sportive drew up its regulations accordingly. A circuit was chosen in the neighbourhood of Le Mans, roughly in the form of a triangle, the corners being at La Ferté Bernard, St. Calais, and St. Mars-la-Brière, which was the point nearest Le Mans. There was trouble at first over the corner at St. Calais, for the road there was very bad, and it seemed as if a neutralisation would be necessary. But the authorities of the little town were so anxious to attract visitors that they undertook to build a wooden track joining the two arms of the circuit, passing through a field, and thus avoiding the town altogether. This satisfied the ACF, and, the circuit once chosen, operations were begun almost immediately. A tunnel was hollowed out, passing under the road, as in the Taunus Gordon-Bennett in 1904, so that spectators could cross without danger. Grandstands were built at Pont-de-Gennes, the roads were put into good repair and tarred so as to avoid dust, and the competitors soon arrived on racing cars of old patterns and began practising over the future scene of the great race. But it was not a course that needed much practice; it consisted practically of three straight sides, connected by corners which were more or less bad. There was a *fourche* – no racing circuit would be complete now without its *fourche* – and the wooden roads at St. Calais and Vibraye were afterwards found to be dangerous at any speed; but for the most part the cars could open out to the utmost over the long undulating straights which seemed to stretch for ever to the horizon.

A large number of entries were received, teams of three cars coming from Renault, Clément-Bayard, FIAT, Hotchkiss, Brasier, Panhard, Darracq, Mercedes, De Dietrich, and Itala. Grégoire entered two cars, Vulpès one, and the list concluded with the veteran Gobron-Brillié, with the faithful Rigolly at the wheel. This car is one of the most remarkable which has ever raced, chiefly on account of its extraordinary longevity. Built early in 1903, its makers had sufficient faith in it to enter it year after year against the constantly improving models of their rivals, and it certainly held its own in the most remarkable way. In the Auvergne in 1905 its performance was equal to, and indeed better than that of a large number of the new cars, and in the Grand Prix it acquitted itself honourably until overtaken by its usual bugbear – radiator troubles.

By the end of June all was ready on the Circuit. Forty miles of palisading had been put up in various places on the course, across side-turnings and in the towns and villages. Two portions of the road were of wood – a stretch in the forest of Vibraye, and the *détour* avoiding St. Calais.

One of the supply stations was placed opposite the Grandstand, so that the spectators had a good view of the competitors as they worked on their cars. The weighing out took place on 25 June, and Barriaux's Vulpès and Tavernaux's Grégoire both failed to appear. The former could not succeed in getting his car down to the weight-limit, and certainly the vehicle had a very ponderous appearance; it was built on the curious Stabilia principle, and was a good example of the abnormal and grotesque type of car that had been developed by racing – a mere engine on wheels.

With the idea of making identification more easy to the spectator, the cars had been numbered in three divisions, A, B and C. The start was at six on the morning of 26 June, and the first man sent away was Gabriel on his De Dietrich; behind him came the rest at intervals of 1½ minutes. The Club was determined that the regulation concerning outside help should be most strictly observed, and from the moment the official start was given to the cars no one but the two men on board was allowed to touch it. Consequently the mechanics of Nazzaro and Weillschott both had to begin work early, for they stopped their engines at the start. The last few men were sent away from the side, as the leading cars were expected to pass at any moment.

The first to reach the tribunes was Lancia, who hurtled through five minutes after de la Touloubre had left. Gabriel broke a radius rod near St. Calais on the first lap, and only escaped disaster by skilfully correcting the swerves of the damaged car. Baras (Brasier) came next, having passed Hémery and Szisz, and having made the record lap of the day. Fabry, on one of the Italas, turned over at Vibraye, and Le Blon ran off the wooden road at St. Calais, and buckled his right rear wheel. Civelli de Bosch on the little Grégoire, and Hanriot on one of the Darracqs, also dropped out on the first round.

At the end of the second lap Baras was still leading, going at a tremendous pace, with Pierry second and Weillschott, the Italian amateur, third, Baras having covered the 129 miles in 105 minutes. But he could not keep up such a speed for long; in the third lap the inevitable trouble arrived, and Szisz went to the top, though another Brasier, with Barillier at the wheel, lay second, with Baras third.

At the beginning of the fourth round some excitement was caused by the passage of Duray and Mariaux together, followed by Nazzaro, who was being chased by Le Blon. After three hours' hard work at the roadside, Le Blon had rebuilt his wheel, using spokes borrowed from Salleron and Shepard, and taken from his other wheels. Szisz kept his lead, and Teste, on a Panhard, worked up to the second place, whilst Shepard, an American amateur driving in his first race, lay third. The fifth lap saw Szisz followed by Albert Clément. Weillschott, who was third, unfortunately could

In 1906 the first Grand Prix, organized by the Automobile Club de France was held at Le Mans. The winner was Szisz with this 90 hp Renault, very much a Veteran design of almost locomotive proportions. *(Cyril Posthumus)*

not stand the strain of the race, and was so exhausted that he failed to hold his car on the road for the last round, running off the wooden road at Vibraye. Edmond, whose eyes, like those of the others, suffered severely from the action of the dust-laying liquid combined with the very fine particles of dust, was also compelled to give in during the last lap, as he was unable to see the road.

Szisz thus kept the lead by steady driving, and shot past the stands just after a quarter to twelve, winning the first day's race of 384 miles by 25 minutes. The second place fell to Albert Clément, and the third to Nazzaro. Lancia, who was the favourite before the race, came in ninth, and in all 17 cars finished, each being taken away and locked up in a specially constructed garage for the night. This park was fenced in and padlocked against all intruders, and during the night a 2,000,000 candle power rotary searchlight played on the racers to ensure their security against any tampering. And it should be here recorded that the Prince d'Arenberg, Comte R. de Vogué, and Sr. Quinonés de Léon, the only members of the Commission Sportive unconnected in any way with the trade, sat up all night on guard, in spite of their hard day's work and the prospect of another on the morrow – a most self-sacrificing act.

The race turned upon the behaviour of the tyres. It was a tropically hot day, and the great heat combined with the tremendous speeds attained over the long straight stretches of the circuit destroyed the tyres in one or two laps, and the drivers became exhausted by the incessant labour of replacing them. Instead of sitting peacefully in their cars while an outside staff changed the tyres, the driver and mechanic were compelled to do all the work themselves in accordance with the before-mentioned intentions of the organisers of the race. Wrestling with heavy covers in a tropical heat, with his eyes inflamed by the tar and dust, and with the strain of driving upon him as well, the lot of the driver in the Grand Prix was not a happy one. The possibility of this trouble had, however, been foreseen by the Renault firm, and in company with the FIAT and Itala they had fitted their cars with detachable rims. And so while their rivals struggled with stiff covers and security bolts they had merely to undo eight nuts, which held eight wedges between the detachable rim and the wheel, and the whole rim, carrying the tyre, came off the wheel. Then a new tyre, ready inflated on its rim, would be slipped on, the nuts run up, the wedges tightened, and the whole operation was completed in less than two minutes, with a minimum of strain on the driver and mechanic.

Some of the firms preferred not to adopt such a novel idea until it had been more thoroughly tested. Others, like the Panhard, would have liked to have fitted it, but were already so near the weight limit that they could not spare the additional 9 kg per wheel which this fitting involved.

Next morning the drivers were sent away on a novel principle – one that simplified the timing considerably for the spectators. Szisz, having completed the first day's run in 4 h 45 min 30$\frac{3}{5}$ sec was dispatched at that exact clock time in the morning, and hence at any time during the race his time was the hour as shown by the clock. The other competitors followed suit, according to the times they had made the day before – Clément at 6 h 11 min 40$\frac{3}{5}$ sec, Nazzaro at 6 h 26 min 53 sec, and so on.

The cars were dragged out of the park by horses – to the great delight of the journalists, who saw infinite opportunity for jests – and brought to the line, where the drivers were allowed the assistance of two mechanics to start the engine, on the word being given to go. It is worthy of note that out of the 17 starters 14 got away without the least trouble in starting their engines – contrary to the opinion of most people, who expected that there would be considerable difficulty in getting the big motors to move. Szisz drove to the Renault depôt, refitted a couple of tyres, took on supplies, and then left, after spending nearly twelve minutes at the *ravitaillement*. Albert Clément got away inside five minutes, and Nazzaro left without stopping at his stand at all. Mariaux subsequently did the same, and Shepard could not get away until he had spent half an hour before the Hotchkiss stand. The only driver who availed himself of the regulations allowing a substitute on the second day was Jenatzy, whose place was taken by Burton. Lancia had intended to do so, but, owing to some difficulty, the substitute was not available, and the famous Italian was compelled to drive after all, starting in his ordinary clothes, as he had not time to change.

Having been dispatched so long before anyone else, Szisz passed the stands at the end of his first round while 11 cars were waiting to be sent off, and even when he got round again there were still four waiting the word to go. The last man to leave was the unfortunate Rougier, who had changed 14 tyres in a single day (on ordinary rims), unaided except for the help of his mechanic. Szisz was so far ahead in the race that he was never in danger of being passed, but Nazzaro and Albert Clément had a great duel for the second place, in the course of which the former made the best time of the second day, nine minutes better than that of Szisz.

The condition of the roads was bad; torn up by the high speeds of the heavy cars on the first day, the corners were seas of loose pebbles, through which the cars ploughed their way as best they could. Shepard ran over

the banking at La Fourche, and smashed a wheel. Hémery, like all the Darracq drivers, had trouble with his valves and only covered one circuit, though he came through very fast when he did arrive. Rigolly retired with a burst radiator, and Teste had a bad smash from a broken back spring hanger. During the third lap Richez retired, and in the final round Rougier at last gave up the struggle against his tyres. Szisz broke a back spring on the last lap but one, but continued steadily and finished at a quarter-past-twelve. Nazzaro came in at a quarter to one, with Albert Clément just three minutes behind. More than an hour passed before Barillier finished, and the rest arrived at intervals, with Mariaux last at 4.38 pm.

It was terribly hard race, for the strain on the men was tremendous. The removable rims decided the fortunes of the day, and Clément must have driven magnificently to have come so close to the leaders, as he lost about ten minutes by every tyre change.

Thus ended the Grand Prix of 1906. As a substitute for the Gordon-Bennett it was not all that had been hoped. The feeling of sport was almost entirely absent, and the international element was nil; it was never a question of the victory of France or Italy; at most it was only a duel between the firms of Renault and FIAT. Undoubtedly the most remarkable performance was that of the Brasier firm, which had all three cars in at the finish – a wonderful record after such a hard race.

The cars competing were all of the same types as in 1905 – new vehicles, certainly, but representing the idea that immense power was necessary to obtain the best results, with the consequent evolution of a huge, ponderous vehicle, destructive to its tyres, and losing in tyre troubles what was gained in speed. The little Grégoires appealed to the engineer as better in principle, but they were so untuned that they were handicapped out of the race.

Another new race in 1906 was the Targa Florio held in Sicily over what became known as the Long Madonie circuit, just over 90 miles in length and initially for touring cars. It attracted rather parochial entries and the Italas of Cagno and Graziana took the first two places. The Tourist Trophy was again for touring cars and held in the Isle of Man; C. S. Rolls won with a Rolls-Royce from Bablot with a Berliet (who had also finished third in Sicily). In the Vanderbilt Cup, a run to the 1000 kg formula, the winner was Hémery (Darracq) and it was the French company's second win in succession in the race. As yet there was no real internationally accepted standard racing

Felice Nazzaro at the last wheel of the 16.25-litre Fiat with chain drive which he drove to victory in the 1907 Grand Prix held at Dieppe over 477 miles. Up until 1906 Fiat had been known as FIAT. The 1907 cars were reactionary and did little to contribute to the technical development of the racing car.

formula, despite what had been laid for 1901 and 'Grand Prix' racing as such still had to be established.

Fiat won the three important races of 1907 and in each race the winning driver was Felice Nazzaro and for each race Fiat produced a different car to comply with the differing regulations. First came the Targa Florio in Sicily, run on a limited bore basis and with a maximum bore for 4-cylinder cars of 125 mm (Fiat ran cars with cylinder dimensions of 124×130 mm bore and stroke). The Kaiserpreis held in the Taunus mountains of Germany prescribed a maximum capacity of 8 litres with a minimum weight of 1175 kg and minimum dimension restrictions to exclude pure racing cars (it was notionally an event for touring cars). Fiat entered cars with cylinder dimensions of 140×130 mm. The Grand Prix in France was now without restrictions other than a fuel consumption limit of 30 litres per 100 kilometres (about 9.4 mpg). For this race Fiat produced a car with cylinder dimensions of 180×160 mm – 16¼ litres – and it was amazing that such a large capacity car could achieve 9.4 mpg under racing conditions. There was no Vanderbilt Cup in

1907. The Tourist Trophy was won by the Rover of E. Courtis.

In 1908 the Targa Florio was won by the Isotta Fraschini of Trucco with the Fiats of Vincenzo Lancia (already established as a motor car manufacturer in his own right) and Felice Nazzaro (destined to become a manufacturer between 1911 and 1916 – but the company bearing his name survived until 1923) in second and third places. Inevitably the most important race of the year and the one that set the standard was the Grand Prix held at Dieppe to a new and complicated formula. This prescribed a maximum piston area of 755 sq cm, with a maximum bore of 155 mm for four cylinders and 127 mm for six cylinders. In fact all the leading contenders had four cylinders and the winning Mercedes represented the state of what was rapidly becoming an advanced art. Although chain drive was retained and there were still brakes on the back wheels only, chassis were much more rigid, braking was much more efficient and roadholding and cornering had reached a standard not to be beaten for many years.

To quote Anthony Bird, 'This race was notable for seeing the first appearance of "pits". They were just that – shallow emplacements dug by the side of the track, lined with timber revêtments and stocked with the necessary spares and tools. The other outstanding feature of the affair was the prodigious consumption of tyres. Since racing began cars had been too fast for their tyres, but the greater speed of the 1908 cars over those of the previous year and the rough state of the track, which had been cut about by the *Voiturette* race (held earlier), showed up the inadequacies of tyre design. The Rudge-Whitworth centre-lock wire wheel had already won favour in England, but the Automobile Club de France barred it from the Grand Prix, apparently for no better reason than that the French makers had not got round to using it. Detachable rims were, however, permitted, and the Mercedes pit staff worked wonders with the six nuts securing each rim to its felloe.

'Had it not been for his 19 tyre failures there is little doubt that Victor Rigal on the Clément-Bayard would have won, his average speed of 63.6 mph brought him to fourth place and represents an astonishing performance in view of his difficulties. The Mercedes were not so destructive (perhaps because of their lighter axles), but there were no spare tyres left at the pit during the last two laps. Fortunately, neither Lautenschlager, nor Poege [who finished fifth] needed more tyres and the former was able to hold first place which he attained in the fifth lap, with the Benzs of Victor Heméry and Richard Hanriot next in succession . . .

'The third Mercedes driven by Salzar . . . had broken the lap record in a time of 36 min 31 sec on the first lap; ignition trouble then set in, the car fell back to 35th place on the second lap and retired on the third. That the two leading German firms took first three places was a sad blow to French pride, but the great cost of Grand Prix racing made all the leading firms quite happy to agree to the suspension of Grand Prix events during 1909 and 1910.'

Brooklands, the World's first permanent circuit had opened in 1907 and it was to be followed by Indianapolis in 1909 but the first 500 Miles race was not held until 1911. With no Grand Prix until 1912 in fact, racing was at a low ebb in 1909 and 1910,

although *Voiturette* racing and such events as the Targa Florio continued. After Watson with a Hutton (a Napier by another name) had won the Tourist Trophy in 1908, even this event was discontinued until 1914. In the United States there was the American Grand Prix at Savannah, first held in 1908, when Louis Wagner won with a Fiat and after no race in 1909 the winner in 1910 was David Bruce-Brown (Benz).

In the Coupe de *Voiturettes* promoted by *L'Auto* magazine, there was a cylinder bore limitation varying with the number of cylinders. In the first three races, in 1906-08, the winner each year was a Sizaire et Naudin, driven by one of the Sizaire brothers in 1906 and by their partner Naudin in 1907-08. In 1906-07 these were single-cylinder cars with a square, 120×120 cylinder and running at up to the, then, quite high speed of 2000 rpm, and although 4-cylinder engines were permitted in 1908, the French company still used a single-cylinder unit. During these years Peugeot had

The winning 12.8-litre Mercedes of Christian Lauteschlager in the 'pits' at the 1908 Grand Prix at Dieppe for a punctured (shredded!) right hand front tyre to be replaced. It was Lautenschlager's tenth puncture. Although centre-lock wheels were prohibited, detachable rims were permitted and fitted to the Mercedes. The design of the Mercedes was by Paul Daimler after Wilhelm Maybach. *(Cyril Posthumus)*

been racing the single-cylinder Lion-Peugeot, taking third place each year 1906-08, but for 1909 built a V-twin, a car described by Clutton as a 'freak', which won in the hands of Guippone.

Marc Birkigt of Hispano-Suiza had built an advanced T-head, 4-cylinder car for the 1909 race, but persevered after his company's defeat and returned to take first and third places (Zuccarelli and Chassagne) in the 1910 race held at Boulogne. A Lion-Peugeot was again second. For 1911 the organisers of *L'Auto* Cup substituted a *Coupe des Voitures Légères* for cars of not more than 3 litres and the 4-cylinder Delages of Bablot and Thomas took first and third places, sandwiching Boillot's Lion-Peugeot. During these years there was also the Catalan Cup at Sitges in Spain in 1909-10 (Goux won with a Lion-Peugeot both years) and the Sicilian Cup held between 1907 and 1910 (a victory for Naudin in 1907 and there followed three successive wins by Lion-Peugeot).

Grand Prix racing resumed on a half-hearted basis in 1911 and there was a Formule Libre Grand Prix de France held at Le Mans, won by Hémery with a 10-litre Fiat, a modified touring car but remarkably, second place went to Friderich with a 1300 cc (65×100 mm) 4-cylinder Bugatti. The Bugatti had run in the Grand Prix because it was too light to be eligible for the concurrent Coupe de *l'Auto* races. Friderich's average speed was 46 mph, compared with the 56.71 mph of the Fiat and the 55.2 mph of the winning Delage in the Coupe de *l'Auto*. The Bugatti, which incorporated many of the design features seen in later racing Bugattis, represented 'the beginnings of the modern high efficiency 4-cylinder light car; a complete contrast to the Lion-Peugeot' (Clutton). It was undoubtedly the most important and influential design of the period.

In the United States in 1911 the first 500 Miles race at Indianapolis was won by the Marmon of Harroun and Patschke and David Bruce-Brown with a 14-litre Fiat S74 won the American Grand Prix at Savannah.

1912-14

Once more the Grand Prix of the Automobile Club de France was held at Dieppe and on a formule libre basis except for a minimum cockpit width of 175

mm. The race was held over a distance of 956 miles and over two days. Despite the technical advances made in *Voiturette* racing and by Bugatti, Fiat and Lorraine-Dietrich were not influenced and produced chain-drive monsters of 14 and 15 litres respectively. They were dinosaurs from the different motor racing world of 1908. Peugeot, however, broke new ground and produced 4-cylinder 7.6-litre cars, with twin overhead camshafts operating inclined valves. Twin overhead camshafts became standard on racing cars from then on. Quite who was responsible for the twin overhead camshaft concept remains a not entirely resolved mystery. For many years Ernest Henry the Swiss engineer employed by Peugeot was given the credit, but latterly it has become apparent that it was the joint work of Henry, together with *Les Charlatans* as they were known at Peugeot, Paul Zuccarelli, (who had raced for Hispano-Suiza), Jules Goux and Georges Boillot, drivers entrusted with the development of the new racing car because of their practical experience.

The last dinosaur – the Fiat S74 driven by American David Bruce-Brown in the 1912 Grand Prix at Amiens. Although Bruce-Brown led at the end of the first day, he hit a dog on the second day, the fuel tank was holed and he was disqualified for refuelling away from the pits.

Although David Bruce-Brown led at the end of the first day from Boillot (Peugeot), the American collided with a dog on the second day, the fuel tank developed a leak and he was disqualified for refuelling away from the pits. Boillot won the race for Peugeot from Wagner (Fiat) and the Sunbeams of Rigal, Resta and Médinger, which took first three places in the Coupe de *l'Auto*, ran concurrently. In addition Zuccarelli with a Lion-Peugeot won the *Voitures Légères* Grand Prix of France at Le Mans, David Bruce-Brown was killed during practice for the Vanderbilt Cup held at Milwaukee (the winner was Ralph de Palma with a Mercedes) and Bragg (Fiat) won the American Grand Prize, which was also held at Milwaukee.

The following year a fuel consumption formula of 20 litres of fuel per 100 km (14.1 mpg), coupled with a weight minimum of 800 kg and a maximum of 1100 kg was adopted. Although Fiat missed the race, there were entries from Delage, Itala, Opel, Sunbeam – and Peugeot. Peugeot produced a 5.6-litre version of the 1912 car and in this 566-mile race at Amiens Boillot and Goux took the first two places with the new cars. Boillot and Goux also took the first two places in the *l'Auto* Cup at Boulogne and Goux won at Indianapolis the same year.

For 1914 there was an engine capacity limit of 4½ litres and a maximum weight of 1100 kg for the Grand Prix. Peugeot – together with Delage, Fiat and Picard-Pictet all adopted four-wheel-brakes. Peugeot was expecting to win again, but instead there was an immense battle between the Peugeots and the latest Mercedes. The story of the Mercedes and the race is

Georges Boillot, at the wheel of the 5.6-litre Peugeot with which he won the 1913 Grand Prix at Amiens. The Peugeot pioneered the twin overhead camshaft cylinder head devised by *Les Charlatans* and Ernest Henry. Note the contrast between the old-fashioned bolster fuel tank and the modern, eared, knock-off hub caps. *(Cyril Posthumus)*

21

told by Anthony Bird (first published by Profile Publications Limited, 1966).

The 1914 Grand Prix Mercedes

The 1914 Grand Prix, of twenty laps of the 23.3 miles Lyons circuit, was run on a capacity limit formula which fixed engine size at 4½ litres and maximum weight at 21 cwt. A look at some of the technical details destroys three of the sacred cows of motoring history:

Firstly – that aero engine practice did not influence car engine design until after the war. Both the 1913 and 1914 Mercedes racing engines had much in common with the firm's well-known aero engines. (And the 1906 'Adams Eight' had been powered by a modified Antoinette airship engine).

Secondly – that 'Hotchkiss drive', ie using the back springs to transmit driving thrust to the frame and to absorb braking torque, was superior to other contemporary systems as it avoided 'rear wheel steering'. This theoretical truth should have been amply disproved by the GP Mercedes, and many thousands of production cars of different makes, which handled excellently despite the use of a torque tube or some other form of torque-reaction linkage.

Thirdly – that rotational speeds much above 3500 rpm were not attainable because the virtue of opening inlet valves before top dead centre had not been realised. This puts the cart before the horse, and it was because metallurgy, sparking plug and valve spring weaknesses held back the practical application of high speed working that some 3000 rpm was regarded as a reasonably safe limit; at this speed there is no advantage to be gained by early inlet valve opening.

Paul Daimler was responsible for the 1914 racing Mercedes; although the firm's traditions were in no sense violated, the Maybach influence, which had been so clear in the 1908 cars, was no longer dominant.

The photographs say all that needs to be said of the way racing cars had changed externally in six years. It must be remembered, however, that the high build and sit-up-and-beg driving positions of 1908 had not been retained purely by conservative adherence to touring car fashions. The very large engines had very large flywheels, and to give 6 or 7 inches clearance beneath a flywheel nearly two feet in diameter dictated a high chassis and floor level; this and other factors brought the driver's eye level some five feet or more from the ground in 1908. On the 1914 Mercedes this dimension had been reduced by some 10 or 12 inches, and the very narrow body (37 in at the widest point) and *coupe vent* radiator helped reduce drag.

Though Mercedes still raced with two-wheel brakes in

1914 (foot operated transmission brake and hand brake acting directly on the rear wheels in accordance with conventional practice), the hand brake mechanisms showed novelty in the use of toggle mechanism, in place of cams, to expand the shoes which were flexible; the drums were also designed to 'give' a little and the greatest possible area of lining thus made contact with each drum. These brakes were probably as good as two-wheel-only brakes could be, and a similar arrangement is to be found on some of the Panhard-Levassors of the 1920s.

The apparently old fashioned exposed valve springs and stems of the engine were retained to aid cooling and make for easy adjustment, but the crankshaft dimensions and combustion chamber and valve ports would have passed as up to date until quite recently. In accordance with the aircraft practice of the firm the ports and water jackets of the individual cylinders (93×165 mm) were separate structures welded into place. This very costly form of construction allowed rigid control of the thickness of metal in all the vital areas and abolished the menace of distortion. Four inclined valves per cylinder allowed good breathing at the relatively low speeds used, and the single overhead camshaft was driven, by bevels and vertical shaft, from the back of the crankshaft to avoid torsional disturbances. The engine was designed to take four sparking plugs per cylinder, fed from two magnetos, though only three were used. This prodigality of sparks not only provided good flame-spread but was a safeguard against misfiring at high speed; sparking plugs were still apt to be unreliable in 1914. The engine was, in consequence, an extremely reliable one and developed 115 bhp at 2800 rpm.

There was a plunger-pump system of pressure lubrication. One of the triple pump barrels drew in a small quantity of fresh oil from an external tank and added it to that already being circulated by the scavenge and feed pumps. In addition a foot-operated pump allowed the mechanic to feed fresh oil to cylinder walls and crankcase.

There was no departures from conventional practice in chassis, steering, or suspension, though the Mercedes face-cam and coil spring rebound dampers were noteworthy and the chassis was rather more rigidly braced than was then usual, with an X member in the centre of the frame. The old scroll clutch had disappeared in favour of a double cone affair and the 4-speed gearbox gave motion to a propellor shaft and live axle. The shaft was enclosed in a tube and driving thrust and torque reaction were delivered to a ball trunnion joint mounted on the X member. Despite the pundits who assure us this arrangement promotes oversteer, the cars steered beautifully.

An uncommon feature of the rear axle was that the pinion shaft carried two driving pinions with the differential mechanism between them; each pinion meshed with a separate crown wheel – one to each half-shaft. This unusual arrangement had been done before and was to be done again; it had the merits of allowing great rigidity in the pinion shaft; the thrust of one driving pinion was counterbalanced by the opposite thrust of its fellow (thrust race bearings were not always as free from trouble as designers would have liked); above all it abolished the tendency to induce wheelspin by transverse torque reaction which, for racing cars particularly, was the most serious drawback of the conventional bevel-geared live axle.

The Daimler Motoren Gesellschaft entered five of these cars (the maximum allowed) for the event, and the preparation, testing and practising were done with a degree of thoroughness not previously seen in motor racing. It was this, and the reliability of the cars, rather than any outstanding novelty or merit of design which gave Mercedes a triple victory. Each car became, as it were, tailored to its driver and to the exigencies of the course. A sufficiency of crown wheels, half-shafts and driving pinions, for example, was provided to allow six different final drive ratios to be tried on each car during preparation. These

The conquering heroes: three of the team of 4½-litre Mercedes outside the Daimler-Benz works at Stuttgart-Untertürkheim. No.28, on the left, is Lautenschlager's winning car.

23

ratios varied only between the narrow limits of 2.1:1 and 2.7:1. Maximum speed claimed was 112 mph and with the 2.5:1 ratio this was reached at 2900 rpm and a piston speed of 3050 feet per minute.

In addition to their painstaking pre-race work, which was soon to pay dividends, the Mercedes team introduced a new element into racing – the absolute control of individual cars by signal from the pit. This robbed the driver of some of his individuality, and, in the opinion of many, took from motor racing its claim to be a sport, but there is no doubt it was an inevitable move and one which some other concern would have made if Mercedes had not.

Toughest opposition to the Mercedes came from Peugeot whose cars were faster round the corners by virtue of their four-wheel brakes. At least one of the GP Mercedes was fitted with front brakes at one stage but at the time of the race all five relied on rear wheel braking only. Max Sailer was given the task of opening up the race and his Mercedes led for the first five laps and had by then gained a 2¾-minute lead over Georges Boillot's Peugeot; but this pace could not be maintained and Sailer went out on the sixth lap with a broken crankshaft. The need to make full use of their cornering and braking ability was already causing tyre trouble on the Peugeots.

From laps 5 to 15 Peugeot seemed to be dominant, and when curiously slow pit work lost Lautenschlager two minutes on the 11th lap the cautious punter might have baulked at putting any money on the Mercedes. On orders from the pit Christian Lautenschlager, Louis Wagner and Otto Salzer now began to close up and harry the opposition. On the 18th lap, which he covered at 68.7 mph, Lautenschlager took a 23-second lead over Boillot who had, by then, little chance of winning and none at all when he broke a valve on the last lap. His was a magnificent attempt; particularly as he had to make eight tyre changes against Lautenschlager's four.

Mercedes had the satisfaction of taking first three places; Lautenschlager at an average of 65.83 mph, Wagner at 65.3 and Salzer at 64.8. The race remained extremely close to the end; fourth place was taken by Jules Goux (Peugeot) at 63.94, and Dario Resta (Sunbeam) was fifth at 62.46.

It has been said that no cheer was raised and no hands clapped as the three Mercedes crossed the finishing line in 1914, and this has been attributed to the tense feelings brought about by the imminence of war. It seems unlikely that the spectators at the Lyons circuit were particularly aware of the terrible doom then preparing, but that the rigid system of control imposed on the Mercedes team left the spectators puzzled and disapproving. The future pattern of racing procedure was drawn and public approval was at first withheld.

Four weeks later the pistol shot which started the war was fired. A macabre twist to the tale is provided by the fact that the chauffeur at Sarajevo who was wounded in the attempt to drive the murdered Archduke out of range was Otto Merz, a Mercedes apprentice, one time riding mechanic to Poege and himself a famous racing driver in the twenties.

Part 2

THE ROARING
TWENTIES, 1919-1930

1919-21

Inevitably there was no racing in Europe during the horror of the First World War (although Indianapolis was run in both 1915 and 1916 before America entered the War) and it was slow to start again afterwards. Indianapolis was run in 1919 with a 300 cu in/5000 cc capacity limit and Edouard Ballot, head of the Paris-based company best known for the proprietary engines that it built for sale to other manufacturers, was persuaded by racing driver René Thomas, to build a team of cars for the race. Former Peugeot designer Ernest Henry undertook the project which is said to have been completed in 101 days and was a magnificent twin overhead camshaft straight-eight. Four cars were entered at Indianapolis, they were fastest in qualifying, but were plagued by tyre problems and only finished in fourth place, driven by Guyot. American Wilcox with a pre-war Peugeot, again designed by Ernest Henry, was the winner. Peugeot also won the revived Targa Florio, the famous Sicilian road race.

For 1920 the Indianapolis formula was changed to capacity limits of 183 cu in/3000 cc and both Peugeot and Ballot entered teams (the Ballots were in effect a scaled-down version of the 1919 cars). Ralph de Palma led with one of the Ballots for 186 of the 200 laps, but was slowed by magneto trouble and the winner was Gaston Chevrolet (Monroe). The *Voiturette* race at Le Mans, the first international race in France for six years, was won by Friderich (Bugatti) and in the Targa Florio the winner was Meregalli (Nazzaro), but Enzo Ferrari, whose real fame was to be as a team manager and manufacturer, finished second.

By 1921 Europe had sufficiently recovered from the ravages of war for the French Grand Prix to be revived (as the 'Grand Prix of the Automobile Club of France', it had been the only Grand Prix as such), but

Magnificent folly and a great influence on later designs of the 1920s – the Straight-Eight 5-Litre Ballot. Four of these cars were entered at Indianapolis in 1919 and here René Thomas is seen at the wheel. The Ballot team failed because of tyre problems, a change in the Indianapolis regulations for 1920 meant that they were little raced and all have now disappeared. Partly because of the lack of European Grands Prix, there was strong interest in Indianapolis by the European teams.

there was now also to be an Italian Grand Prix. Racing was run to the same 3-litre formula as Indianapolis. The French race was held at Le Mans and attracted entries from Ballot, Mathis (another French company) and the Sunbeam-Talbot-Darracq Anglo-French conglomerate, together with a team of American Duesenbergs, one of which was driven by Jimmy Murphy. The Duesenbergs were fitted with four-wheel hydraulic brakes and Murphy won a duel from fellow-American de Palma with a Ballot. Milton (Frontenac) won at Indianapolis, Masetti won the Targa Florio and then came the Italian Grand Prix, held on a triangular road circuit near Brescia. There were only six starters and Goux (Ballot) was the winner after the retirement of the Fiat of Pietro Bordino.

1922

European racing now adopted a maximum engine capacity of 2 litres, a minimum weight of 650 kg and a riding mechanic was still carried. As Indianapolis continued with a 3-litre limit for another year, this helped create a divide between European and American racing that was not bridged until the 1960s when British teams began to build special cars for the

500 Miles race. There were, of course, exceptions such as Wilbur Shaw's wins with a Maserati at Indianapolis in 1939-40 and Ascari's appearance there with a Ferrari in 1952, but they were very much exceptions.

That Grand Prix racing was increasing in popular appeal and was attracting manufacturers in much greater numbers became very evident in 1922. There were five serious contenders, Ballot, Bugatti, Fiat, Rolland-Pilain and the Sunbeam-Talbot-Darracq Group and entries also appeared during the year from Aston Martin, Diatto and Mathis. In addition to Grand Prix racing there was the Tourist Trophy in the Isle of Man for 3-litre cars (won by Chassagne's Sunbeam) and the Targa Florio in Sicily, a Formule Libre race (won by Masetti with a Mercedes). The new Avus circuit at Berlin and the Monza Autodrome in a park in Milan were both opened – the latter after 100 day's frantic work.

Manufacturers raced ostensibly for publicity reasons, but the expense of building and racing a Grand Prix team was such that the directors had to be great racing enthusiasts and the decision to race was rarely based on purely commercial reasons. The Italian Fiat company had been racing since the dawn of motoring

Jimmy Murphy acknowledges the crowd after winning the 1921 French Grand Prix at Le Mans. Although not evident in this photograph, the road surface was appalling and in parts little more than a rough track. Murphy's win was the first in a European Grand Prix with an American car and in effect it was also the last. Much later wins by American teams were with cars designed and built in Britain.

and its beautifully constructed 6-cylinder Tipo 804, designed by Fiat technicians Cappa, Cavalli, Bertarione and Becchia under the direction of Fornaca outdated its contemporaries and proved the dominant car of the year winning both the French Grand Prix at Strasbourg (the driver was Felice Nazzaro who had also won the 1907 French race) and the Italian Grand Prix at Monza (driver Pietro Bordino). The Fiat was another highly influential design that was widely copied. Of Fiat one Italian authority stated, 'Fiat did not copy; it taught after having created.' The French race was the first in Europe to adopt a massed start (as at Indianapolis) instead of releasing the cars singly or in pairs.

Louis Hervé Coatalen, engineering chief of Sunbeam-Talbot-Darracq, however, copied prolifically. The 1921 8-cylinder Sunbeams had been the work of former Ballot chief design engineer Ernest Henry and was closely related to his work for Ballot, while the

Friderich at the wheel of his 'streamlined' Bugatti at the 1922 French Grand Prix at Strasbourg. The 'hole' in the nose was matched by a (smaller) outlet in the long pointed tank. The similar Ballots sported even more bulbous noses because these also housed the spare wheel.

Beautifully engineered and constructed, the Fiat 804 was the dominant car in 1922. This is Felice Nazzaro at the French Grand Prix. Undoubtedly Fiat were the technical leaders of the early 1920s. *(Cyril Posthumus)*

equally unsuccessful 4-cylinder 1922 cars were again designed by Henry and inspired by his work for Peugeot and Ballot. In contrast the Bugatti Type 30 (Ettore's first serious racing straight-eight) and Ballot's 2LS featured innovative 'aerodynamics'; both had cowled radiators and long pointed tanks. The aerodynamics can have been little less effective than a dustbin and whilst Bugatti and Ballot surprised everybody, they influenced nobody. The Bugattis were not unsuccessful however and the cars were second and third in the French race and third in the Italian. In design the Ballots dated back to 1920 and were, nominally at least, private entries, for Ballot had officially withdrawn from racing at the end of 1921 to concentrate on the production of passenger cars which became ever-drearier until the company was finally taken over by famous car and aero engine manufacturer, Hispano-Suiza. Another French contender was the Rolland-Pilain, built at Tours, a fairly low-slung, 'classic' straight-eight of unremarkable fragility.

1923

The money spent by manufacturers on new cars was immense and there was a barrage of new models and innovations. Fiat, still leading the field technically, produced the very fast, supercharged Tipo 805, which although it was to fail in the French race, was in fact the car of the year. The evolution of Coatalen's new Sunbeam is told shortly. Both Bugatti and Voisin (a famed aircraft builder) produced apparently eccentric, carefully conceived aerodynamic cars. Voisin's 6-cylinder cars incorporated a metal-reinforced wooden chassis of aero industry origins, but the cars were hopelessly underpowered. Benz (still to merge with Daimler) built a mid-engined car, one of which finished fourth in the European Grand Prix at Monza. From Alfa Romeo came the P1, designed by Giuseppe Merosi, but the first car crashed at Monza with fatal results for the driver, Ugo Sivocci and it was not raced. Louis Delage, who had built two 5-litre cars for sprints and hill climbs, revealed his new V12 car designed by

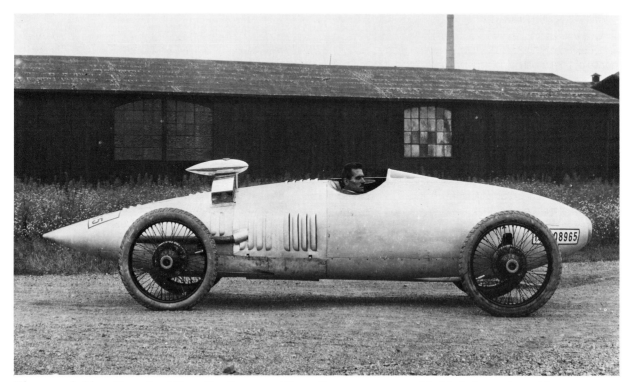

The remarkable mid-engined Benz *Tropfenwagen*. The radiator was mounted behind the engine with a streamlined header tank above it in the air stream.

Charles Planchon, apparently a cousin of Delage, at the French Grand Prix, but it failed and its day was to come later. Rolland-Pilain still raced, but with as little success as before.

At the French Grand Prix Henry Segrave (later Sir Henry) scored a remarkable victory with his Sunbeam and this account of the race is from *Sir Henry Segrave*, (B.T. Batsford Ltd, 1961) and is reproduced with the kind permission of the author and the publishers.

The 1923 French Grand Prix
by Cyril Posthumus

Reviewing 1922 through the eyes of those S-T-D directors who supported racing, the sweetness of facile victory in the Isle of Man, at Le Mans, Brooklands and Barcelona, helped to allay the bitterness of Sunbeam's failure at Strasbourg. But the memory of that race rankled with Louis Coatalen, to whom victory in the Grand Prix was the zenith of achievement. He had never forgotten the shattering pace of those lovely little red Fiats, nor how they eclipsed his Sunbeams, and when full Fiat teams of 2-litre and 1½-litre cars were entered for the inaugural Grand Prix and voiturette races at the new Monza track in September, 1922, he discreetly withdrew his Sunbeam and Talbot-Darracq entries from those events.

Looking ahead to 1923, Coatalen could foresee no chance of victory with the Henry-designed 2-litre, 4-cylinder Sunbeam, however much it might be improved. Never a man to dither, he saw what he had to do, and did it. By offering a better salary than Fiats were paying, he enticed one of their key engineers, Vicenzo Bertarione, away from Turin to join Sunbeams and design a new 2-litre car for the 1923 Grand Prix, to be run at Tours on 2 July.

Not surprisingly, Bertarione's Sunbeams were 'sixes', closely resembling the Fiat power units of the previous year, though they embodied sundry improvements. The engines were on the test bed by April, and the first car, stark in unpainted aluminium, ready for testing early in May. And by June, all three were ready for the fray, to be driven by 'Bill' Guinness, de Hane Segrave and Albert Divo.

Segrave took the Grand Prix extremely seriously; it was his first race of 1923, and none could be more important. He was thoroughly familiar with the new car's design through every stage of its transition from paper into metal, had driven the prototype whenever possible, and before the team had even settled properly at the Hotel de Bordeaux at Tours, was driving round the course in a touring Sunbeam.

He found the Touraine circuit was of the usual roughly triangular shape, but with a considerable variety in fast and slow corners. He disliked it at first, finding it heavily cambered, bumpy, dusty, and rather narrow, with soft road verges, all too often bounded by paling fences, always a hazard to whirling hubcaps. Practice in the new Sunbeams showed that they slewed uncomfortably at high speed, and although the front track was widened to increase stability, they remained tricky to hold on the faster stretches.

Weighing up the opposition, and bearing in mind the undeniable fact that in numerous past races the fastest cars failed to finish whereas the one driven with something in hand survived to win, de Hane resolved on this occasion to hold back at the beginning, and see how things shaped. He practised assiduously, taking endless trouble at the corners, even getting his mechanic Paul Dutoit to clock him through certain sections, then later timing other rivals and comparing performances. The pair also put in much time at pitwork practice, striving to save vital seconds on refuelling and wheel-changing.

Troubles with the Sunbeams were few, and morale high during the training. They had the legs of the Rolland-Pilains, the Bugattis and the Voisins, and only the Fiats remained an unknown quantity. The Italian cars were late to arrive. They were driven all the way from Turin to Tours, over the Alps by road, and did not arrive until late on the fourth training day, giving themselves two days of official practice only.

Yet, as in 1922, they caused a major sensation. They looked slightly larger and longer than the Strasbourg cars, and instead of six cylinders now had eight, emitting a harsh tearing roar behind which was a strange whining note. Their drivers, Bordino, Salamano and Giaccone, practised hard, and the tempestuous Bordino staggered everyone by lapping in 9 minutes 56 seconds, an average of 85.6 mph, which was 34 seconds faster than Segrave, quickest of the Sunbeams!

Was it to be Strasbourg all over again, with Britain's high hopes dashed once more by the brilliant Fiats?

The Italians' secret was the supercharger, then a new and strange device which, literally, crammed the petrol-air mixture into the engine instead of letting the engine suck it in, notably augmenting the power output. Its use in Grand Prix racing for the first time was the greatest technical sensation of a sensational race.

July 2nd was dry and uncomfortably hot, and the crowds thronged in their thousands to the Touraine circuit. Once again there was the panoply and splendour of *the* Grand Prix, the brightly coloured flags of the nations on the vast grandstand, the bustling, eager crowds, the gendarmerie and soldiers. Then the arresting strains of the 'Marseillaise' sounded, heralding the inevitable State dignitaries, amongst them the Minister for War, M. Maginot, whose famous 'Line' was to afford France such false security in later, war-torn years.

Once again the rolling start as at Strasbourg – but this time there were no delays, and at 8 am to the second the Chairman of the Racing Board of the ACF, the Chevalier René de Knyff, raised a yellow flag, then swept it down, and the pilot motor-cyclist shot off with the pack of seventeen throbbing cars at his heels.

With the race under way, de Hane found himself sixth, just ahead of Divo, while out in front went Bordino in the supercharged Fiat, setting an amazing pace, and being clocked at 122 mph though a 3-kilometre stretch on his first round. For eight searing laps the fiery Italian led, followed by Kenelm Lee Guinness, driving an inspired race. Then the Fiat suddenly faltered, choked and died, small stones and grit doing fell work as they were pumped, largely unfiltered, into the engine by the supercharger.

Now Guinness led for Britain, while de Hane, still sixth, became a worried man on lap 4 when clutch slip set in at over 4500 rpm, so that on one lap he clocked a mere 61.2 mph through the measured distance! On the 12th lap Guinness ceded his lead by stopping for fuel, oil and water, the two surviving Fiats of Giaccone and Salamano snarling past. Then KLG's Sunbeam, too, was afflicted with clutch slip, dropping him even behind Segrave.

The next excitement came when Giaccone's Fiat suffered a similar fate to Bordino's and retired. Albert Divo moved to the fore, but Salamano caught him three rounds later after a pit stop, while Segrave, fed up with the slipping clutch and almost contemplating retiring, found himself a tardy third and continued plugging along.

Then a remarkable thing happened. There came a 'crack' from within the cockpit, more felt than heard above the noise of the engine, but Dutoit, looking down, could see nothing amiss. At the same time an elated de Hane suddenly found his clutch gripping fully, and Dutoit, seeking further, discovered that a metal stop bolted to the gearbox to control rearward movement of the clutch pedal, but actually restricting it, had come away, letting the clutch fully out. Segrave now had a car in full and fine fettle, and although the Fiat was many miles ahead, de Hane drove flat out in an effort to close the gap on Divo and Salamano.

Coatalen then brought him in to refuel, and de Hane and Dutoit effected a model pit stop, spoiled when somebody handed Segrave an oil funnel with the dust cover still in place. It took him several seconds to remove it, which so annoyed him that he flung the offending cover into the pits, giving those responsible a deserved spattering of oil.

Fate now picked on the unfortunate Divo, who struck infuriating trouble when, on lap 30, he pulled in for refuelling and, in his haste, jammed the quick-release filler cap solid. The hapless driver and his mechanic Moriceau

wrestled furiously with the cap, first Moriceau using a hammer while Divo stood on the cap to hold the spring down. Then a wrench, hack-saw and cold chisel were all tried without success; the cap was well and truly jammed. The adjacent Fiat pit watched operations with much interest, and there came a caustic comment from designer Fornaca, 'I will send them a proper design for a cap', obviously intended for Bertarione's ears.

Meanwhile Segrave was picking up seconds which quickly grew into minutes, and while his brother Rodney, helping in the Sunbeam pits, handed out tools to the desperate Divo, de Hane slashed past the stationary Sunbeam into second place. Then at last, after losing 18 minutes, poor Divo had to resort to the small reserve tank, stopping each lap to refill. And as he set off, there came fresh drama when Salamano in the leading Fiat came to a halt about 2 kilometres from the pits.

The hubbub in the Fiat pits became a positive uproar when Feretti, Salamano's mechanic, was seen running towards them. He managed to pant 'benzina, benzina!' before falling against the counter, completely exhausted, but when the Fiat team manager despatched a fresh mechanic with a bidon of fuel, the race jury ruled that this was not permissible, and an official stopped him, insisting that the original mechanic must return to the car. Poor Feretti, still gasping for breath, thereupon took the bidon and grabbed a bicycle, only to be stopped again and told he must make the journey on foot.

This action aroused the ire of the crowd, who whistled and catcalled indignantly, while in the Fiat pit all was consternation. Alas for Salamano, the spluttering engine which forced him to stop was not suffering from fuel shortage, but, like its sister cars, from seriously damaged internals. The superchargers which had given the Fiats their pace also proved their undoing.

It was amidst this crisis for Fiat that a distinctly Torinese accent, which could only have been Bertarione's, was heard from the Sunbeam pits to remark, 'I will send them a proper design for bearings to stand up to supercharging.'

But what of de Hane Segrave, flogging his No 12 Sunbeam around that long, dusty, stony circuit? On lap 33, with only two to go, he seemed a certain second, the highest he had ever been in a Grand Prix. Then, as he crested a rise near Semblancay, his heart leapt when he saw, stranded on the right, a red car which could only be Salamano's Fiat. He hardly believed it until Dutoit shouted in his ear, 'C'est le quatorze qui est en panne. Nous sommes en tête!' ('No 14 is broken down – we are leading!').

As he tore past the pits with only two laps to cover, the entire Sunbeam ménage was up on the pit counter waving

Making history: Segrave crossing the line at Tours, the first ever British driver of a British car to win the French Grand Prix – a feat unequalled for 37 years, when Brabham's Cooper won the 1960 race. *(Cyril Posthumus)*

him on exultantly, though they had to jump down again pretty quickly as Divo came in for his regular *bidon*, slinging it in with the engine running, and dashing off again, anxious to preserve his hard-won second place.

Even then, Fate hadn't finished. While Segrave fled round, half expecting the Fiat to roar past at any moment, poor Bill Guinness became the undeserving target for misfortune. He was lying third, his clutch still slipping, the engine misfiring occasionally, and his second gear out of action, when he inadvertently stalled at La Membrolle. He and Perkins had the greatest difficulty in getting going again owing to badly burnt valves, so that Friderich's Bugatti went past, splitting Sunbeam's 1-2-3 order.

In the Sunbeam pits the atmosphere was electric as de Hane ran out his last lap. Then up went the relieved cry, 'Here he comes', and although the ACF were either too late, or too tired, to wave the official finishing flag for him, a fine roar of applause went up as Segrave and Dutoit in the green No 12 shot across the line at over 100 mph to win the 496¼-mile race in 6 hours 35 minutes 19.6 seconds, at 75.3 mph.

Completing an extra lap, the victors pulled up, tired,

grimed but elated, and clambered from their car, instantly to be 'fired' at by a battery of cameras. From these they turned and crossed the course to the Tribune of Honour, where the War Minister, M. Maginot, and other dignitaries waited to congratulate the Grand Prix winner.

Then out rang 'God save the King' for the first time ever in the greatest of Grands Prix, a thousand hands seemed to offer themselves for shaking, until at last Segrave and Dutoit joined the Sunbeam equipage in the Hartford pits. There they were embraced by the excited Bertarione and, much to de Hane's disgust, offered champagne, which he disliked. All he wanted was a glass of cold water – but they hadn't any!

Back in England, at St. John's Wood, that Monday evening, Doris Segrave made a telephone call to Reuters' news service in London. 'This is Mrs Segrave. Have you any results, please, of the Grand Prix motor race at Tours?'

'Grand Prix motor race, madam? Just a moment, please.'

A pause, then the voice returned, pitched higher with excitement. 'Hello, madam; yes, we have the Grand Prix results. Your husband, Major Segrave, was the winner!'

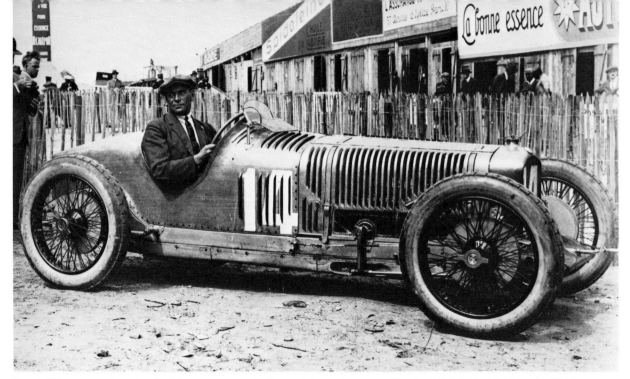

Louis Wagner at the wheel of the very complex but, ultimately, very effective V12 2-litre Delage in 1925. Delage dominated the French race after withdrawal of the Alfa Romeo team. *(Cyril Posthumus)*

1924-25

By 1924 Fiat's interest in racing was waning, partly perhaps because of the loss of important personnel, Bertarione to Sunbeam and Vittorio Jano to Alfa Romeo, and the team achieved little. Racing turned into a duel between Jano's new P2, which is fully described on Pages 00-00 and the Planchon-designed Delage V12. The 1985 cc Delage was a formidable piece of machinery and constantly modified by his assistant Albert Lory who assumed full responsibilities following Planchon's departure later in 1924. During the year the Delages, still not fully developed, finished second and third in the French Grand Prix and third at San Sebastian. The Alfa Romeos won the French and Italian races.

In the absence of both Alfa Romeo and Fiat, Segrave with the new 8-cylinder supercharged Sunbeam was the winner at San Sebastian in Spain, Britain's last Grand Prix success until Tony Brooks won the 1955 Syracuse Grand Prix at the wheel of a Connaught. Mercedes scored a rare success when Christian Werner won the Targa Florio at the wheel of a Ferdinand Porsche-designed supercharged M7294 car and the Schmid, the 1923 Rolland-Pilain with Swiss 'cuff-valve' engine designed by Dr Albert Schmid and Ernest Henry, could manage no better than fifth

and sixth places in the Italian Grand Prix. The year also saw the appearance of the new straight-eight Bugatti Type 35, the archetypal racing car of the 1920s, but its successes were to come later.

For the last year of the 2-litre formula in 1925, there was one change, riding mechanics were no longer carried. The Delage V12 was now supercharged and developed a stupendous 180 bhp at 7000 rpm (compared with 120 bhp in unsupercharged form). Alfa Romeo withdrew from the French Grand Prix after Antonio Ascari's fatal crash and Delage took the first two places (Benoist/Divo followed by Wagner/Torchy) and Delage took the first three places at San Sebastian in the absence of Alfa Romeo. Delage however withdrew from the Italian race. Constantini won the Targa Florio for Bugatti, but overall it was again an Alfa Romeo year. The following account of the all-conquering P2 by Peter Hull and Luigi Fusi was first published by Profile Publications Ltd in 1967.

The Alfa Romeo P2 Grand Prix Car

It is a surprising fact that the full technical details of the P2 Grand Prix Alfa Romeo were not made known to motor racing enthusiasts in general until some 40 years after the car's inception in 1924. The famous P2 cars were seen in action mainly in their native Italy, and made successful appearances in France, Belgium, Switzerland, North Africa and Czechoslovakia, but never in Great Britain or the USA. If only one had come to Brooklands, no doubt its secrets would have soon been unlocked; T.A.S.O. Mathieson tells us that Captain George Eyston tried to buy one around 1930, but instead he was persuaded by the Alfa Romeo factory to take over a rather special 1750, with which he obtained records at Brooklands in 1930 with R. C. Stewart, the actual owner of the car.

Prior to the advent of Alfa Romeo's P2, the most successful Italian Grand Prix marque since the pioneer days was Fiat, their unbeatable 6-cylinder Type 804, built for the 2-litre formula which commenced in 1922, being an acknowledged landmark in racing car design. Segrave's 2-litre Sunbeam, which won the 1923 French GP at Tours after the Fiats had had trouble with the vane-type superchargers fitted to their new straight-eight Type 805 models, was designed by the Italian ex-Fiat designer Vincent Bertarione, and thus was said to owe much in its layout to the Type 804; in the same way the P2 Alfa Romeo, the work of the ex-Fiat designer Vittorio Jano, was said to have been based on the Type 805.

However, one of the authors of this Profile (Luigi Fusi) was from its earliest days a member of the design department created by Ing. Nicola Romeo to be responsible for the P2, and he feels bound to point out that although Jano naturally availed himself of his Fiat experience, the conception of the car and the advanced techniques which brought about its final success, were a result of Jano's own original genius. It is significant to remember that it was the superiority of the P2 in racing which caused Fiats to withdraw from competitions.

The part which Nicola Romeo himself played in the creation of the P2 should not be underestimated. Born at San Antimo, near Naples, on 28 April, 1876, Romeo graduated in civil engineering at the Naples Polytechnic in 1900, and then went to Liège in Belgium where he obtained a degree in electrical engineering. In 1902 he set up a business in Milan concerned with compressed air mining machinery and earth moving equipment and was responsible for the drilling of the Appenines tunnel for the Bologna-Florence railway. During the 1914-18 war he prospered, took over the ALFA motor car factory in Milan and generally became something of a captain of industry, producing RO (Romeo) aircraft in Naples, railway wagons and all sorts of engineering equipment besides Alfa Romeo cars.

To spread the name of Alfa Romeo abroad, he gave Jano the full backing of all his resources for the design and construction of the P2 and closely followed its development with his collaborators in the venture, Ing. Giorgio Rimini, Ascari, Campari, Ferrari, Bazzi and Rescalli. Jano was

helped in the design department by Signor Molino who, from 1926 to 1956, was to be in charge of design at Fabbrica Automobili Bianchi of Milan.

Enzo Ferrari was born in Modena, in the Italian province of Emilia-Romagna, and in his memoirs he has said that Turin, the capital of the province of Piedmont and the home of Fiat cars, creates a breed that is quite different from that in other towns in Italy, although today it is debatable whether it was the Torinese that made Fiat or Fiat that made the Torinese. With their racing record it is hardly surprising that the Fiat works attracted some of the finest automobile engineering brains in Italy.

A genius in overalls. Vittorio Jano, acknowledged as one of the world's greatest automobile designers, who led the team which designed and built the P2. *(Luigi Fusi)*

After the 1914-18 war Ferrari found himself in Turin and applied for a job with Fiat, though without success. He did, however, get a job with a firm there that sold light truck chassis to coachbuilders for conversion into touring cars, which were in short supply at that time. His work often took Ferrari to Milan and in a great meeting place of the sporting fraternity in that city, the Bar Vittorio Emanuele, he met Ugo Sivocci, who was chief tester at the CMN (Costruzioni Meccaniche Nazionali) car works at Milan, a make then fitting war surplus Isotta Fraschini engines into new chassis. It was Sivocci who persuaded Ferrari to leave Turin and settle in Milan. Sivocci took Ferrari in hand at the CMN works, and they both raced these cars in the 1919 Targa Florio. The CMN firm later transferred to works in Pontedera, Tuscany, where the Vespa scooter eventually came to be produced.

At this time another motor firm in Milan, later to be world-famous, was just starting to make a name for itself in competitions. This was Alfa Romeo, and their Chief Designer, Giuseppe Merosi, also came from the same region as Ferrari, though his birthplace of Piacenza is in the far north on the borders of Lombardy, of which Milan is the capital city. Back in 1904 Merosi had worked for a year in the racing car design department of Fiat in Turin, though he had been with ALFA (later Alfa Romeo) since 1910.

It was to Alfa Romeo that Ferrari went after leaving CMN, and Sivocci joined him there after driving for Fiat in the 1921 Italian GP at Brescia. In October 1920 Ferrari drove in the Alfa Romeo team in the Targa Florio, and finished second in a 40/60 hp model that had originally been designed by Merosi before the war.

Before long Ferrari, backed up by the racing and sales manager Giorgio Rimini, had made himself the driving force behind the Alfa Romeo team which scored many successes in Italian events with pre-war designed cars driven by Antonio Ascari, Giuseppe Campari and Ugo Sivocci. Their first big international win, however, was in the 1923 Targa Florio, won by Ugo Sivocci in Merosi's new post-war design, the 3-litre six-cylinder push-rod ohv RL model.

Ferrari, like Coatalen of Sunbeam, realised that it would be a shot in the arm for Alfa Romeo hopes of breaking into Grand Prix racing if he could attract to Milan one of the team of brilliant young technicians working for Fiat. His first success in this direction was with Luigi Bazzi (later to design the famous Bi-Motore Alfa Romeo), who left Fiat for Alfa Romeo following a disagreement with his chief, Ing. Fornaca, after the 1923 French GP at Tours.

Bazzi immediately set to work to assist Merosi in completing the design of the six-cylinder Grand Prix P1 Alfa Romeo, like the 1923 Sunbeam inspired by the invincible Type 804 Fiat. A team of P1 cars was entered for the 1923

Italian GP at Monza in August 1923, but unfortunately Ugo Sivocci was killed in one of them in practice, so that the entire team was withdrawn from the race by Nicola Romeo as a mark of respect.

The following month Ferrari was climbing the stairs to a flat on the third floor of an unpretentious house in the Via San Massimo, Turin, the home of Vittorio Jano. Luigi Bazzi had suggested that Ferrari should make the call, for Jano was a young and very promising technician at Fiat. Jano's wife, Rosina, answered Ferrari's ring, and, when he told her that the reason for his visit was to tempt her husband away from Fiat, she said she was sure her husband was too much of a Piedmontese ever to leave Turin. However, Vittorio Jano himself soon arrived and listened to Ferrari's proposition. The following day he signed up with Alfa Romeo, and brought other lesser members of the Fiat staff with him.

Vittorio Jano was born on 22 April, 1891, in Turin, where his father was Chief of the Arsenal. Young Jano entered the car industry in 1909 as a technical draughtsman with STAR (Societa Torinese Automobili Rapid), a firm founded in 1904 by Giovanni Battista Ceirano to manufacture Rapid cars. Jano stayed with Rapid until the spring of 1911, when he went to Fiat.

There is no doubt that Jano was a genius amongst automobile designers, and Nicola Romeo first gave him the chance to prove it. At Fiat he had been on the design staff for both touring and racing cars and was chief of their racing department in 1923.

Ferrari says Jano introduced an almost military-like discipline at Alfa Romeo, which enabled him to produce the P2 in a few months. Jano was almost 20 years younger than Merosi, and the latter was not too pleased when Jano replaced him as Chief Designer of both touring and racing cars in 1926. Merosi then transferred to Mathis at Strasbourg, who had once had Ettore Bugatti as his Chief Designer; not that this was probably much consolation to Merosi.

In the words of the late Laurence Pomeroy, the P2 Alfa Romeo followed the conventions established by Fiat in 1922 not only in respect of engine design, but also in both bodywork and general external appearance.

On the straight-eight engine the same welded-up steel construction for the cylinder jackets was followed as pioneered by Mercedes and later adopted by Fiat. So far as the supercharging went Jano had carried out some development work by supercharging one of the P1 cars in 1924, thereby raising its output from 80 bhp to 118 bhp.

The supercharger on the P2 blew air into the carburettor on the Mercedes principle instead of drawing mixture from it to blow into the engine, an arrangement pioneered by Sunbeam in 1924 and later universally adopted by other manufacturers, though Mercedes did not go over to it until the 'thirties. The supercharger pressure was about 10½ lb and delivery from the front of the engine was to a single Memini carburettor at the rear of the engine via a large ribbed aluminium pipe.

Unlike the later Jano Alfa Romeos, the valve operation from the overhead cams was through fingers on the P2, as on the 1922 Fiat and the P1 Alfa Romeo (and also the single ohc Type 35 Bugatti). The valve angle was 104 degrees, compared with 96 degrees on the 1922 Fiat and 90 degrees on the P1.

Like the Fiat both the P2 and the P1 had roller bearings, whilst it is interesting to compare the output of the original P2 of 134 bhp in 1924 with the 146 bhp of the Roots blown straight-eight Type 805 Fiat and the 138 bhp of the 1924 Roots blown 6-cylinder Sunbeam, a development of the 1923 unblown car.

As for appearance, the P2 certainly resembled the Fiats, even to the extent of having a bull-nose radiator cowl. The gearbox was in unit with the engine, whilst the back springs were unusual in not being visible externally as they narrowed towards each other at the rear in plan view to follow the taper of the pointed tail of the car, their front mountings actually being inboard of the chassis members, which also tapered towards the rear.

In March 1924, the first P2 engine was running on the bench, and on 2 June at 6 pm the first car was completed. Campari and Ascari tested it at Monza first, then over the Parma-Poggio de Berceto road, and on 9 June the car made its racing debut in Ascari's hands at the Circuit of Cremona race over 200 miles, which it won with ease from a Chiribiri and a Bugatti at 98.31 mph. It was timed at over 121 mph over the 10-kilometre straight, and the riding

mechanic on this occasion was Luigi Bazzi, who had assisted Jano in the design of the car.

Campari's P2 should undoubtedly have won the first of the long series of races on the Pescara Circuit, which took place on 13 July, and Ferrari, driving an RL Targa Florio Alfa with Campari's cousin, young Eugenio Siena, as riding mechanic, was constantly watching his mirrors to let the P2 through. However, Campari had burst a tyre and carried no spare (though Ferrari says he dropped out through gearbox trouble) and he hid the car up a lane to conceal it from the Alfa Romeo team's rivals. Fortunately, Ferrari saved the day for Alfa Romeo by winning the race on his RL from a Mercedes and an SPA. Eugenio Siena was destined to lose his life in the 1938 Tripoli GP at the wheel of a 12-cylinder Alfa Romeo.

On 3 August, 1924, the P2 cars made their debut in a Grande Épreuve when a team of three took part in the European Grand Prix at Lyons, the drivers being Antonio Ascari, Giuseppe Campari and Louis Wagner. A fourth car, to be driven by Ferrari, was withdrawn when Ferrari fell ill. Ascari's car was unusual in being cut short at the back, a single spare wheel behind the seats replacing the long, streamlined tails of the other cars. Perhaps Ascari was bearing in mind Campari's experience at Pescara.

Although this was their very first Grand Prix, the Alfa Romeos were always amongst the leaders. At first Segrave's Sunbeam led from Ascari until the Sunbeam dropped back with a faulty magneto. Then Bordino's straight-eight Type 805 Fiat assumed the lead with Ascari still second, and held it until the 12th lap when Bordino stopped with brake trouble. On the 17th lap of the 35-lap race, Lee Guinness's Sunbeam took the lead from the Alfa Romeo when Ascari stopped to change wheels. When

The first P2 ever built, photographed, still unpainted, on 2 June, 1924, a week before it won the Circuit of Cremona race. *(Luigi Fusi)*

Guinness later retired with transmission failure, Ascari led from Campari, then came the two unsupercharged V12 Delages driven by Divo and Benoist, followed by Wagner's P2. The unsupercharged Type 35 Bugattis were delayed by tyre trouble.

With just three laps to go Ascari made a pit stop and, despite much pushing by his mechanic Giulio Ramponi, he could not restart the engine and had the heartbreaking misfortune to retire with a cracked block. As a result the stout Campari was the victor, finishing less than a mile ahead of Divo's Delage which was followed home by Benoist's Delage, Wagner's P2, Segrave's Sunbeam, Thomas's Delage and the Bugattis of Chassagne and Friderich.

This, together with the 1914 French GP over a similar circuit at Lyons, is generally acknowledged to have been one of the greatest Grands Prix ever held due to the quality of the entry and the closeness of the racing and Alfa Romeo's victory in their first GP was unprecedented in the annals of the sport.

It also proved to be the hardest fought GP the P2 cars ever contested. In the Italian GP at Monza a month later the only opposition was from a Mercedes team which was withdrawn after one of their drivers, Zborowski, was fatally injured in a crash. Ascari, making up for his misfortune at Lyons, won by 16 minutes from Wagner, with Campari a close third. The first car of a rival team to finish, a Schmid, crossed the line three quarters of an hour after Campari. This was the last year mechanics were carried in GP races, though two-seater bodywork continued to be specified for 1925.

This 1924 Grand Prix of Italy, on 19 October, saw more power being produced from the P2 engine by the adoption of two Memini carburettors instead of one. With one Memini the engine had produced 134 bhp at 5200 rpm, but with the two carburettors the power went up to 145 bhp at 5500 rpm. Due to the higher fuel consumption caused by the two carburettors the oil tank was moved from its position in the scuttle and was situated under the passenger's seat, whilst a reserve 5½-gallon fuel tank was placed in the scuttle. All the Grand Prix races of 1924/5 were 500 or 600 miles in length, but none of the races the P2s contested between 1926 and 1929 were longer than about 300 miles, so the reserve tank was dispensed with during these years, and the oil tank was returned to its original position in the scuttle.

The 1925 season commenced with a walk-over for the P2s in the European GP at Spa on 28 June, in which all three team cars carried a spare wheel at the back in place of a streamlined tail. Here the Delages formed the only opposition, but all retired through not fitting blow-off valves for their new superchargers. As the Frenchman, Louis

Wagner, had gone over to Delage, Count Gaston Brilli-Peri took his place in the Alfa Romeo team, but he had the misfortune to retire with a broken spring at Spa. Ascari was again the victor with Campari second, and they were the only finishers. During the race the Alfa Romeo drivers stopped for a five-minute impromptu meal round a table whilst their cars were washed and polished – Jano's method of getting his own back on the Belgian crowds, who were jeering at the Italians for their easy victory.

The French GP at Montlhéry in July was a tragedy, for Ascari crashed and was killed whilst in the lead. Although Campari then led by four minutes from the nearest Delage and Sunbeam, the whole Alfa Romeo team was withdrawn from the race.

Despite the fact that the Italian GP at Monza on 6 September decided the newly instituted World Championship, Delage did not enter, and two centrifugally-blown straight eight Duesenbergs from the USA were the only apparently effective challengers to the P2s, apart from some Type 35 Bugattis linered down to 1½ litres in anticipation of the 1926 Formula. By now the streamlined tails on the P2s had been modified, having been shortened by 150 mm, with three elongated holes in the rather blunter point, this latter modification having first been used at Montlhéry on the longer-tailed cars. The holes were to allow the escape of air at high speed.

It was Brilli-Peri who brought the World Championship to Alfa Romeo when he won from Campari by 19 minutes. Costantini's little Bugatti was third and Milton's Duesenberg fourth. In fifth place came the third P2 of the team, driven by the American Peter de Paolo, which was only running on one carburettor. De Paolo had won at Indianapolis the previous May with his Duesenberg, but refused an invitation to enter it at Monza as he was unwilling to have the cockpit of his pencil-slim single seater widened to two-seater width in compliance with the European regulations. Instead he accepted the invitation to drive a P2 which, he said, did not handle as well as his Duesenberg.

A relatively unknown driver called Tazio Nuvolari was reserve for the P2 team, but he crashed in practice when his gearbox seized and injured himself.

As the P2 had won the title of World Champion for Alfa Romeo, a laurel wreath was added as a surround to the radiator badge on *all* Alfa Romeo models from 1926 onwards.

The 1½-litre GP Formula was not a success, so that many important races during this period were run under *formule libre* rules and P2 Alfa Romeos frequently took part in them. In fact in Volume 1 of his classic work *The Grand Prix Car* (Temple Press Ltd) Laurence Pomeroy was moved to comment in the caption to a photograph of a P2 engine that the P2 Alfa Romeo was the most successful road

A practice scene with a Manx-tailed P2 before the 1925 Grand Prix d'Europe at Spa. Campari looks back down the road, whilst Ascari, the eventual winner, eats out of a pot – *not* his crash helmet! *(Luigi Fusi)*

racing car in Europe for the five years following its inception in 1924, a statement which must have caused several copies of his magnificent great volume to drop with a thud from the nerveless fingers of Bugatti admirers.

Although Count Brilli-Peri, Count Bonmartini, Tazio Nuvolari and the Swiss driver J. Kessler (who bought his car from Campari) all obtained places or wins with P2s during these years, it was one car driven first by Campari and then by Achille Varzi which scored the most successes. Believed to be the winner at Lyons in 1924, the main modification when it was in Campari's hands was the external fitting of a spare wheel to the nearside of the tail, necessitating a kink in the exhaust pipe to pass underneath it. This was one of the four positions utilised for carrying a spare wheel on the P2. Campari bought this car from the works, and with it he won the Coppa Acerbo at Pescara in both 1927 and 1928. In 1928 he sold the car to Achille Varzi, and, sharing the driving with him, came second in the European GP at Monza behind Chiron's Bugatti.

The following year Varzi, with his new acquisition, won the Monza GP and the races at Rome, Alessandria and Montenero and became Champion of Italy for 1929. He finished second at Cremona to Brilli-Peri in a 2006 cc P2, who averaged 138.77 mph on the same 10 km stretch over

which Ascari had averaged 121 mph with the 1987 cc P2 back in 1924.

At the end of the year Varzi, like Brilli-Peri, sold his car back to the factory, who completely modified it for 1930 in order to run it as part of a team together with two other similarly modified P2s.

These modifications were quite substantial and incorporated several parts from the 6C 1750 Gran Sport sports car. These included the front and rear axles and the brakes. The back springs were now parallel to the car's axis instead of being inclined as before, and both front and rear springs were outside the chassis members and very near the wheels to improve the springing. Although the wheelbase was the same as before, the modified car was no longer slightly crab-tracked like its predecessor. The oil tank was fitted under the passenger's seat, as on the 1925 P2 car, and the fuel tank, forming the tail of the car, was modified by making a longitudinal slot in it for housing the spare wheel. The cockpit was also made larger by widening it at the aperture, though the body width was the same as in 1924.

On the engine the magneto drive was altered owing to troubles encountered in the previous year, whilst the supercharging system was modernised by making the supercharger draw the mixture from the carburettor instead of blowing through it. The capacity was also increased slightly to 2006 cc and the output went up to 175 bhp. Finally the cars were given inclined squarish radiators similar to those on the 6C Gran Sport 1750 Alfa Romeos.

The modified P2 was no beauty, but showed its effectiveness at Alessandria early in 1930 when Varzi, on what had been his old car, won the race from Juan Zanelli's Bugatti.

Two of the modified cars were entered for the Targa Florio, but they were so fast and difficult to handle it was decided to scratch both the cars, which were to have been driven by Varzi and Campari. Campari was quite happy with the decision, but Varzi insisted on starting in the car he drove at Alessandria. It is interesting to note that for the Targa Florio his car's induction was modified back to the old system whereby the supercharger blew through the carburettor.

In the drive of his life, during which his car lost its spare wheel, and caught fire at the back when the mechanic was trying to refuel it whilst in motion, Varzi won the race at record speed and beat the old lap record.

Tyre troubles defeated the three square-radiatored P2s in the final of the Monza GP, and their power undoubtedly exceeded their road holding abilities. Despite this they did well in the Consolation Race and Borzacchini was second in the 3000 cc heat. In the Coppa Acerbo Nuvolari came fifth in his P2, whereas Borzacchini was third behind two

Maseratis in a 6C 1750 Alfa. The first Czechoslovakian GP at Brno was the P2's last race. Two modified cars were driven by Nuvolari and Borzacchini. After his own car had retired, Nuvolari took over Borzacchini's and was leading the race, but he slowed some six miles from the finish and toured over the finishing line in third place behind privately owned Bugattis, his radiator blowing off clouds of steam.

Alfa Romeo supported Grand Prix racing almost continuously from 1924 until 1951, an era that began and ended with two remarkably successful designs – the P2 and the Type 158/159. By the greatest of good fortune examples of the two types of P2 still survive and can be seen by visitors to Italy. An original 1924 P2 is on display at the Alfa Romeo Museum at the factory at Arese, just outside Milan, whilst Varzi's modified 1930 Targa Florio winner is in the Biscaretti Automobile Museum in Turin. Even more encouraging is the fact that it is the policy of the Alfa Romeo Museum to keep all their exhibits in running order, and to exercise them on occasions.

1926-27

For 1926 the Grand Prix Formula changed to 1500 cc with a minimum weight of 600 kg and a minimum width of 80 cm. The change in the formula meant that Alfa Romeo, Fiat and Sunbeam all withdrew, as did several other manufacturers, although, as has been narrated, the P2 Alfa Romeos continued to be seen in Formule Libre events. In Britain underfinanced efforts were made by Alvis (with remarkable and very promising front-wheel-drive cars that were never fully developed), Aston Martin, Eldridge (E.A.D. Eldridge was a prolific and successful special builder) and Halford (Major Halford was a brilliant aero engine designer). The first (Diatto-based) Maserati appeared and another Italian company, OM, built an 8-cylinder car. Racing in 1926 was, however, fought out between three French teams: Delage with their new straight-eight that achieved little in 1926, but won every major race it contested in 1927 – and the cars were to win many more in later years; Bugatti who largely dominated the year; and the unsuccessful Bertarione-designed Talbot 8-cylinder – it was also raced as the Darracq, but was built at the S-T-D factory at Suresnes near Paris – and the truth was that the company could not really afford to race.

The 'World Championship' was held for the second time in 1926 and dominated by Bugatti (who raced the Type 39A, a Type 35 derivative) with wins in

the French Grand Prix, the Spanish Grand Prix (at San Sebastian) and the Italian Grand Prix at Monza – together with dozens of other, lesser events. Bugatti could hardly have lost the French race at Miramas, as the only entries were three Bugattis! Indianapolis was a round in the Championship and won by Frank Lockhart with a Miller and the only European round which Bugatti did not win was the RAC Grand Prix at Brooklands where victory went to Delage.

There were detail changes to the regulations for 1927: minimum weight was increased to 700 kg and there was a minimum width of 85 cm. By 1927 Albert Lory had the Delage V8 perfected and it was unchallenged throughout the year. This is the full story of these brilliant cars, as told by Cyril Posthumus (first published by Profile Publications Limited, 1966).

The Delage 1½-Litre, 1926-27

Amidst the infinite and fascinating variety of racing cars produced during the past seventy years, some stand out from the ruck as veritable milestones along the hard, unending road to perfection. One such was the 1926-27

Perhaps the most successful racing car of all time – the straight-eight Bugatti Type 35. This is Jules Goux on his way to a win in the 1926 Grand Prix d'Europe held at San Sebastian. *(Cyril Posthumus)*

1½-litre straight-eight Delage, the French car which won every major race it contested in 1927, carrying Robert Benoist to an unassailable European Championship, and with which the British driver Richard Seaman defeated all the modern *Voiturettes* in four major International races during 1936.

It was the last and, in many eyes, the greatest of racing designs emanating from the Delage factory at Courbevoie-sur-Seine, whose founder, Louis Delage, believed implicitly in the value of racing. Delage laurels included the 1908 GP des Voiturettes, 1911 Light Car GP at Boulogne, 1913 GP de France, 1914 Indianapolis 500 Miles race, and the 1925 French and Spanish GPs, but the straight-eight 1500 was to surpass all these feats. When he had money, the flamboyant Louis Delage spent if freely. His Château de Pecq at St Germain was one of his more famous indulgences, but the 1926-27 GP Delage was another on which no expense was spared, and which has perpetuated his name in the automobile world.

A Remarkable Engine

The 1926-27 Delage's forté was its engine. After much experience in developing the Planchon-designed 2-litre V12 Delage of 1923-25, Ingénieur Albert Lory, who came from Salmson with Robert Benoist, plumped for the simpler straight-eight layout when designing a new Delage for the 1500 cc GP Formula of 1926-27. This required a minimum weight limit of 600 kg, two seats (though one was unoccupied) and a minimum body width of 80 cm (31½ in), the weight being raised in 1927 to 700 kg, and the second seat no longer being required.

Lory's engine had an iron cylinder block with fixed cylinder head on an alloy crankcase, twin overhead camshafts operating sixteen valves, a bore and stroke of 55.8×76.0 mm (1488 cc), twin Roots-type superchargers, and a one-piece counterbalanced crankshaft running in ten big roller races. The lavish indulgence in roller and ball races was eloquent of Lory's determined fight against friction. In all, no less than 62 were used in this remarkable engine! The big ends, camshafts, and the train of 21 timing and auxiliary gears driving oil pumps, water pump, magneto and camshafts all ran in roller or ball races. The two finned superchargers, mounted centrally alongside the engine on the nearside, were driven from the driving train by one internal shaft on the left, and the magneto by another shaft on the right, both running in ball races.

Lubrication was on the dry sump system, with the main bearings fed by direct jets and the big ends by centrifugal force. Generous water passaging to ensure maximum cooling at vital points was provided, the overall

Innovative, but unsuccessful – the front-wheel-drive Alvis raced in 1926-27. This is the car in 1927 form. Alvis of Coventry justified their racing activities for a whole host of reasons including '... we think it right and patriotic to pit British cars against foreign ones on all possible occasions.' Alvis claimed that Delage spent 25 times as much as they did on racing during the 1927 season.

result being that this engine turned at over 8000 rpm, a prodigious crankshaft speed at that time. The revolution counter read to 9000 rpm, the instrument being marked green from 6000 to 7500 rpm, orange from 7500 to 8000 rpm and red from 8000 to 9000 rpm. An unprecedented piston speed of 4000 ft per minute was attained, and the power output was over 165 bhp in 1926. This figure was attained on a petrol-alcohol-benzole-ether fuel, with the twin blowers compressing at only 7½ lb per sq in. That it could stand considerably higher internal pressures was proved ten years later when Giulio Ramponi, testing Seaman's engine on the brake with 12 lb psi supercharging, inadvertently let it exceed 9000 rpm for several minutes without mishap.

The engine drove through a multi-plate clutch and a 5-speed gearbox in which fourth was direct and fifth speed an overdrive, intended to reduce stresses at sustained high speeds. The gearbox also drove a mechanical brake servo. An open propeller shaft transmitted the power to the bevel final drive on the rear axle.

The Chassis

With that remarkable (but heavy) engine, Lory's genius was largely expended. His chassis was unduly slender and whippy, thereby impairing roadholding. It is generally but incorrectly believed that the engine of the 1500 cc Delage in its earliest (1926) form was offset in the frame with the objects (a) of exploiting the 'no-mechanics' rule introduced the previous year, and (b) of finding more room for the driver. Credit for doing this must go, in fact, to the Delage's rival, the 8-cylinder 1½-litre Talbot-Darracq, which had its engine desaxé from its inception. The Delage engine and transmission were central, as confirmed by the starting-handle hole in the radiator. None the less, the driver was seated lower than the propeller shaft on his left, with little room to spare, and the exhaust system was uncomfortably close to the scuttle and pedals. Just how uncomfortably was soon to be revealed.

The radiator, broad, squarish and similar to the 1925 GP type, was mounted vertically, but very low and well ahead of the front axle. Suspension followed the conventions of the day in being semi-elliptic with short, hard leaf springs and Hartford friction shock absorbers. Streamlining was helped by a full length undertray and flush fuel filler caps. Finish was in pale blue, with darker wheels. It has been estimated that building the team of four for the 1926 season cost Automobiles Delage something like £36,000. Nor was it their final expenditure.

Travelling Ovens

The unreadiness of the new Delages contributed to the fiasco of the 1926 French GP at Miramas on 27 June.

Their withdrawal, together with that of the Talbot team, left three Bugattis to dispute a farcical race. But four weeks later the cars from Courbevoie were at San Sebastian, in Spain, to face the seasoned Bugatti team in the GP of Europe. Freak equatorial weather added to the drama, for temperatures of 110 deg F laid appalling stress on a serious Delage defect – that exhaust pipe lurking so snugly on the offside of the body was turning the drivers' cockpits into veritable furnaces and their pedals red hot.

That the new cars were very fast was established from the start, but after ten laps or so their hard-won lead disappeared as the Delage drivers pulled in one by one for relief from stifling heat and fumes. Holes were cut in the scuttles and cowls to coax extra air in, and second drivers took over. Morel collapsed with sunburn and burnt feet and went to hospital, Benoist and reserve driver Wagner needed medical treatment, and Bourlier lay inert behind the pits, while the cars stood silent in the scorching sun and the Bugattis moved farther and farther ahead. Then the elements relented, a cooling wind sprang up, the team revived and Robert Senéchal, a last-minute volunteer relief, shared one car with Bourlier to snatch second place from the Bugattis. The other Delages placed fourth and sixth, while Wagner set the fastest lap.

Having cost Delage the year's most important race, that unanticipated design defect very nearly cost him the next one. This was the British GP at Brooklands held on a hot August day, and Lory's devilish exhaust pipes again cooked the drivers so that they stopped periodically to douse their scorching feet in bowls of water. 'One could actually hear their boots hissing as they went into the water' wrote Major H. O. D. Segrave, a member of the rival Talbot team, afterwards. The exhaust set fire to the bodywork of Wagner's car and he had to retire it, later relieving Senéchal to share victory in an exhausting race, pursued by a Bugatti and another Delage.

No Delages ran in the 1926 Italian GP. Instead they were sent back to Courbevoie for drastic rebuilding. Lory redesigned the engine to bring the exhaust valves and that troublesome exhaust system to the nearside. Next, varying Talbot's example, he offset the entire engine-transmission-final drive line four inches to the left, thus gaining more cockpit room but squeezing the twin blowers out of their place on the nearside of the engine. Instead Lory produced a long single blower of identical capacity, mounted it high ahead of the engine and drove it from the timing gear train. To accommodate the repositioned starting handle the radiator had to be remodelled, so while he was about it Lory designed a handsome new one, taking another leaf from Talbot's book by inclining it and improving the streamlining.

Five Victories – and a Small Setback

In this improved form, and with that superb engine now delivering a full 170 bhp, the Delage team and their No 1 driver Benoist proved unassailable in 1927. They kicked off early in the season with a damp but easy victory in the GP de l'Ouverture at Montlhéry, Benoist driving a car with a modified 1926 radiator as the new ones were not ready yet. After this preliminary canter, the team turned out in full strength for the French GP, also at Montlhéry, where Benoist, Bourlier and Morel outpaced the trouble-fraught Talbots to score a 1-2-3 victory. In the Spanish GP at San Sebastian, Benoist met tougher opposition from the audacious Italian Emilio Materassi in a factory-entered Bugatti, which was faster than the Delages through the turns but slower along the straights. The result was a tremendous duel which ended only when Materassi overdid things at Bascardo's Corner and crashed into a wall when leading with nine laps to go. The Delage, close behind, rushed into the blinding dust, missed the Bugatti by inches, and spun, Benoist in his confusion restarting the reverse way of the course! Resuming the proper direction, he went on to win, with Bourlier's Delage third behind Conelli's Bugatti.

Three weeks later occurred the only set-back to total Delage supremacy that season, in the minor GP de la Baule, a 62-mile beach race for unlimited capacity racing cars. Driving the only 1500 cc Delage entered, Edmond Bourlier led until half-distance, then spun and stalled. Oiled plugs delayed his restart and he was caught by G. E. T. Eyston's 2.3-litre Bugatti.

Undeterred, in fact with insolent confidence, Delage sent only one car, driven by Benoist, to the GP of Europe at Monza, Italy, to face OM, Miller and Duesenberg, but no Talbots or Bugattis. In pouring rain, Benoist just ran away with the race, finishing 22 minutes ahead of an OM, with a Miller third. The full team then came to Brooklands for the second British GP, scoring another devastating 1-2-3 success, well in front of the rival Bugattis. Louis Delage was present to watch their triumph, which clinched the European Championship for Robert Benoist. The winning car proudly appeared on the Delage stand at the Olympia Motor Show a few days later.

A superb shot of the straight-eight Delage in the pits at San Sebastian in 1926, the first race for the new car. Robert Senéchal is about to take over the car driven by Benoist who had been overcome by the heat and was receiving medical attention. Delage were still sorting out their problems. This car eventually finished second.

To Further Glory

On the crest of the wave, but with hard economic times looming, Louis Delage decided to sell his beautiful watch-like cars at the end of 1927. Malcolm Campbell acquired one, winning the Junior GP and the 200 Miles Race at Brooklands, and the Boulogne GP, all in 1928. The following year Louis Chiron took a Delage minus its front brakes to Indianapolis, USA, placing seventh in the famous 500 Miles Race against the specialised American track machines. W B Scott acquired the Campbell car for a successful spell of racing and class record-breaking at Brooklands, while Earl Howe acquired two Delages and won 1500 cc class races at Dieppe in 1931, Avus in 1932 and Nürburgring in 1933. His was also the first 1½-litre car to finish in the Grand Prix class Acerbo Cup race in Italy in 1932, but shortly afterwards this car was written off against a tree during the Monza GP. Howe raced his other Delage until 1935, placing third that year in the Albi and Berne races.

Rejuvenation

It was at that Berne race of 1935 that the idea of acquiring Earl Howe's Delage was first put to Dick Seaman by his head mechanic Giulio Ramponi and team manager Tony Birch. After initial resistance on the grounds that it was too old, Seaman agreed to buy the car plus another engine and many spares. That winter the Delage underwent a course of rejuvenation eloquent of the advances made in racing design and metallurgy in ten years.

Weight reduction was a prior aim, for which Ramponi prescribed new duralumin wheels saving 7 lb per wheel, a new radiator saving 20 lb, a new combined fuel tank and tail, 95 lb lighter than the old, and a change in gearbox from the heavy ENV epicyclic fitted by Earl Howe to a 5-speed Delage gearbox 70 lb lighter, as used in the 1925 V12 GP cars. Lockheed hydraulic brakes replaced the old mechanically-operated type, higher compression Hepworth and Grandage pistons were fitted, the blower pressure increased to 12 lb psi and the valve timing meticulously checked and modified by Ramponi.

Brake-tested by Laystall, the engine now gave over 185 bhp which, combined with Seaman's skill, placed it on a par with the more modern ERA, and Maserati 1500s. New, outrigged front springs and a rebuilt front axle, and the packing of the dumbirons with hard wood to resist chassis twist were other modifications. The whole car was painted a sinister black, with silver wheels, then taken by Seaman to Nürburgring, Germany, for a fortnight's testing before its debut in racing.

The black Delage's first meeting was at Donington Park in May, 1936, where it ran in two short races and won both. Then Seaman began serious work with the RAC 1½-litre race at Douglas, IOM, which the Delage won non-

First in Italy in 1927. Benoist yet again, his lone Delage in the centre of the front row, between the American Cooper Special and an OM. *(Cyril Posthumus)*

Robert Benoist with the straight-eight 1½-litre Delage after winning the 1927 RAC Grand Prix at Brooklands – his fourth major win of the year. Behind the car, holding the flowers, is Robert Senéchal.

stop, defeating nine modern ERAs. Car and driver then went abroad, briefly leading the Eifelrennen at Nürburgring before leaving the road, winning their heat at Picardie but crashing in the final (Seaman was unwell), then winning the Pescara and Berne 1500 cc races. After that, with no time for detail maintenance, the Delage was returned to Britain for the 200 Miles Race at Donington, in which Seaman won both the 1500 cc class and the race outright, defeating many larger cars.

Sadly, while Seaman was re-enacting the Delage invincibility of ten years earlier, private tragedy had assailed Louis Delage. His company failed and was absorbed by the

Delahaye concern, who paid Delage a small monthly pension and bade him keep away. He sold his possessions one by one and died, virtually destitute, in 1947.

When Dick Seaman joined the Mercedes-Benz Grand Prix team in 1937, his famous black Delage was purchased, together with the ex-Scott car, and all available spares, by Prince Chula of Siam for his cousin B. Bira to drive. Alas, in striving to modernise the design with independent front suspension and a new frame designed by Lory, the princes broke its winning spell. They abandoned if for their ERAs, but during the war Reg Parnell acquired the car plus many parts, reassembling the Seaman car with its old chassis, and producing two 'spare-parts' Delages from the rest, using the two frames built for Chula.

All three were raced in the early post-war period of racing, but R.R.C. ('Rob') Walker retrieved the Seaman car from the circuits for a major rebuild, restoring it to as near 1936 condition as possible, using a spare engine and gearbox and a new body. Only one GP Delage survives in its original 1927 form, in the United States, this being the car brought to Indianapolis by Chiron in 1929. Although inaccurately finished and wearing modern tread tyres, it stands as a cherished memorial to an unforgettable racing car.

Before the 1½-litre formula had ended, however, one other car had made a single and successful outing. The supercharged 12-cylinder Fiat Tipo 806 had been driven to victory in the 1927 Monza Grand Prix by Pietro Bordino. After this win Fiat withdrew from racing and for reasons that remain inexplicable destroyed all Type 804, 805 and 806 cars. It was vandalism on a grand scale and as Denis Jenkinson has written of Fiat, 'Their engineering expertise was outstanding, and had they put as much effort into actually racing as Delage, Bugatti or Alfa Romeo did we may have seen the whole history of Grand Prix racing reading very differently.'

1928-30

For 1928 Grand Prix racing was *almost* Formule Libre, with a minimum weight of 550 kg and with a maximum of 750 kg and with a maximum race distance of 600 km. The ever-increasing World depression meant that there was little support for Grand Prix racing, no new cars and no real incentive and most of the competing teams withdrawing. As a result racing was dominated by the well established straight-eight Bugatti in Type 35B (2270 cc

The car that could have been a world-beater: the 1927 Fiat Tipo 806 with 12-cylinder engine. Bordino drove it to victory in the Monza Grand Prix, but then it was destroyed along with other Fiat racing cars.

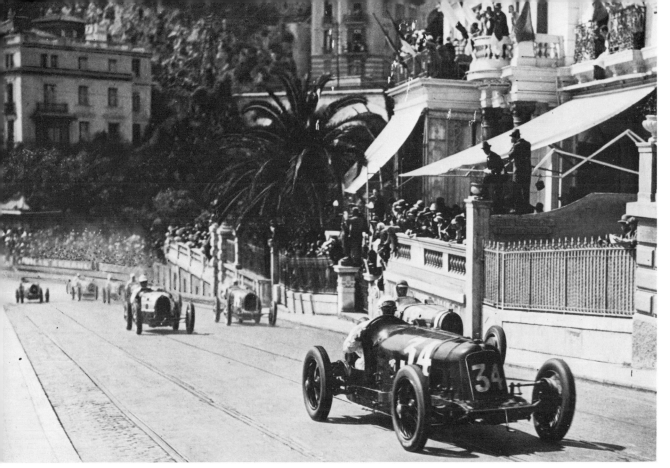

In the 1930 Monaco Grand Prix Luigi Arcangeli with a 2-litre Maserati leads a horde of Bugattis up the hill from Ste. Devote corner. Arcangeli retired and Bugattis took the first six places.

Luigi Arcangeli at the 1930 Rome Grand Prix with the new 8C-2500 Maserati, one of the most successful of the Maserati brothers' early designs. He won the race from Bouriat's Bugatti.

unsupercharged) form, and there was a fall-off in the number of races held. Monégasque driver, Louis Chiron (who was still racing as late as 1955) won both the Spanish Grand Prix at San Sebastian and the European Grand Prix – but the French Grand Prix was held as a handicap race for sports cars and the German Grand Prix, now in its third year, remained another sports car event. The Bugatti Type 35 and its derivatives probably won more Grands Prix, great or small, than any other model, mainly because of the lack of real opposition. It was, however, a reactionary design that changed little over the years.

It was to prove much the same story in 1929. Again, for this year and 1930, there was a change in the regulations. There was a minimum weight limit of 900 kg and two-seater bodies with a minimum body width of 100 cm were specified. More importantly, there was a fuel and oil consumption limit of 14 kg per 100 km. In 1929 commercially available fuel only was allowed, but this was changed for 1930 to permit up to 30% benzole. This formula was adopted in 1929 only for the Spanish and French races, but other events were run to what might loosely be described as Grand Prix rules. Williams and Bouriano took the first two places at Monaco with their Bugatti Type 35Bs, Williams also won the French Grand Prix at Le Mans and Chiron led home a Bugatti 1-2-3 in the Spanish race at San Sebastian. During the year the obsolescent Alfa Romeo P2s won minor events in Italy and Tunisia. An interesting development was the Maserati V4 with two 2-litre straight-eight engines mounted on a common crankcase and developing 300 bhp at 5500 rpm. The new car ran in only two Italian races during

the year and retired in both.

The most significant development in 1930 was the appearance of the Maserati 8C-2500, a much improved straight-eight car developing 174 bhp at 6000 rpm and their model achieved six wins during the year, albeit in minor races: the Rome Grand Prix (Arcangeli), the Coppa Ciano at Livorno (Fagioli), the Coppa Acerbo at Pescara (Varzi), the Circuit of Avellino (Fagioli), the Monza Grand Prix (Varzi) and the Spanish Grand Prix (Varzi). In addition Borzacchini won the Formule Libre Tripoli Grand Prix with the twin-engined V4. He also drove the V4 at Indianapolis, but the car was emasculated by the removal of the superchargers and retired with electrical problems. The Alfa Romeo P2s, now entered by Scuderia Ferrari which had been formed on 1 December 1929 to run the works cars for the Portello factory, achieved another year of minor successes. Bugatti, however, still dominated much of the year with the Type 35 and Molsheim won the Monaco, Belgian and French Grands Prix, in addition to many minor races. During the year Ettore Bugatti introduced the Tipo 45, another twin-engined car, but with the difference that the two 2-litre cylinder blocks were mated to a common crankshaft. These cars ran in hill climbs, they cannot be regarded as a success, but the chassis formed the basis for the Type 54 raced the following year.

By the end of 1930 Grand Prix racing was sick, very sick, but an improving economic climate led to new cars and new enthusiasm and it was to enjoy a rapid renaissance in the early 1930s.

Part 3:

ALFA ROMEO AND THE SILVER ARROWS, 1931-40

1931

For the years 1931-33 there was another change in the regulations, to a 'free formula' in which the only restriction was a minimum length of ten hours. It would have turned all Grand Prix races into major feats of endurance, save for the fact that it was adopted only for the French, Belgian and Italian races.

Racing continued to be supported by the same three companies, Alfa Romeo, Bugatti and Maserati and all three introduced new models during the year. At Monaco Bugatti produced the Type 51, the Molsheim company's familiar straight-eight, but with two overhead camshafts and a power output of 180 bhp at 5500 rpm. Louis Chiron drove one of the new French cars to victory at Monaco, the first of the year's important races held over a distance of 100 laps (195 miles).

Next came the Italian Grand Prix brought forward to 24 May so that the ten hours would be run in daylight. From Alfa Romeo came two new cars; there was a team of three two-seater racing versions of the beautifully engineered Jano design which had finished second in the Mille Miglia 1000-mile road race in sports form. Campari/Nuvolari and Minoia/Borzacchini took the first two places with these new cars and as a result of this victory it became known as the 'Monza'. It was to prove one of the most famous racing cars of all time. Alfa Romeo also produced at this race the Tipo A with two 1750 6-cylinder engines mated together. Sadly Luigi Arcangeli was killed when he crashed this car in practice. At this race Bugatti also produced the 4.9-litre Type 54, one of which was driven into third place by Achille Varzi. The ten-hour

French Grand Prix at Montlhéry was won by the Bugatti Type 51 of Divo/Bouriat and the Belgian race, another ten-hour marathon, was won by the Type 51 of Williams/Conelli.

In the remaining races of the year the results were mixed. Not unexpectedly Nuvolari won the Coppa Ciano at Livorno with a Monza, but two unexpected victories followed. Rudolf Caracciola, who had already stunned Italy by winning the Mille Miglia road race for sports cars with his brutish Mercedes-Benz SSKL, repeated this victory in the German Grand Prix at the Nürburgring with the same car, while Campari won the Coppa Acerbo at Pescara with the Tipo A Alfa Romeo. Luigi Fagioli won the Monza Grand Prix at the wheel of the new 8C-2800 Maserati with enlarged engine and the haughty Italian was leading in the Czechoslovakian Grand Prix at Brno with the same car when he crashed into a bridge – Chiron won with his Bugatti.

What was clear above all else was that the leading teams had lost their sense of direction, almost encouraged in their high-powered, but ill-handling follies by the 'free formula'.

1932

In a year in which the only major change in the regulations was a reduction in race length to a minimum of five hours and a maximum of ten, Alfa Romeo's new 'Monoposto' almost completely dominated. The Monoposto or P3, again the work of the brilliant designer Vittorio Jano, was another straight-eight, of 2.6 litres, with a power output of 190 bhp (the makers claimed rather more) and single-seater

47

The Bugatti Type 51 of Divo and Bouriat in the 1931 French Grand Prix at Montlhéry. Albert Divo is cleaning the aero screen and Guy Bouriat is standing at the rear of the car.

bodywork. By the standards of the time it handled well (better than the Bugatti and Maserati opposition), it was more than adequately powerful and Scuderia Ferrari, entering the cars on behalf of Alfa Romeo, was well organized.

Nuvolari won at Monaco from Caracciola, with a white-painted entry prepared by Scuderia Ferrari, but ostensibly privately entered. Thereafter wins followed in quick succession in the Targa Florio (Nuvolari) and the Eifelrennen (Caracciola). These successes were with the Monza as the Monoposto did not appear until the

Monégasque driver Louis Chiron at the wheel of his 4.9-litre Bugatti at the 1931 Monza Grand Prix. Chiron finished second in his heat.

Italian Grand Prix at Monza. Nuvolari won the Italian race from Fagioli's new, larger capacity twin-engined Maserati and he won again in the French Grand Prix, with other Alfas second and third, Caracciola won the German Grand Prix and then Nuvolari won three Italian races in succession, the Coppa Ciano, the Coppa Acerbo and a minor race at Avellino. In the Czechoslovakian Grand Prix the Monoposto suffered its only defeat of the year by another make and the winner was Chiron (Bugatti). Caracciola won the Monza Grand Prix, and Raymond Sommer (Monza) won at Marseilles from Nuvolari (Monoposto). It had been a marvellous year for Alfa Romeo and although the Monopostos were withdrawn for part of the 1933 season for financial reasons, the successes of 1932 heightened the team's complacency when the 750 kg formula came into effect in 1934.

1933

So the leading Scuderia Ferrari drivers Nuvolari and Borzacchini were forced to resort to the now obsolescent Monzas with engines bored out to 2.6 litres. The strongest opposition came from Maserati who introduced a much improved car with 2992 cc (69×100 mm) engine claimed to develop 210 bhp at 5600 rpm. All Maserati racing cars had been two-seaters, as were the first two of the new 3-litre cars (8C-3000s), but all subsequent cars were Monopostos (8C-3000M).

Alfa Romeo's problems were highlighted when Varzi (Bugatti Type 51) won the Monaco Grand Prix – the first European race in which starting grid positions were determined by practice times. Varzi again won at Tripoli and at Avus (with the 4.9-litre Type 54), but Nuvolari enjoyed an easy win in the

French driver 'Phi-Phi' Etancelin at the wheel of his Alfa Romeo Monza in the 1932 Dieppe Grand Prix.

Eifelrennen. Campari (Maserati) was the winner in the French Grand Prix at Montlhéry (the works Bugatti team had withdrawn) and for Nuvolari this, coupled with the subsequent failure of his Monza at Barcelona and Reims, brought a parting of the ways. At the Belgian Grand Prix he appeared at the wheel of a Maserati and won from the Bugattis of Varzi and Dreyfus. He won again with a Maserati at Livorno. By the Coppa Acerbo at Pescara, a very important race for Alfa Romeo, the Portello team had relented and the Monoposto reappeared in the hands of Luigi Fagioli. Fagioli won from Nuvolari, won again at Comminges in France (Nuvolari was not entered), Chiron won for Alfa Romeo at Marseilles (Fagioli was second) and Fagioli won the Italian Grand Prix with Nuvolari second.

It was a tragic day for motor racing, however, as in the Monza Grand Prix, held later in the day, Campari (Monoposto) and Baconin Borzacchini (Maserati) were fighting for the lead in their heat, skidded on oil dropped in an earlier heat by Trossi's Duesenberg and both crashed. Whilst Campari was killed instantly, Borzacchini died shortly afterwards. In the next heat Count Czaykowski was killed when he crashed his Bugatti. Both Borzacchini and Campari were great national heroes.

There remained two major races. Chiron won the Czechoslovakian Grand Prix with his Monoposto, and also the revived Spanish race at San Sebastian. At San Sebastian Bugatti introduced his new 2.8-litre Type 59. But the Monopostos were unbeatable − or at least everyone in Italy thought so.

The Years of Power

For the years 1934-36 (subsequently extended until the end of the 1937 season) the AIACR (Association Internationale des Automobiles Clubs Reconnus) responded to the general apprehension about the rising speed of racing cars by introducing the 750 kg Formula. Whilst there was no limit on engine size, the 750 kg (14.73 cwt) weight limit excluded driver, tyres, fuel, oil and water. There was also a requirement that the bodywork should present a minimum cross-sectional area of 85×25 cm at the driving seat and races were to be over a minimum distance of 500 kilometres (310 miles).

The weight restriction was very much in line with successful contemporary cars, the Alfa Romeo P3 Monoposto (700 kg), the Bugatti Type 59 (760 kg) and the Maserati 8CM-3000 (a little over 750 kg). Although these new regulations were announced in October 1932 and some information about German plans was published in 1933, the existing teams showed no real response, although Bugatti increased engine size of their Type 59 from 2.8 to 3.3 litres.

It should also be remembered that whilst Scuderia Ferrari, who increased capacity of the Monopostos to 2.9 litres, fielded a serious team of works Alfa Romeos, Bugatti fielded works cars and there were works entries from Maserati, many entrants were wealthy private owners racing with or without works support. To be a racing driver was to be a sportsman rather than to follow a sporting career. There was no World Championship as such and a few major and many minor races throughout the year.

1934

The first important race of the year was the Monaco Grand Prix held on Easter Monday and this was a straight Alfa Romeo–Bugatti–Maserati struggle. Algerian driver Guy Moll won with his Scuderia Ferrari Alfa Romeo from team-mate Louis Chiron and Marcel Lehoux (Bugatti Type 59, still with 2.8-litre engine). There followed races at Alessandria in Italy, Tripoli in Libya and Casablanca in Morocco and Alfa Romeo won all three.

Both of the new German teams, Auto Union and Mercedes-Benz were entered in the Avusrennen at Berlin on 27 May, but only Auto Union started. This car was the work of Dr Ferdinand Porsche, originally to be known as the P-Wagen and to be raced by Porsche's own team. However, Auto Union (the conglomerate formed by the merger of Horch, Audi, Wanderer and DKW) learned of Porsche's plans and it was agreed that they would take over the project. Both Auto Union and Mercedes produced designs of high power and low weight that made a nonsense of the weight restrictions imposed by the new formula. This was achieved by using rigid, lightweight tubular chassis and independent suspension front and rear. The traditional teams retained a flexible, girder-type chassis

The Bugatti Type 59 was one of the most beautiful racing cars of all time and was characterised by its wire wheels; the wheel rim was supported by the radial spokes and driven by serrations on the brake backplate. The road cars in the background and the driver's visor reveal that this is not a contemporary photograph. It was taken at Prescott hill climb in the 1960s. (*Guy Griffiths*)

Because Alfa Romeo would not, initially, sell the Monoposto to private purchasers, the 8CM Maserati was much in demand. Whitney Straight is seen at the wheel of one of four cars ordered from the factory at the 1934 International Trophy at Brooklands. At Brooklands Straight was fastest on scratch. By the cockpit, wearing a beret, is the famous mechanic Giulio Ramponi, who lived well into his nineties. Straight's cars were extensively modified by Reid Railton, painted white and distinguished by the shield-shaped air intake.

frame with stiff suspension by rigid axles (an approach to design that had remained unchanged for close to 15 years). Porsche's design, the Type A, featured independent suspension by torsion bars at the front and leaf springs at the rear, a V16 supercharged 4360 cc engine developed 295 bhp at 4500 rpm and this engine was mounted behind the driver. It was strictly speaking mid-engined, although always referred to as rear-engined, and the layout had been inspired by the rear-engined Benz *Tropfenwagen* developed in 1922-23.

Both Auto Union and Mercedes-Benz ran their cars on exotic and secret fuel brews produced jointly by the oil and chemical industries and so noxious were the exhaust fumes that onlookers in the pits would complain of nausea, headaches, breathing problems and irritated eyes. Likewise both designs featured carefully developed aerodynamics that made the square-rigged opposition look obsolete. Although Germany's racing colour was white, Auto Union chose to paint their cars with aluminium paint to give a silver appearance and for reasons that will be explained, Mercedes-Benz did likewise.

To run these teams cost vast sums of money, but very little of it came from Hitler's government, although Hitler supported and encouraged it. In his brilliant *Racing The Silver Arrows* (Osprey Publishing Ltd, 1986), Chris Nixon quotes the following from *Mannschaft und Meisterschaft*: 'The Führer has spoken. The 1934 Grand Prix Formula shall and must be a measuring stick for German knowledge and German ability. So one thing leads to another: first the Führer's overpowering energy, then the formula, a great international problem to which Europe's best devote themselves and, finally, action in the design and construction of new racing cars.' Hitler offered the annual sum of 500,000 Reichsmarks (450,000 as a subsidy and 50,000 as prize money) to the company that built a German Grand Prix team. This 450,000 Reichsmarks was eventually split between Mercedes-Benz and Auto Union and in today's values they each received about £400,000 a year. In pre-war years this subsidy was a closely guarded secret, but obviously much more money was needed to finance the teams. However, as German military might was rebuilt, there were lucrative contracts which helped subsidize the two teams.

But back to Avus, a high-speed circuit near Berlin composed of long straights connected by slightly banked loop roads (it gained notoriety as a dangerous course only later when a steep banked corner was substituted for the northern loop). The Auto Unions failed and Moll (Alfa Romeo) won from Varzi (Alfa Romeo) and Momberger (Auto Union). Moll drove a streamlined Alfa Romeo specially built for this race. In August Moll was killed in the Coppa Acerbo at Pescara. Enzo Ferrari has described the young Algerian as 'one of the most capable drivers he had ever met.'

The Eifelrennen at the Nürburgring, the most difficult circuit in Europe, was held only six days later and the new Mercedes-Benz W25 was ready. The W25, designed by Dr-Ing. Hans Nibel, featured a square-tube chassis and independent suspension front and rear (at the rear by less than satisfactory swing-axles). The straight-eight 3360 cc engine developed 345 bhp at 5800 rpm and the W25 was of course front-engined. When the W25s were weighed the Mercedes team manager, the great Alfred Neubauer, was confronted by the fact that the cars were 1 kg over the weight limit. The white paint, together with a considerable amount of filler was removed, and the cars were given a thin coat of aluminium paint. Thereafter, like Auto Union, the Mercedes-Benz teams raced in silver and the tag *Silberpfeile* ('Silver Arrows') was given to the cars by the press. This unofficial name strictly relates only to Mercedes-Benz and not to Auto Union.

Manfred von Brauchitsch won at the Nürburgring from Stuck (Auto Union) and Chiron (Alfa Romeo). It was the start of a new régime. In their next race, the French Grand Prix at Montlhéry, the German cars disappointed, however, lacking both speed and reliability. None finished the race and the Alfa Romeos of Chiron, Varzi and Moll/Trossi took the first three places. Thereafter the German cars took all the major races, with Stuck (Auto Union) winning the German Grand Prix at the Nürburgring, Fagioli (Mercedes-Benz) the Coppa Acerbo at Pescara, Stuck the Swiss Grand Prix on the new Bremgarten circuit at Berne, Caracciola/Fagioli (Mercedes-Benz) the Italian Grand Prix, Fagioli the Spanish race and Stuck in Czechoslovakia. The two German teams had withdrawn from the Belgian Grand Prix because of the

The 1934 Mercedes-Benz W25. It was very aerodynamic by the standards of the time, but aerodynamics had a long way to go.

Twenty-four year-old Guy Moll with his Scuderia Ferrari Alfa Romeo Monoposto on the starting grid for the 1934 Coppa Acerbo at Pescara, the race in which he was killed.

onerus customs duty that was to be imposed in respect of the teams' special fuel. At the Italian race the Maserati factory introduced the new Tipo 34 car with 3326 cc engine in the existing chassis. It was driven by the great Tazio Nuvolari, but performed poorly.

1935

From the experience gained in 1934 both German teams modified their cars for 1935. Auto Union's Type B now featured a 4950 cc engine developing 375 bhp at 4800 rpm and torsion bar rear suspension. The W25 Mercedes-Benz was bored out 3990 cc and now developed 430 bhp at 5800 rpm. The most significant changes were, however, made to the Italian cars, but this did little to achieve success – although the season was to see one notable exception.

Because of the worldwide depression Alfa Romeo had been in financial difficulties for some years. In 1931 control had passed to the Instituto di Liquidazione, but two years later ownership passed to the Instituto Ricostruzione Industriale, which meant government ownership and it stayed in government

Tazio Nuvolari with the new Tipo 34 Maserati before the Italian Grand Prix at Monza in 1934. To the left of the cockpit is Guerrino Bertocchi, nominally 'head mechanic', but the mainstay of Maserati racing activities for so many years. The new Maserati was uncompetitive and did nothing to stem the tide of German racing domination.

hands until its recent acquisition by Fiat. Although the IRI was in theory, at least, autonomous, it was influenced by Benito Mussolini's fervent enthusiasm for motor racing and his desire to match German racing successes. As a result Alfa Romeo did have some degree of financial support, but it was never enough to tip the balance. In 1935 the Monopostos were raced with engines enlarged to 3.2 litres and also featured Dubonnet-type independent front suspension (by trailing links steered with the wheels and mounted on the ends of a tubular axle). Other Alfa Romeo developments were the monstrous *Bimotore* built by Luigi Bazzi for Scuderia Ferrari (with Alfa's approval) and powered by front and rear-mounted Monoposto engines. It was of course eligible for Formule Libre events only. Later in the year Alfa Romeo produced the 8C-35, with 3.8-litre engine, independent suspension front and rear and a clumsy attempt at body aerodynamics.

Maserati had handed their racing activities over to the private Scuderia Subalpina and eventually their V8RI with 4.8-litre V8 engine, independent

suspension front and rear and 'streamlined' body appeared, but it was doomed to failure. Bugatti had in effect opted out and the only change was the adoption of a 3.8-litre engine for the Type 59.

The first major race of the 1935 season was the Monaco Grand Prix and, in the absence of Auto Union, Luigi Fagioli won for Mercedes-Benz. Achille Varzi won at Tunis for Auto Union (his was the only German car entered), Caracciola won the Tripoli Grand Prix for Mercedes-Benz (it was a Formule Libre race to permit the *Bimotore* to run, and driven by Nuvolari it finished fourth) and Fagioli won the Avusrennen. The Eifelrennen at the Nürburgring was won by Caracciola (Mercedes), he won again in the French Grand Prix at Montlhéry and the Belgian Grand Prix at Spa-Francorchamps, while Fagioli was the winner in the Penya Rhin Grand Prix at Barcelona. It was proving a year of Mercedes domination, partly because Auto Union temporarily withdrew because of caburation problems with their enlarged engines. Next came the German Grand Prix at the Nürburgring, a race that completely upset the form book. This description of the race is from *Alfa Romeo, A History* by Peter Hull and Roy Slater, one of the very best of 'one-make' books, first published by Cassell in 1964 and more recently reissued in revised form by Transport Bookman Publications.

The 1935 German Grand Prix

It will be remembered that towards the end of the 1934 season the 2.9 Monoposto Alfa Romeos were being beaten by both the 3.3 Type 59 Bugattis and the 6-cylinder Maseratis. Now, with their enlarged engines of 3.2 litres, hydraulic brakes and new suspensions the Alfa Romeos were more than a match for these cars. Unfortunately it seemed unlikely they would ever be able to beat the much more powerful Mercedes and Auto Unions, and the Germans were undoubtedly of this opinion when the 1935 German GP was held at the Nürburgring on 28 July.

The Ferrari Alfa Romeo drivers entered for this race were originally the front ranking trio of Nuvolari, Chiron and Dreyfus, but in the actual event Dreyfus was replaced by the less experienced though very talented Brivio. All three had cars with the later enlarged 3.2-litre engines, independent front suspension with hydraulic brakes and reversed quarter-elliptic springs at the rear. It was these improvements, combined with Nuvolari's genius and determination, which made the 1935 German GP become a motor racing legend that has already been described in so many books on the subject. The Scuderia Subalpina Maseratis, Taruffi's 3.3 Bugatti, the Mays/Delius 2-litre ERA and other independents on Maserati and Alfa Romeo were complete also-rans, and the race developed into a fight between Nuvolari versus five Mercedes (Caracciola, von Brauchitsch, Fagioli, Geier and Lang) and four Auto Unions (Stuck, Rosemeyer, Pietsch and Varzi). Nuvolari had a mere 265 bhp, the 16-cylinder Auto Unions about 350 bhp and the straight-eight 3.9-litre Mercedes over 400 bhp. Caracciola led on the first lap, but Nuvolari followed only 12 seconds behind him, and just in front of Fagioli. During the second lap Rosemeyer came up through the field and Nuvolari was somewhat overwhelmed, so the order was Caracciola, Rosemeyer, Fagioli, von Brauchitsch and Nuvolari. By the fourth lap Nuvolari had slowed a little, allowing Chiron past him, and when Rosemeyer ran off the road and had to change a wheel Chiron was fourth and Nuvolari was sixth. Meanwhile Brivio retired with a broken differential, and before long Chiron also went out with transmission trouble leaving Nuvolari on his own. Just before Chiron retired, Nuvolari had put on speed, and between the sixth and ninth of the 22 laps of the race he passed Rosemeyer, Chiron, Brauchitsch and Fagioli and on the tenth lap he even got past Caracciola to take the

lead. At the end of the 11th lap, half-distance, the five leading cars headed by Nuvolari came into the pits to refuel, and change wheels. Here the big drama of the race took place, for von Brauchitsch got away in 47 seconds, but the handle of the refuelling pump in the Ferrari pit broke, so Nuvolari's car had to be refuelled from churns. Whilst this was going on Nuvolari got out of his driving seat and danced around in a great frenzy of excitement, and finally drove off after an eternity which amounted to 2 min 14 sec. Brauchitsch's lightning stop had put him into the lead, so on the 12th lap Caracciola was second, Rosemeyer third, Fagioli fourth and Nuvolari was back in fifth position. Instead of making him lose heart, the infuriatingly slow pit-stop acted as a goad to Nuvolari who, by the 14th lap, had climbed back to second place, and was 1 min 46 sec behind Brauchitsch. Brauchitsch had been going very fast, and put in a record lap of 80.73 mph, but he then slowed down, thinking his lead was secure whilst Nuvolari gradually gained ground by as much as 16 seconds a lap. With one lap to go he was still 35 seconds behind, so a victory for Brauchitsch seemed fairly certain, the only worry being that one of his tyres was already showing the white breaker strip. On that very last lap the inevitable happened, the left-hand rear tyre burst and, whilst Brauchitsch skilfully kept control, Nuvolari passed him to win a race to which that much over-worked adjective fantastic could truthfully be applied. Nuvolari won at 75.25 mph and finished 2 min 14.4 sec in front of Stuck's Auto Union in second place. Caracciola was third, Rosemeyer fourth, von Brauchitsch fifth and Fagioli sixth. Nuvolari's virtuosity in this race had always been allowed to overshadow the merits of his car. With its light weight, excellent cornering, good brakes, reliability and slightly increased power output, it proved itself better suited to the Nürburgring than the Auto Unions. The chicanes in the French Grand Prix seemed to show that the Alfa Romeo in Nuvolari's hands handled better on the slower corners than the Mercedes in its 1935 form, whilst the wet roads which prevailed on the Nürburgring probably made the extra power of the Mercedes an embarrassment for its drivers at times.

It has been said Nuvolari was lucky to win because of Brauchitsch's burst tyre which was true enough, but Brauchitsch had built up his lead largely due to Nuvolari's delayed pit-stop. What did run in Nuvolari's favour in his battle against the Mercedes was the fact that the two leading Mercedes drivers were not properly on form, for Fagioli was delayed by shock-absorber trouble and Caracciola was feeling unwell. On balance it was a thoroughly well deserved victory both for Nuvolari and for Alfa Romeo, as luck was not on their side all the way.

During the remainder of the year, but only in the absence of German entries, Alfa Romeo dominated.

The agitated Nuvolari urges his pit crew to hasten refuelling his Alfa Romeo, half way through the 1935 German Grand Prix when he was leading. The handle of the fuel pressure pump had been broken by an over-enthusiastic mechanic and the car had to be refuelled from churns. *(Cyril Posthumus)*

The straight-eight Alfa Romeo engine, as fitted in 3.5-litre form to the 8C-35. This was the car raced in post-war days by Dennis Poore. *(Guy Griffiths)*.

The improved 8C-35 was driven on its début in the Italian Grand Prix by Tazio Nuvolari. At Monza he chased the German cars hard, worked his way up to second place, but retired because of piston failure.

These were of course all victories in lesser events. Varzi won for Auto Union in the Coppa Acerbo at Pescara (no Mercedes were entered), Carraciola won at Bremgarten, and Stuck beat the Mercedes at Monza to take a fine victory for Auto Union in the Italian race. Mercedes-Benz finished 1-2-3 in the Spanish race at San Sebastian. Varzi and Rosemeyer took the first two places in the absence of Stuttgart in the Czechoslovakian Grand Prix at Brno. Former racing motorcyclist Bernd Rosemeyer was one of the sensations of the 1935 season; in his too short racing career he was only to drive for Auto Union and it was at Brno that he met Elly Beinhorn, the famous pilot, who soon became his wife. In 1935 there was a new European Championship for drivers and this was won by Caracciola.

1936

For 1936 Auto Union introduced the Type C with 6006 cc engine developing 520 bhp at 5800 rpm and the roadholding had been much improved. The latest version of the Mercedes-Benz W25 had a 4740 cc engine with a power output of 494 bhp at 5800 rpm. The Italians were unable to match the power of the two German teams, although the 12C-36 Alfa Romeo introduced during the year and with a V12 4060 cc engine developing 370 bhp in the existing chassis achieved a measure of success.

Early in the year it seemed as though Caracciola and Mercedes-Benz would dominate once more and the Mercedes driver won at Monaco from the Auto Unions of Varzi and Stuck. Varzi and Stuck took the first two places for Auto Union at Tripoli, but Caracciola won again in the Tunis Grand Prix. The first of Nuvolari's three defeats of the German cars came in the Penya Rhin Grand Prix held on the Montjuich Park road circuit. Caracciola was soundly beaten into second place.

Young Bernd Rosemeyer's first win of the year was in the Eifelrennen at the Nürburgring, a race run in heavy rain and mist. He drove magnificently to win from Nuvolari and became known as *Nebelmeister* (Fog Master), just as Caracciola was frequently referred to as *Regenmeister* (Rain Master). A second victory for Rosemeyer followed at Budapest. A single Auto Union was entered for Varzi in the Milan Grand Prix, but

Nuvolari beat the German car into second place. Varzi was permitted to run an Auto Union in certain Italian races as a private entrant. This enabled him to keep all the starting and prize money, thereby circumventing the German government's rule that money was not to be taken out of the country.

The Belgian Grand Prix was cancelled, the French event was held as a sports car race and the next important race was the German Grand Prix. Rosemeyer led almost all the race and Stuck finished in second place. Only Auto Union of the two German teams ran in the Coppa Ciano at Livorno, but the cars had received no attention after the German race. The 12-cylinder Alfa Romeo of Nuvolari broke shortly after the start and he took over team-mate Brivio's 8C-35 to start a chase of the Auto Unions which were running 1-2-3. The odds were very much against him, but he caught and passed all three to win the race. As the brakes of Auto Unions, not relined since their last outing, faded, so Brivio and Dreyfus were also able to get past to make it an Alfa Romeo 1-2-3 finish. In the Coppa Acerbo the following weekend Nuvolari retired and Rosemeyer led home an Auto Union 1-2-3.

Rosemeyer seemed destined to win the European Championship, but it was a title that Caracciola was prepared to yield only with great reluctance. In the Swiss Grand Prix Caracciola took the lead at the start, but Rosemeyer's Auto Union was soon right behind the Mercedes. The Auto Union was handling better, Rosemeyer was faster through the corners, but the cars were closely matched on the straight, and it was quite impossible for Bernd to pass. Eventually, the Clerk of the Course was persuaded to show Caracciola the blue flag, the Mercedes driver was obliged to let Rosemeyer go ahead and he won the race from team-mates Varzi and Stuck. The incident caused bad relations between the two drivers and it was only some six months later, after a dinner party given by Goebbels in Berlin, that Rosemeyer was to forget and forgive. Mercedes did not enter the Italian Grand Prix, Rosemeyer won the race from Nuvolari and took the European Championship. At the end of the year Nuvolari competed in the Vanderbilt Cup race, a revival of a race held at Long Island, New York between 1904 and 1910 and later at other circuits. In the absence of German opposition Nuvolari won from Wimille (Bugatti).

Dick Seaman drove this V8RI Maserati entered by Scuderia Torino in the 1936 German Grand Prix. He was eliminated by brake problems. He is seen at the Karrussel, the slightly banked, tight curve.

Bernd Rosemeyer rapidly became the star of the Auto Union team. He is seen in the 1936 German Grand Prix at the Nürburgring which he won. It was very much an Auto Union year.

Although Rosemeyer had been the outstanding driver of the year, Nuvolari had been far from overshadowed with his V12 Alfa Romeo and by any standard he was the most consistently successful driver of the 1930s and successful almost regardless of how competitive was his car. This fine appreciation of Nuvolari by Cyril Posthumus was first published in *The Motorist's Weekend Book* (B.T. Batsford Limited, 1960).

The Farmer's Son
by Cyril Posthumus

Correrai ancor piu veloce per le vie del cielo. These words were inscribed in huge letters above the entrance to the Cathedral in Mantua where, in August 1953, the funeral service for Tazio Giorgio Nuvolari took place. Meaning: 'You will travel still faster upon the highways of heaven', they were read with awe, sadness and a reverence amounting almost to love by the many thousands of Mantuans who followed the cortège through the streets to pay tribute to Italy's greatest driver.

The crowd which thronged the cathedral that day was immense; estimates of the number varied between 25 and 55 thousand, but whatever the true figure may have been, there was no denying their universal grief at the passing of Mantua's most famous citizen. The same words were engraved upon Nuvolari's tomb, to which he was taken, clothed in his famous canary yellow jersey and blue overall trousers, with racing goggles, gloves and helmet accompanying him, and escorted by a procession of mourners which stretched for nearly a mile and a half through the streets.

What manner of man was this, then, whose funeral could bring out a town almost in its entirety, and whose death put a nation into mourning?

Tazio Nuvolari was not simply a racing driver. To Italy he became an idol, a demi-god, a legend, epitomising all that young Italy aspired to be; the man who 'did the impossible', not once but habitually, the David who slew the Goliaths in the great sport of motor racing. He was *Il Maestro*.

Italians today, only too aware of their country's current lack of motor racing talent, turn perforce to the glories of the past for comfort, and warmly recall the feats of the old Italian masters. There were so many in Italy's golden years... Varzi, Farina, Trossi, Fagioli, Bordino, Nazzaro, the Ascaris father and son... Yet in 99 cases out of the hundred, one name will come to their lips before any of these – that of their beloved Nuvolari, the farmer's son who came from Ronchesana, near Mantua.

That little man, barely over five feet tall, deceptively frail and narrow in build but seemingly strung together with high-tensile steel wire, with his long narrow chin and prominent jaw, dark piercing eyes, toothy grin and greying hair, endeared himself to all, not solely by his indomitable fighting spirit and wizardry at the wheel, but for his innate goodness.

Italy loved him for his quiet and gentlemanly mode of living; he was kind, generous, thoughtful and modest, completely free of the *prima donna* complex which could so easily affect a racing ace, a lover of home life and immensely devoted to his wife and family – traits which all won the hearts of the ordinary people.

As a driver he was, of course, unique. Possessed himself of tremendous vitality, he seemed to infuse his very car with the same restless energy. As he raced, he grimaced, bared his teeth, grinned, puffed out his cheeks, talked to his car, and patted it now and then. He wasn't playing to the gallery, to which he was entirely oblivious, but simply being his natural dynamic self and doing all those things which characterised the Maestro, the master of motor racing.

I was too young to appreciate my first sight of Nuvolari. It was down at Brooklands in autumn, 1933, when I was a school-boy. He looked so small, so yellow, and so cold despite a thick 'teddy bear' coat, and when he took it off and climbed into a 2.3-litre Bugatti he seemed to shrink still further. Then he drove out on to the Mountain circuit, and I followed the concerted rush down to the Fork hairpin to watch. To me, he looked most excitingly dangerous, the Bugatti skittering round in brief, jerky slides, but I don't think he cared much for that short, bumpy and unnatural circuit. I spent the savings of several weeks to attend the race meeting a day or two later, and was bitterly disappointed when Nuvolari did not drive after all.

I was more versed in Nuvolari 'lore' when I saw him again, in the Donington Grand Prix of 1938, and was thrilled to the core by the sight of him in action. A skimpy, yellow-clad figure almost lost in the cockpit of his silver Auto Union, he contrived to look far 'busier' than any other driver, not only through the corners but even when motoring down the straights. Up to a point, of course, he *was* 'busier' – busy outpacing the entire Mercedes-Benz team and winning a glorious race, giving some 60,000 spectators the thrill of their lives.

Without a doubt, he was Italy's greatest racing driver of all time – but was the legendary Flying Mantuan the *world's* greatest, as has so often been suggested?

To borrow the late Professor Joad's well-worn phrase, 'It all depends on what is meant by "greatness". The number of outright victories gained by a driver are far from being the sole criterion of greatness, which in motor racing means much more: the ability to go very fast and remain on the road, for instance; the ability to drive with your head as well as your hands and feet; to fight, and to go on fighting no matter how hopeless the odds may seem; and to do all these things just a little better than your rivals, without wearing your tyres down to the breaker strip or blowing up your engine. . . Nuvolari qualifies all right, but so do others.

Statistics help little. They show that Nuvolari won a round 50 race victories of importance in 17 seasons between 1924 and 1946. In contrast, Juan Manuel Fangio, who is considered by many to be Nuvolari's sternest rival as the world's greatest driver, scored 55 in nine seasons between 1949 and 1957. Alberto Ascari, whose brilliant career was cut short after eight years, gained 43 wins between 1947 and 1955, Rudolf Caracciola scored 26 major victories between 1926 and 1939, while Stirling Moss already has over 45 important wins to his credit, and doubtless plenty more ahead of him. Yet comparison is misleading since, on the average, more races per season have been held in post-war years than in the 'thirties, and more in the 'thirties than the 'twenties.

What the results tables do not reveal is that, first, Nuvolari's ratio of retirements to successes is higher than the others, attesting to his notorious 'win or bust' outlook; and secondly, that a large proportion of Nuvolari's victories were achieved on cars slower than the opposition. The only year in which he consistently had one of the fastest cars was 1932, when he was a member of the official Alfa Romeo team with the then new and invincible *monoposto* Alfa Romeo straight-eights. For most of his other victories he was fighting unequal odds – and loving it.

All great drivers have the *chef d'oeuvre* – the masterpiece of their career; Caracciola's was probably the 1931 German GP, Fangio's the 1957 German GP, Ascari's the 1949 GP of Europe, Moss's the 1955 Mille Miglia or the 1959 Italian GP. The trouble with Nuvolari was that he had several! By tradition his greatest triumph was the 1935 German GP, when he defeated nine modern German cars – five Mercedes and four Auto Unions – with his basically four-year-old Alfa Romeo – a wonderful feat indeed, the story of which has been told and retold in motor-racing literature.

Yet there were other achievements by Nuvolari, lesser known and lesser chronicled, testifying to his matchless fighting spirit, his fierce refusal to recognise defeat, and his uncanny ability, reinforcing his right to a very high pedestal in motor-racing history.

Naturally one as indifferent to danger as he suffered numerous accidents during his long career, and talking his way out of hospital and competing in races heavily swathed in bandages or plaster became a notably Nuvolari habit. There was no false heroics about this, but simply his tremendous will to race defying common sense. Pain he could tolerate when there was a goal ahead, but inactivity he could not bear; his volatile temperament would not allow it.

After being flung through a wire fence at Monza when he crashed in a P2 Alfa Romeo during a trial by the works in 1925, his injuries included a severely lacerated back, promising a month or so in a hospital bed to recover. But Nuvolari wasn't having any – not with the vital motor cycle Grand Prix of the Nations meeting at Monza six days hence. He persuaded the medicos to bandage him in such a way that he could be seated on his 350 cc twin ohc Bianchi and push-started. He duelled fanatically in pouring rain with Britain's famous Wal Handley, and when the latter's Rex-Acme gave out under constant pressure from the Bianchi with half a lap to go, Tazio scored a triumphant victory for Italy.

At Alessandria early in 1934 the Maestro broke a leg when his Maserati crashed on treacherously wet roads, owing to the fact that his true line through a corner came suddenly to be occupied by a disabled Alfa Romeo. After four restless weeks in hospital, Tazio could endure the inactivity no longer, and against his doctor's earnest advice, entered to drive a Maserati in the Avus GP near Berlin.

He had the pedals modified so that all three could be operated with one foot, the other still being in plaster, and then, despite the entreaties of his wife, friends and doctor, he hobbled out for practice on crutches, having to be helped in and out of the cockpit. In a devastatingly fast race dominated initially by the new Auto Unions and later by the Ferrari Alfas, Nuvolari pressed on, tortured by cramp and plagued by tyre trouble, eventually finishing a modest but hard-won fifth.

One place ahead of him in another Maserati was the great British sportsman Earl Howe, who was moved to comment on Tazio's drive: 'Let any who say it was foolhardy at least be honest and admit it was one of the finest exhibitions of pluck and grit ever seen. By such men are victories won!'

Two years later, while practising for that other high-speed race, the Tripoli GP in North Africa, a wheel of Nuvolari's 4.1-litre 12-cylinder Alfa Romeo caught a marker stone at over 125 mph. The tyre burst, the big Alfa lurched, then turned over, ending up in the desert sand bordering the circuit. Nuvolari was flung high in the air, to land by good luck in a heap of drying grass. Would-be helpers who rushed to the scene faced a puzzle – the wrecked car lay there, smoking and steaming, but where was its driver? They found him deep in the grass ten minutes later, unconscious, with damaged ribs and severe bruising.

At the hospital he was put into plaster and told he would have to rest for several days.

'But of course,' said Nuvolari. 'After the race I shall do

so.' Next day, curiously immobile because of his plaster 'corset', he drove a replacement Alfa into seventh place. Foolhardy perhaps, but typical Nuvolari 'guts'.

Few victories can have been sweeter to the Maestro than those he snatched from the powerful German teams in the mid-'thirties. He never enjoyed an uneventful race or a secure victory; he loved a battle, and in adversity became positively inspired. The classic example, of course, is that 1935 German GP at the Nürburgring, yet the following season saw him administer defeat upon the German teams, not once, but three times, and it is only because the races concerned were not Grandes Épreuves that their history is less known than the great German race.

On paper in 1936 Nuvolari hadn't a chance. The rear-engined Auto Unions from Zwickau were turning out over 500 bhp from their 6-litre, 16-cylinder engines, while Mercedes-Benz of Stuttgart had 490-plus bhp beneath their sleek bonnets. In contrast the high, heavy-looking 12-cylinder Type C Alfa Romeo just introduced could barely exceed 400 bhp. In road holding and weight distribution, however, it was equal if not superior to the German cars, while the sheer virtuosity of Nuvolari in the cockpit, plus the awe in which he was held by the rival teams, were jointly worth a good few bhp on a Grand Prix circuit, particularly if there were plenty of corners.

Give Nuvolari a corner, and he contrived somehow to get through it fractionally quicker than anyone else; his habit of twitching the wheel as he approached a corner fast, deliberately provoking a skid, then using that skid both to slow the car and place it correctly for rapid exit from the corner, was something unique, calling for an ultra-fine sense of balance. Given bends galore, and Nuvolari in the Alfa was on a near-equal footing with the theoretically superior German cars.

The result was an unexpectedly interesting 1936 Grand Prix season. Surprises began at Barcelona, three weeks after Tripoli. His plaster corset now a mere memory, Tazio was on top form and rarin' to go. Two Mercedes and two Auto Unions faced him, but on the twisty Montjuich circuit he was undaunted. From flag-fall he flung his cumbersome-looking Alfa into combat with Caracciola's Mercedes, the pair waging one of the season's most memorable duels.

Two pit stops to Caracciola's one weighed against Nuvolari, but the Mantuan devil shot back into the fray, broke the lap record, and caught up with the Merc. again. The last 20 laps were merciless, German and Italian masters both giving of their awe-inspiring best, and tension rose to an unbearable climax when, on the last lap of all and the Alfa leading, it began to spit and bang as the fuel tank emptied. Desperately Nuvolari nursed it round in top gear, still staving Caracciola off, to flee across the line the victor, by 3 seconds on an all but dry tank.

Striving to hold the duellists at Barcelona, Auto Union's new star Bernd Rosemeyer smote a lamp-post heartily, after which fifth place was the best he could manage. At Nürburgring in the Eifelrennen a week later, however, he turned the tables on Tazio and won a famous victory in the fog for Auto Union. But the irrepressible Italian was second home, way ahead of two Mercedes and three other AUs, so that *Deutschland über Alles* only just prevailed.

Then came the one and only International Hungarian GP, run on a circuit in the Budapest gardens – and a gripping race it proved to be. This time there were full three-car teams from Mercedes-Benz and Auto Union for Nuvolari to cope with, and in the coping he aroused the hundred thousand-strong crowd of spectators to the wildest Tzigane frenzies of excitement.

It was the meteoric Rosemeyer who set the opening pace, with Caracciola worrying at his heels and Nuvolari following, while the leading pair wore each other out. 'Caratsch' went first, retiring at half-distance, whereupon Tazio moved up to challenge the Auto Union. Then Brauchitsch's Mercedes, a lap behind, got in the way until Nuvolari's persistent presence on his tail so demoralised the German that he spun off and crashed through a barrier.

With the road clear Nuvolari soon closed on Rosemeyer, then applied the same treatment to him, repeatedly nosing up level on the corners until the harassed Bernd overslid his Auto Union when accelerating too hard. In a trice Nuvolari was through, thereafter pulling away to the extent of 14 seconds when the chequered flag flew for another remarkable Nuvolari victory.

One week later he gave Auto Unions something more to think about, by beating his celebrated rival Achille Varzi in the Milan GP. This was more a personal battle between the pair than a serious inter-marque struggle, and Varzi's second place with the unwieldy rear-engined Auto Union on so serpentine a circuit was, in fact, a fine effort. Nevertheless it signified one more defeat of a German car by an Italian, and in spite of the much-vaunted accord along the Rome-Berlin Axis, the southern partner enjoyed rubbing it in.

No doubt Auto Unions felt a lot better after their great 1-2-4 victory in the German GP, and it was perhaps in the flush of this success that they decided to rush three cars to Leghorn for the Ciano Cup race the following Sunday. It proved a rash decision, for they suffered the humiliation of 100 per cent defeat by Alfa Romeo, with old campaigner Nuvolari the chief artificer of victory.

At the start things looked black for Italy, with the big silver Auto Unions of Stuck, Varzi and Rosemeyer thundering off into the lead, while Tazio's V12 Alfa clanked to an impotent halt on the very first lap with a broken differential. But this was just the sort of situation to arouse the devil in Nuvolari. Instead of glumly removing his helmet and climbing on to the pit counter to watch the rest of the race, he leapt up and down, shouting at designer-cum-pit chief Vittorio Jano to call in one of the other team cars for him to take over – but *'Presto! Presto!'*

Out went the signal, and in came Pintacuda with one of the older eight-cylinder 3.8-litre Alfas; 'Pinta' was frantically motioned out, and in sprang Tazio. As he tore off he had a 66 seconds deficit to make up on the German cars in the lead.

He whipped that Alfa round the Leghorn course to such effect that he quickly broke Stuck's new lap record – and already Stuck had retired. The Maestro's pace goaded the German pit into signalling 'faster' to their drivers, who were already finding it tough going owing to failing brakes. Hans Stuck took over from Rosemeyer and shot back to support Varzi, now leading the race from Brivio and Dreyfus in Alfas. His effort made no difference, for behind came another Alfa, demoniacally driven by Nuvolari, and gaining, gaining, all the time.

One by one the Maestro picked them off; Stuck, Dreyfus, Brivio and finally Varzi in the Auto Union, now virtually brakeless after two hard races without adequate maintenance in between. The hapless Germans tasted deeply the bitterness of defeat that day, for soon Varzi retired also, and Stuck became the sole Auto Union survivor, a disconsolate fourth behind the three Alfa Romeos.

But the glories of Barcelona, Budapest and Leghorn in 1936 could not easily be repeated, and even Nuvolari the master could not continue to combat the German teams with an out-dated Alfa Romeo. In the end he had to join the Germans for a chance to win. He went in mid-1938 to Auto Union, whose team were demoralised after Rosemeyer's death early that year. It took him three races to find his form with the tricky rear-engined cars, and then, at Monza in the Italian GP and at Donington Park, England, he scored two remarkable victories, administering to Mercedes the heartiest double trouncing that august marque had known for a long time.

Capping Nuvolari's pre-war career came his Belgrade GP victory on the very day Britain and France declared war

Nuvolari with the 12-cylinder 12C-36 Alfa Romeo leads the Auto Unions of Rosemeyer and Stuck in the Italian Grand Prix. The Italian finished second behind Rosemeyer, but Stuck crashed.

– 3 September, 1939 – and with a record such as his, the Maestro could well have made Belgrade his swan-song and retired honourably from racing. But to have done so would have seemed to Nuvolari like signing his own death warrant.

'Aren't you afraid of dying in a racing car?' he was once asked.

'I suppose you expect to die in bed?' Nuvolari retorted.

'Yes, indeed, I hope so,' was the reply.

'In that case,' snorted Nuvolari, 'I wonder you dare to go to bed at night.'

Nuvolari was 54 when he resumed racing in 1946, commemorating his return by a win in the Albi GP. But his health and morale were not what they used to be; his two sons Giorgio and Alberto had died, while he himself suffered acutely from the effects of fumes on his chest.

Yet the old indomitable 'do or die' spirit still lay underneath, and was to emerge the following spring, with Nuvolari's remarkable drive in Italy's famous 1000 miles sports car race, the Mille Miglia. Run in relentless, teeming rain, this was a fit man's race if ever there was one, yet the old fire and skill took Nuvolari out in front, and sheer will power kept him there. Driving an *open* 1100 cc Cisitalia he led the field until 180 miles from the finish, against opposition which included Biondetti, Villoresi, Cortese, Taruffi and other younger stars. Only the intrusion of water into the Cisitalia's ignition halted his fantastic drive, and in the end the gallant Nuvolari finished second, haggard, soaked through, and utterly exhausted, 15 minutes behind Biondetti's 2.9-litre saloon Alfa Romeo.

Clemente Biondetti threw a blanket around Tazio's shivering form and led him gently off to warmth and rest at his hotel, while to those who congratulated him on his Mille Miglia victory he retorted, 'I did not win – I merely finished first. The just and deserving winner is Nuvolari, the greatest racing driver in the world.'

Biondetti was not alone in that view. Said Giuseppe Farina, one-time team-mate to Nuvolari: 'He was the perfect driver, incomparable in skill and spirit. To follow him for a few laps was the finest education of all.' Said René Dreyfus, another erstwhile team-mate, 'Nuvolari? – an artist to the very finger-tips. . . the greatest racing driver of our day and any other. . .' Said Luigi Villoresi, whose Maserati Nuvolari shared in his very last Grand Prix drive, at Reims, in 1948: 'An unsurpassed fighter, an artist at the wheel, extremely popular, intensely human; possessed of a "je ne sais quoi", an aura, which fascinated and dominated other drivers. . .' Lastly, Nuvolari's greatest rival, Achille Varzi, is reported to have called him 'the boldest, most skilful madman of us all'.

Was Nuvolari the world's greatest racing driver?

Of course he was!

1937

By Mercedes-Benz standards, 1936 had been a poor year indeed, but Stuttgart supremacy reasserted itself in 1937, and both Auto Union and Alfa Romeo were overshadowed. From Mercedes-Benz there was the new W125 with 8-cylinder 5660 cc engine developing 646 bhp at 5800 rpm and a resurrection of the de Dion rear axle to be a standard feature on racing cars for many years. The power to weight ratio of the W125 was not to be matched for nearly 20 years. The Auto Union Type C was unchanged apart from a slight power increase to 545 bhp. Alfa Romeo continued with the 12C-36, although a 4.5-litre car appeared – without success – later in the year. The efforts of Maserati and Bugatti can be largely ignored, for Maserati were struggling with financial problems and Bugatti was turning to sports car racing.

The first race of the year was the Tripoli Grand Prix won by Lang (Mercedes) and then came the Avusrennen, now incorporating the banked North Curve. Both Mercedes-Benz and Auto Union entered streamlined cars and rising star Hermann Lang won for Stuttgart at 162.61 mph, the highest speed ever recorded in a race – and faster by over 30 mph than that other high-speed race, the Tripoli Grand Prix. The season continued with Auto Union initially looking strong with Rosemeyer scoring a rare victory over Caracciola in the Eifelrennen, Nuvolari winning at Milan (the only German car entered was an Auto Union for young Rudolf Hasse who finished fourth), Rosemeyer won the Vanderbilt Cup and another Auto Union victory was scored by Hasse in the Belgian Grand Prix at Spa-Francorchamps.

Then the new Mercedes-Benz came to the fore again. Caracciola won the German Grand Prix (but sadly Auto Union driver Ernst von Delius crashed and suffered fatal injuries); von Brauchitsch–Caracciola–Kautz made it a 1-2-3 for Mercedes at Monaco; Caracciola–Lang–von Brauchitsch repeated this performance at Bremgarten; and Caracciola won both the Italian Grand Prix (with Lang second) and the Czech Grand Prix (with von Brauchitsch second). Caracciola was again European Champion. Mercedes-Benz had won seven races (five by Caracciola, two by Lang), while Auto Union's total was four (excluding the Vanderbilt Cup) and Hasse won in Belgium because most of the 'stars' were not yet back from the Vanderbilt Cup and there were only seven starters. The team from Chemnitz had added to their score with wins by Rosemeyer in the Coppa Acerbo at Pescara and the International Grand Prix at Donington Park.

In 1937 British driver Dick Seaman had joined the Mercedes team and his friend George Monkhouse of Kodak was a welcome guest at Stuttgart and attended most of the year's races. This led to Monkhouse's superb book *Motor Racing with Mercedes-Benz* covering the 1937 season and reissued in post-war days by G.T. Foulis & Co Limited with additional sections covering the 1938 and 1939 seasons. This extract describing the 1937 Coppa Acerbo held on the magnificent Pescara circuit also relates one of Rosemeyer's few victories in 1937.

The 1937 Coppa Acerbo

by George Monkhouse

The Coppa Acerbo is held at the little seaside town of Pescara, about half-way down the Adriatic coast of Italy. The race was inaugurated 12 years ago by Minister Acerbo. The circuit is probably one of the finest in Europe from the drivers' point of view, being 16 miles in length, although the cars do not come round often enough to make it really interesting for the spectators.

On leaving the grandstands the road continues straight for about half a mile and then starts a really twisty up-and-down section of about eight miles. This is followed by two four-mile straights, there being a chicane in the middle of each. These chicanes were introduced in 1935 to give the slower Italian cars a better chance, as without them the German cars would be out of sight in one lap.

All the hotels are shut up for the year with the exception of the one week in which the Coppa Acerbo takes place, and except for a few local inhabitants Pescara is completely deserted. The natural result of this is chaos for the race week. One is lucky to get anything to eat at all or even a bed. I was singularly unlucky in my choice of the latter. The bedroom was filled with mosquitoes, and the bed itself appeared to be a fleas' nest. I learnt afterwards from Earl Howe that I had myself entirely to blame. He goes to Pescara equipped with a mosquito net, two Flit sprays, and a large pot of Flit oitment, which makes the human body a less delectable morsel to such fierce insect life.

I arrived at about five o'clock on Wednesday afternoon to find Seaman looking remarkably fit although his face was still pretty bad and his nose was a hideous sight as it

seemed to have absorbed large pieces of the road. The bone had set in his thumb, but he was considerably inconvenienced by a large blister which had grown there due to the catapult device they had affixed at Adenau.*

I discovered that the reason Seaman had been asked to go to Pescara was because Lang was ill and Seaman was the only other Mercedes driver who knew the circuit intimately, having won the 1500 cc race in both 1935 and 1936.

We were sitting outside talking when suddenly a beautiful low-winged monoplane appeared and circled round above us. In this was Rosemeyer, who had flown from Genoa in his wife's Messerschmitt Taifun. Before her marriage to Bernd she was Elly Beinhorn, the famous German airwoman...

...Practice on Thursday was officially at half-past seven in the morning, but there was quite a long delay while the chicanes were put straight. Most of them had been run into and demolished by the sports cars, which had started their practice at six o'clock. Nobody recorded very fast times except Seaman and Rosemeyer, who did about 11 min 11 sec. Seaman had an unfortunate experience. Coming down the last straight the off-side front brake locked on when braking for the chicane, and he had to mow down a string of flags across the road to avoid the risk of running into the chicane. Caracciola's car did not appear to be going very well and after fiddling about with it for quite a long time, trying to get the carburation right, the mechanics pushed Rudi off once again. He completed one more lap when the car arrived back firing on seven cylinders, making a most peculiar noise. The engine was dismantled after practice, and it was found that number eight piston had burnt through.

Carburation is terribly difficult on a circuit such as Pescara. As I have said, it has a very twisty section as well as two long straights, so a compromise has to be made. If the mixture is correct or rich enough for full throttle on the straight without the engine overheating, then the car does not accelerate quickly at low engine revolutions on the twisty section, and, conversely, if the mixture is too weak, giving good acceleration at low engine revolutions, the engine is liable to overheat at full throttle on the straights.

The Mercedes mechanics worked all Thursday on Caracciola's car and had it ready in time for Friday's practice, when it seemed to be going very well, and he did a lap in 11 min 7 sec. Seaman's first lap on Friday was 11 min 16 sec, and he started off on his second lap. Eleven minutes passed, and still no sign of Seaman, then 12 minutes and Caracciola appeared, drew into the pits, and said that Seaman had crashed in Cappelle village, but that although the car was very badly damaged Seaman appeared to be quite all right. This news was confirmed

*The results of an accident in the German Grand Prix.

later by Stuck, who with his usual good nature had stopped and had a talk with Seaman.

Seaman's experience must have been frightening, for on approaching the village at over 100 miles per hour, he braked and the near-side front brake locked on and stayed on. He held the car through the first bend in the village, but was so badly placed for the next one that the car ran straight into a house, tearing the near-side front wheel right round and pushing it into the back end of the bonnet, the front cross member of the chassis being broken right through as though a giant had severed it with an axe. The car was obviously beyond repair. This was terribly bad luck for both Mercedes and Seaman as there was no spare car, so the Mercedes team would be reduced to two. The incredible part about the whole thing was that Seaman was not even scratched.

This was Seaman's third accident since driving with Mercedes, and all of them had in some way or another been connected with the number thirteen. The series of thirteens were so strange that one wonders if there is not something in this superstition after all. Starting with his accident at Monza, his room number at the hotel was 113 and twice he had sat down thirteen to dinner, when he remarked that 'something was obviously going to happen to someone'. He arrived back from America on 13 July, flew to Nürburgring to practise for the German Grand Prix and owing to his second place in the Vanderbilt Cup Race had 13 marks for the British Racing Drivers Club gold star – he crashed in the race. Now he had crashed at the thirteenth kilometre post during practice for the thirteenth Coppa Acerbo on Friday 13 August – an amazing sequence.

In the meantime, Rosemeyer, who seemed bent on breaking Varzi's 1936 lap record of 10 min 44 sec had taken out Muller's car. At the end of ten minutes we stood on the pit counter looking over the top of the far chicane for the sun to flash on Rosemeyer's screen as he came up the straight at nearly 200 miles per hour. Ten and a half minutes passed, but still no sign of Rosemeyer, but at the end of 11 minutes the car appeared going relatively slowly, rounded the chicane, and drew into the pits with oil streaming out of the back.

The Auto Union mechanics quickly produced quantities of rag and cleaned the outside of the car. Leaning nonchalantly against it, they pretended all was well, even though oil was still pouring out underneath. Rosemeyer was a little more explicit and he said that coming down the last straight he heard a 'ping' and saw a puff of smoke in his driving mirror. This was shortly followed by some rather louder noises from the back, indicating something adrift inside the engine. This 'something' had apparently poked itself outside – hence the oil.

Stuck did the fastest lap on Friday in 11 min 1 sec,

Fagioli and Müller, who were driving the other Auto Unions, being quite a lot slower, as was Brauchitsch who did not know the circuit at all well. Just as practice was about to end, the loudspeakers announced that the new Alfa Romeos were on their way up to the circuit and practice would be extended for another half hour. This news brought a cheer from the Italian crowd, who expected great things. Suddenly there was a shout of 'Viva Nuvolari', as the 'Mantovano Volante' arrived. The new car was certainly much lower than its predecessors, although the front and rear suspension appeared to be the same as on the old 12-cylinder, and for that matter the engine also did. I was assured, however, by various optimistic Italians that this was absolutely the last word in Grand Prix cars, and that now at last Nuvolari would be able to show the Germans a thing or two. As far as I could see the only real difference between the new car and the old one was that it was much lower and that the petrol tank, instead of being at the back, was now situated in the middle of the car in the form of a saddle over the driver's legs.

We waited expectantly while the plugs were changed and the car started up. It was driven round for a lap by Guidotti, the head tester, from the Alfa Romeo works. These new cars had been officially entered by the works and not by Ferrari. After this Nuvolari, amidst cheers, donned his blue helmet and climbed into the driving seat. He drove round for several laps, in around 12 minutes, but the car did not seem to be going at all well – all rather disappointing.

At Saturday's practice four Auto Unions appeared once again, as they had replaced the engine of Müller's car, which Rosemeyer had blown up, with a spare they had brought. Mercedes, of course, were now reduced to two cars. Rosemeyer enlivened proceedings considerably by taking off his shirt, wearing only a linen helmet, goggles, gloves, shorts, and a pair of sandals. In this attire he got into his Auto Union, which was pushed backwards down the road by the mechanics to the last chicane so that he could get a flying start past the timing box. He was obviously bent on breaking the lap record, and on this occasion succeeded by no less than 12 seconds, going round in 10 min 32 sec. In conversation with him afterwards, I asked him if he thought he could go any quicker than this. He said that if he cut off later on the straights he thought that he could knock off another five seconds, bringing his time down to 10 min 27 sec. Pretty hectic it sounded to me!

The two Mercedes drivers, Caracciola and Brauchitsch, recorded 10 min 56 sec and 11 min 5 sec, Stuck in an Auto Union being three seconds slower. Two of the new Alfa Romeos appeared for Saturday's practice. The second one, driven by Farina, was not going at all well. Nuvolari after trying extremely hard for five laps, only managed to get round in 11 min 25 sec. This obviously annoyed him, for he came into the pits and poured a bucket of cold water over his head. After practice the Targa Abruzzo sports car race took place, in which there were 53 Fiats, one Lancia and six Alfa Romeos. The winner was Cortese in an Alfa.

The big race on Sunday was preceded by a 1500 cc event. During the first lap there was a terrible accident in which four spectators were killed, two having their legs completely severed. This was not at all surprising to me, because during practice I had noticed people sitting on the edge of the straights drinking coffee, while Mercedes and Auto Unions flashed by at 190 miles per hour within a few feet of them.

Seaman's Mercedes had already been withdrawn and it was announced that Farina's Alfa Romeo was not going to start, which was not surprising considering its performance in practice.

The front of the grandstands was decorated with paper strips bearing the words 'Viva Nuvolari', 'Viva Rosemeyer', 'Viva Caracciola', 'Viva' all the other drivers, and 'Viva Il Duce', and a huge portrait of the latter surmounted the pits. A fierce-looking but untidy barbed wire entanglement had been erected between the grandstand and the road to keep the crowd back.

The big cars were lined up for the start as follows:

STUCK	CARACCIOLA	ROSEMEYER
Auto Union	Mercedes	Auto Union
BRAUCHITSCH		MÜLLER
Mercedes		Auto Union
NUVOLARI	FAGIOLI	RUESCH
Alfa R 12-cyl	Auto Union	Alfa R 8-cyl
SOMMER		BELMONDO
Alfa R 8-cyl		Alfa R 8-cyl

Just before the start Marshal Balbo arrived and shook hand with all the drivers, Nuvolari getting out of his car. Balbo is a great motor-racing enthusiast and seems to be immensely popular with all the drivers. As the flag dropped, Caracciola, calm as ever, nosed his Mercedes in front of the two Auto Unions on either side of him, and held the lead until the cars were out of sight. Rosemeyer, however, passed him and came round on the first lap in 10 min 48 sec, with Rudi only two seconds behind. Stuck was third, 18 seconds behind Caracciola, and Brauchitsch 15 seconds behind him. The rest of the field were fairly well strung out with Nuvolari in ninth place, 50 seconds behind Rosemeyer, the new Alfa obviously misbehaving itself. Rosemeyer now decided that Caracciola was far too close to be pleasant and trod on the gas, accomplishing the second lap in record time for the race, 10 min 36 sec.

On the fourth lap Brauchitsch passed Stuck, who dropped rapidly behind owing to the fact that his engine was not going too well. Nuvolari in the new Alfa had great difficulty in passing Ruesch in an 8-cylinder Alfa Romeo, and on the fifth lap came into the pit, when a plug was changed and the car taken over by Farina. It was a heavy disappointment to the Italians that their hero Tazio had to give up so soon. In the meantime Sommer and Ruesch had been having a private dust-up, which ended in Ruesch turning round on the twisty section of the course and retiring.

Stuck's Auto Union appeared at the pits on the sixth lap very much out of breath. The mechanics changed both rear wheels, filled the tank with petrol, and changed a large number of plugs, during which Stuck talked with Paula his wife, and drank a bottle of Pellegrino mineral water. This stop lasted 4 min 20 sec. On being pushed off the Auto Union proceeded to give the spectators a firework display, the engine emitting clouds of smoke and intermittent bangs – most exciting. Stuck eventually got under way and managed to stagger round for another lap before calling it a day. Farina was having further trouble with the new Alfa and retired before half distance. Rosemeyer had been increasing his lead over Caracciola, and by the end of the seventh lap had a lead of 58 seconds.

There was great excitement at the end of the eighth lap when the leaders were expected to come in for tyres and petrol. Suddenly Rosemeyer appeared with a rear tyre in absolute shreds and made a rapid stop at the Auto Union pits, immediately followed by Caracciola who made an even quicker one at the Mercedes pit, gaining 20 seconds on the deal and reducing Rosemeyer's lead to 38 seconds. The crowd were obviously getting rather worked up because it looked as if Caracciola was now setting out to catch Rosemeyer.

The whole scene changed as the loudspeakers announced that Rosemeyer had come into the Auto Union tyre depot on the far side of the circuit and that Caracciola had passed him and was in the lead. Needless to say a buzz of excitement went round the grandstand, but as Rosemeyer had just changed tyres it was a little difficult to understand how this could possibly have happened. I discovered afterwards from Rosemeyer that he knew that he had lost a lot of time on the eighth lap, both by coming into the pits slowly with the tyre in ribbons, and also on the tyre change. So he had set off in a great hurry to pull up his lead again. He braked too late for a corner on the twisty section of the course and struck the tenth kilometre post with his offside rear wheel. Fortunately he managed to get the car back on the road again, and continued, but at the 13th kilometre stone (Rosemeyer's lucky number is 13) the tyre complete with rim and spokes flew right off the car, letting it down on the brake drum, on which he was able to run to the tyre depot about 200 yards down the road, his arrival being announced by the rim itself that got there first! A new wheel was then put on and Rosemeyer set off in pursuit of Caracciola, who by this time had a lead of 31 seconds. Nothing daunted, Rosemeyer went after Caracciola and reduced his lead to 17 seconds by the end of the tenth lap. As Caracciola passed the pits it was all too obvious that his engine was dying and that the car was only firing on seven cylinders – what really bad luck!

At the end of the 11th lap Rosemeyer and Caracciola came round together, the latter making straight for the pits, shouting that a piston had gone. Zimmer and Lindenmaier tore off the bonnet and changed number seven and eight plugs with great rapidity. The car was pushed off again with the engine still spluttering. Caracciola completed one more lap when he came in and handed over to Seaman. This was the 13th lap, so something was bound to happen to him, and about half-way round the twisty section of the circuit the engine caught fire, so Seaman stopped on a downhill section, switched off the engine, and waited for the flames to die out before restarting. This constant back-firing and the ensuing flames from the induction pipe not only burned a hole in the bonnet but the fumes very nearly stifled Seaman, who just managed to 'waffle' into fifth place. Brauchitsch, who had driven very steadily throughout, finished 1 min 41 sec behind Rosemeyer, who won the 13th Coppa Acerbo in record time at 87.61 miles per hour. Müller's Auto Union was third, 6 minutes behind Rosemeyer, with Fagioli fourth. The only Italian car to finish was an Alfa Romeo driven by Belmondo, a good last, miles behind. Fagioli seemed very tired and had to be lifted from the car.

My photographic activities were somewhat curtailed by the police, who were in a flat spin owing to the accident during the one-and-a-half-litre race. I had walked up to the big chicane at the end of the straight and was promptly taken by force by the police and placed behind the chicane, where I could not even see, let alone take photographs, although I shouted in my best Italian 'photografico!' When they were not looking I managed to dodge away to take a picture or two, and after about ten minutes I decided to venture back on the circuit again. This had disastrous results, as I was immediately manhandled by two excited policemen, one of whom I punched in the chest, and the other I pushed into a nice slimy puddle of water. This seemed to amuse the crowd even more than the motor-race, but the result was most frightening for me as one of them produced a nasty little knife, so that I was forced to take to my heels and run back to the pits for safety. Here I complained to Agnoli, the assistant director of the course, who told me that exactly the same thing had happened to

him and that the pits were the only safe place in the circuit as the police had gone berserk. This consoled me, especially when I heard that Fumagalli, the official photographer for the RACI, had also been manhandled.

The new Alfa Romeos, about which such a song and dance had been made in the Italian press, were pathetic. One can only hope that the Alfa Romeo factory was as disappointed as the Italian crowd who had come to watch the new car, and Nuvolari who had to drive it.

When in Italy I asked many people whom they considered to be the best driver; most of them being patriotic naturally said 'Nuvolari'. The best answer was, I think, from the gentleman who summed up the situation as follows: 'Rosemeyer *says* he's the best driver, Caracciola obviously *thinks* he is, but by this time Nuvolari must *know* he is...!'

Seaman and I left Pescara directly after the race and spent the night at Riccione, a seaside resort on the Adriatic with a wonderful bathing beach. Next day we set off for Milan where we stayed two or three days, and drove out to the famous Monza circuit. Monza has been the Waterloo of many famous drivers, including Materassi, Borzacchini, Campari, and Czaykowski. Seaman showed me the tree which he had run into when practising earlier in the year, and there were still some small fragments of aluminium lying about on the grass.

1938

For 1938 there was a new Grand Prix Formula which combined weight minima and a limit on engine capacity. There was a sliding scale of weight from 400 kg to 850 kg (excluding engine oil, fuel and water). Supercharged cars could be between 666 cc and 3000cc and unsupercharged cars between 1000 cc and 4500 cc. In practice all cars were of 3000 cc supercharged or 4500 cc unsupercharged. The formula in fact unfairly handicapped the unblown cars.

Mercedes-Benz produced the W154 with a chassis similar to, but lower than, the W125 and powered by a V12 2962 cc engine developing 468 bhp at 7800 rpm. From Auto Union came the Type D, in which Dr Ferdinand Porsche was not involved, as all his energies were now concentrated on the Volkswagen. The Type D was also a V12, of 2990 cc and developing 420 bhp at 7000 rpm, still rear-mounted and in a chassis with Porsche torsion bar front suspension and a de Dion axle at the rear.

In 1938 Alfa Romeo set up their own racing department, Alfa Corse, and produced cars with 8, 12

The 1938 3-litre supercharged Mercedes-Benz W154, the car which scored the most wins during the year.

In 1938 Bugatti produced the Type 60 3-litre supercharged car, based on an earlier chassis. Jean-Pierre Wimille on the right of the car, drove it in the Cork Grand Prix, but it retired because of an engine misfire.

and 16-cylinder engines mounted in the chassis first seen in the latter part of 1937. To try to run three different engines diluted the team's efforts and little success was gained. Maserati, now under the control of the Orsi family, produced the 8-cylinder 3-litre supercharged 8CTF and although this was very fast, it also proved mechanically unreliable. The 8CTF's greatest successes were wins at Indianapolis and in the 500 Miles race Wilbur Shaw drove one of these cars to victory in both 1939 and 1940. In France both Talbot (a straight six) and Delahaye (a V12) built unsupercharged cars and the rarely seen French SEFAC, originally built for the 750 kg Formula, made a few appearances with 2770 cc supercharged engine. Bugatti also built a 3-litre supercharged car, but it appeared only a couple of times.

Motor racing suffered a devastating blow in January 1938 when Bernd Rosemeyer was killed at the wheel of his Auto Union during a record attempt on the Frankfurt-Darmstadt *Autobahn*; the car had been caught by a gust of wind while travelling at around 250 mph and blown off the road. Rosemeyer's death shook Auto Union and although Tazio Nuvolari was persuaded to join the team, it won only four races in the years 1938-39.

The Mercedes-Benz team dominated racing during these two years, although the first race of the

Giuseppe Farina in practice for the 1938 Swiss Grand Prix with the V12 Alfa Romeo Tipo 12C-312. Farina finished fifth at Bremgarten ahead of team-mates Taruffi and Wimille. These later Alfa Romeos still proved no match for the German opposition.

new formula was to give a different – and misleading – impression. The Pau Grand Prix was won by René Dreyfus (Delahaye) from the Mercedes-Benz shared by Caracciola and Lang, partly because Dreyfus was able to run through without refuelling and partly because the German car was plagued by plug trouble. Thereafter the Mercedes-Benz record read: 1st (Lang), 2nd (von Brauchitsch), Tripoli Grand Prix (Auto Union did not enter); 1st (von Brauchitsch), 2nd (Caracciola), French GP; 1st (Seaman), 2nd (Caracciola/Lang), German Grand Prix; 1st (Lang), Coppa Ciano, Livorno; 1st (Caracciola), Coppa Acerbo, Pescara; 1st (Caracciola), 2nd (Seaman), 3rd (von Brauchitsch), Swiss Grand Prix. On the strength of these successes Caracciola was again European Champion. The Mercedes-Benz team ran into mechanical problems in the Italian Grand Prix and the International Grand Prix at Donington Park at the end of the year and Nuvolari won both these races for Auto Union.

1939

Although the clouds of war were gathering, racing continued in 1939. Mercedes-Benz raced the W163 with new engine developing 485 bhp at 8000 rpm and Auto Union adopted two-stage superchargers which boosted the power of the Type D to 485 bhp at 7000 rpm. The Stuttgart steamroller carried on and Hermann Lang, one-time mechanic but now a National hero, won the first four races of the year at Pau, Tripoli (to which reference will be made shortly), the Eifelrennen and the Belgian Grand Prix. The Belgian race was marred by the death of Dick Seaman. He crashed, the car caught fire and unable to release the steering wheel which was necessary to get out of the car, he died in the inferno. At Reims all three Mercedes-Benz entries retired and Müller and Meier took the first two places for Auto Union. Caracciola won the German Grand Prix, Lang led a Mercedes-Benz 1-2-3 at Bremgarten and then came the Yugoslavian Grand Prix at Belgrade. On the day that

Tazio Nuvolari joined Auto Union after Rosemeyer's death in a record-breaking attempt early in 1938. He is seen in the Italian Grand Prix at Monza which he won.

the second World War broke out, 3 September, 1939, Tazio Nuvolari with his Auto Union won from the Mercedes of von Brauchitsch. There were no more Formula 1 races in 1939, and Lang was European Champion. Racing continued in Italy until that country entered the war in 1940. The W163s survived the war and were driven in two Formule Libre events in the Argentine by Fangio, Karl Kling and Lang in 1951, part of the Mercedes-Benz learning curve before re-entering sports car racing in 1952. Carburation problems, lack of suitable fuel and tortuous circuits took their toll and they were easily defeated by Froilan Gonzalez with a 2-litre supercharged Ferrari.

Voiturettes.

Parallel with the growth in strength of the German racing teams there had been a growth in interest in *Voiturette* racing, for cars of up to 1500 cc

Another win for Nuvolari and his Auto Union followed in the 1938 International Grand Prix at Donington Park, postponed from September until October because of the Czechoslovakian crisis. This photograph shows off to advantage the superb lines of the 3-litre V12 Auto Union.

A new car to appear at Reims in 1939 was this monoposto Talbot driven by Raymond Mays. Its fuel tank sprang a leak in practice and repeated this in the race. This 4.5-litre unsuper-charged Talbot was the forerunner of the cars that plodded their way to a good measure of success in post-war days.

supercharged. The leading contenders were the British ERA and the Italian Maseratis, but as the German stranglehold increased on Grand Prix racing, so in 1938 Alfa Romeo produced the Tipo 158 or *Alfetta*. This was a straight eight, based on one half of the Alfa Corse V16 3-litre engine and designed by Giaocchino Colombo with Enzo Ferrari acting as consultant. The *Alfettas* won two races in 1938 (and failed in two others).

The most numerous Maserati was the Tipo 6CM with 6-cylinder engine. This photograph was taken at a Vintage Sports Car Club meeting at Castle Combe in Wiltshire in 1965.

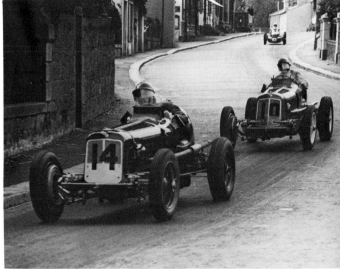

A category for *Voiturettes* had existed since the early years of the century, but the 1500 cc category became extremely popular from 1934 onwards as a cheaper category of racing. The two most successful marques were the British ERA and the Italian Maserati. These two ERAs are seen competing in post-war days in the 1948 Jersey International Road Race. Geoffrey Ansell leads the eventual winner, Bob Gerard. Gerard's car, R14B, featured a lowered radiator and bonnet line. (*Guy Griffiths*)

The 1939 Tripoli Grand Prix was held as a *Voiturette* race and Mercedes-Benz stunned the opposition by racing their new W165 V8 1500 cc cars. Here Lang with his W165, the eventual winner, leads Caracciola away from the start. No. 44 is an Alfa Corse-entered Tipo 158 and No. 38, the special streamlined Maserati that retired early in the race.

The Italian authorities were sufficiently impressed that in an effort to maintain the country's *amour propre*, all single-seater races on Italian soil in 1939 were held to *Voiturette* rules. Unfortunately for the Italians, Mercedes-Benz produced the W165 1493 cc V8 cars with a power output of 278 bhp at 8250 rpm in the first race at Tripoli (Libya then counted as Italian soil) and Lang and Caracciola took the first two places, while three of the four Alfas retired because of overheating. The W165s were raced only the once and without this opposition Alfa Romeo 158s won three

more races in 1939, together with the 1940 Tripoli race (before Italy entered the war).

Although not a great deal of progress had been made, Auto Union was also planning a 1500 cc car. Both German teams had appreciated the imbalance of the existing Grand Prix formula and foresaw that it would be replaced by a new formula for 1500 cc supercharged/4500 cc unsupercharged cars. This eventually came into force for 1947, when Germany was banned from international racing, and the *Alfettas* were to achieve domination.

Part 4

SUPREMACY OF THE SUPERCHARGER, 1946-51

1946-48

Motor racing resumed after the war with a Formule Libre ('free formula') race held in the Bois de Boulogne in Paris. Initially the *official* formula was a continuation of the pre-war Formula A for cars of 3 litres supercharged and 4.5 litres unsupercharged. There was a minimum race distance of 500 kilometres (311 miles). In reality the races were contested by a rather mixed bag of pre-war *Voiturettes* (the 1500 cc supercharged equivalent of modern Formula 2), 3- to 4.5-litre unsupercharged cars (French Delage, Delahaye and Talbot) and the odd 8C-308 3-litre supercharged Alfa Romeo. From 1947 there was a new formula, soon to be called Formula 1, but originally again known as Formula A, for cars of 1500 cc supercharged and 4500 cc unsupercharged. The minimum race distance remained unchanged.

A World Championship for Drivers was introduced in 1950 with a scoring system of 8, 6, 4, 3 and 2 points for first to fifth places with an additional point for the fastest race lap. At the same time the minimum race distance was reduced to 300 kilometres (186 miles) or three hours. This meant that the Monaco Grand Prix, a very 'slow' race on a street circuit could be reintroduced after a two-year interval and form part of the World Championship series. The Indianapolis 500 miles race counted as a round in the World Championship until 1960, although during that period no Indianapolis driver competed in a Grand Prix and there were only a couple of half-hearted efforts to run European cars in the American race.

First raced in 1938, the Alfa Romeo 158 *Voiturette*, a straight-eight twin overhead camshaft supercharged 1479 cc design proved even more dominant than it had before the war. After a first appearance in the 1946 St. Cloud Grand Prix, run through the streets of a suburb of Paris, in which both the Italian cars retired, the 158 won every race entered between 1946 and 1950 – three in 1946, four in 1947, four in 1948, the team gave the 1949 season a miss and 11 in 1950.

During these years power output of the 158's engine rose from 225 bhp to 350 bhp and the team had a star-studded list of drivers that included Frenchman Jean-Pierre Wimille and Italians Achille Varzi and Giuseppe Farina. One of the greatest drivers of the era – and in pre-war days – a name now almost completely forgotten was Varzi, superbly portrayed in this article by Cyril Posthumus published in 1964.

The Man Who Crashed Twice: Achille Varzi

By tradition the Italian racing driver in action is an excitable character given to shouting, gesticulating, waving his fists, baring his teeth and in general giving way to his emotions. Tazio Nuvolari filled the role splendidly, and so did Luigi Fagioli when he got worked up. Campari and Farina complied well with the national trait, while in more recent years Castellotti and Musso could get amply emotional under stress.

There were exceptions, of course. The gentlemanly Count Trossi, for instance, or his fellow nobleman Count Antonio Brivio of the Sforza family. But an even more remarkable exception was Achille Varzi of Galliate, outside Milan, a man who, though he contributed so much to the drama of racing in the late twenties and early thirties, was the very antithesis of Latin ebullience. His calm was Nordic to extreme, he was cold and unsmiling, his eyes dark and brooding, his manner aloof; to all except his closest acquaintances, he seemed a formidable, intimidating and unapproachable man.

Although Varzi smiled only with difficulty, his forbidding mien concealed a gentlemanly charm and a sardonic sense of humour, while with his noted fondness for women, he was undeniably human! His methods on the circuit echoed his manner. When in command of the race, he drove with a calculated machine-like perfection, followng his own wheeltracks to the inch for lap after lap; when at bay he was magnificent, driving with grim, ice-cold ferocity, immensely fast but never making a mistake. In a career lasting 14 years he drove in over 70 major races, won 28 of them, and crashed but twice.

At the circuits, Varzi was a distinctive figure, broad-shouldered, well turned out in impeccable blue racing overalls, his straight hair parted exactly in the centre, and with a cigarette dangling eternally from his lips. Like all the best inter-war Italian drivers Varzi graduated from the tough school of motor-cycle racing. Between 1923, when he was 19, and 1927 he won many important Italian races, riding Sunbeam, Norton, Garelli, Guzzi and Frera machines, and so impeccable was his style that his compatriots called him 'the motor-cycling Nazzaro', a compliment indeed in a country where Felice Nazzaro was revered for his smooth, effective gait.

It is not generally known that this brilliant Italian rode five times in the world-famous Isle of Man TT races. On his first attempt in 1924 he crashed when avoiding a fallen rider, thereby gaining the special Nesbit Trophy award 'for a sporting action'. In 1925 and 1926 he won *The Motor Cycle* Visitors' Cup for the best performance by a foreign entrant, and British riders remarked on his taciturn single-mindedness when in the Island; he didn't mix with rivals, nor join in parties, but just stuck to the formidable job of learning the 37½-mile Manx circuit.

Unusually for one so dedicated, Varzi never had pressing need to earn a living. As the second son of a wealthy textile engineering family, he could have played the dilettante amateur, but that was not his way. It was on two wheels that Varzi first met the meteoric Tazio Nuvolari, 19 years his senior, and the legend flourished through the years that these so brilliant yet so contrasting Italians were deadly rivals. This was true at one stage in their careers, but not permanently; they were friendly opponents in their motor-cycle days and in 1928 actually became partners in one of the first car racing *scuderie* to be formed.

As an old hand who had raced his first car in 1921, Tazio was No 1 with Achille as the 'learner', paying his own way. Both drove red-painted Bugattis, Varzi's being prepared by a Mantuan named Guido Bignami, who was to act as Varzi's chief mechanic and *aide* throughout his racing career. The team went to Tripoli, Pozzo, Messina,

Cremona and Pescara, the net result being four wins for Nuvolari and just one second place for Varzi.

But 24-year-old Achille was learning fast, and at Pescara his attention was riveted on the winning car, Campari's grand old P2 straight-eight Alfa Romeo. This was the very Alfa with which Campari had won the historic French Grand Prix of 1924, and after seeing the car perform again at Montenero, Varzi took the plunge and bought it from Campari for 75,000 lire. This was a lot of money – about £800 – but Achille managed it somehow. Three weeks later in the European GP at Monza, he was the *rivelazione* of the race, battling with stars such as Chiron, Brilli-Peri and Materassi and taking the lead in his venerable P2. Then tragedy intervened. On lap 18, Materassi's Talbot left the track at 125 mph and plunged into the crowd, killing 27 and injuring 21, the driver also dying. Two rounds after this calamity Varzi handed over to Campari as prearranged, whereupon Louis Chiron snatched the lead from the Alfa. Seven laps later Varzi took over again, but his first place was now irretrievable and he finished two minutes behind the flying Bugatti.

After that performance, the Alfa Romeo factory took a special interest in Varzi, gave him official backing, and kept his P2 in razor-edged tune. Came 1929, a black year for Wall Street and International finance, but not for Achille Varzi and his P2. The Bordino Cup, Rome GP and the Montenero Cup all fell to him, and jointly he won the San Sebastian 12 Hours race in Spain with Zehender in a 1750 cc sports Alfa. Next came Italy's premier race, the GP at Monza, and there the new star Varzi and the P2 outpaced everyone to win at 116.83 mph from Nuvolari, his triumph clinching for him the Italian Championship.

Italian Champion in his second season! That was something even Nuvolari did not achieve, and the little Mantuan felt it keenly. Their rivalry flared into the open early in 1930, when both joined the Alfa Romeo team. Their first encounter as team mates, the Mille Miglia 1000 Miles race, accentuated the problems of having 'two cocks in one farmyard' as one Italian journal put it. Starting one minute apart, Varzi preceding Nuvolari, the pair ran virtually level 'on paper' until Ancona, about two-thirds distance. Then the Alfa team control, anxious that both rather than neither should finish, kept Varzi back with assurances that he was holding Nuvolari – and the latter roared into the finish at Brescia a comfortable winner.

Varzi was furious. A week later he beat Nuvolari in the Bordino Cup race, both driving P2s, and two weeks later Varzi and the P2 won again in the Targa Florio. This was one of his greatest victories, in which Nuvolari with a 1750 Alfa could not better fifth position. The pair met again in P2s at Rome, but this time both had to retire when well behind Arcangeli's 2.5-litre Maserati. Varzi's cold,

Varzi at work winning the 1930 Targa Florio with the Alfa Romeo P2, one of his finest victories. *(Cyril Posthumus)*

calculating eye fastened keenly on this fine new Italian machine after the race, and he saw more evidence of Maserati pace at Leghorn [Livorno] where the P2s again perished in the wake of one driven by Fagioli.

Two weeks later Varzi surprised his opponents by appearing at Pescara, not in the P2, but in one of the new Maseratis! Moreover, he won the race at record speed, with the P2s well back, third and fifth. A month after that came the Monza GP, but whereas Nuvolari's P2 retired, Varzi fought a tigerish battle for the lead with Arcangeli, both in 2.5 Maseratis. Plug trouble had cost Varzi 1 minute 50 seconds early on, but he rejoined the race in an ice-cold fury, made up the time loss in 60 tempestuous miles, broke the course record on 11 consecutive laps, and caught the astonished Arcangeli on the last corner of the last lap, to win a desperately exciting race by one-fifth of a second!

That Monza coup earned Varzi the title of Italian Champion for the second year, but he capped his season with yet another victory for Maserati in the Spanish GP at San Sebastian. With three wins in three drives, one would have expected Varzi to sign up with Maserati again in 1931, but instead, he surprised and aggrieved many of his countrymen by 'going French' and joining the Bugatti team.

Things began well when he won his first 1931 race

driving the new Type 51 2.3-litre twin ohc Bugatti before a vast North African crowd in the Tunis GP at Carthage. Next he took the Bordino Cup race, beating Nuvolari in the new 2.3-litre 8-cylinder Alfa. But the Mantuan turned the tables on the Galliatese a week later, he and Borzacchini in Alfas defeating Varzi in the Targa Florio – or perhaps, more accurately, the weather beat him, for it rained and though Varzi led three laps of the four and made fastest lap, he had no mudguards on his Bugatti and, becoming plastered with mud from head to waist, and half-blinded, he was caught by his Alfa rivals, who had the foresight to fit rudimentary wings to their cars. This decline in Varzi fortunes prevailed more or less for the next two years, though he shared first place with Louis Chiron in the gruelling 10-hour French GP of 1931, and won the Tunis GP the following spring. But 1933 opened with the most famous Varzi-Nuvolari duel of all, in the Monaco GP, when the blue Bugatti and the red Alfa literally ran nose to tail for 99 of the 100 laps. Then Varzi made a superhuman effort, cut the lap record by two *whole* seconds, and passed Nuvolari – and the Alfa Romeo blew up and stopped in a cloud of smoke while Varzi howled over the line the victor.

Less creditable was Varzi's win in the subsequent Tripoli GP, an apparently desperate affair in which he and

Nuvolari crossed the line one-tenth of a second apart. In truth the pair were partners with Borzacchini and Campari in a plan whereby their finishing order was agreed in advance. In order to popularise the 1933 Tripoli race on the new Mellaha circuit, a huge national sweepstake was held, and the man who drew the ticket with Varzi's name on it ventured to approach the great man, and offered him half his potential prize, totalling over 3,000,000 lire or about £30,000, if he managed to win the race!

£15,000, even split with three or four accomplices, was big money. Varzi promptly contacted the other drivers, and a strange race ensued: Borzacchini and Campari retired, while Nuvolari, leading, contrived to run out of fuel with two laps to go, and stopped for a refill. As for Varzi, he had been delayed by ignition trouble, and stammered past on six of the Bugatti's eight cylinders to 'win' from Nuvolari by a foot or so! Somehow news of the dubious transaction leaked out, and the drivers concerned were 'admonished'.

But there was nothing 'phoney' about Varzi's next victory, the Avus GP in Berlin. The Nazi party had just taken over governmental control in Germany, and Adolf Hitler himself was present, together with some 300,000 spectators. Varzi's mount was the big, brutish but very fast 4.9-litre Type 54, and a similar car, privately owned, was driven by the daring Count Czaykowski. The pair immediately engaged in an exciting duel, averaging 123 mph and leaving the big Mercedes and Alfa Romeos behind.

An old hand at this sort of thing, Varzi 'played' his adversary pitilessly, forcing the pace ever higher – 128½ mph, 130, 132, 133 mph, until on the penultimate lap, the grim-faced Italian closed right up on Czaykowski in one of the wide turns, then slowly, inexorably, drew ahead and tore on to victory by perhaps two yards. His last, stupendous lap was at over 136 mph.

For 1934, the ace from Galliate left Bugatti to drive Alfa Romeos for the Scuderia Ferrari; and in that single season he scored seven victories, the same number he had won during three hard years with Bugatti. Yet 1934 was the year in which Germany re-entered GP racing with the remarkable new Mercedes and Auto Unions, and by the latter half of the season Ferrari's proud Monoposto Alfa, monarch of all it surveyed since 1932, was dethroned at last.

That winter Auto Union approached Varzi, and with little hesitation, he joined the Germans for 1935. They paid him a retainer of about £4000, a share in all winnings, and gave him a big white Horch 'prestige' car – and were glad to get him at the price. The Auto Union, with its big 16-cylinder engine in the tail, was a brute to handle, but Varzi took to it well and won his first race with the car, the Tunis GP, at a canter.

Varzi beating Guy Moll to first place in the 1934 Tripoli Grand Prix by one-tenth of a second. Both drivers were in Alfa Romeo Monopostos.

Next came another old favourite of his, the Tripoli GP, and by lap five he was in the lead. The pace was staggering, and with laps in the hot African sun at 125 mph tyres were hardly lasting 10 laps, though Varzi still led by lap 35, with five to go. Then a tread flew with a sharp crack, the tyre burst and he hobbled round to the pits while Caracciola's Mercedes screamed triumphantly into the lead. Re-shod, Varzi tore back in pursuit and by the final lap had the Mercedes in sight when another tyre burst. He was placed second, and none but Bignami, with a lighted cigarette ready, dared approach him as he coasted in.

Avus came next, and again tyres beat Varzi; he had to make three changes during the 125-mile final, and finished third with one cover down to the canvas. In the Eifelrennen Varzi was said to be suffering from appendix trouble and withdrew, and in the German GP, also on the Nürburgring, he went poorly and came eighth. 'Ill health', said the reports, but other sources suggested something very different. Varzi the bachelor was in love, they said, and certainly he was now seen repeatedly with the wife of one of the German drivers. He won his next race, the Acerbo Cup at Pescara, yet in ensuing events something of his noted precision in handling a car seemed to go; his pace became erratic, his concentration and his interest wavered.

Only one more victory came his way when in the Auto Union team, and that was in the Tripoli GP, the following year. Though they were team mates, Varzi and Hans Stuck fought a bitter duel until, with four laps to go, Stuck in the lead was slowed by his pit – and Varzi suddenly loomed large in his mirror after a fantastic lap at 141.3 mph and thundered past to win by 4.4 seconds.

The livid Stuck was scarcely comforted on being told by his team manager that it had been deemed politically better for an Italian to win this race in Italy's 'empire', but upon Varzi, the news when it reached him had a shattering effect. Having received no 'ease off' signal like Stuck, he had gone all out to win. The pride of this strange, uncommunicative man was bitterly wounded, and the upshot was that, in the effort to find rest and peace of mind, he was persuaded by his girl friend to try morphine drugs.

One week later the Tunis GP brought the first crash in Varzi's racing career. A sudden gust of wind caught him unawares while travelling virtually flat out. His Auto Union left the road at about 180 mph with one prodigious leap, pitched Varzi out, then somersaulted over and over, pounding itself into a battered heap of scrap metal. Miraculously, Varzi suffered only a few cuts, bruises and shock, but the subsequent reaction to such a violent accident caused him to resort again to drugs. It was the end of Varzi as an ace.

His performances during the rest of 1936 were mediocre, although at Pescara the old Varzi peeped through with a record lap at a savage 183.64 mph through the flying kilometre to complete an Auto Union one-two-three victory after troubles delayed him. Even so, his season's winnings totalled 380,000 lire, and with nine fruitful seasons behind him he was now a wealthy man. Sadly, the will as well as the need to race had now gone, Auto Union's contract ended, and Varzi was not seen at a circuit for months.

Then suddenly, in July 1937, he drove a *Voiturette* – a 1500 cc Maserati – for the first time in his life, in the San Remo GP. *Infra dig*, perhaps, for a man of his fame and reputation, but Varzi won his heat by a lap and the final by almost a minute from two Italian amateurs. Six weeks later Auto Union gave him a drive in the Italian GP at Leghorn. He went well in practice but the long, tiring race betrayed his lack of form, and he finished sixth, woefully exhausted. Defaulting in two more 1937 GPs, he again essayed a return to racing in 1938, driving a new 3-litre Maserati in the Tripoli GP, but the Maserati's transmission failed early on. Nominated for the Ciano Cup and Italian GP races he non-started in both and after that he really gave up trying.

Others did not, however, and with the patience and persuasion of several close friends during the war years, Achille Varzi was completely cured of his drug addiction.

He married in 1941, and when Grand Prix racing returned in 1946 he returned with it, now a veteran, but still impeccably turned out, still the *grand seigneur*, still grim of mien, with the cigarette on his lips, and Bignami in attendance. The silver Mercedes and Auto Unions had gone, but in their place the Type 158 Alfa Romeos ruled the racing roost – and there, sitting in one on the grid at Geneva for the 1946 GP of the Nations, was Achille Varzi.

His come-back was marred by engine trouble, and he could only finish seventh whereas his team mates Farina, Wimille and Trossi scored a triumphant one-two-three victory. But he won the Turin GP and took a second at Milan, and then, early in 1947, Varzi and a 3-litre 8-cylinder Alfa Romeo crossed the South Atlantic for the first Argentinian *Temporada* series of races. Villoresi beat him in the Buenos Aires GP but Varzi reversed the order at Rosario, reviving old tactics by running level with Villoresi on the final corner, then sprinting for the finish. Perhaps really happy again for the first time in a dozen years, the old Galliatese wizard beat Villoresi again at Sao Paulo, won at Interlagos, then returned to Europe.

With brilliant team-mates like Jean-Pierre Wimille, victory in the Alfa team was rationed, and Varzi's turn came in the Bari GP alone, though he was second at Berne, at Spa, and at Milan. That winter he again did the Argentinian round – he was developing a great liking for that country – this time wielding a rebuilt 4.6-litre 12-cylinder Alfa Romeo. He took second at Mar del Plata and won the Sao Paulo GP again, and it was during this second visit that Varzi met a very fast, rather rugged local driver named Juan Manuel Fangio. He gave him much good advice on handling a car, and in race tactics, and Fangio took it very seriously. 'I hung on his every word', he later wrote – with the result that is so well known.

Varzi returned, almost reluctantly, to Europe. His first engagement with the Alfa team was the GP of Europe at Berne, and during practice the Galliatese took out the newest, more powerful Type 158 to try to improve his times. It had been pouring with rain, and on the tricky Jordenrampe left-hander, his sleek red Alfa Romeo suddenly skated sideways on the glass-like surface and charged a wooden barrier tail first. It bounced off, spun, and hit the barrier again head on, then rolled over, casting Varzi out on to his head, protected only by a linen helmet.

Seconds later Louis Chiron in his big blue Talbot screeched to a standstill and rushed, aghast, to help his friend and former team-mate. But Achille Varzi was past help; he was dead.

In 1949, when the Argentine AC sent a team of drivers, headed by Juan Manuel Fangio, to contest European Grands Prix they called their team the Squadra Achille Varzi in memory of the great Italian. By courtesy of his father, Menotti Varzi, their HQ was at Galliate, in Achille's old house and workshops, and their team manager was Guido Bignami, his right-hand man.

It was not until 1948 that there was any real challenge to Alfa Romeo, for the 4-cylinder Maserati opposition, entered only by private teams, was outclassed (although winning many races when Alfa Romeo did not compete). In 1948 Maserati introduced their 4CLT/48 model with new tubular chassis and twin-stage supercharging and always known as the 'San Remo' after the Grand Prix in which it first appeared; from the French Talbot concern came a new 4500 cc 6-cylinder single-seater (they had built one single-seater before the war), also raced only by private owners; and at the 1948 Italian Grand Prix held at Turin the new Ferrari V12 made its first appearance in Formula 1 form. In 1947 the great French hope, the CTA-Arsenal

Although no match for the all-conquering Alfa Romeos, the unsupercharged 4.5-litre Talbots were consistent performers and won races when no Alfas were entered. The French cars were private entries, but as here, in the 1950 British Grand Prix, usually appeared in entry lists under the name 'Automobiles Talbot'. This is the veteran French driver, Philippe 'Phi-Phi' Etancelin who retired in this race. (*T. C. March*)

had appeared, but it was a primitive design and absolutely nothing was achieved. Another car to appear in 1948 was the British Alta, the first example of which was supplied to George Abecassis, a British motor dealer of Portuguese ancestry. It incorporated many of the features of pre-war Alta *Voiturettes*, but with new all-independent suspension by wishbones compressing on to rubber blocks. Neither it, nor its successors, also sold to private owners, achieved anything and the fact is that even with an intensive and well-financed development programme it lacked the inherent potential for success.

1949-50

In the absence of Alfa Romeo, it was expected that Ferrari's constantly modified V12 cars would dominate, but in the first major race of the year, Louis Rosier at the wheel of a lumbering Talbot came through to win – mainly because the good fuel economy of the French car meant that he could run the whole race without a refuelling stop. Later in the year supercharged Ferraris won the Swiss and Dutch Grands Prix and the International Trophy race at Silverstone.

Ferrari soon learned his lesson and put in hand the development of an unsupercharged car, the first version of which with a 3.3-litre engine ran in the 1950 Belgian Grand Prix, a 4.1-litre car ran at Geneva and by the Italian Grand Prix in September the full 4.5-litre Tipo 375 car was ready.

While Alberto Ascari and Luigi Villoresi struggled through Ferrari's second learning curve, Alfa Romeo, with what was basically a 12-year old design and a famous team of drivers, the 'three Fs', Farina, Fangio and Fagioli swept all before them in the Milan company's now much bigger racing programme.

The first Drivers' World Championship was won in 1950 by Giuseppe Farina, a veteran whose racing career started seriously in 1933, and as the following portrayal of his career shows, a man of erratic moods, professional jealousy and with more than a streak of ruthlessness.

The First World Champion
Giuseppe Farina, 1950

Over 40 years after he won the first World Championship, Nino Farina is both a legend and something of an enigma. When Farina was racing, drivers simply got on with the job of driving, only if they had journalistic leanings did they pen their own autobiography and it was rare indeed for a driver to collaborate with a journalist, rarer still for him to have a close enough friend to write his biography. Very little of what Farina felt about racing ever became known, there was no explanation for his harsh, forceful driving that sometimes bordered on ruthlessness or for his moods that on occasion resulted in him giving up the race in the middle of a chase and made life so difficult for his team manager.

Farina was born in Turin on 30 October, 1906. He took his doctorate in political economy at Turin University and was related to Pinin Farina, the greatest of all Italian coachbuilders. In Turin, in the Corso Tortona, he ran with his brother his own coachbuilding company known as Stablimente Farina. The business flourished in post-war days and was responsible for a number of bodies fitted to early Ferraris, but as Ferrari turned to the Pininfarina concern more and more for new coachwork for his cars, the fortunes of Stablimente Farina gradually faded.

Giuseppe Farina is best remembered for his style of driving; the relaxed, inclined position and outstretched arms that was to influence a whole generation of drivers. Even in post-war days, when Farina was driving for the Alfa team, many of his contemporaries still sat crouched, fighting with the wheel. While the great stylist Farina applied art and intelligence to the driving of his car, the 'Pampas Bull,' Argentinian Froilan Gonzalez, would hunch over the wheel of his Ferrari and urge it along with great heavings of his ponderous frame.

Farina's parents had comfortable financial means; there was always a car in the family and before he was ten-years-old he was a rabid motoring enthusiast. Although his parents tried to steer him towards a more academic career, young 'Nino' was determined to become a racing driver. His first race, of a very unofficial nature, came in 1921 when he was only 15-years-old. He and his brother raced through roads near Turin with a brace of Temperino 1200 cc cycle cars – there is, however, no record as to who won, but that this race did take place was substantiated by a photograph in Farina's family album.

While at University 20-year-old Farina decided to buy a racing car without his family knowing. The only problem was money and Nino tried to raise this by speculating on the stock exchange. Soon he had accumulated almost all the money needed, but then disaster struck, his final speculation failed and he found himself hopelessly in debt. There was now only one thing that he could do – tell his father the full story. By this time Farina senior had become reconciled to his son's plans to become a racing driver. He paid off all the debts and agreed to buy Nino the Alfa Romeo he wanted, but on the understanding that he, too, should have one so that they could compete together.

Their first event was the 1927 Aosta-Gran San Bernardo hill climb. Nino's run was first, but in a burst of over-exuberance he lost control at a corner, turned the car over and was taken off to hospital with a broken shoulder. At this point Farina senior put his foot down and decreed that Nino could forget cars and racing and concentrate on his studies. It was not until 1933 that Nino could afford another car for competitions work, an 8C-2300 Alfa Romeo which he drove into third place in the Naples Grand Prix. The following year he crashed again in a hill climb, hitting a wall at the first corner, less than 200 yards from the start. This accident helped to tame his wild driving. He took his racing more seriously and later in the year switched to a Maserati 1500 cc *Voiturette,* with which he scored a number of successes including a win in the Circuit of Masaryk in Czechoslovakia and third place in the Circuit of Biella, a minor Italian 'round the houses' race. Both of these successes were gained at the wheel of cars entered by the Scuderia Subalpina on behalf of the works and he continued to drive for this team the following year.

In the early part of the 1935 season he handled a 3.7-litre version of the new 6-cylinder Maserati that had made its debut in the hands of the great Tazio Nuvolari at Monza the previous year. This car proved hopelessly unreliable, as did the 4.8-litre V8 Maserati which he handled later in 1935. Perhaps Nino's best drive of the year was in October in the Donington Grand Prix (the first international Grand Prix to be held on a road circuit in England) which he led on a rain-soaked course for the first 100 miles until his V8 Maserati expired with a broken half-shaft. Farina had become friendly with Tazio Nuvolari and the great Italian helped and encouraged the young Maserati driver.

Farina's driving greatly impressed Enzo Ferrari who later wrote of him: 'He was a great driver, but I could never help feeling apprehensive about him, especially at the start of a race and one or two laps from the end. At the start, he was not unlike a highstrung thoroughbred, liable to break through the starting tape in its eagerness. When nearing the finish, he was capable of committing the most astonishing follies, although it must be admitted in all justice that he risked only his own safety and never jeopardised that of others. As a consequence he was a regular inmate of the hospital wards.' *(The Enzo Ferrari Memoirs)*

Ferrari's remarks are of considerable interest, but it is

impossible not to question whether one can trust what he wrote of Farina, any more than one can trust his undoubtedly prejudiced descriptions of Fangio or Fangio's equally prejudiced comments on Ferrari. Certainly Farina was involved in many accidents, so many that he could not remember them all, but his moments of folly came mainly in later years when both he and Ascari were driving for Ferrari (to be beaten by the younger man was more than his pride could stomach). In pre-war days Farina appeared to be gripped by a ruthless determination to succeed, a man who had made a scientific study of motor racing and drove with forethought and precision. If he took a risk, it was a calculated risk and not a chance.

Enzo Ferrari invited the slim, austere Farina to join the Scuderia for 1936. At this time Italian motor racing was in a very sick state. Since the introduction of the 750 kg Grand Prix Formula at the beginning of 1934, a Formula imposing a maximum weight but no maximum engine size, the German teams, Mercedes-Benz and Auto Union, had been racing cars of considerable technical complexity. Their annual racing budget was many times greater than that of Alfa Romeo, the leading Italian contender that had dominated racing in the early 1930s. The outcome of so much effort applied was inevitable; there was a Teutonic stranglehold on Grand Prix racing that the Italians could rarely break and Farina's chances of success in Grand Prix racing with Alfa Romeo were slim.

Farina's first drive for Scuderia Ferrari was in the Mille Miglia road race in April and at the wheel of one of the new 2.9-litre supercharged Alfa Romeo sports cars, closely based on the design of the team's Grand Prix machinery. He finished a bare half-minute behind team-mate Brivio whose car had covered the last 25 miles of this 922-mile race, the latter stages run in the dark, with smashed headlamps. In Grand Prix racing he achieved a fourth in the Eifelrennen at the Nürburgring and thirds at Milan, Modena and Barcelona, but his year was marred by a horrible accident in which he was not blameless. In the Deauville Grand Prix, in the absence of opposition from the German teams, Farina was leading the race with his 8-cylinder Alfa Romeo when he collided with the ERA of Marcel Lehoux which he was lapping. The accident cost the life of Lehoux whose car caught fire.

For 1937 Farina remained with Scuderia Ferrari, finishing second in the Mille Miglia with a 2.3-litre unsupercharged Alfa Romeo, taking other second places in the Circuit of Turin and Milan and winning at Naples. Alfa Romeo decided to resume racing cars on their own behalf in 1938 and Farina now drove for this works team proper which was given the name of Alfa Corse. 1938 started badly for Farina; he crashed in the Mille Miglia and at the Tripoli race he was involved in yet another fatal accident when he

collided with the Maserati of Laszlo Hartmann who was killed. In this first year of a new Grand Prix Formula the latest German cars were not entirely *au point*, and it was for this reason rather than any other that Farina achieved more Grand Prix successes than in the past. In the Coppa Ciano at Livorno he took second place to Hermann Lang's Mercedes, a fortnight later he finished second to Caracciola's Mercedes in the Coppa Acerbo at Pescara, he was fifth in the Swiss Grand Prix and second again in the Italian race. For the second year running he was the winner of the Italian Championship.

From an Italian point of view the most significant event of 1938 had been the introduction of the new Alfa Romeo Tipo 158 1500 cc *Voiturette* which, after teething troubles in its early days, was to enjoy a run of racing success that persisted until the end of the 1951 season. In 1938 these cars had appeared in four races and won two of them, but Farina did not drive a 158 until 1939 when all major Italian races were held for 1500 cc racing cars and the Tipo 158 spear-headed the Alfa attack. At Tripoli the 158s were trounced by two new *Voiturettes* from the Mercedes factory, cars that no one knew existed until shortly before the race. After an early effort in which he held second place ahead of Caracciola's Mercedes, Farina retired with engine trouble.

The new Mercedes only appeared the once and in the remainder of the year's *Voiturette* races Alfa Romeo had a comparatively easy time. The Dottore won the Coppa Ciano, after leading the race for the whole distance, took third place in the Coppa Acerbo and won the *Voiturette* class of the Swiss Grand Prix. Farina drove a fantastic race at Bremgarten, for in the final in which the *Voiturettes* and Grand Prix cars ran together, he was in second place to Lang's Mercedes at the end of the first lap and it took seven laps before Caracciola could force his Mercedes past into second place. At the finish he was still leading a works Mercedes and a works Auto Union. In the whole of his career this was the race that gave Farina the greatest satisfaction. One final victory in 1940 before Italy entered the war and Farina joined the army, came in the Tripoli Grand Prix in which he again drove a Tipo 158.

Alfa Romeo – and Giuseppe Farina – returned to racing in June, 1946, in the St Cloud Grand Prix run through the streets of a Paris suburb and incorporating a half-mile long tunnel – much longer than the tunnel at Monaco. The Alfas were driven by Farina and Jean-Pierre Wimille, but both retired with clutch trouble; a direct result of the cars' long hibernation during the war years. What was remarkable about this failure was that it was the only post-war defeat of the 158s until Gonzalez pushed Fangio back into second place at the 1951 British Grand Prix.

The Alfa's second outing was at the Grand Prix des

Nations, on a street circuit at Geneva the following month and here Farina's team-mates were Wimille and Achille Varzi, two of the greatest drivers of all time, and Count Felice Trossi. The race was run in two heats and a final, and at the end of the first lap Nino came round in second place behind Nuvolari's Maserati, gesticulating wildly and it was apparent to everyone that Tazio had been baulking him every inch of the way. Farina pushed his way past on the next lap and won the heat from team-mate Trossi. In the final, Nuvolari succeeded in ramming Wimille's leading Alfa which spun off and rejoined the race in third place and Farina was the winner, again leading Trossi home.

Farina retired with transmission trouble on the very first lap of the Turin Grand Prix and the race was won by another Alfa driven by Varzi. At this time there was a great deal of dissension in the Alfa team because the company insisted on picking the winner, and quite often signalled the leading Alfa driver to ease off and let another Alfa driver overtake him. The usual practice when teams were running three or four cars for fairly evenly matched drivers would be to let them sort out their placings for themselves in the opening laps and then signal them to hold position, a much fairer arrangement. At Turin, Wimille was forced to ease off to let Varzi win and as a result of the altercation after the race he was dropped from the team at the Milan Grand Prix. In this race Farina finished first on the road in his heat, but was penalised a minute for jumping the start and classified third. It seems that Trossi was supposed to win the final and after a few laps Achille Varzi let him through to the front. A furious duel between Varzi and Farina developed in which Varzi appeared more concerned in stopping Farina from going after Trossi than holding on to second place. Farina's brakes began to play up and when he spun at one of the corners, instead of carrying on in a safe third place he retired in a 'huff' because he was not being allowed to win. 'During the evening after the race, in the cafe in the Galleria della Duomo,' wrote John Eason Gibson, 'Farina put on a terrific act: aloof and sulky.'

The net outcome of these nursery antics was that Farina was told by Alfa Romeo that they no longer required his services, thank you very much, and when Farina failed to appear on the circuits in 1947 everyone concluded that he had retired. Nino bounced back again in the South American Formule Libre races early in 1948 and won the Mar del Plata Grand Prix with a 3-litre Maserati. In European races he drove Maserati 4 CLT/48 cars for two seasons and soon revealed that he had lost none of his old sparkle. In 1948 he won the Grand Prix des Nations at Geneva and the Monaco Grand Prix, but despite driving really hard in 1949 his only success was second place in the International Trophy race at Silverstone. He appeared at the 1949 Italian Grand Prix at Monza at the wheel of a

new version of the Maserati known as the 'Milano', one of two cars built by the Scuderia of that name to win the special starting money prize of six million lire (£3000) offered to any entrant of two new cars. The Milano, with an engine much more powerful than that fitted to standard Maseratis, proved really fast, but it still lacked the speed to catch the latest Ferraris which were also making their debut in this race. Yet again Farina's difficult and disagreeable temperament let him down. He was in third place when he retired in a 'huff', merely because he could not catch the two leading Ferraris – one of these retired and if only he had had the sense to keep going, he would have finished second.

After a year's absence Alfa Romeo returned to racing for 1950 and there is no doubt that they were desperately short of drivers. Of their old team, both Varzi and Wimille had been killed in motor racing accidents and Count Trossi had died of cancer. At the time Alfa Romeo must have felt that they were scratching about rather when they signed up promising Argentinian Juan Fangio, who had but one season of European racing behind him; veteran Luigi Fagioli who was another driver thought to have retired; and, as team-leader, Nino Farina who was given another chance.

As events turned out, this trio proved to be one of the most successful that had ever raced together, and more than a match for the Ferrari opposition driven by Ascari and Villoresi. Just as in 1947 and 1948, the Alfa team won every Grand Prix entered and Farina took the Drivers' Championship, newly inaugurated for that year, with victories in the British, Swiss and Italian races. Nino also scored victories in non-Championship races at Bari and Silverstone. At Monaco he spun on water that had broken over the sea-wall, hit the wall and rebounded broadside across the road where his Alfa was rammed by Gonzalez's Maserati. This triggered off the multi-car accident that eliminated half the entry. He fell back with gearbox trouble to finish fourth at Spa and after fuel pump trouble was classified seventh in the French race. At the Grand Prix des Nations he crashed his car into the straw bales to avoid Villoresi who had lost control, hit a kerb and was thrown out.

In 1950 Farina was at the peak of a career which now went into a gradual decline. The following year he won his heat of the International Trophy race at Silverstone, but the final was abandoned because torrential rain flooded the track. At the Swiss Grand Prix, another race run in heavy rain, he drove a car which bulged with supplementary tanks to get him through the race without refuelling. All the extra tankage affected its handling and he fell back to finish third behind team-mate Fangio and Taruffi with one of the new 4.5-litre Ferraris. A minor victory in the Ulster Trophy race in

Classic Farina: leaning well back in the cockpit and with plenty of room for the arms to work the wheel. The race is the 1950 British Grand Prix which Farina won with his Alfa Romeo 158. (*T. C. March*)

Northern Ireland followed, and setting the pace right from the start, he won the Belgian Grand Prix at Spa.

His Alfa was delayed by tyre trouble in the French Grand Prix and with his car crippled in the closing stages of the race by a faulty magneto, he finished fifth, banging his fists in frustration on the sides of the car as he tried to snatch fourth place on the last lap from Parnell's 'Thin Wall' Ferrari which had been slowed by transmission problems. His car expired with an under-bonnet fire in the British race, the gearbox failed at the Nürburgring and at Monza his Alfa retired after only five laps. Farina took over team-mate Bonetto's car and started a frantic chase after the leading Ferraris. When he stopped to refuel, the Alfa was stationary for two minutes, an inordinately long time, all the ground he had gained was lost, but once more he began to fling his Alfa round Monza in vain pursuit of Gonzalez's Ferrari. His car had developed a fuel leak, he stopped again for the tanks to be topped up and as he accelerated away from the pits, fuel could be seen spewing from the tail of the Alfa. Despite the fire risk, the Alfa was not black-flagged, and after one of the most gallant and hard-fought races of his career Farina took third place. In the last round of the Championship at Barcelona he again finished third.

When Alfa Romeo withdrew from racing at the end of the 1951 season, Giuseppe Farina signed up with the Ferrari team. For the next two seasons he fought a personal battle to beat Ascari, a battle that he was bound to lose, for Ascari was by far the better driver; more controlled, faster

The World Champion with his 158 Alfa Romeo at Monza for the 1950 Italian Grand Prix.

82

and more precise. At 45 Farina found that his ability was waning, he could not match Ascari's lap times, and time and time again he threw away good placings by overdriving his car. At Marseilles in 1952 he took the lead when Ascari stopped for new tyres and carried on at undiminished pace until he shot into the straw bales and wrecked his front suspension; at Montlhéry in the Paris Grand Prix he was overtaken by team-mate Taruffi and while trying to regain the lead, he ended up in a ditch and was disqualified for receiving help in getting the car back on the track; at les Sables d'Olonne he was eliminated in a multi-car crash that was no more his fault than anybody else's; and he crashed again at La Baule in August. His best performances during the year were wins in the Naples and Autodrome Grands Prix, and in Championship races he finished second at Spa, Rouen, the Nürburgring and Zandvoort.

1953 was to be Farina's last full racing season. At the beginning of the year he was involved in a horrible accident in the Argentine Grand Prix when his Ferrari mowed down a crowd of spectators who nad strayed over the safety barriers to watch the race from the edge of the track. Ten onlookers lost their lives. After such a terrible accident, however little he was to blame personally (the real fault was lack of crowd control) many a driver would have felt unable to carry on driving. But only a fortnight later Farina reappeared at the same circuit with a Ferrari and won the Buenos Aires City Grand Prix. Shortly afterwards another accident, albeit of a minor nature, cost Farina a race; he was leading at Pau when he 'over-cooked' a corner, spun off, stalled and buckled a wheel. Once the European Championship season, as such, was under way Farina seemed to take a grip on himself and his driving became more restrained. He finished second to Ascari at Zandvoort, retired with engine failure at Spa, crossed the line in fifth place at Reims (which meant that in this close-fought race he was only a couple of seconds behind the winner) and took a sound third place at Silverstone.

At the Nürburgring, generally recognised as being the most difficult of European circuits, Farina drove with rare brilliance, displaying much of his skill of earlier days. After Ascari's leading Ferrari had lost a wheel, the Dottore sped past Fangio's Maserati and team-mate Hawthorn to score his first World Championship race victory since the 1951 Belgian Grand Prix and the last in his career. He followed this up with another good drive in the Swiss race in which he finished second, and he was second again in the Italian race after Ascari had spun at the last corner of the last lap. In sports car racing in 1953 he co-drove with Ascari the winning Ferrari in the Nürburgring 1000 kilometres race.

For 1954 Farina remained with the Ferrari team, finishing second in the Argentine Grand Prix, co-driving the winning car with Maglioli in the Buenos Aires 1000 kilometres sports car race and winning at Siracusa in the first European Formula 1 race of the season. In the Mille Miglia he drove one of the new and monstrous 4.9-litre Ferrari sports cars, but crashed into a tree not long after the start while trying to avoid a spectator who had run on to the road. Farina's injuries included a broken arm and although he reappeared two months later at the Belgian Grand Prix he was not really fit. He had another bad crash during testing at Monza and did not race again until 1955. After running without conspicuous success during the first few months of 1955, Farina was still badly troubled by leg burns and once again withdrew from racing. He was entered with one of the Lancia V8s which Ferrari had just acquired at that year's Italian Grand Prix, but non-started after tyre trouble in practice.

Farina was now approaching his 49th birthday, older even than Fangio when he retired, but, admittedly, not as old as that motor racing wonder Tazio Nuvolari who drove in his last Grand Prix at the age of 56. He decided that the time had come to hang up his crash helmet for good and he never raced again. He had hoped to round off his career by running at Indianapolis, a life-long ambition, but failed to qualify in 1956 or 1957 when he appeared with cars entered by American Ferrari concessionaire Luigi Chinetti.

Giuseppe Farina was not a great driver by the standards set by Nuvolari, Fangio, Moss and Clark, but he was a very fast driver of great courage and determination. He was too audacious and too temperamental perhaps for his own good, sometimes too obstinate when the odds were weighted heavily against him, sometimes throwing in the towel before the race was lost. Farina died on 30 June, 1966 when he lost control of his Lotus-Cortina on a slippery road near Chambery in France while driving to the French Grand Prix. His car went off the road and demolished two telegraph poles and Nino was killed outright.

1951 Onwards

For 1951 Alfa Romeo retained Farina and Fangio, and their efforts were supported by 'guest drivers'. An improved version, the Tipo 159, appeared and although power had now increased to 405 bhp at 10,500 rpm, the drivers were restricted to 8500 rpm (9500 rpm and 385 bhp if the situation was really desperate), fuel consumption had risen to 1½ mpg, much of the fuel consumed was used for internal cooling of the engine and in some races the cars needed two refuelling stops. The cars could run with increased fuel tankage of 75 gallons, but this affected handling and made refuelling stops even more protracted. The introduction of a de Dion rear axle at the Belgian Grand Prix did little to improve the roadholding.

The Alfa Romeos suffered a 'technical knock-out' in the International Trophy at Silverstone, the final of which was abandoned because of a torrential rain and hail storm. The 159s were slowed because their superchargers were sucking in water and when the race was stopped Reg Parnell was leading the field with Tony Vandervell's Ferrari 'Thin Wall Special'. Although Parnell was awarded the prize money, there was strictly speaking no winner and the Alfa Romeos remained unbeaten. Defeat was not, however, far away. Fangio won the Swiss race, Farina won in Belgium and Fangio took over Fagioli's car to win in the French race. In the British Grand Prix the Alfa Romeos were trounced by Froilan Gonzalez with a 1950 Ferrari (that is with a single sparking plug per cylinder instead of the two of the 1951 cars) and Ascari won for Ferrari both the German and the Italian races. Tyre problems plagued the Ferraris in the Spanish race, Fangio won the race and clinched his first World Championship. This is Fangio's own account of his Championship year from *My Twenty Years of Racing* (Temple Press Limited, 1961)

My First World Championship

by Juan Manuel Fangio

After the Italian Grand Prix I went back to Argentina, terribly disappointed at my ill luck. But the warmth of my compatriots' welcome made up for it.

When I arrived at Balcarce my family received me with all their usual affection. I promised my brothers and sisters that, one day or another, I would win that World Championship.

Before the end of 1950, I tackled three South American races and won them all: the Grand Prix of the City of Parana, Grand Prix of Santiago, Chile (in which I drove a Ferrari) and, finally, the Argentine 500 Miles at Rafaela where, for the first time, I raced a Talbot.

A good start but not remarkable, especially when I was the favourite on paper. In fact, 1951 began with a disappointment: the Grand Prix of Buenos Aires, on the Costanera Norte, when for the first time, I had a Mercedes-Benz*. Another was driven by Hermann Lang.

Froilan Gonzalez took the lead and held it to the end, to the wild enthusiasm of the crowd. Lang came in second, I was third, happy that Froilan, at his best that day, had scored such a success.

Six days later came the second Grand Prix of Buenos

*Mercedes-Benz had sent two of their 1939 3-litre W163 Grand Prix cars to South America, part of the learning curve before re-entering sports car racing in 1952.

Froilan Gonzalez battles with the single-plug 4.5-litre Ferrari on his way to a resounding, but unexpected win in the 1951 British Grand Prix. (*T. C. March*)

Aires. But the Mercedes were not up to their European reputation. I retired, while Gonzalez's Ferrari carried him to victory again with a big lead over Kling and Lang, the other two Mercedes drivers.

I began to think I should never win at the wheel of a European racer on Argentine soil.

First... second... third... retired. Several races went like that, Giambertone [Fangio's racing manager], a sort of electronic brain, counted them up and can tell you I raced about 200 times in all. I won those I deserved to win, was placed 61 times, and retired in 47 other races.

At this point in our memoirs, Giamba and I looked at each other, worried to see the pile of notes and documents still waiting to be thumbed through. We asked ourselves whether readers, no matter how enthusiastic for motor racing, would not be bored by this endless series of descriptions. The vocabulary is always the same and the story mostly a succession of races on closed circuits, between rivals duelling in similar circumstances.

For the man behind the wheel races are never dull. Even in a car that is technically superior, there is always the unforeseen which can put the favourite out of the running. But it is a different matter to describe them without always respecting the order in which they happened.

I went back to Europe once again. In my first race in 1951, I was beaten... by rain. The International Trophy Race at Silverstone had no interest, really, as a very violent thunderstorm obliged the organisers to call a halt after the sixth lap. My Alfa was third at that moment, and kept that position, behind Reg Parnell and Duncan Hamilton. Our only consolation was winning the first heat, the second one going to Farina.

I was no luckier in the Grand Prix of Monza, in which I gave up after eight laps, due to repeated engine trouble with my Ferrari. Ascari won with ease in his 4.5-litre Ferrari at 115.53 mph.

My spirits began to droop when I had to retire once more in the Grand Prix of Paris, in the Bois de Boulogne on 20 May, due to the capricious behaviour of my Simca. Let me say here that I owe a big debt of gratitude to Amédée Gordini, who, although he did not know me, let me drive his cars.

The first 1951 race with Championship points was the Grand Prix of Switzerland, on the Bremgarten circuit at Berne. Four Alfas were lined up for the start, driven by Farina, Sanesi, de Graffenried and myself, and there were three new Ferraris, driven by the famous trio of super-Champions: Ascari, Villoresi and Taruffi.

A cold persistent rain was falling. The tarmac was dangerously shiny. I thought, 'If I don't get out in front immediately, I shall be blinded by spray splashed up by the other cars.'

One of the greatest of all drivers, Juan Fangio, seen here at the 1950 British Grand Prix with the Alfa Romeo chief mechanic. (*Guy Griffiths*)

So I concentrated on the start and managed to take the lead. The worst was over. Except for that brief, necessary moment of refuelling, I kept my place. Behind me the other drivers struggled in a disagreeable mist of water. Villoresi was so blinded by it that he went off the road at the end of the 13th lap, fortunately without bodily harm. I won, followed by Taruffi and Farina, and made the fastest lap. The nine championship points gained seemed a good omen.

Just the same, experience had already taught me never to rejoice too much about a first success. In fact, in the Grand Prix of Belgium, on the Spa-Francorchamps track on 17 June, Nino Farina won brilliantly, beating Ascari and Villoresi. As for me, I was put out of the running by the most stupid of incidents. We could not remove one of my rear wheels and had to change the tyre itself on the rim. I lost the race, finishing a sad ninth. I consoled myself with one Championship point for the fastest lap. Farina had 12 points and I was close behind with ten. When I saw Giamba he said, 'Don't worry. This year you'll win that title!'

I hugged him as an answer. The World Championship had become a sort of race by stages, taking place throughout the season on different circuits. That business of changing a tyre, which had cost me 14 minutes, could cost me the title.

Bad luck dogged me. Six days later, I joined Rosier to

drive a Talbot in the Le Mans 24 Hours. We took turns at the wheel, maintaining a good position for about eight hours. Then we were out of the race with lubricating trouble.

With all that bad luck hanging over me, I entered the French Grand Prix on 1 July without confidence. I was determined to make every effort to break my bad-luck cycle but it proved exceedingly difficult.

Twenty-three cars lined up; four Alfa Romeos, five Ferraris (three sent by the factory and two privately owned), seven Talbots, four Simcas and three Maseratis.

At the start I managed to take the lead, surprised to see that Farina had trouble getting away. Ascari began a great duel with me. We passed each other several times, Farina pursuing us strongly. The lap record could not last at that speed. I was first to beat it. Then Farina performed miracles several times. The race was sensational. It was had to breathe, the heat was so suffocating, and tyres literally burned on the corners, sending up puffs of acrid smoke which choked us.

Alberto's Ferrari pulled up at the pits. I learned later that his gearbox had been out of order. Scarcely had I grabbed the lead again when I had ignition trouble. Swearing quietly, I stopped at my pit. The mechanic opened the bonnet cried, 'Magneto,' in relief and sent me back on the track in about ten seconds.

Now Farina had take the lead, followed by Villoresi. I was third and getting ready to cut down the distance when ignition trouble brought me into the pits again. The mechanics decided to change the magneto, demagnetized by the heat. While I waited impatiently, Fagioli was stopped by a peremptory signal and I was invited to take his car. I gave Fagioli a friendly handshake for sacrificing his own chances for me and took off in his car, having lost only 58 seconds while the mechanics changed the four wheels and filled the tank.

Ascari re-entered the race at the same time in Gonzalez's Ferrari. Desperately, I put my foot down. On the 32nd lap, I lowered the record, averaging 118 mph. I passed Villoresi, then Ascari. Quick reckoning told me that I could not reach the finishing line without refuelling again. It was better to stop immediately. Villoresi seized the chance to pass me, but I didn't have much trouble overtaking and passing him when I restarted. Meanwhile, Fagioli was back on the track at the wheel of my repaired Alfa.

On the 44th lap Farina, still in the lead, had an unpleasant surprise. The tread of his left tyre came off and wound around the brake drum. After a stop at his pit to change his wheels (a stop during which I took the lead), Farina's tyres played him the same trick again. He must have been cornering too fast. Ascari was on my tail. Then he had brake trouble and was no longer a serious menace for the rest of the race. Sanesi, driving the fourth Alfa, was

immobilized by ignition trouble near the end (the same trouble that I had had) but managed to push his car to the line, finishing sixth.

With a great sigh of relief, I crossed the line first, followed by Ascari, Gonzalez, Villoresi, Parnell and Farina, in that order. I had recaptured the championship lead with 15 points. Farina had fourteen, Ascari nine.

It was immediately after the French Grand Prix that the Ferrari engineers finally had their 4½-litre unsupercharged engine ready to beat the supercharged 1½-litre Alfas. We had the proof in the British Grand Prix at Silverstone on 13 July.

In the front row stood two Ferraris, those of Ascari and Gonzalez, and two Alfas, driven by Farina and myself. In the second, the Ferrari of Villoresi was next to the Alfas of Sanesi and Bonetto. Farina was the only Alfa driver to have a de Dion rear end and extra tanks.

From the start it was a fight between Gonzalez and myself, and it was fun to duel with my old friend like that. I stayed in the lead until the 30th lap, then Gonzalez passed me. I stopped to refuel, losing precious time, as the Alfa carried 65 gallons of fuel, much more than the Ferrari. On the 60th lap, Gonzalez was filled up in 23 seconds flat, and thus kept his lead. That day he won triumphantly, while I finished second. Farina had to retire after 85 laps with his clutch on fire, losing a well-earned third.

The Grand Prix of Germany, held on 29 July on the classic Nürburgring circuit, fully confirmed the technical significance of the Silverstone race and the superiority of the 'unblown' Ferrari engine.

The Ferraris in practice made better time than our Alfas. Trying to beat the lap record just set by Ascari, I almost had a serious accident, going off the road on the hill leading down to Adenau. I still remember that instant of terror. I knew there was an extremely steep drop, just beyond the corner where my car began to skid, and came on to it as though leaping from a spring-board. By chance, a tree trunk stopped the machine as I managed to swing across the road. No damage to the car and not even a scratch on me. All alone, I put the car back on the road. Thirty feet from me, a spectator standing behind the tree trunk drank half a bottle of brandy to recover from his fright.

When the actual race started, I got out in front for three laps, pitilessly tailed by Ascari. Then he passed me. Close behind me were Gonzalez and Farina until Nino had to retire with mechanical trouble.

By mid-race, I was back in the lead, shortly after the German driver Pietsch went off the road, spectacularly, without hurting himself in the least. Then I had to stop for refuelling and Ascari took the lead, gaining a big advantage. I threw myself into the pursuit, making the fastest lap, but I was not able to do better than finish

Obsolescent, over-complex, over-stressed, but still unbeaten, until the 1951 British Grand Prix: the Alfa Romeo 'Alfetta'. Fangio strives with his 159 to catch Gonzalez' Ferrari at Silverstone. (*T. C. March*)

second, again behind Alberto. But, at least, I had increased my championship points.

If only for prestige, the fifth Grand Prix of Bari gave Alfa Romeo a chance to make up for having been beaten in the last two races. Ascari and Villoresi were eliminated immediately. A backfire set fire to Ascari's car but he wasn't hurt. An ordinary breakdown stopped Villoresi. So, again, I found myself duelling with Gonzalez. For a time he lost ground, then made it up, staying 14 seconds behind me. During that time my gears were not in the best of shape, Nevertheless I managed to win, after a refuelling stop of only 12 seconds.

Gonzalez, his ruddy face brightened by a quick smile as the race finished, was second, 1 minute 10 seconds behind me. I cite that figure because, at that time, part of the Italian Press, without any justification, contended that Gonzalez was 'timid' in his driving during the last part of the race.

They went so far as to reproach him for being unwell during the race yet refusing to be replaced. No one who knew Froilan could have believed that for a moment. And some observers, evidently short of arguments, even dragged out that old business about Italian cars being driven by Italian drivers, rather than by Gonzalez and myself. Nationalism in motor racing is an easy way to become chauvinistic. All that unpleasant business was made up for by some 100,000 cheering spectators massed along the Bari circuit and by favourable comments in the more serious Italian and foreign Press.

There were still on the international calendar two races towards the World Championship. I was at the head of the list. Perhaps because of that, there was some animosity due to national jealousies. I admit that, for weeks, I had been anxious to see the whole business come to an end. When I had begun racing, several years before that, if someone had even suggested the possibility that I might become world champion (a title that did not exist at the time), I should have said, 'You're crazy.' Yet, in that hot month of September 1951, I found myself favourite for the title while the traditional strength of Alfa Romeo seemed to decline.

The Grand Prix of Italy, held on 16 September at Monza, was for Alfa Romeo what Waterloo had been for Napoleon. Ferrari put his four official cars among the first five.

At the start, I was in the first row, alongside Farina and Ascari. My first duel was a very lively one with Alberto, but it ended on the 13th lap. The tread of my tyres came off abruptly and I had to limp to my pit. A few laps later, I managed to pass some of the other cars but exactly half-way through the race mechanical trouble that could not be repaired cut short my efforts. The race was triumphantly carried off by Ascari, followed by Gonzalez. After my retirement, my only consolation was that I was still in the lead on Championship points with 27, followed by Ascari with 25, Gonzalez with 20, and Farina, 17.

It was clear that the Grand Prix of Spain, on 28 October would decide whether Ascari or I would capture the world title. Neither Gonzalez nor Farina had enough points to hope to catch up.

I deeply admired the graceful, pleasant style of Alberto's driving. He was a real champion and merited the title for his class, worthy in every way of his father's. I felt it was a great honour to have him as a rival. Added to that was the technical superiority of the Ferraris in the last races. In such circumstances, I was not sure of having much chance.

I have read in a 100 newspaper or magazine articles that I was a self-controlled driver, impassive in the face of anything. That is probably the impression I give on the outside. I succeeded and still succeed in controlling myself, it is true. But that cold exterior is only the result of an effort to analyse my own feelings, even the most instinctive, trying to find solutions to my problems.

You may imagine my state of mind as we lined up for the start of the Spanish Grand Prix. As in the year before, I might lose that title at the very last minute. In practice the Ferraris had given dazzling performances and Ascari was as dangerous as ever.

Alberto took the lead right from the start, with Farina and I right behind, then came Bonetto, Gonzalez, de Graffenried and Taruffi. The Avenida General Franco, known more familiarly by the people of Barcelona as 'the diagonal,' was an extraordinary straight on which our cars could touch nearly 160 mph. Ascari, just ahead of me, was going like an arrow. I decided not to duel immediately but to hold on, up in front, without pushing my car too hard. My main worry was refuelling. The Ferrari had huge extra tanks, which meant a minimum number of stops, while our Alfas would have to refill more often.

Gonzalez spun right round, luckily without hurting himself. I sighed with relief. Right after that, a tiny piece of rubber flew off one of Ascari's tyres and hit me in the face, not harming me in the least. I was surprised. How could the tyres of his Ferrari wear out so fast? I understood when I realized that the Ferrari mechanics had put 16-inch tyres on their cars – too small a size, evidently, for the weight of the extra tanks and the very high speeds we were achieving on 'the diagonal'.

In those conditions, I decided to take the offensive at the exact moment my rivals began having tyre trouble. The moment came soon. On the sixth lap, Taruffi's rear wheel came off but he managed to get it patched up and continue, losing a lot of time. On the seventh lap, I saw Villoresi arrive at his pit, haltingly, his tyres in shreds. Now is the time, I thought, and put my foot down to take on

Ascari, who reacted immediately.

What I had foreseen happened. On the ninth lap, Ascari's tyres were in such a state he had to stop at the pit to have them all changed. I did not let up until my pit signalled that I was more than a minute ahead of Ascari. Then I slowed up a little, allowing myself 10 seconds more than my fastest lap, to prevent excessive wear on my own 18-inch tyres. I was in front and tyre trouble might cost me the victory. I kept saying to myself, 'You're not sure of winning until you cross the finishing line.'

Behind me, Alberto was badly handicapped, having to change tyres every nine laps. All the other Alfas were doing well, except de Graffenried's, which had to pull up half a dozen times for radiator repairs. It looked as though the Ferraris, triumphant at Monza, were bound to lose this time because of those unlucky tyres. In fact, all of them were lacerated several times. In addition, Villoresi had to retire with severe transmission trouble and Taruffi with a broken half-shaft. The only Ferrari still in the running was Gonzalez, but he was too far behind to be an immediate threat.

In the final scoring for the world title, I had 31 points. Ascari, whose score stayed at 25 points, congratulated me like the sportsman he is, although his tyres had let him down. That is the way it goes in racing. Rarely does a driver make technical errors; his equipment often betrays him.

I have a habit of humming as well as chewing gum, during a race. This time I spat out my gum and began to pray, silently. My prayer was answered. The voices of 300,000 yelling fans accompanied me on the lap of honour. I was deeply thrilled at the sound of a crowd shouting in Spanish. It seemed as though I were in Buenos Aires.

'World Champion' was being shouted everywhere. The lap of honour seemed terribly long. Coming towards me from my pit I saw Alessio, the engineering director of Alfa Romeo. He was emotional and it looked as though the mechanics had suddenly gone crazy. Alessio embraced me and I, too, had a lump in my throat.

I was brought before General Franco's representative, who gave me the cup for the Grand Prix of Spain. I found myself face to face with Sojit, the giant-sized Argentine radio reporter who had glued millions of our compatriots to their loudspeakers with his exciting reporting.

I will spare you all the banquets, receptions and speeches. Gonzalez was as happy as I. He had finished second in the Grand Prix and third in the World Championship. In the Spanish race, Farinal had come third, Ascari fourth. All the others had been lapped.

A nervous reaction to the occasion made me feel suddenly very tired. I realized I should not race again in 1951.

I went back to Argentina where enthusiastic crowds

welcomed me at Buenos Aires. Balcarce [Fangio's home town], by contrast, was no less than a volcano. I threw myself into it with relief. The next morning, I realized I was already thinking about the 1952 season.

At the end of 1951 Alfa Romeo withdrew from racing. The company was state-controlled and there were simply no funds available to develop and race a new car. The British BRM, described below, had failed to achieve a raceworthy status and there was every indication that racing would be completely Ferrari-dominated. Reluctantly the decision was made to run the World Championship in 1952 and 1953 to Formula 2 rules.

The existing Formula 1 officially lasted until the end of 1953, but very few races were held to this formula and none of these was of any real importance. The main contenders were improved Ferraris occasionally entered by the works, but more usually by private owners, Tony Vandervell's much modified and immensely potent 'Thin Wall Special' and the BRM.

The BRM, Britain's great racing hope had been hyped by its sponsors and in particular by that inveterate optimist Raymonds Mays – and ridiculed by the popular press. It was an expensive, protracted, but nevertheless very exciting, failure. This account of the BRM by David Hodges and Harry Mundy (first published by Profile Publications Limited in 1967) superbly encapsulates its stormy history.

The V16 BRM

During the thirties Raymond Mays and Peter Berthon were largely responsible for Britain's most successful single-seater racing car. In 1939 their association with ERA ended and they had the extraordinary idea that Britain should become a power in the then very exotic sphere of Grand Prix racing; before the end of the Second World War they formulated tentative plans; after the war, with varying assistance and backing, they doggedly produced a Grand Prix car. To all intents and purposes, the story of that first BRM stretched over a decade; while it may not be literally true, it seems that during half of that period more print was devoted to it than to any other racing car, ever. Recollections of its vicissitudes still tend to blur objectivity...

Mays and Berthon had a company, Automobile Developments Ltd, on which to found their enterprise and as the war in Europe ended Mays approached British industry, principally the motor industry, for support in cash and kind. Initial contributions and support from Oliver Lucas and Alfred Owen – to whom BRM was eventually to owe its very existence – gave impetus to the appeal, and during 1946 over 100 companies gave their backing to the project. The SMM and T firmly withheld its 'official' support, but as orders for components were placed, Sir Stafford Cripps authorised a statement to the effect that the Government was convinced of the importance of motor racing and by the granting of permits and the exercise of influence was prepared to facilitate the production of a team of BRMs. Although at the same time it was stressed that the entire responsibility rested with private enterprise, contrary impressions were not dispelled; these gained a firm hold on the Continent and lingered on embarassingly for years – some were convinced that the BRM was Government-sponsored, others even thought of it as a Rolls-Royce GP car (that company collaborated in the design and manufacture of a centrifugal supercharger for the engine).

In the summer of 1947 the British Motor Racing Research Trust was set up to act in an advisory capacity and also to take some of the load from May's shoulders. Then, as almost always, the project was going through a difficult period; during the ensuing months of delay, the advantages of a committee with some authority, which inevitably spawned sub-committees, proved dubious. But, slowly, work went ahead, and one of the most complex Grand Prix cars ever contemplated began to take physical shape in the hands of a group with relatively scant Grand Prix experience, albeit with as much as any in Britain – but then there had not been a whole-hearted British venture into racing's premier class for over 20 years.

From this distance in time the resources considered adequate seem almost ludicrously inadequate. The first financial target had been £25,000 plus contributions in kind; annual expenditure had been expected to run at around the same figure, although by mid-1947 this estimate had been doubled. When design work started at Bourne in 1946, the only facility was an unheated drawing office contrived in a derelict malting barn – even the relatively meagre facilities of the one-time ERA workshops were not available. Throughout, the design of the engine, chassis, transmission, in fact every detail, was in the hands of four senior designers and three junior draughtsmen; there was no development department as such (apart from a single engine test dynamometer); machine shop personnel and fitter-mechanics totalled no more than 30. When judging the venture in perspective, the 200 engineers and 300 machine shop and assembly personnel employed by the

Daimler-Benz racing department to prepare for their return to GP racing in 1954 should be borne in mind . . .

In theory at least the decision to adopt a design incorporating many novelties – not least a complicated supercharged V16 engine – was absolutely right. In practice, however, the post-war design which was eventually to succeed was to be an uncomplicated, unsupercharged V12, and one cannot but speculate on the course of the BRM story if Berthon had followed less perfectionist design lines (alternatives were not seriously considered at this stage, nor during the life of the car, when attention to the V16 was to demand more time than was available!). The project had become public knowledge early in 1946 but little information was released, so the form which the car might take became the subject of intensive guessing games (nevertheless, *The Motor* was inspired to remark, *sotto voce:* 'A possible danger, which must be guarded against, is over-elaboration'). Some basic facts were released towards the end of 1947.

The parts came together frustratingly slowly, so that the first car was not completed until December 1949. In the same month it was demonstrated to the Press, and by its 'popular' representatives hailed as an immediate world-beater. Better qualified journalists were more realistic – '[Few projects] can have been faced with so many hazards as those anticipated for BRM in the months to come' (*The Motor*). '. . . much remains to be done before a team of three cars can appear on the starting line in international contests' (*The Autocar*). Both journals reiterated the importance of BRM to national prestige; *The Motor* coldly assessed the probable cost of a season's racing at £73,000 – nearly three times Mays' original estimate, although, even allowing for depreciating values, not near enough to the six-figure truth of the fifties.

The first BRM unveiled on the bleak airfield at

The immensely complex V16 engine of the BRM. (*T. C. March*)

Raymond Mays, the 'father' of the BRM V16, demonstrates the new British challenger at the 1950 British Grand Prix. (*T. C. March*)

Folkingham (where BRM had a test circuit) proved to be an impressively low, smooth and compact car. It was designated 'Type 15', this merely signifying 1.5 litres not that it was the 15th design of a series.

The V16 Engine

The 16-cylinder engine, with its banks at an included angle of 135 degrees, was reasonably orthodox in layout and was, of course, in perfect balance. The cylinder blocks, in groups of four, were arranged to permit an approximately half speed drive from the centre of the crank to the clutch. Also from the centre, a system of increasing gears took the drive forward to a two-stage centrifugal supercharger (produced with considerable assistance from Rolls-Royce). Originally the supercharger was designed to run at 3.25 engine speed, but because of engine breathing restrictions this was later increased to 4.0 times engine speed.

The magnitude of these restrictions can be judged from the fact that while the original estimated power output of the engine (with 3.25 blower ratio) was 600 bhp at 12,000 rpm, the maximum achieved in practice was 485 bhp at 10,000 rpm with the higher ratio of 4.0:1 (Rig work at Rolls-Royce proved estimates of blower performance.)

The engine was originally designed for a fuel injection system, but this was fitted for only a brief initial period and was not subsequently used. Throughout its life, therefore, the engine operated on two 2.5-in diameter SU carburettors, which were considerably smaller than the original single throttle proposed for fuel injection.

However, the greatest restriction in breathing was undoubtedly the valve gear which, contrary to popular belief, and after an initial design error in geometry was rectified, proved extremely reliable. To obtain this, by keeping maximum valve acceleration to 52,000 ft/sec, the lift was only 0.25 in, and this throttling effect undoubtedly explains why the gains of power achieved when the supercharging speed was increased were small. Had the engine breathing matched supercharger performance, drivers' critisms of poor torque in the middle range would have been overcome. Moreover, the even greater criticism of a continously rising torque curve with its peak at the point of maximum power – which meant that when accelerating through a fast corner the limit of tyre adhesion could be reached with the car under the influence of considerable cornering forces, with loss of sideways adhesion – would have been alleviated by the use of supercharger vortex throttling, if the original Rolls-Royce power estimates had been achieved. These vortex throttles – which were designed and made, but never fitted – regulated the boost pressure above a pre-determined speed so that an optimum degree of supercharge pressure could have been achieved, without excessive boost above 10,000 rpm; this was never realised, because of the poor engine breathing.

One other major defect in the engine was responsible for unreliability and major failures. The cylinder liners, although very short because of the 1.90-in stroke, were located in compression by their top and bottom flanges. It proved impossible to machine eight of these per bank absolutely square and to maintain an equal 'nip' at the cylinder head gasket over a wide range of thermal gradients. As a result, water leaked into the cylinders, hydraulic locks were formed and the liners disintegrated with disastrous results (not as the result of sparks induced between the ignition leads, as was stated at the time).

The transmission – the 5-speed gearbox was mounted transversely at the rear – and the de Dion rear suspension (except for the Lockheed air struts) were based on the 1938-39 Mercedes GP cars and proved successful and reliable. At the front the Porsche type of trailing link suspension – retained in principle from the C and E Type ERAs – was given more rigidity and movement by lengthening the arms and increasing their spacing. However, they still suffered from considerable deflection and contributed substantially to the poor handling of the car.

The complete vehicle was too heavy – the dry engine, including supercharger (54 lb), weighed 525 lb, compared with around 285 lb for the unsupercharged 1.5-litre Coventry Climax V8 of 1961-65; the dry chassis weight of the Mk 1 BRM was 1624 lb, compared with 1010-1050 lb for the 1.5-litre F1 BRM of 1962. Nevertheless, it was only marginally heavier than the Type 158C Alfa Romeo, the contemporary car to beat.

Racing Debut

The racing world was impatient for the car's first race appearance. It was hoped that this would be in the British GP in May 1950, but here a car was simply demonstrated and exhibited. It should have been in the Silverstone International Trophy in August, but only a single car of the pair entered was ready, and then not in time for practice; it did not leave the line at the start of its Heat when a drive shaft failed as Sommer let in the clutch (for which that great driver was unjustifiably vilified). So the real debut came at Goodwood on 30 September, in two short spring events which were nominally 'international'. Reg Parnell drove the BRM to win both without difficulty (although his achievement in keeping his difficult car pointing in the right direction should not be belittled), and its sponsors were thus encouraged to venture onto the Continent and to enter two cars for the GP of Penya Rhin at Barcelona.

Here the flaws in the BRM make-up became apparent, for while it was demonstrably faster than its principal rivals, works Ferraris, over 1 km of the long

Pedralbes straight (highest speeds, 186 mph and 178 mph respectively), it was slower through and out of corners, to the extent that its flat-out advantage was more than offset (best BRM practice lap, 94.9 mph, best Ferrari lap 98.2 mph). In the race both BRMs started badly, Parnell was fourth at the end of the first lap but retired on the next with supercharger drive failure; Walker worked the second car up to fourth by half-distance, but he too retired.

So far, then, the BRM had little to show but promise – and even allowing for the material problems and shortages of the late forties as well as for the advanced nature of the car, one might have hoped that in the four years since work had commenced something more might have been achieved. Undoubtedly, the organization was beset by difficulties – technical, financial, organizational, personal – but some of these appeared to be of their own making, certainly some should have been avoided. Be that as it may, none contributed towards making the car raceworthy, while a predeliction for testing it privately on an English airfield rather than expose it to true circuits and to races may well have served to retard its development . . .

In 1951 the cars were entered first for the Swiss and French GPs, but were withdrawn. The home match of the year, the British GP, could hardly be ignored – yet even

First – and only – Grand Épreuve. Reg Parnell in the 1951 British Grand Prix at Silverstone. He finished fifth, almost roasted in the cockpit. (*T. C. March*)

then, eight and a half months after they had last been raced, a late failure and late preparation meant that the BRMs did not reach the circuit until the morning of race day. They were allowed to start; that they finished fifth and seventh, five and six laps behind the winner, was due to the courage of their drivers, Parnell and Walker, in bearing infernal cockpit conditions. These were to be the only places ever gained by V16 BRMs in the Grandes Épreuves.

For very valid reasons the cars entered for the Italian GP were withdrawn three hours before the race. But outwardly this incident smacked of fiasco, and this the BRM organization, living on an overdraft of acrimony and dissension, could ill afford, for it was also running short of another, most valuable intangible – goodwill. This much was clearly indicated by the falling membership of the BRM Association (later to become ORMA).

Tests at Monza after the Italian GP showed that the poor handling characteristics (ie shortcomings attributable to the Porsche trailing link system) evident at Barcelona a year earlier were still present – indeed, on this fast circuit to which it was theoretically well suited, the BRM appeared to have lost ground to the Italian cars. During the winter the hitherto imprecise steering was modified and Girling disc brakes were fitted in place of Girling three-shoe drums; outwardly, the smooth body was altered as air intakes were improved (to the radiator) or introduced (to the cockpit).

During the next few months, developments in international racing could well have ended the life of the BRM Type 15 (and hence, one might speculate, of BRM?). These stemmed from Alfa Romeo's withdrawal from racing, which apparently left Formula 1 wide open to Ferrari's 4.5-litre cars. Many organisers chose to run their 1952 Grands Prix for unsupercharged 2-litre F2 cars. BRM assurances that they would contest Championship events and provide some worthwhile opposition for Ferrari were received with scepticism, and doubts were strengthened when their entry for the early-season Turin GP was withdrawn, although the équipe had but recently been at Monza for further tests.

Despite this sweeping change, which in effect removed all purpose from the V16 project, the BRM Trust decided to carry on and race the cars in such Formula 1 events as were run and in others open to them, formule libre races around the perimeter tracks of redundant British airfields. Driving strength suddenly became impressive, for two established GP stars agreed to drive the V16s, together with an English *comingman* and two stalwarts – Fangio and Gonzalez, Moss, Parnell and Wharton.

At last, too late, BRM achieved a fairly full racing season. But fortunes were mixed. At Albi and Dundrod the BRMs were clearly faster than any other cars, but failed to finish; at Silverstone Gonzalez set a new circuit record, but this was equalled by Taruffi in the 'Thin Wall Special' 4.5-litre Ferrari entered by C. A. Vandervell, an erstwhile member of the BRM Trust; at Boreham there was not even a fastest lap to compensate for retirements.

Then the BRM won its third race, its first for nearly two years, at Turnberry. At the end of September, the 1950 Goodwood success was repeated; here, for the first time, a three-car team was run and in the main event Gonzalez, Parnell and Wharton finished first, second and third, while Parnell set a new lap record. An ideal result, but in a minor 15-lap race on a secondary circuit and therefore without real significance. It was followed by an ignominious defeat, at Charterhall. By an ERA . . .

In the world of commerce, BRM Ltd would have been considered an ailing concern, ripe for the attentions of the Official Receiver (writing in the Financial Times in 1966, Sir Alfred Owen recalled that annual expenditure in the early fifties was around £130,000 and that the greater part of this sum was not recouped). Before the season was over the BRM Trust had decided to sell BRM Ltd; in the late Autumn the assets – and liabilities – were taken over by the only whole-hearted bidder, Alfred Owen on behalf of the Owen Organisation.

1953 Season

The decision to keep the V16s 'on the active list' in 1953 cannot have been lightly or easily taken. Yet, stubbornly, the promise of a shatteringly effective racing machine was still there. In particular, the power unit was giving a minimum of 450 bhp, with reasonable reliability. The problems involved in fully utilising this power remained, for it was available through only a very narrow rev range (peak power at around 11,800-12,000 rpm virtually nothing below 9000 rpm) and this meant that drivers had to make excessive use of the gearbox, while at the same time coping with handling which was still somewhat odd. One result of the decision was, in effect, a series of 'match races' between the V16 and the Thin Wall Ferrari.

Above all, though, there was one more Continental outing, to Albi at the end of May, to meet 'works' Formula 1 opposition on a true road circuit for the last time. Latter-day assertions that sheer power is a racing be-all and end-all are based on dubious premises, but there can be no doubt of its attractions for spectators in the days of 'hairy' front-engined cars – and if any post-war car qualified for that adjective it was the V16 BRM. The spectacle promised as Ascari ('works' Ferrari), Farina (Thin Wall), Fangio, Gonzalez and Wharton (BRMs) practised on the Circuit Raymond Sommer drew an immense crowd on race-day. In fact, the promise was good for only a few laps of the formule libre heat, then the principal Ferraris retired. Gonzalez's BRM threw a rear tread (as it had in practice)

and he finished fifth, but Fangio won at 110.84 mph (faster than the existing lap record) and Wharton was a good second. The Final opened with the BRMs running 1-2-3, but then a rash of tread-throwing cost them the one Continental race in which they started as clear favourites – the cars were exceeding 180 mph on the straight and consequently braking and acceleration stresses were accentuated, the day was hot, the exhausts played directly on to rear tyres. Gonzalez' car lost two tyres, yet he still raced aggressively and finished second, Fangio lost a tread when flat out and his damaged car was retired, Wharton lost a tread at about 130 mph and he was thrown, uninjured, from his car (No 3) before it wrote itself off.

The season had started with a victory at Goodwood and two defeats. After Albi the 'Owen v Vandervell series' continued, honours going to the BRM at Charterhall, to the Thin Wall at Silverstone and twice at Goodwood. Wharton also drove the V16 to victory over negligible opposition in two races at Snetterton and at Castle Combe.

As the season ended so, officially, did the Formula to which the V16 BRM had been designed. In ideal conditions it was probably the fastest car of the Formula, although in practice, ie in a race around any given circuit, this generalisation cannot reasonably be applied despite the fact that it gained several circuit records. Comparisons are hardly valid if the yardstick is inadequate; the Thin Wall was the only other F1 car developed into 1953 and it remained a match for the BRM, not least by virtue of its superior handling, and it too held circuit records.

Logically, the story of the V16 BRM should end at this point, especially as a new 2.5-litre BRM for the new Formula was being developed. But the supercharged cars were still raced, to keep the team's hand in and develop components (and certainly to enliven National events). Moreover, two Mk II cars appeared. These were lighter, with tubular space frames, shorter, and had smaller wheels (thus disappeared one BRM feature which had appeared dated) and slightly modified suspension. Only one, the fourth Type 15 BRM to be built, was new; the first BRM was converted to Mk II specification, thus becoming in effect No 1/5.

Before the Mk II appeared, Wharton took a Mk I to New Zealand on an expedition which was scarcely worthwhile. The new Mk II was first raced at Goodwood at Easter, when a Mk I car was raced for the last time. Wharton and Flockhart drove throughout the season; as ever the BRMs enjoyed mixed fortunes, but at least the continuing duel with the Thin Wall drew crowds, and generally they were given value for money.

The cars came out again five times in 1955, when Peter Collins gained their only victory. On 1 October the scream of 16 tiny BRM cylinders was heard in anger for the

Ken Wharton with the V16 in the Formule Libre race at Silverstone in July 1953. By this time the cars were painted dark, instead of light, green and the bodywork featured not only a much larger intake, but was heavily louvred. Wharton finished third behind Farina (Ferrari Thin Wall Special) and Fangio (with another V16 BRM).

The lighter, shorter-wheelbase Mark II BRM seen at the Easter Goodwood meeting in 1954. Ron Flockhart is at the wheel and he finished fourth after falling back because of magneto trouble.

last time, in a minor event at Castle Combe.

The first and last BRM, No 1 or No 5 or No 1/5 was the last to run, driven by Flockhart and Rivers Fletcher on test at Folkingham in 1957. Nearly ten years later this car was overhauled and was driven in a demonstration at the 1967 British GP meeting.

Summing Up

The first BRM failed in that it did not win a single Grande Épreuve – indeed, it was not even run on most of the classic circuits of Europe. At first glance, the record does not look too bad: 73 starts, 19 firsts, 14 seconds, 8 thirds and 8 other placings to set against 24 retirements. But these figures mislead, for the number of starts in Championship races under the Formula to which the car was built is negligible and far outweighed by its record of withdrawals from events of this calibre.

In retrospect, mistakes were made in the conception of the BRM – in particular, the project was far too ambitious in relation to the funds and facilities available. The direct return – in terms of race successes – on an expenditure of labour, money and resources which was nevertheless prodigious, cannot justify the BRM Type 15. So what is left? The splendid basic conception, and hence a fund of advanced engineering experience, the foundation of an establishment which has since proved of no small value to British industry, and, for ordinary race spectators, memories of occasional glimpses of flashing speed and an exhilarating sound. And around this car, the creation of Britain's first full-blooded GP team for decades, which through the faith and perseverence of a few, notably Sir Alfred Owen, was eventually to attain the goal set in the forties.

Failure it may have been, National disgrace it was not (although the daily press wanted the public to see it that way), but the BRM did much to encourage general interest in motor racing and stimulated serious enthusiasts, notably Tony Vandervell, in their desire to build a serious Grand Prix contender.

Part 5: THE SUBSTITUTE FORMULA, 1952-3

Background

Formula 2, originally known as Formula B, had been introduced as a subsidiary formula, the equivalent of the pre-war *Voiturettes*, for the 1948 season and was open to unsupercharged cars of up to 2000 cc and 500 cc supercharged cars. Very few attempts were made at building supercharged cars and none was successful.

Initially the two leading contenders in the formula were Ferrari with V12 cars and the British HWM team. HWM (Hersham & Walton Motors) was a garage business at Walton-on-Thames in Surrey run by John Heath and George Abecassis, both of whom were great racing enthusiasts. In 1949 Abecassis raced without success the first of the new Alta Formula 1 cars

and Heath was seen at the wheel of a neat 2-seater 'special' known as the HW-Alta and which he entered in both racing and sports car events with great promise. From 1950 a full team of these low-cost, home-built cars were entered in races all over Europe as the team chased from race to race, in their efforts to obtain starting money. And not all these events were Formula 2, for the team also competed in Formula 1 with success. This account of how HWM competed in the 1950 Bari Grand Prix gives a marvellous insight into the team's 'shoe-string' efforts and is from *Alf Francis, Racing Mechanic* written in collaboration with Peter Lewis (G.T. Foulis & Co 1958), a new edition of which is to be published by G.T. Foulis in late 1991.

The original HW-Alta seen on its début at the Goodwood meeting on Easter Monday 1949. It was simple, effective and remarkably successful and encouraged Heath and Abecassis to run a full team of HWMs in 1950. (*Guy Griffiths*)

A Thousand Pounds Is A Lot Of Money

During the Reims race Tony Hume (HWM Team Manager) took me aside in the pits. 'Look, Alf,' he said, 'you know the Bari race. Well, we have just been offered a fantastic sum – a thousand pounds for the whole team to start. Can you get the cars down there in time for practice next Friday?'

I knew there was this Bari fixture, but had no idea where the place was and I told Tony Hume I should have to study the map first.

'Well,' he said, 'everything depends on you. If you can make it, the money is ours. If not, then it's too bad. But you know as well as I do that we don't often get a chance like this to make a thousand pounds.'

I don't mind admitting that I brought myself up with a jerk when I saw from my map that Bari was some eleven hundred miles from Reims. We could just about make it by driving the whole way non-stop, providing there was nothing much to do to the cars once we arrived there, so I gave Tony Hume my answer.

'Everything depends on how the cars behave here. If they finish in good order, then we will get them to the start line in Bari. But I cannot guarantee they will be properly prepared.'

This did not worry Hume.

'It does not matter,' he said. 'A thousand pounds is a lot of money.'

This was my biggest problem to date, and whilst the Reims race ran its course I worked out a rough plan in the pits. To start with there was the old problem of ready cash. We did not have enough to be able to leave immediately after the race on Sunday night, and in any case I had a fairly formidable bill to settle at the hotel, and another one in the local cafe where we had taken our meals.

I knew that I could not possibly move off until all the bills had been met, and I also knew that I should not be able to obtain sufficient French francs until the Automobile Club paid us our starting money on Monday afternoon. However, it seemed crazy to have to waste so much precious time, waiting for the cash, before we could leave Reims. So I decided to fill up the big lorry on credit at the local garage, and to send it off with two cars first thing on Monday morning, with Rex and Frank. I would leave my own lorry and one car as security in the garage whilst I collected the cash.

I took Rex and Frank aside immediately after the race and told them the plan.

'I want the cars loaded in the lorries. We are not going back to the garage, except to fill your lorry with petrol, and sharp at 7 am tomorrow morning I want you to leave Reims. All you have to do tomorrow is reach the Hotel Cosmopolitan in Aix-les-Bains. As soon as you arrive go straight to bed and get some sleep. I shall wait here until Monday evening, pay all the bills, collect some money from John Heath and then drive all Monday night to catch you up. I hope to be with you on Tuesday morning, and Frank Nagel can then take over my van whilst I have a sleep, and we crack on to Italy.'

After the race, there were the usual parties in Reims – particularly at the Hotel Welcome – and at about two o'clock in the morning, when I had finished working on the accounts, I decided that it was time I had a drink myself. I went into the Welcome Bar and there was John Heath with the usual crowd of enthusiasts, hangers-on and well-meaning friends one always finds after a race. I say 'well-meaning' because Rex and Frank were there, when they should have been in bed, basking in the limelight of HWMs very creditable performance and collecting drinks left, right and centre. I wonder if those people would have kept them up so late had they realized what a journey lay ahead of us. Anyway, John Heath came over to me.

'Can you remind them that they have a long journey tomorrow?'

I wanted to tell John Heath that he should have sent Rex and Frank packing hours ago, but I kept my temper and got them out of the bar. I had already arranged with the hotel porter to wake them at 7 am but it was 9 am before they finally moved off. They certainly did not look as though they would reach Aix-les-Bains, and appeared so ill and tired that I almost felt sorry for them.

In the afternoon I met John Heath after he had collected the starting money. We went through the accounts and he then reimbursed me. At last I was able to pay all the bills and get the small van out of pawn. I then met two Englishmen on holiday with an MG and as their knowledge of France was limited they asked if they might follow me as far as Aix. Naturally I agreed, as I was only too glad to have companions for the journey, and we set off in the evening just after 5 o'clock.

With three hundred odd miles to cover there was no time for hanging around; I put my foot hard down and kept it there. I really thrashed the van, and to such purpose that the MG driver flashed his lights and signalled me to slow down. They had trouble with their carburettor and, once that had been put right, informed me that I was going too fast for them.

'OK,' I said, 'why don't you go ahead, but try to keep going at a fair speed.'

I very soon found they were going too slow for me, and when we arrived in Dijon just after midnight they promptly decided to call off the marathon. In a very friendly manner they pointed out that they were on holiday.

'We want to avoid killing ourselves if we can,' said the

older of the two, who had been driving.

So I said good-bye to them and continued the journey, refreshing myself during the early hours of the morning with several stops at village pumps and numerous swigs from the brandy flask.

Soon after daybreak, about 20 miles from Aix-les-Bains, I suddenly stood on the brakes. I could not believe my own eyes. There was the transporter, parked neatly on the grass verge by the side of the road; I pulled in, expecting to find that it had broken down.

These was no sign of life whatsoever and everything was peaceful and quiet until I neared the cab of the lorry. I have never heard such a cacophony of snoring. Rex and Frank were slumped in the cab, absolutely out to the world; I felt like committing a double murder and then maybe shooting myself.

There were the two bright boys who were supposed to reach Aix-les-Bains and have a good night's sleep in a decent bed so that they would be fresh enough to handle the two trucks between them next day whilst I had a sleep. And Bari was still more than eight hundred miles away!

So I banged on the sides of the lorry and woke them up. They had their excuses, of course, and maintained that the carburettors had given trouble. This may well have

been the case because on our way to Reims the previous week the lorry had run out of petrol and we had used racing fuel, which had naturally upset the whole system. However, I was not entirely convinced that part of their trouble was not due to a hangover. I put my cards on the table.

'One thing is sure,' I said 'we have to press on and not one of us is even going to see a comfortable bed, let alone sleep in it, until we get to Bari.'

We arrived in Aix-les-Bains soon after 10am and I suddenly felt the steering behaving in a most erratic manner. The front axle was no longer joined to the chassis! The whole front end had become a flexible platform and was moving where it wanted, not where I wanted it to move. I was almost too tired to realize what would have happened if the axle had gone during my marathon run the night before – but not quite. I have a vivid imagination.

So I nursed the lorry along to a garage and told Rex and Frank to get some sleep at the Cosmopolitan, in spite of my ultimatum by the roadside, whilst the broken brackets were welded to the chassis. I knew the job would take four or five hours.

We left Aix-les-Bains in the late afternoon for the Mt Cenis Pass and what a journey we had over the Pass. I wrote in my diary: 'What a life. Why on earth did I ever

Stirling Moss with one of the original HWMs in the Formula 1 International Trophy at Silverstone in 1950. He finished sixth overall, a magnificent performance by a 2-litre unsupercharged car. (*T. C. March*)

undertake such a job. It is worse than working in the salt mines of Siberia. We had snow and fog on the Mt Cenis. It seemed that everything was against us. It must have been the worst night ever on the Pass. I am absolutely worn out.'

Mt Cenis is normally a fairly easy Pass to cross but it seemed on that particular night that the elements decided to play hell. And it was Hell. Somehow we got through to Italy and then it was just a question of pressing on. Rex and Frank drove the large transporter, changing drivers every three or four hours, whilst I continued in the small van non-stop. I had not slept since snatching three hours on Sunday night in Reims.

It was crazy to carry on like that but we had no alternative. I could not do it these days and when I think of the miles we covered on that trip in little more than four days I realize what a wonderful team spirit there was with HWM.

At Piacenza, on the road to Bologna, we stopped for a cup of coffee and were sitting at a table on the sidewalk when we saw John Heath's Light Fifteen Citroen. Whoever was driving gave us a toot on the horn, whilst the other occupants waved and gave us a thumbs up signal.

Two thoughts crossed my mind when the car had gone. First, I ruminated on the pleasant life that drivers lead compared with mechanics, and then I realized that we must have made faster time from Reims, in spite of our delays, than they had in the Citroen. Not bad for a couple of clapped out lorries and a bunch of bearded mechanics who were beginning to look like the Long Range Desert Group.

I decided at Piacenza that we would take time off for a bathe, once we reached the Adriatic coast. Quite apart from anything else I was beginning to itch. It would refresh us for the long run down the coast road through Pescara to Bari. So off we went again on the non-stop marathon, through Modena and Bologna to Ancona. Not far from Ancona we left the large transporter by the side of the road and took the small van down a little used track to the sea.

We stripped and plunged into the Adriatic. None of us had a swim suit, but a girl's school outing on that very beach would not have stopped us taking that well-earned dip. We relaxed for an hour or two, stretched out on the warm sand, and the sunshine did us a power of good.

In spite of the rest, we were all very tired and, with another night of driving ahead, I decided that we must change lorries from time to time, so that each one of us would be able to get some sleep and also some variety in driving to ease the monotony. A change of lorries is as good as a rest. I had at last reached the end of my tether. I just could not drive any more and asked Frank to take the small van whilst I climbed into the big transporter with Rex and settled down to have a sleep.

I told Rex to keep an eye on Frank, particularly as it was getting dusk when we moved off. I don't know how long I slept but I remember waking with a start as we rounded a sharp corner and asking Rex if the other van was behind us.

'Looks like it,' he replied, and we continued for another mile or two. Suddenly Rex looked in the mirror. 'I don't think Frank is there,' he said. 'Those lights I thought were his must have belonged to someone else.'

We stopped and waited. Ten, 20, 30 minutes. Still no sign of Frank. After two hours we were desperate. I felt as depressed as when I had found the lorry beside the road outside Aix. Where was the gun? Where was Bari? I knew the answer to the second question – a hundred and fifty miles away.

There was only one thing to do. Turn the lorry round and search for Frank. We drove back some 20 miles before reaching a fairly large village, and in spite of the fact that it was now well past midnight there were plenty of people still around. Sometimes I wonder just when the Italians do sleep. Yes – they remembered a lorry with 'Lucas' on the side but could not say which way it had gone. Why not stop and have a cup of coffee? There is always tomorrow. It was a typical Italian attitude.

However, our luck was in at last. Groping around in the dark we found the tyre marks of the small van leading up a minor road. We knew it was Frank because the tyres were military pattern with a distinctive tread. So off we went again, tearing along the narrow country road in the transporter and keeping our fingers crossed at every blind corner.

At last, after 15 nerve-shattering miles, we came to another village and, believe it or not, there was a petrol station still open – at 4 am. I asked the attendant, in a pantomime of sign language and schoolboy French, whether he remembered a lorry with 'Lucas' on the side. Yes, he had seen one, and sure enough when we searched the village there was the van parked in a small square. Frank was sound asleep.

I shook him and his relief at seeing us when he opened his eyes was so great that he burst into tears. You can imagine his feelings. He had only joined us at Reims and this was his first journey with the équipe. He could not speak Italian and was, in any case, so tired when he arrived in the village that he had forgotten where we were going. So he could not even write 'Bari' on a piece of paper. His memory just did not work any more. What else could he do but hope and pray that we would find him.

I wonder what would have happened if he had remembered and been directed back along that narrow country road. It could have resulted in a pile up on one of the blind corners, involving the whole HWM team of cars.

Rex and I were so pleased we had found Frank that not a single cross word was spoken. Like the famous Crazy Gang we were together again, and looking back on that hectic journey I reckon we were like the Victoria Palace comics in more ways than one.

We arrived in Bari just before lunch on Friday, one day earlier than we had expected, having completed eleven hundred miles since leaving Reims on Monday. After the Reims race I had told John Heath that we would make the trip under one condition. 'We shall have to scrap the first day of practice because I am sure we shall not make it by Friday.' John Heath agreed and promised that, even if we did arrive on Friday, he would be quite happy to practise only on the Saturday. This was sensible because in any case it was a Formula 1 race of 200 miles, and our competitors were far more powerful than the HWMs. I knew as well as he did that we were racing at Bari for a £1000 starting money and for no other reason.

Bari is the sort of city where if you have a racing transporter everyone knows of your arrival as soon as you reach the outskirts. By the time we pulled up at the Automobile Club, Heath and the drivers were waiting for us.

They were all very relieved – particularly Stirling – that we had arrived without mishap. We looked, and felt, like tramps. We had not shaved or washed properly for four days and I for one was not at all surprised that the Italian police gave us some very strange looks as we drove towards the Club.

Then John Heath dropped a bombshell. He insisted that we ought to get one of the cars ready for practice. Quite apart from anything else it meant fitting new tyres, for the HWMs still carried the Reims treads and they were badly worn.

'We must give the boys a chance,' said John Heath.

I looked across at Rex and Frank. They were almost asleep on their feet.

'Frank . . . Rex,' I said, in a loud voice. 'Go straight to the hotel and get to bed.'

At once, Stirling ranged himself alongside me.

'I can take them in the Citroen,' he said.

I hoped this would have the effect of reminding John Heath of his promise, but he had made up his mind to practise and, whilst Stirling drove Frank and Rex to the hotel, I got down to it and changed a set of wheels on one of the cars. I can remember very little about the practice. If we had any trouble I certainly cannot recollect putting it right.

I have never been so glad to get to bed as I was after that damned practice session, even though I found myself sharing a small room with Frank and Rex. The Alfa Romeo mechanics were staying in the same hotel – twenty-eight of them – and they not only occupied most of the rooms

John Heath and mechanic try to resolve a problem with the Weber carburettors on the 1953 HWM. The photograph was taken at the British Grand Prix that year. (*Guy Griffiths*)

but monopolized the restaurant at mealtimes.

According to my diary I woke up on Saturday morning feeling very much better, having had quite a good night's sleep in spite of the combined snoring of the other two. A good breakfast cheered me up a lot and the marathon run was becoming a memory. It was not easy to be miserable in such glorious sunshine.

During the Saturday practice session, it was decided to fit 4.0:1 axle ratios on all the cars. Bari is a 3¾-mile 'round the houses' circuit, with race averages around 80 mph and uses part of the promenade on the sea front. It is a combination of several different types of surface, comprising patches of cobble, granite stone and smooth stretches.

After the practice the cars were prepared finally for the race. I always insisted on the team being absolutely spick and span, and ready to be pushed on to the starting grid, before we went to bed on the night before a race.

My work plan was one I had evolved at Reims when Frank Nagel joined us. I looked after the three engines, whilst Frank and Rex were responsible for everything else on the chassis. I was whistling to myself and checking the carburettors on Fischer's car in a fairly leisurely fashion, for we were well ahead with our preparation, when suddenly there was an explosion and a sheet of flame. The car was on fire.

Having changed the axle ratio, Rex had started to

clean up whilst I worked on the carburettors, and was washing the cockpit with petrol. In those days the cars carried batteries for the self-starter, etc, and whilst he was scrubbing the cockpit with a paint brush dipped in petrol, the metal ring on the handle touched the solenoid switch on the starter. It shorted at once and created a large enough spark to cause a fire, particularly as the cockpit had been soaked in petrol and Rex was also holding a tray of petrol in his hand.

As soon as I heard the explosion, I ran over to the bench for the fire extinguisher, banged it on the floor and waited for a stream of fluid. Nothing happened? I lifted it and realized at once that it was empty. I picked up another extinguisher and this also was empty!

Meanwhile, the fire had gained a hold and there was so much smoke and flame that I could not see Rex Woodgate, who was gallantly trying to put out the fire with the small and almost useless extinguisher from the car. Both he and Frank were separated from me by a barrier of smoke and flames and any minute now three HWMs each with some 35 gallons of fuel in the tank, were going sky high. I could almost see the headlines in Equipe: 'HWM team destroyed in garage fire! Disaster kills three.'

I ran into the street to find help and the first person I met was the garage proprietor. He was waving his arms about like a drunken sailor and shouting 'Santa Maria. Mia Garagio.' In spite of the hysterics he carried a fire extinguisher which he had borrowed from a neighbour. I snatched it from him and he immediately turned tail and disappeared as I advanced on the burning car and directed a stream of fluid over the cockpit.

By the time the local Fred Karno outfit arrived – in the form of the resident fire-fighters – we had the fire under control. Rex Woodgate was badly burned and we lost no time in getting him to hospital. He was not detained but it was obvious that, with his hands bandaged, we could not expect any help from him in the pits during the race.

The fire was the cause of major blunders on the part of Frank and myself. When the explosion occurred, Frank was just about to fill the back axle on Macklin's car, having changed the ratio. In the confusion that followed the fire, he forgot all about it and the car went to the grid without any lubricant in the back axle.

For my part, when all the excitement had died down, I forgot to finish checking the carburettors on Fischer's car and consequently the float chamber container was not properly tightened. The fire was, therefore, the real cause of both these cars retiring in the race, and it also kept us working, repairing the damage, until 6am. However, we managed to get two hours' sleep.

In the race Macklin was very lucky. When the axle went solid he was travelling at his maximum speed –

about 120 mph – and spun round and round on the straight like a ballerina. Fortunately, he was able to hold the madly spinning car, and also keep out of the way of other drivers.

Moss drove one of the finest races of his career at Bari. He finished third (and remember it was a Formula 1 race) in front of all the two-stage Maseratis and the Ferraris. The 158 Alfa Romeos beat him (Farina first, Fangio second) but there was one occasion, in the early stages of the race, when Moss was ahead of Fangio and in second place.

This may not have been the most successful appearance of HWM during the season but it was certainly a magnificent drive on the part of Moss. Both Macklin and Fischer, before being forced to retire, mixed it with the 'big boys' but Stirling just walked away from everyone else with the exception of Farina and Fangio.

At this time Stirling was still a boy off the circuit, but once in a racing car he was very different. He became part of the team, and his ambition – as it was with all of us – was to prove HWMs were the best cars in their class.

He was in every way a first rate member of the HWM team – an ideal partner – and was not out for personal glory. I liked him, too, because he took a real interest in the work done by the mechanics and tried to help us with our problems by giving suggestions and ideas.

On Monday we had our usual conference to sort out the accounts, and I had a coffee with John Heath and Stirling Moss. This was my first social occasion with Stirling over a cup of coffee, but by no means the last. He described his experiences at the prizegiving, which we had not attended as we were only too glad to get to bed after the race and are not, in any case, usually invited to prizegiving ceremonies.

As Stirling described how he danced with Miss Italy, or maybe it was with Miss Bari, I thought to myself: 'This is the other Moss. Still very much a youngster at heart. Very different from the cold, calculating machine in the HWM cockpit yesterday afternoon.'

Alf Francis was chief mechanic to HWM until the end of 1951 and later he was mechanic to Stirling Moss and ran Rob Walker's team. Although HWM achieved many successes in their early years and the team 'brought on' some fine drivers including Moss, Lance Macklin and Peter Collins, by 1952 decline had set in. They struggled all year and by 1953 the team's fortunes had sunk so low that the organisers of the German Grand Prix refused their entries. That year HWM introduced a Jaguar-powered sports-racing car and it was with one of these cars that John Heath was killed in the 1956 Mille Miglia road race in Italy.

1952

Although the decision to run World Championship Grands Prix in 1952 to Formula 2 was made late, there was no shortage of contestants. Almost inevitably however racing was Ferrari-dominated. The Maranello team had produced in 1951 the Tipo 500 1980 cc 4-cylinder car designed by Aurelio Lampredi and Tipo 500s were driven for the works by Alberto Ascari, Luigi Villoresi and Giuseppe Farina. Other drivers were brought into the team from time to time and it was Piero Taruffi who won for Ferrari the first of the year's Championship races, the Swiss Grand Prix at Bremgarten, while Ascari was competing at Indianapolis. Ascari won the remaining six Championship races that year and he was undisputed World Champion. He also won the first three Championship races of 1953 and this record of winning nine consecutive World Championship races remains unbroken. Ferrari also won ten non-Championship races during 1952 and suffered a sole defeat at Reims where the unexpected winner was Jean Behra (Gordini).

The French Gordini team could have provided a serious challenge all season if the *patron* Amédée Gordini had been provided with sufficient finance, but he was forced to run his twin-cam straight-sixes as another 'shoe-string' operation. Maserati produced a

British Formula 2 cars: Cooper-Bristol with Mike Hawthorn at the wheel in the International Trophy at Silverstone. In this race he retired because of a broken gear-lever, but later in the season he achieved some good Championship finishes. (*T. C. March*)

ERA G Type. Stirling Moss contracted to drive this promising new car and is seen in the British Grand Prix at Silverstone. Sadly it proved a complete failure, but it later formed the basis of the successful Bristol 450 sports-racing cars. (*T. C. March*)

Alberto Ascari was head and shoulders above the opposition in 1952-53 and completely dominated the World Championship. Here he is on his way to a win in the 1952 British Grand Prix. (*T. C. March*)

Connaught A-series. Dennis Poore in the 1952 British Grand Prix in which he finished fourth. Beautifully engineered, but underpowered, the Connaught achieved a good measure of success in minor events. (*T. C. March*)

new 6-cylinder A6GCM car, but it was not until the Italian Grand Prix at Monza that it showed real promise and Froilan Gonzalez with a new twin-plug version shook the Ferrari team by leading until he made a refuelling stop and he eventually finished second. The British contenders were the Alta, Aston-Butterworth, Connaught, Cooper-Bristol, Frazer Nash and HWM. Young Mike Hawthorn's performance with his Bob Chase-entered Cooper was sensational and included fourth in the Belgian Grand Prix, third in the British and fourth in the Dutch and led to his invitation to drive for Ferrari in 1953. None of the other British marques, the Italian Osca or the Maserati-Platé (rebuilt versions of the old Formula 1 cars) achieved much. But certainly the starting grids were full that year.

1953

The year proved a straight fight between Ferrari and Maserati, but with the Maranello team always having the edge – until the very end of the year. Ferrari still raced the Tipo 500 in slightly improved form with a team consisting of Ascari, Villoresi, Farina and Hawthorn, while Maserati had a much improved version of the A6GCM and now fielded a full team consisting of Fangio, Gonzalez and, usually, Felice Bonetto, with ostensibly private entries driven by Swiss Emmanuel de Graffenried and Argentinian Onofre Marimon. Generally the Ferraris handled better, but the Maseratis were slightly faster in a straight line, but handicapped by a rigid rear axle. After Ascari had won the first three Championship races of the year, came the French Grand Prix. At this stage in the season young Hawthorn was being much criticised for his 'lack lustre' performances, but his win at Reims made him a hero in Italy. This is Hawthorn's account of that victory (from *Challenge Me The Race*, revised edition, Aston Publications Ltd, 1988).

The 1953 French Grand Prix

After Monza, we went straight back to France for the French Grand Prix on 5 July at Reims, where I was destined to become the first Britisher to win this great classic since Segrave won in 1923. I suppose whatever else I do, this will always be regarded as one of my greatest successes – indeed, a lot of people seemed to think it was one of the most exciting motor races ever run – yet it simply did not occur to me at the time; I was much too busy to think about it.

Up to a short time before the start it was very doubtful whether Ferrari would let us start at all owing to an unfortunate incident during the 12-hour sports-car race which preceded the Grand Prix. The 4½-litre V12 Ferrari driven by Maglioli and Carini was in the lead, and had set up a new sports-car lap record at 114.7 mph for the circuit which had just been increased in length to 5.19 miles.

In the early hours of the morning the car was seen to be running without side-lights before the permitted time for switching off and after a re-fuelling stop it was pushed for a short distance when it re-started. The Ferrari personnel argued that other people had also switched their lights off and the pushing at the re-start was simply to get the car clear of spilt fuel which might have started a fire. However, the organisers took the extraordinary course of announcing that no further times would be taken for the car, while still permitting it to go on running.

Eventually, after an extraordinary series of half-hearted – and incorrect – efforts to stop it the car was called in and withdrawn. Whereupon the French crowd booed and hooted and jeered in an extraordinary demonstration against the race officials. The decision was final, however, and the race was won by Stirling Moss and Peter Whitehead, driving one of the disc-braked C-type Jaguars which had won at Le Mans and that at almost the same average speed.

The incident aroused extremely bitter feelings and right up to the start of the Grand Prix we were uncertain as to whether we would be instructed to withdraw or not. Fortunately we got the go-ahead.

The usual Ferrari team, Ascari, Villoresi, Farina and I, faced Maseratis driven by Fangio, Gonzalez, Marimon, Bonetto and de Graffenried, and the ranks were filled up by HWM, Connaught, Cooper-Bristol, Gordini and Osca. Gonzalez, who had started with his tank only half-full, rushed off into the lead as pace-maker and in chasing him Ascari, Villoresi and I got involved in a private duel among ourselves.

At one point I passed Ascari and he shrugged his shoulders as if to say: 'Take it away; I can't go any faster!' Positions were changing several times a lap. I had the lead and then Villoresi came past, and sometimes we would be hurtling along three abreast; at 160 mph, down an ordinary French main road. It was a bit frightening to see the nose of one of the other cars come alongside, then drop back again as the driver decided he could not make it before the next corner. The cars were evenly matched and could only get past each other by slip-streaming. The trick was to tuck in close behind the other man, get a tow from his slipstream, ease back the throttle as far as possible without losing position, and then suddenly tramp on the pedal and use the sudden surge of urge to nip out and pass him. Whereupon he would try to get into position to return the compliment.

Shortly before half-way mark, Fangio and Farina caught up with us and then we really started mixing it. It was a situation in which the slightest misjudgment by one driver could have meant disaster for everybody, but even so, we usually managed a quick grin at each other when we passed – all except Farina, who sat scowling with concentration.

After 28 laps, Gonzalez had to pull in for fuel and lost his lead to Fangio and I. We saw him just preparing to re-start as we passed the pits. Fangio and I now drew ahead of the rest of the group and began a private scrap which was to last without a second's respite for the remaining 32 laps of the race. At the time I did not dream that I had any chance of winning the race; I thought Ascari, Farina and Villoresi were just letting me keep Fangio occupied and were watching for the moment to come up and take over nearer to the end of the race. At one time I got in front of Fangio and as we accelerated away from the Thillois corner he dropped back several hundred yards, as though he had missed a gear change.

I thought: 'Good, now I can disappear!' but as I went round the long, fast right-hander under the bridge after the pits, I found Behra right in front of me in the Gordini. I had to slow down for a moment and as I went past I spotted

Fangio right on my tail again; the old wheel-to-wheel struggle began once more. Officially we were limited to 7000 rpm with the Ferraris, but lap after lap I was getting 7600 on the straight and the engine stuck it without missing a beat.

We would go screaming down the straight side by side absolutely flat out, grinning at each other, with me crouching down in the cockpit, trying to save every ounce of wind resistance. We were only inches apart, and I could clearly see the rev counter in Fangio's cockpit. Then once, as we came into Thillois, he braked harder than I had expected and I shunted him lightly, putting a dent in his tail. That shook me for a moment, for I thought it would take some living-down. 'New boy shunts Fangio,' they would say. But he showed no resentment at all; he just kept on fighting every inch of the way, according to the rules, in the way that has earned him the admiration and respect of everyone in motor racing.

I did have one anxious moment when he pulled across fairly sharply just as I was trying to come past on the right but I was quite sure it was unintentional. Another time we were running abreast when we came up behind a much slower car and I pulled right over, clipping the grass, so that we could pass him in line abreast. All this time I had no idea what was going on behind us, for the pit had ceased hanging out signals. I heard afterwards that the mechanics were jumping around gibbering with excitement and even Ugolini seemed ready to throw his pencil away.

Perhaps ten laps from the end, I suddenly thought:

The wheel to wheel battle in the 1953 French Grand Prix between Mike Hawthorn (Ferrari) and Juan Manuel Fangio which Hawthorn won by the narrowest of margins.

'Good heavens, I could win this race!' and I began to think out ways of crossing the finishing line first. If I came out of Thillois first, with Fangio in my slipstream, he could always find the extra spurt to beat me over the line. If I tailed him round the corner and stayed in his slipstream, I could probably spurt past him at the critical moment; but he was too old a hand to be caught by a simple trick like that. The only hope was to stake everything on getting into Thillois first and pulling out with a sufficient lead to keep him out of my slipstream.

Then I had a totally unexpected bit of luck. As we swung into the last lap, it suddenly dawned on me that Fangio had not changed down into first gear for the Thillois turn. Perhaps he was having trouble with the gearbox and could not get the gear in. Wheel to wheel we flashed round for the last time and I knew that everything was going to depend on perfect timing of that last change into first gear on the last corner. We were only inches apart as we braked, changed down and down again. Then I slipped into first, cut round the apexes close in as possible, straightened up the wheels and simultaneously slammed the throttle wide open. The engine screamed up to peak revs, but the tyres gripped; I gained the precious yards I needed and I was leading by a second as the chequered flag came down.

During the last lap I had realised, almost subconsciously, that we were no longer alone. Gonzalez and Ascari had been fighting a second duel only a short distance behind us and on the last sprint for the line Gonzalez, driving with colossal determination, had closed the gap so that he finished only a few feet behind Fangio. Ascari was only 3.2 sec behind Gonzalez!

Just to show how remote the driver, concentrating on his job, can be from what is going on round him I will quote what Rodney Walkerley wrote in *The Motor* about the end of the race:

'I shall not attempt to describe the final laps. The whole thing was fantastic. The crowd was yelling, the commentators were screaming. Nobody paid much attention to the rest of the drivers at all and the drivers themselves slowed up to watch this staggering display.'

And *The Autocar* said: 'It was a battle which exhausted even the spectators with its intensity and duration.'

Yet, whenever I was able to give it a thought, I was chiefly worried because it must be rather a boring sight for the spectators, just watching two cars passing and re-passing. I was still concerned about having shunted Fangio earlier in the race, but as we coasted down the road after the finish, he came alongside grinning broadly and gave me the boxers' handshake, which made me feel a lot better. Then we stopped and I was engulfed in a fantastic reception. Maybe it had not been so boring after all.

I was not in particularly good form at the start of the race, because of the sports-car race dispute and the uncertainty about permission for us to start in the Grand Prix. Nor is the Reims circuit one of my favourites. Made up of French main roads closed for the occasion and linked by sections of private road, it measures 5.19 miles to the lap. Its main features are two long straights, two acute slow hairpin corners and some very fast curves where spectacular four-wheel drifts are possible at about 120 mph, but the advantage gained on the fast corners can easily be lost if someone manages to get into your slipstream on the straight.

A lot of people concluded from the way I was crouching down in the cockpit that I must have been as excited as the spectators seem to have been. The possibility of beating Fangio was exciting enough for anyone, but doing a race like this you have to concentrate so hard on saving every fraction of a second and on thinking out the next moves that there is no time to feel excited. I adopted a rather hunched driving position quite early in my driving career as most of the cars I drove were too small for me and I had to keep down to keep out of the wind. Gradually it became a habit and I tend to do it even when I am in a car which gives me room to sit back in the conventional modern position.

Later in the year Ascari won the British race, showed complete mastery in the German race at the Nürburgring until his car lost a wheel (Farina won for Ferrari) and won the Swiss Grand Prix now held in August. Then came the Italian Grand Prix. This race proved a titanic duel between Ascari and Fangio. At the last corner on the last lap Marimon who had rejoined the race after a pit stop and was helping his team-leader harrass the World Champion nudged the tail of the leading Ferrari; Ascari spun off and Fangio scored his only Championship race victory of the year. Ascari was again World Champion (he had won 11 of the 15 Championship races held in 1952-3). In addition Ferrari won five non-Championship races in 1953.

At Monza Ferrari had produced the new Tipo 553 *Squalo* (shark), so-called because of its bulbous side tanks and a development of the 4-cylinder theme to be raced in 1954. None of the other teams achieved much in 1953, although Ken Wharton tried hard with a works-supported Cooper-Bristol and after struggling for much of the year with a special Cooper-Alta designed by John Cooper (Sports editor of *The Autocar* and not to be confused with John Cooper of Cooper

The battle for the lead in the 1953 Italian Grand Prix with Fangio (Maserati) leading the Ferraris of Ascari (No. 4) and Farina (No. 6) and the Maserati of Marimon.

Cars, although the car was Cooper of Surbiton-based), Stirling Moss switched to a normal Cooper-Alta; running this on nitromethane fuel additive Moss rose to fifth place at Monza and was running at speeds that were higher than the tyres could withstand.

Although run to a substitute formula, Grand Prix racing in 1952 and 1953 had proved successful and did much to popularize the sport. Lower costs had encouraged many more competitors and there was little doubt that the new 2500 cc Formula of 1954 onwards would prove even more successful.

Part 6: BRITISH REVIVAL, 1954-60

1954

For the years from 1954 to 1960 Grand Prix racing was run to a Formula of 2500 cc unsupercharged and 750 cc supercharged, although in practice only a handful of cars were built for the supercharged category and none was remotely successful. The supercharged alternative was only included at the request of BRM who toyed with the idea of racing a car powered by an engine based on their disastrously unsuccessful V16 1500 cc supercharged design. There were no other restrictions except that there was a minimum race length of 300 kilometres (186 miles) or 3 hours. This new formula had been proposed as long ago as 1951 and reflected the success of the 2000 cc Formula 2 that had been introduced for the 1948 season.

Although the German Mercedes-Benz team was known to be returning to Grand Prix racing for the first time since 1939, and British contenders were planned by BRM, Connaught and Tony Vandervell (the Vanwall), most critics expected to see Ferrari and Maserati continue as the dominant marques in racing. Despite a number of inaccuracies, the following two articles by Roy Pearl that appeared in the May 1954 issue of *Motor Racing* magazine give a revealing picture of the state (and status) of motor racing in Italy at the time.

Exclusive from Modena

Why does Italy lead the world in motor racing design and technique? How do the famous stables find the money to cover the tremendous costs involved? To answer these vital questions, MOTOR RACING went to Modena, home of Ferrari and Maserati. Here, in 'Racetown' itself, we spent many hours in the factories and on the test track. For eighteen hours of every day we were in the company of the World's most famous designers and drivers. Here is our report:

These words are typed in the no-man's land of the sixty-room Hotel Albergo Reale, known by its frequenters as 'The Pub'. It stands in the centre of Modena, midway between the factory of Maserati and the offices of Ferrari. To this hotel come all the 'names' of motor racing for their food, vino and shop-talk. The resident of Room 16, with monopoly of the best bath, is Mike Hawthorn.

Modena stands on the Plain of Lombardy, sheltered by the snow-capped Apennines, 115 miles south of Milan. It is a clean, sunny, dreamy town radiating a web of long, flat roads inducive to speed. A mile-and-a-half from its centre is Modena Autodrome. Here, on the 1.38-mile, 75 mph rectangle, much of Italy's car and motorcycle testing is done.

Ten miles west of the Autodrome, and close to the mountains, is the village of Maranello, where, divorced from the town office, is the factory of Scuderia Ferrari.

Our fellow-guests in this hotel are Reg Parnell, Isobel Baird and Leslie Hawthorn. They are here to bring back to England the ex-Baird Ferrari, now with 2½-litre engine. Also present are Sidney Greene and Roy Salvadori, who are making final arrangements for the delivery of the FI Maserati. Stirling Moss' mechanic, the renowned 'Alfred', has checked in too.

Our first visit was to the Ferrari factory at Maranello where Mike had fixed to show us round in company with Reg Parnell and Leslie Hawthorn. Mike's fellow-guide was Enzo Ferrari's son Dino. He greeted us at the gates of the closely guarded ultra-modern Ferrari fortress from the cockpit of the new 5-litre sports car which is being prepared for the Mille Miglia. Although he later relented a little we were told firmly not to take photographs.

As we stepped from the courtyard into the factory itself we discovered most of the answers to our 2000-mile quest. For here, over a floor area of some 75,000 square feet, was a superbly equipped plant. The tools to do the job are right there on the spot and so are the men.

The ultra-modern building covers the sides of an approximate square, with a courtyard and rest house in the centre. It was built, we were told, during the war as a machine tool factory for Enzo Ferrari and later given to him by the Italian Government. Now it houses only the racing car side of Enzo's diverse business interests in Italy. At this works no other activity of any kind is pursued; tales that sub-contract work on other products is executed here to help pay for the racing business are quite untrue.

Dino Ferrari was indignantly emphatic in denying that the Scuderia currently received any form of financial assistance from the Italian Government. He also told us that the Scuderia and its assets were the private property of his father. It is clear, however, that Ferrari receives very strong support from the trade, particularly fuel and tyre companies, in the form of success bonuses. We gained the impression that the total probably exceeded £100,000.

In 1954 Froilan Gonzalez was the man most able to shake Mercedes-Benz superiority. He is at the wheel of his Ferrari 553 *Squalo* at the International Trophy at Silverstone early in the year. (*T. C. March*)

Dino Ferrari confirmed that about 150 Ferrari sports cars were made and sold every year. The ex-factory price of these cars is about £5000. Another manufacturer told us that the cost of making those cars would be about half that amount.

It would seem, therefore, that Ferrari has an income from car sales of at least £750,000. We found that it was generally agreed that starting money and prizes would, in a normal season, cover travelling expenses and drivers' remuneration. Therefore, even without outside support, Ferrari would seemingly be left with £350,000 to meet development and construction costs of new racing cars; this is on the assumption that his £100,000 yearly wages bill is mostly covered by sports car manufacture labour charges. From these estimated figures it might be thought that Ferrari is more than covering his expenses. This is the general impression among Modena people. Many say that Ferrari's personal gain is about £200,000 a year. Although that is only talk it does not hide the fact that the real key to this business is the sale of sports cars.

We were unable to obtain any convincing reasons for Enzo Ferrari's statement of last October that he was withdrawing from racing because of financial difficulties. We believe that this move many have been actuated by an attempt further to improve sports car sales, to increase bonus money and entrance fees, since sport and trade authorities would fear the loss of, respectively a spectacle and a star to hitch up with.

As we entered the number one machine shop, some 500 feet by 50 feet, Dino told us that the Scuderia employed 220 mechanics. Each is supplied with bright blue overalls by Pirelli. The layout of the shops is scrupulously clean and ultra-modern. In this first section were over 100 large new machine tools including £10,000 gear cutters and drills, borers, lathes and milling machines.

Work was proceeding on parts of the 5-litre's V12 engine and various four-cylinder types. In view of last year's rumours on Ferrari 'Sixes' we were interested in a new six-cylinder block being machined in this shop. Of ten chassis in the stores at the end of the shop, six were for 2-litre sports cars and four for 4½-litre vehicles. We were surprised to learn that Ferrari do not build their own chassis; bodies are built by Pinin Farina.

In the second machine shop were 100 smaller machines producing smaller components, engine and gearbox assembly was also in progress. The entire shop was flanked by component test rooms. In one was a rig for running-in back axle and gearbox, operated through a crankcase and clutch housing.

In another of these gallery 'shops' new 2-litre four-cylinder sports engines were being assembled. We noted that the dynamo was placed vertically between the two magnetos, it had four Weber carburetters, water pump at rear and bottom of the sump, the usual hair-pin valve springs, inserted valve seats.

Our next surprise was to find that Ferrari had financed the construction of his own foundry, a 5000 square feet affair. As yet, only such things as brake drums and gearbox shells are being cast at Maranello. Cylinder heads and blocks are still produced by Maserati.

The racing shop was not filled with new projects. Two F1 'side-tank' cars were there and we noted the de Dion tube was forward of differential-gearbox unit instead of behind it as on last year's type cars. Also in the shop were five of last year's type cars (2½-litre), all ready for Syracuse. These included Mike's, easily distinguishable with his customary four-spoked steering wheel.

Then came the Ferrari pièce de resistance. Hawthorn was to test the 5-litre sports car with Mille Miglia axle ratio. He passed, as he drove through the guarded gates, Dino's new Mediterranean hue Farina-bodied Fiat 1100. The seats were clothed in the black and yellow check of the Scuderia. Earlier, Dino had been driving the big car round the factory perimeter as a temporary 'hack'.

Mike lined up the car on the secondary road outside the factory. There was a sudden deafening roar and two very black lines of thick rubber scored the highway behind the blurred red monster. Reg Parnell measured them later at more than half-a-mile long.

While waiting for Mike to return from the Autodrome designer Lampredi told us something of the car. The V12, he said, develops 340 bhp at its maximum of 6000 rpm. The top speed is over 175 mph. Unusually big brake drums (which surprised even Parnell) were noticeable, as was the bulge over the tail fairing enclosing the extra large fuel tank. The throttle lever, we noticed, runs in a roller bearing, and Weber carburetters are fitted. That was all we were allowed to discover, except that we got an impression of accessibility to engine and axles.

A roar in the distance indicated that Mike's autodrome was *our* 20-foot road — strewn as it was with bullock carts, Vespas, bicycles, and pedestrians.

Words can never describe the incredible effect of the blinding speed of Mike's first run. 'Pop' Hawthorn had never seen anything like it; nor had we. Parnell remarked dryly that, 'He must have been doing more than 100.' Lampredi smiled laconically.

Once, twice more Mike did it. The roadside became lined quickly with the Ferrari mechanics who had helped to build the car. Each run was more awesome and more frightening than the last. Then Mike came in. His speed, he said, was 'about 180 mph at 5300.' It is not hard to appreciate that this 'sports car' is even faster than the FI Ferrari.

Soon after dawn next morning we were at Modena Autodrome watching Roy Salvadori trying out the FI Maserati. His own car was receiving its green in the paint shop so he was driving Fangio's car. Although Roy had never driven this F1 car before he completed 15 laps in impeccable style. He was not assisted by the track surface – on one corner this slowed him to walking pace, he said. Roy told us that he was taking things easy and was not driving the car flat out. Yet three times he equalled Ascari's 4.5-litre Ferrari lap record of 1 min 4.5 secs. (A Maserati test mechanic has been timed by the Automobile Club at 1 min 2 secs unofficially.) Salvadori drove with a full 40-gallon tank. He was completely happy with the car and full of praise for it. He could not raise a single point of criticism and he believed he could get round the Modena circuit very much faster.

Our tour of the Maserati factory was prefaced by an interview with Sig. Orsi, designer of the racing-car section of the Maserati industrial combine. We asked him why Maserati races.

'Maserati started with racing cars 25 years ago,' he said, 'we hope to keep up the tradition.' As Maserati make motorcycles, lorries, machine tools, and many other components, it is obvious that they currently benefit from their car racing publicity – so long as it is not too costly.

Sig. Orsi believes that it is possible to make a profit out of motor racing and that profit and loss is relative to success in races and in selling race cars and their derivatives. We gathered that although Maserati are not making a profit yet, they are not losing very much either, despite the fact that they consider themselves independent of trade 'bonus' support. This is because of their considerable sports car income. The company wishes to return to its pre-war system of selling racing cars throughout the world. Ferrari will not do this.

Although Maserati are currently selling about 85 sports cars per year at a cost to the customer of about £5000 each they plan to widen this activity. Their ultimate aim is to produce a production sports car 'to compete with the Jaguar' type, using the racing department to create prestige.

The other activities of Maserati, said Sig. Orsi, do not subsidise the racing department.

Sig. Orsi believes that Italy owes her racing car success to the fact that the country specialises in the production of racing cars. Every racing car part is made in Italy by racing car specialists and this, he said, is not the case in other countries, where proprietary brands invariably are used.

Inspection of the factory showed that, although Maserati racing car activity occupies much less floor area than Ferrari's, Maserati construct their own chassis and build their own bodies. It was also evident that full use of other Maserati resources, such as machine tools, forges and presses was made.

At the time of our visit the cars for Moss and Wharton appeared set for delivery before these words appear.

In the racing shop was the mock-up of an aerodynamic F1 cockpit cover which may see service this year. Under development is a new 1½-litre sports car, an example of which is to be bought by Sidney Greene. We were not allowed to see a new 2.5-litre sports car which was in the body builders. This may be entered for the Mille Miglia and Le Mans. Roy Salvadori's F1 Maserati has only a modified 1953 engine. The 1954 power-unit will be installed at the beginning of June.

Maserati's probable 1954 team will consist of Fangio, Marimon and Baron de Graffenried. Their second team will include Schell, Bira, and Mieres. The only British Maseratis to receive works assistance will be the Greene/Salvadori machines. Both Moss and the Owen Organisation are

paying the full price of about £5000 for their F1 cars – a total of over £10,000 each including import duty and purchase tax.

The Moss car will have fuel injection. Moss is entering the car at 26 meetings including Monza, and Stirling plans to fly to Italy as soon as the car is ready and test it at Monza for two days or so.

Sig. Orsi told us that is was too early for his équipe to reveal their racing plans. He considered that Monza was the true test of all cars and that, in Italian eyes, it was the only race which really showed which was the best car of the year.

We did not go to Lancia. It is generally appreciated that this company, 49 per cent owned by Fiat, plans to race solely to promote sales of its existing models. We did, however, go to Milan to talk to Alfa Romeo.

Alfa's had raced as a publicity medium for their cars. But in recent years they have established themselves on a world-wide basis as manufacturers of marine, industrial,

Stirling Moss with his new Maserati 250F waits on the starting grid for his wet heat at the 1954 International Trophy at Silverstone. (*T. C. March*)

stationary, and aero engines. They are also building heavy lorries and trolley buses. These products, in themselves are creating publicity and also demanding increasing promotional expenditure and technical effort. The production of the car section, being satisfactory, it was decided temporarily to shelve racing activities and devote these resources, both financial and technical, to other products. At the moment there are no plans to re-enter grand prix racing for 1954. Developments in 1955 have not been decided but, in view of the current production rate of 6000 Model 1900 Alfa Romeos per year, an early resumption of sporting activity seems unlikely.

In particular we were impressed by the admiration for Ferrari. It confirmed our view that rumours of upsets over Government policy towards the two companies are quite unfounded.

Italians make it pay

Roy Pearl interprets our Modena report: the background factors which help to maintain Italian supremacy are vital to the future of British motor racing.

Italy has no magic formula for motor racing. There is no hidden secret to explain why there are more works teams in Italy than in any other country. Above all, there is no fairy godmother behind the scenes to pay for Italian superiority.

The explanation is straightforward. Consider the relevant facts in the Modena report.

Ferrari is in motor racing for big business – but he is inspired by a burning enthusiasm for motor racing just the same. Ferrari builds race cars (with big trade support) to sell his sports cars at high prices.

Maserati are in motor racing by tradition. The Maserati car business was originally built upon racing successes. That integral enthusiasm persists; besides it is good publicity for the sale of other products. But don't forget that Maserati build race cars to sell – Ferrari doesn't.

Lancia have restarted racing because sales need a boost and pride of ownership plays a big part in the Italian motor market.

Nationalised Alfa Romeo would come back into racing (and I believe they will when their industrial problems have been straightened out) if it was commercially advisable to do so. Since government organisations are not normally fired with great enthusiasm, there is little chance of Alfas merely following tradition and making an earlier comeback.

So, the Italians set out to make their racing pay. There is a commercial approach running through all Italian motor racing but there is much more important traditional,

psychological background without which big time motor racing in Italy would not flourish. It is that national demand for motor racing ensures big prize money and big starting money, big trade bonuses for works teams and official encouragement.

Without taking into account Stanguellini's projects or OSCA's sports cars there are three formidable Italian contenders for first-class honours in 1954. Not any two of the three are in motor racing for the same reason but each one of them trades on the all-important factor – Italian enthusiasm for motor racing. That is the hard fact that we must face.

The Italians love motor racing, they love racing cars and they are all little Farinas. Motor racing gets publicity. Motor racing has an influence upon their motoring and their motor cars.

Vast Pool of Specialists

Compare that with our own situation. We have designers of outstanding ability and we are not behind in original thought, nor backward in studying designs and improving upon them. We have good mechanics but what chance have they of gaining real racing experience in the big class? We have not been in the top flight of GP racing for thirty years, and that has left us without a comparable number of specialists upon which to draw.

We are motor-racing enthusiasts too but in Italy the sport has been going on seriously for so much longer – fifty years in fact.

'We have specialists in Italy with years of racing experience on every sort of job,' said Maserati's director, Orsi. That surely is one of the answers to quick development.

British drivers are good, and fortunately one has had the good sense to go to an established Italian team to learn – we hope that eventually he will have the opportunity of bringing his experience to the assistance of British motor racing.

Enthusiasm for the sport amongst the ordinary people is the key.

To every Italian the names Ferrari, Maserati, Alfa Romeo, Nuvolari, Farina, and Ascari mean just as much as do the names Len Hutton and Stanley Matthews to the British. With that background the Italian motor industry in the broadest sense must take a keen interest in racing. Pride of ownership plays an important part in car sales.

We Want Serious Challenger

Since there is no real national interest in motor racing in this country we must decide whether enthusiasm of a relative few is really enough to back the challenge. We must decide whether it is possible in the circumstances to challenge the Italians, even if we found financial ways and means.

I believe in British ingenuity, resourcefulness, determination, and creativeness sufficiently to say that we can. But – should we, if we could, follow the Italians' pattern – or should we think up a new one for ourselves?

Our old methods and our present plans just will not do if we are to make a serious challenge.

I commend our clubs and club members and club drivers for their enthusiastic performances, and I believe we could lick the Italians at autocross, 750 cc or vintage racing and I know we can beat them with 500s but we still need a serious challenger for World Championship Formula racing.

It seems that in this country we must find an excuse for racing motor cars on a basis comparable with Ferrari. Very few amateurs could afford to construct, develop and race a team of cars in Formula 1 events. Since to race one team of three successfully each weekend would require nine or ten fully prepared cars.

The Italians do not need an excuse, that nation must have motor racing, a fact which establishes immediate commercial importance. I believe, and so do the Italians who know him well, that Enzo Ferrari will never lose his enthusiasm for racing, and whilst it continues to be profitable he will not give up. Further, I believe that if perforce Ferrari, Maserati and other Italian stables dropped out, then others would come in, encouraged by the less formidable competition and having themselves that integral enthusiasm, natural know-how and pool of specialists. Motor racing is part of the Italian make-up.

Even though they do not need an excuse the Italians will find ways and means for making motor racing pay.

We should be able to make motor racing pay. If Ferrari can afford to run a racing team to publicise his sports cars so could British sports car manufacturers.

If Maserati can run a team on profits from the sale of racing cars, then so could British racing car manufacturers if they had comparable plant and machinery.

If Lancia can boost sales in Italy by racing a team then British popular car manufacturers could boost exports, but they need to be convinced.

This last method would undoubtedly be the cheapest because our racing teams would have giant manufacturing facilities. The first method would be almost in the same category and both would be dependent upon the initiative of British car makers, whose advisers the SMM and T are not convinced of motor racing's commercial value.

Can British racing car manufacturers adopt a Maserati/Ferrari plan, and sell both racing and sports cars for profit?

British Resources Inadequate

Our Connaughts, Coopers, and HWMs suffer from a common drawback – lack of funds with which to set themselves up with machinery for building good Formula 1 cars and for developing them quickly. If funds are not forthcoming and they are to survive there must be a commercial or nominal link with industry – not necessarily with car manufacturers but with some allied industry which would benefit from publicity, or development.

There are other small perquisites which would automatically follow a real effort to produce a challenger. To begin with at least four British drivers might buy British cars. British promoters would become interested and perhaps pay better starting money. The trade might be tempted to support teams as well as, or even instead of, individuals.

It seems then that the aim can be the same – to make motor racing pay, but with such a different background our formula cannot be the same, with perhaps the one exception – Ferrari. The trade and national inducement could provide the tools – the Connaughts, Coopers and HWMs could do the job – well.

Juan Fangio again drove for Maserati in the early part of 1954, winning the First World Championship races of the year at Buenos Aires and Spa-Francorchamps (in Belgium), but he had contracted to drive for Mercedes-Benz when the new German cars were ready. Originally Maserati had not in fact planned to enter a works team throughout the year, but by the time that they had decided to do so, there were driver problems and in mid-season Stirling Moss, together with his own private Maserati, was brought into the Modena team. Ferrari won most of the minor races during the year, but had proved unable to match the Fangio/Maserati combination.

The Mercedes-Benz come-back took place in the French Grand Prix at Reims, a high-speed circuit well-suited to the very fast W196 cars with streamlined full-width bodywork, but, initially, suspect roadholding. This description of the French race is from *Motor Racing:*

The 1954 French Grand Prix

On 4 July Hermann Lang watched his 24-year-old compatriot Hans Herrmann raise the Reims lap record to 121.38 mph. Fifteen years before in a 3-litre Mercedes-Benz Lang had likewise established a lap record on the same circuit, but neither of them had won the race. Unlike 1939

First World Champion: Giuseppe Farina at the wheel of the Alfa Romeo 158 in the 1950 British Grand Prix at Silverstone. He won the race, the first ever World Championship event, from team-mates Luigi Fagioli and Reg Parnell, the British driver's only appearance for Alfa Romeo. (*Guy Griffiths*)

First British car to win a World championship race: Stirling Moss (Vanwall) in the 1957 British Grand Prix. He took over from team-mate Brooks to win the race. (*T.C. March*)

Jack Brabham, World Champion in 1959, 1960 and 1966. He became the first and only driver to win the Championship at the wheel of a car bearing his own name.

Below: In 1960 Jack Brabham won his second World Championship at the wheel of Cooper-Climax cars. This photograph was taken late in the year at Esso Bend at Oulton Park during the non-championship Gold Cup major race. *(David Phipps)*

On the banking at Monza in the 1961 Italian Grand Prix is Giancarlo Baghetti with the 120-degree V6 engined Ferrari nominally entered by Scuderia Sant' Ambroeus. Baghetti won his first three Grands Prix, the non-Championship races at Siracusa and Naples and the French Grand Prix in 1961, but never won another race. (*David Phipps*)

In 1962 BRM made good and Graham Hill won his first World Championship with the dark green V8 cars. In this race, the French Grand Prix at Rouen, he retired and the winner was Dan Gurney with the flat-8 Porsche. (*David Phipps*)

John Surtees at the wheel of his V8 Ferrari in the 1964 Dutch Grand Prix at Zandvoort. Surtees finished second to Clark (Lotus) in this race and went on to win the World Championship by a margin of one point from Graham Hill. (*David Phipps*)

Although the Brabham team achieved little success during the years of the 1500 cc Grand Prix formula, Dan Gurney scored a fine victory in the 1964 French Grand Prix held on the magnificent Circuit des Essarts at Rouen. (*David Phipps*)

Jim Clark dominated the 1963 and 1965 seasons with the Lotus-Climax in 25 and 33 forms. Clark is seen in the 1965 German Grand Prix which he won. (*David Phipps*)

Jochen Rindt (Lotus 72) leads Chris Amon (March 701) in the 1970 French race at Clermont-Ferrand. These drivers took first and second places, but the moral victor was Jean-Pierre Beltoise (Matra V12) wh fought his way through to take the lead only to fall right back because of a puncture. (*Nigel Snowdon*)

Also seen in the 1970 French Grand Prix is Jackie Stewart with the March 701 car raced by Tyrrell as an interim measure until his own car was ready. Stewart won the Spanish race in 1970 with the March, but at Clermont-Ferrand he finished ninth after slowing because of ignition trouble. (*Nigel Snowdon*)

A great driver, a great character – and for many a great hero: Ronnie Peterson, seen here with the March 711 in the 1971 Monaco Grand Prix. He finished second and with three other second places that year (but no wins) he took second place in the Drivers' Championship. (*Nigel Snowdon*)

In 1973 the Tyrrell team regained its dominant edge and Jackie Stewart won the World Championship before retiring with a record total of 27 Grand Prix wins. Here he is seen in the Spanish Grand Prix at Montjuich Park, from which he retired because of front brake failure. (*Nigel Snowdon*)

Above: The winner of the 1973 Spanish race was the 1972 World Champion, Emerson Fittipaldi – despite a deflating tyre.

The 1975 season proved a largely Niki Lauda and Ferrari benefit and the new 312T car from Maranello was more than a match for the opposition. Lauda is seen in the Monaco race which he won. *Nigel Snowdon*)

when Mercedes lost to their pre-war rivals Auto Union, in 1954 all other opposition melted before Herrmann's team-mates Fangio and Kling.

The ACF Grand Prix has been a significant race in Mercedes history from the time of their first victory in 1908 to their previous last victory in 1938. In 1914 a brand new car romped home first, in 1934 the first of the fabulous 750 kg formula cars failed miserably, in 1954 a team of new Formula 1 GP machines made their first appearance and again dominated the world's oldest Grand Prix motor race.

Unprecedented traffic clogged all routes to Reims (the fastest road circuit) whilst those who were up in time to see the finishing stages of the 12-hour Sports Car race were breakfasting mainly upon champagne, which is as plentiful as water in this district.

Those who in political circles would be classified as 'informed observers' predicted that Mercedes would not last one hour. This prophecy arose from the surprisingly troublesome showing of the German cars in practice, when they were beset with fuel bothers. As they had whined, with a note similar to the BRM, past the pits straight at speeds approaching 180 mph, the engines would momentarily cut out almost as if the ignition had been switched off. Neubauer had no public comment to make but it was significant that next time the cars were refuelled, chamois leather covered the funnels.

What went on behind the guarded doors of their headquarters was not revealed but it proved so effective that during the race neither Fangio's nor Kling's car missed a beat. Instead it was the opposition, Ferrari, Maserati and Gordini which suffered such *terrible hecatombe* and only seven cars finished out of 23 starters in 61 laps.

It is really an understatement to say that Mercedes dominated the race since it was Gonzalez alone, with one of the 'side-tank' Ferraris who was ever any match for the silver German cars. Even he was 7 seconds behind Fangio at the end of five laps and 14 seconds behind after ten laps. Two laps later the over-extended 4-cylinder engine had had enough.

With a capacity of 2496 cc rising from a bore of 76 mm and stroke of 68.8 mm the Mercedes engine can turn happily at more than 8000 rpm and the driver has five speeds in the rear-mounted gearbox. With the exception of compression-ignition engines this was the first time that fuel injection direct into the cylinders has been used successfully at high revs. Air is fed into the eight inlet ports through a collector-pipe controlled by one master butterfly valve and eight separate feeder pipes.

The fuel pump and injector nozzle are by Bosch as is also the magneto which fires two plugs per cylinder. Drive to the overhead camshafts, together with the fuel pump, is mounted amidships.

To reduce frontal height, and at the same time to provide sufficient off-set for the propellor shaft, the engine has been installed on its side, forward of the tubular spaceframe type of chassis. Just ahead of the cylinder block are the front brake drums, cooled by means of peripheral fins, connected to the wheels by universally

On their début in the 1954 French Grand Prix, the new Mercedes-Benz W196 cars shattered the opposition and Fangio and Kling took the first two places.

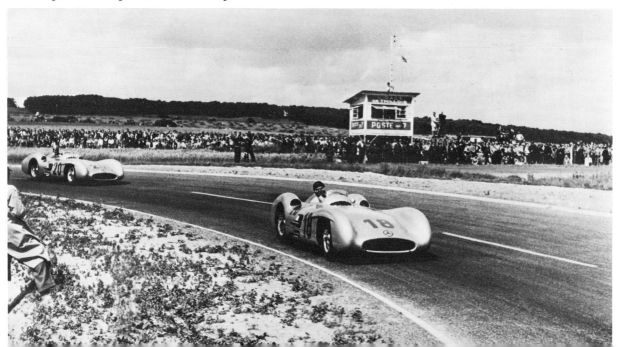

jointed shafts. The outboard universal joints take large-diameter front hubs and wheel nuts are two-lobed as against three-lobed at the rear.

The front wheels are carried on wishbones but at the rear Mercedes have remained faithful to swing-axle design, although the system has been improved and carried to its logical conclusion by mounting the wheels on arms independent of the drive-shafts and by placing the pivot point low down, under the gearbox. A form of Watts link provides fore-and-aft location and torsion bars are used all round as the axle-springing medium.

Another traditional Mercedes feature is the detachable steering wheel on a splined shaft, but quite unorthodox is the arrangement whereby the starting handle is inserted into the tail of the car to engage with the gearbox. To start the engine a fuel pump must be operated by a handle in the cockpit.

At Reims the enclosed tyres gave no trouble but care has been taken to provide air-ducts for tyre cooling whilst the aperture on the scuttle in front of the windscreen is to collect air for cooling the rear brakes. These scoops may make the body profile less efficient than it would otherwise be but there is a full-length under shield which is exceptionally smooth. Forty-four gallons of nitro-benzine-based fuel were carried at Reims, which means that the cars averaged over seven mpg – a creditable figure.

Even though the Germans dominated the race there was no doubt right to the end as to who would eventually win. During the closing stages neither Fangio nor Kling did anything to enlighten the spectators who would finish first, indeed, they were breathless at the speeds achieved whilst they swopped places every few laps. They screamed along the straights side by side and no one knew whether they were driving to team orders for an all-German win, for Fangio to finish first or whether the ultimate result was left to the two drivers. It was only when they accelerated away from Thillois Corner for the last time that Fangio put his car half-a-length ahead to cross the line first. Both cars completed a lap of honour and, ignoring the reception committee, motored straight to the paddock to go into the waiting lorries.

The Mercedes failed in the British race at Silverstone a fortnight later where Argentinian Froilan Gonzalez and Mike Hawthorn took the first two places for Ferrari. By the German Grand Prix at the Nürburgring the Mercedes team were racing cars with squarish, unstreamlined bodywork and Fangio won for Stuttgart here, in Switzerland and Italy (although Moss led the Italian race for Maserati until an oil pipe failed). Mercedes-Benz failed again in Spain in October when

It was a different story in the British Grand Prix a fortnight later and Juan Fangio struggled hard to finish third, his streamlined car battered on the oil drums that then marked Silverstone's corners. (*T. C. March*)

Hawthorn won with an improved Ferrari. On the strength of his two wins earlier in the season with Maserati and three with Mercedes-Benz Fangio won the Driver's World Championship for the second time.

At the Spanish race in 1954 the V8 Lancia D50 car designed by veteran engineer Vittorio Jano made its long awaited race début. The Lancia drivers were World Champion Alberto Ascari and veteran Luigi Villoresi. The D50 was the most technically advanced car of its time and its design features included the use of the engine as an integral stressed member with the chassis (something 're-invented' by Colin Chapman on the Lotus 49 in 1967) and pannier fuel tanks. It soon became clear that it was still far from fully developed and that the potential of the chassis was well ahead of contemporary tyre technology. The Lancias failed at Barcelona and again at Buenos Aires in January 1955, although they gained success in minor events in 1955. At Monaco Ascari's car plunged into the harbour while leading the race because of brake trouble, and the Italian World Champion was killed in a practice accident at the Monza Autodrome four days later. By this time Lancia were in deep financial trouble, the young Italian driver Eugenio Castellotti drove a single car in the Belgian Grand Prix and then the entire Lancia équipe was handed over to Ferrari.

1955

In 1955 the Mercedes-Benz team was joined by Stirling Moss, the team also competed in sports car racing and their stranglehold on the Grand Prix scene was even greater. Mercedes won both the Argentine Grand Prix and the Formule Libre Buenos Aires City Grand Prix, their sole failure was at Monaco where two of the cars retired because of engine problems and another victory followed in Belgium. Next came the horrific Le Mans race in which Levegh's Mercedes collided with Macklin's Austin-Healey, plunged into the crowd and more than 80 spectators were killed. As a result of this accident the French, German and Swiss Grands Prix were cancelled (and motor racing was permanently banned in Switzerland). The only Championship Grands Prix that remained were the Dutch, British and Italian and Mercedes-Benz won all three. Fangio and Moss took the first two places in the Driver's Championship.

In *Autosport* for 23 December, 1955 there appeared a fascinating article by Jerry Ames, former Public Relations Officer to Daimler-Benz AG in the UK. The article is reproduced with the kind permission of *Autosport*.

What Makes the 'Silver Arrows' Go

The brief incursion of Daimler-Benz into motor racing during the past two seasons could teach several very interesting lessons, which might throw light on the reasons why some racing cars that showed great promise failed to make the headway expected.

My job as Mercedes PRO in England gave me something of a bird's eye view of the Company's foreign policy and an insight in to many of the methods used by the Daimler-Benz racing organization. For I was on the receiving end of much confidential information and came to know many of the directors, designers, drivers, team manager, technicians and mechanics.

To understand the plan behind the Daimler-Benz 18 months' onslaught on the important races of 1954 and 1955, you must appreciate that this huge firm is a commercial undertaking which must make a profit. It does not go motor racing just for the fun of it!

Racing Brings World-Wide Prestige

Make no mistake, Dr Koenecke and his fellow directors are shrewd businessmen, who realize the importance of capturing world markets now, for future prosperity. Remember, this firm manufactures diesel engines, marine engines, agricultural machinery, commercial vehicles, buses and trolley buses, as well as motor cars. For all these vehicles and equipment, they sought a means of gaining rapid, world-wide prestige and sales stimulus. At the same time it was desired to test certain technical ideas under the hardest possible conditions, which, if successful, could give Daimler-Benz a tremendous lead in engineering knowledge.

Their past experience told them that a successful racing campaign, if conducted on a big enough scale, could achieve all these objects. Their chances of success were great, because still with the company were men like Nallinger, Uhlenhaut and Neubauer, men whose knowledge, experience and skill it would be difficult to match anywhere. If given a free enough hand they could produce results at least commensurate with those achieved before the war. But now Daimler-Benz stood to gain even more because of the greater world-wide interest in motor racing. The cost was to be enormous. Something like a million pounds was actually spent, but the results proved it to be money well spent, for the products of Untertürkheim gained a glamour, a prestige far greater than anything yet achieved in every useful market in the world. In Great Britain alone their sales were more than ten times greater than those of pre-war years.

Other prizes came their way. They learned much about petrol injection, desmodromic valves, suspension and brakes. And they obtained in a few months valuable engineering data that would otherwise have taken years to learn.

Now that their objectives have been gained and order books are full for a very long time ahead, the directors have decided to speed up production in every department to take the fullest advantage of their successes. However much some people may deplore their complete withdrawal from racing, looked at from a strictly business viewpoint, now is the time to consolidate their gains and cash in on receptive world markets. But Mercedes will be back again in racing with new ideas, new cars and a new challenge.

'The System' Examined

There are several reasons why Mercedes achieved the successes they did. Many are not beyond the resources or ability of British firms. Collectively they add up to a method, call it formula if you like, that could spell success for any company.

An essential point to bear in mind is that Mercedes go

motor racing in a professional manner. This entails a certain amount of discipline with regard to the preparation of the cars and for the whole team, including the drivers. It works and brings results. They abhor the slaphappy ways of some of their rivals, both British and Continental. This inefficiency by other firms or individuals has more than once made a present of a race to the Untertürkheim cars.

Pit-Work is Outmoded

To succeed in racing it is essential to start off with a good practical design that is not too complicated; this, of course, includes engine, gearbox, chassis, suspension and brakes. Mercedes nowadays are also of the opinion that if it is necessary to work on the car during a race the chances of winning are practically nil, and there must be something wrong either with the design or the preparation of the car which should have been rectified before it was entered in the race. Nor do they believe that they know all the answers about racing. The other man can, and sometimes does, teach them something, whether it is tactics or design. Let us remember that we have designers in England just as capable as the Germans, if given the opportunity.

Mercedes have found in practice that it is better to departmentalize the racing section and the team under very competent specialists.

At the head of the entire Daimler-Benz racing establishment is Dr Fritz Nallinger, who is also a director of the company. It is he who controls the racing design staff and lays down the racing policy of the firm. He decides the form the engines will take, also the final layout of the racing cars and the performance they are to produce. Needless to say he is a brilliant engineer. Although much in evidence behind the scenes in the racing shops, only rarely does he travel to races with the team. In the event of any disagreement among the drivers, team manager or racing construction department, Dr Nallinger has the last word.

Working closely with him is Dr Rudolf Uhlenhaut, also a director of the company, responsible for the construction of all racing cars, also their preparation. He too is a brilliant designer, but unlike Nallinger he travels with the team to every race and has been doing so for more than 20 years, wherever Mercedes have been racing. Consequently his experience and store of technical knowledge would be almost irreplaceable. That is the reason he is not allowed to race, although his skill as a driver matches that of Fangio and Moss. Last season he even improved on the lap record of the Nürburgring, one of the most difficult circuits in Europe.

One of his jobs is to devise any modifications on the spot, should they be necessary, and he decides on the amount of equipment and spares to be taken to a race. Unlike some of their rivals, Mercedes would rather take too

much equipment than be short of a small part that might easily cost them a race. Mercedes mechanics are taught to be independent and to provide all their working needs from their own equipment van. They are not expected to borrow from other competitors or teams. And I have never known them to be short of spares – a lead that could be followed with advantage by some British firms which have been known to try to borrow from other competitors even during a race. You can't expect to win like that.

Unlike some firms, Mercedes do not regard drivers as necessary evils and rather a nuisance. Instead, they are encouraged to take an interest in the performance and handling of their cars and report on them. Any suggestions for improvements are listened to with interest, although often drivers have suggested ideas that Uhlenhaut has already tried out at some time or other, because there are not many possibilities that escape his fertile brain. But Mercedes are great believers in comfort for their drivers and will endeavour to carry out any special wishes or alterations so far as is practicable, especially if they may help the driver to give of his best. To quote just one example; during practice for one of the Argentine races Stirling Moss happened to mention one evening to Uhlenhaut that he thought the pedal pressure needed for the brakes was a little excessive. The next morning when he went to look over his car, he found a servo motor had been fitted. A small point, but it does illustrate how well Mercedes like to look after their drivers. More British firms could adopt this attitude with advantage to themselves.

Daimler-Benz was the oldest company racing this season. It is probably true to say that it has more experience and greater technical knowledge of this subject than any other firm. They know, for instance, that it is a waste of time and money to send badly prepared cars to the starting line. The chances of success would be nil. Yet it is amazing the number of firms seriously concerned with racing who do just that. Some British organizations in the past have been guilty of sending worn-out motor cars to races time and time again. The harm it does to their reputation and to the British motor industry in general, when the public sees how badly the cars perform, is worthy of second thoughts.

Mercedes do not believe in the dangerous practice of racing tired machinery. On their Grand Prix cars they expect highly stressed parts such as engines, gearboxes and axles to run only about 600 kilometres. After that they are changed, even if the cars are thousands of miles from the factory. This usually works out to a race and one or two practice sessions.

The night before the British Grand Prix of 1955, the garage used by the team at Southport was seething with activity when I walked in at midnight. Kling's car was stripped to the frame. Seeking out Kosteletsky, Uhlenhaut's chief assistant who was in charge of all the work, I asked what was the matter, for the car had seemed to perform well during the practice that day. 'Just a routine change of engine, gearbox and axle,' he said. Apparently the car had covered its 600 kilometres and Kling was to have new units for the race. I wondered how many other competitors, British and foreign, were in a position to make such complete changes away from their own factories. Now you can begin to appreciate the importance of all the spares and equipment that Mercedes carry around to races. They don't do it for amusement, but because they have found in practice that it helps them to win.

Naturally all the major units such as engines, axles and gears are carefully inspected and thoroughly tested before being crated as spares, so that everything to be fitted whilst the car is away from the racing shops is, as far as it is humanly possible to make it, a known quantity. I was very interested to learn what became of the old engines and other units replaced. Kosteletsky told me that on arrival back at the works they are completely dismantled and carefully examined. If there are any parts not worn and really serviceable they are built up into new units. The rest is scrapped.

Not only do Mercedes send ample spare equipment to a race, but they also send enough men. For the British Grand Prix this year they sent no less than 21 mechanics, plus specialists who look after such items as injectors, fuel, tyres and brakes. Each car is under the care of a foreman with his own team of mechanics, and they in turn can call in any of the specialist technicians. But they are all under Kosteletsky, who works directly with Uhlenhaut. When the cars are ready they are handed over to the team manager, Neubauer, to race.

Many of the present generation seem to know very little about this large, dynamic personality who weighs over 20 stone. He is not a German as many people suppose but was born in Czechoslovakia. Alfred Neubauer is a trained engineer and in the early twenties was a works driver of no mean ability for Austro-Daimler. He competed in the 1922 Targa Florio for this company with distinction.

Since 1925 he has been team manager for Mercedes and has proved to be a tower of strength in their racing organization through its most successful periods. He was made a director last year. Besides being concerned with team control, tactics and lap times, he has many difficult decisions to make during a race; for instance, when to press home an attack, or when to conserve his tyres to avoid unnecessary pit stops. He also has to keep his eyes open for young drivers with a promising future and to make a move at the right moment as soon as he thinks they have the ability to win races for him.

As soon as the new season's calendar is announced, usually in October, team manager Alfred Neubauer and another director of the company carefully plan their races for the coming season. Although some firms will enter any race if the starting money is good enough, Mercedes are only interested if the race is important and there is a reasonable chance of winning. Every time the team races it is with a definite objection view; even the Formule Libre race at Buenos Aires was a full-scale exercise in testing the engines of the then unraced SLR for the Mille Miglia.

No Last-Minute Entries

Meanwhile policy, the types of events they will enter, has already been discussed with Nallinger and Uhlenhaut. When the new season's list of races has been drawn up this is submitted to the Managing Director, Dr Koenecke, and finally approved by the Board. Once this has been done, Neubauer can finalize his plans and it is very rare for him to add extra races to his list unless they affect the broad policy that the racing department is following.

An example this year was the Tourist Trophy. At the beginning of the year I had pleaded hard with both Dr Koenecke and Alfred Neubauer for cars for this race. Stirling Moss also tried to persuade them to enter, for he was keen to drive an SLR at Belfast. But the answer was 'no,' they were committed to a definite programme and there would not be the time to prepare effectively the cars for this race. Further, Neubauer, quite rightly, will not allow the cars to be controlled by anyone other than himself during a race. If he cannot lay on the full Mercedes organization he feels it must lessen the chances of victory and therefore savours of dabbling, which is not good enough for Daimler-Benz.

But after Le Mans and shortly before the British Grand Prix, when it was learned that the Panamericana race was off and Mercedes stood an excellent chance of winning the World Sports Car Championship. I received a telegram from Neubauer urgently requesting copies of the TT regulations and large-scale maps of the circuit. I despatched the regulations to him the same day and telephoned Gordon Neill of the Ulster Automobile Club in Belfast. He had also received a telegram for large-scale maps, which were despatched within a couple of days. And then the Mercedes organization swung into action arranging garage, hotel accommodation and a thousand and one jobs connected with each race that come under the team manager. But by the time the TT race was run I was no longer handling their press relations, and so did not go to Ireland with them.

This, then, was the organization behind the Daimler-Benz racing department, with specialists in every key position. However, you must remember that even with this

Stirling Moss won the 1955 British Grand Prix for Mercedes-Benz and led home a 1-2-3-4 Mercedes domination of the race. (*T. C. March*)

The 100 mph transporter used by Mercedes-Benz to rush a single car to a circuit when it was needed in a hurry.

organization the German firm does not win every time. On several occasions its cars have been severely trounced by their Italian competitors.

The System is Tested

After the war, when Daimler-Benz began to think about competitions again, it was felt that the once efficient racing department might have become somewhat rusty. Therefore with typical thoroughness it was decided to give the whole of this section a dummy run during 1952, in order to test its abilities in post-war competition. That season they decided to run in most of the important sports car races with a team of 300SLs. One fact brought to light was the remarkable lack of German drivers of top grade ability, otherwise the old organization soon seemed to settle down into its stride.

They would have liked an all-German team for prestige purposes, but quickly realized this was impossible as no German driver was capable of beating men like Fangio and Ascari, the post-war champions. Therefore they made every effort to persuade Fangio to sign up with them to lead the team.

Twenty-one years ago Mercedes had been faced with a similar problem and solved it very successfully by inducing the Italian driver, Fagioli, to act as team leader and impart some of his knowledge to the promising German drivers until they were ready to take over.

In 1954 Fangio led the new team with Kling and Herrmann supporting him. In this fashion they achieved several successes, but there were times when they only just managed to scrape home first, and twice they were beaten in no uncertain manner. So changes were decided on for the following season. Already Neubauer had his eye on Stirling Moss, whose career he had been following with interest, realizing that here was a driver who could possibly give Fangio greater support. Once the directors had agreed about the inclusion of other non-Germans in the team, Neubauer lost no time in getting in touch with Stirling Moss. Indeed some of the people at Untertürkheim were really on tenterhooks until the British driver had signed up with them.

Neubauer's wisdom was soon proved by Stirling Moss's prowess, and as the chances of finding equally skilled German drivers was becoming even more remote, other foreigners were added to the team until finally it became almost a League of Nations, with drivers from no less than six countries. But the company considered it more important for Germany to win, than for German drivers to be the winners. The essential aim at all times was international prestige.

The First Announcement

It was not until early 1954 that the company confirmed the existence of its Grand Prix cars, but stated that they would not be raced until absolutely ready.

I had known for some time that the expected target date for their first appearance was the French Grand Prix on 4 July. Meanwhile the air was full of rumours. I went to Stuttgart nearly ten days before the race, but did not see a Grand Prix car until I had been there two days. One evening one of the test drivers dashed into my hotel and asked if I would come with him as the first car was ready and it would be shown to me. I couldn't get there quickly enough, in spite of his hectic driving. Proudly the car was wheeled out and placed on the wind-tunnel rollers. Fangio's car was ready for the race at last.

The next day, Monday, I was taken to the engine test bed and shown the engine of Herrmann's car during its final period of testing. The noise defies description, as it was run up to 8500 rpm, although most of the time it was running at 7200 and that was bad enough. I found half-an-hour in that inferno of noise quite enough. The next day the whole team departed from Reims complete with travelling workshop.

During a conversation I had with Uhlenhaut before we left for the race, I learned a few technical details about the new cars and 'Rudi' very kindly worked out the maximum speed for me with the Reims gear ratios. It was 182 mph – a bit shattering for 2½-litres unblown!

After the cars had run in the first practice and a delighted Fangio had really pulverized the lap record, to the intense excitement of the crowds present, it was decided to increase the fuel tankage to allow the cars to run non-stop. Much more worrying was a modification necessary to the oiling system, which had to be incorporated without the usual thorough testing. Uhlenhaut went back to the works and brought the essential parts for the first car, Fangio's, and then rushed the completed car over to Montlhéry and gave it a hard belting for an hour. There was no time to test the other cars.

All the hard work, the skill and thorough preparation that had gone in to the cars proved to be well worth while, for the impact they made on the racing world and the general public was tremendous. But this was only a fore-runner of future successes.

One of the most helpful ideas that has proved extremely useful at courses like Monza, Monaco and Aintree is Uhlenaut's very ingenious plan of the circuit. It always accompanies the cars and drivers to the course. First, an exact scale plan of the circuit is drawn on a sheet 36 ins by 24 ins. If the details of the circuit are not known to Uhlenhaut, he can usually obtain them from Neubauer's department. The radius of every curve is plotted exactly.

Distances are clearly marked in metres. Now comes the important point. The suitable axle and gear ratios having been carefully calculated by Dr Uhlenhaut, the exact point at which drivers will change gear is marked on the chart, and the rpm which they will attain before changing up or down is also indicated. The rpm figures are shown on the chart, progressively, so that every driver will know what engine speed he should use at any point on the course. It should be appreciated that although the engine rpm are shown on the chart for perhaps every 200 or 300 yards of the course, it is not necessary for the drivers to adhere to them rigidly. They are there for guidance.

This chart is made out in Uhlenhaut's office at Untertürkheim, and enables him to work out the most suitable gear ratios for the circuit. As no two drivers handle a car exactly alike, slight changes to gear ratios are sometimes made at the request of individual drivers.

The portion of the road where the brakes will be applied is shown on the chart by shading. This scale plan of the circuit is not only very helpful to drivers, but invaluable to the technicians and people who are responsible for the brakes, as wear of the linings can be fairly accurately calculated. This is just another example of the thoroughness of the team that helps it to win races.

Perhaps the foregoing may give some idea of the importance the German firm attaches to careful preparation, and how well it pays to send only properly prepared cars to the line, with the idea of winning – not merely to draw the starting money. Grand Prix racing has changed very considerably since I first became interested, in 1925. Then, it was largely a sport and a grand spectacle. Now, it is still a grand spectacle but the sporting side has largely given way to business – the stern business of capturing world markets for an industry. Firms now race for national prestige, not just for fun. A team of racing cars must be run efficiently and with proper backing, like any other business; then it can succeed, as Daimler-Benz have proved.

When the German firm next returns to Grand Prix racing it will most likely be with turbo racing cars. The time is closer at hand than many people realize. Will we be able to challenge them successfully? We ought to be able to, because we have the designers and engineers. Surely the resources and good team management are not beyond us when the future prosperity of the British motor industry needs it?

In fact Daimler-Benz did not race again until 1988 when the company 'adopted' and gave full technical support to the Sauber team in Group C sports car racing.

The British Teams

While Mercedes-Benz were dominating racing, three British teams were taking Grand Prix racing very seriously. Tony Vandervell, founder of the Vandervell 'Thin Wall' bearing company had previously raced Grand Prix Ferraris and in 1952 had started work on his own Formula 1 contender. This featured a 4-cylinder engine with cylinder head incorporating 'Manx' Norton racing motor cycle design practice and a Rolls-Royce military crankcase and cylinder block; the gearbox incorporated Porsche synchromesh and other internals; the tubular chassis was built by Cooper Cars of Surbiton and used Ferrari – style suspension; there were Goodyear disc brakes developed in conjunction with that company's aviation division and an external surface radiator mounted on top of the nose.

The car, known as the 'Vanwall Special', first appeared in 1998 cc form with Alan Brown at the wheel in the International Trophy at Silverstone in May 1954, but retired because of a broken oil pipe. By the British Grand Prix on the same circuit in July engine capacity had been increased to 2236 cc and the driver was Peter Collins, but again the car retired, because of a leaking cylinder head joint. The first 2490 cc engine was wrecked during endurance testing on the test-bed and Collins drove the car with 2236 cc engine and conventional radiator into seventh place in the Italian Grand Prix at Monza. The car ran with success with the 2490 cc engine at Goodwood and Aintree, but Collins non-started in the Spanish Grand Prix because of a practice crash.

Mike Hawthorn had driven the 'Vanwall Special' at both Goodwood and Aintree and the works Ferrari driver was so impressed that he did not need much persuasion to join Vanwall for 1955. Originally Peter Collins had also said that he would drive for Vandervell, but had already changed his mind and signed for BRM. His place in the team was taken by competent all-rounder Ken Wharton. The cars were now known simply as Vanwalls and were fitted with fuel injection. It proved a disastrous year for the team. Wharton crashed badly in the International Trophy race at Silverstone and suffered burns that put him out of racing for two months. Hawthorn retired at Silverstone and in the Monaco and Belgian Grands

Prix. It was only too obvious that the cars were underdeveloped and on the evening of the race Hawthorn, his tongue loosened by a couple of beers too many, told Vanwall team manager David Yorke that the team was a shambles and that he no longer wished to drive for it.

In his autobiography, *Challenge Me The Race*, Hawthorn expressed the situation rather more delicately: 'We all admired the immense drive and effort Tony Vandervell had put into creating a British Grand Prix contender, at enormous expense to himself, and it was very difficult for him to accept the fact that the car was still not ready for top-line international racing, but that was the hard truth and there was still a great deal to be done before it could reach the level of performance and reliability which has since been achieved.'

Hawthorn returned to Ferrari and his place in the team was taken by Franco-American driver Harry Schell. Although the cars performed abysmally for the rest of 1955 in major international events, encouragement came from wins in minor races at Snetterton and Castle Combe.

Nineteen fifty-six was to prove another year of disappointment for the team (despite some startling performances by Schell), but the Vanwall was to prove in 1957 the car that broke the Italian stranglehold on Grand Prix Racing.

The Connaught team, based at Send in Surrey, had been involved in Formula 2 racing since 1950 and the combination of chief designer Rodney Clarke and engine specialist Mike Oliver, backed by the personal finance of Kenneth McAlpine, had produced the workmanlike, but inevitably underpowered A series car with Lea-Francis-derived engine. For 1954 Clarke secured the exclusive use of the Alta 2460 cc 4-cylinder twin overhead camshaft engine, a much improved version of the engines that had powered HWM and Alta's own Formula 2 cars. Although Clarke had ambitious designs, including a projected rear-engined Grand Prix car, for expediency he settled on a simple tubular chassis, the Alta engine, initially running on fuel injection later on Weber twin-choke carburettors, was mated to a preselector gearbox and there were Dunlop alloy wheels and disc brakes. The most striking feature of the car was the one-piece alloy streamlined full-width body, conceived independently by Clarke and not in any way influenced by Mercedes-Benz.

Harry Schell with the ever-improving Vanwall in the 1955 British Grand Prix at Aintree. This is Ken Wharton's car which Schell took over. Although Schell finished ninth – and last – he was too far behind to be classified. *(T.C. March)*

Connaught designer Rodney Clarke cleans his goggles before testing the first streamlined B-series car, B1.

In the paddock at the International Trophy meeting at Silverstone in 1955. Three mechanics hold the complete streamlined body shell of the car to be driven by Jack Fairman.

Although the new B series Connaught was first revealed to the press in the late summer of 1954 (when it was fitted with spoked wheels and drum brakes), it did not race until the Easter Monday meeting at Goodwood in 1955. Two cars appeared at Silverstone in May and throughout the year, when the cars were raced at British events only, it was obvious that they possessed immense potential. Because of financial difficulties the team was already thinking of giving up racing when an invitation was received to run in the Syracuse Grand Prix held in Sicily in October. The starting money of £1000 a car was simply too much to refuse. The following account from *Autosport*, reproduced with that magazine's permission was written by John Risely-Prichard, a close friend of driver Tony Brooks and also his entrant in British races with an older private Connaught. By this stage Connaught had decided to abandon the streamlined bodywork as impractical, mainly because of the high cost of repairs and one car had already been converted to normal 'monoposto' style.

The Syracuse Story

I did not imagine, when Tony Brooks telephoned me some 10 days before the race to tell me that he had been invited to drive a 'works' Connaught in the Syracuse Grand Prix, that this was the beginning of a headline story.

Tony takes his job very seriously and motor racing is a hobby from which he derives enormous pleasure, but he did not relish the idea of flying by himself to a country where he did not speak one word of the language, to drive a car he had never driven before on a course he had never seen. It was, however, an opportunity that he should clearly not miss, and I agreed to accompany him if Connaught's would put up with me.

Up to this time, the only single-seat racing car which Tony had driven was my four-year-old 2-litre Connaught on about six occasions during the latter part of this season, and although in each race he had driven the car superbly, a modern Formula 1 machine is quite a different proposition. However, Rodney Clarke evidently shared my complete confidence in his ability.

A day or two later, we were told that the entry had been confirmed, and that we should make arrangements to be in Syracuse not later than Thursday evening before the race for practice on the Friday and Saturday. Two cars were being sent, the open-bodied car which first appeared at the *Daily Dispatch* Gold Cup meeting at Oulton Park in Reg Parnell's hands and a streamlined machine. Les Leston was to be the other driver and he had sportingly said that as Tony had driven for Connaughts before (the 1½-litre sports car at the September Aintree meeting, when he just beat Leston in Peter Bell's car for second place in the 1½-litre race after a terrific scrap) he should have the choice of cars.

It was at the proverbial 11th hour that the organisers definitely decided to hold the race – only, in fact, after they had received confirmation of a full works Maserati team – and Connaughts had little time to prepare the cars. They were both taken to Goodwood for a final test run and loaded straight into the transporters from which they emerged, very dusty, at Syracuse about a week later after a journey of nearly 2000 miles.

When we arrived in Syracuse on the Thursday evening, there was no sign of the transporters or of Mike Oliver, that delightful and brilliant 'back-room boy' who seldom attends race meetings but who, on this occasion, came out to take charge of the team. As the first practice session on Friday approached, there was still no sign of the cars, so Tony, Les Leston and I, after much haggling in sign language (as none of us spoke Italian) hired three Vespas and proceeded to do several reconnaissance laps, much to the astonishment of the race officials and the bewilderment of the polizie who were endeavouring to clear the roads of an intelligently inquisitive local populace.

The Syracuse event is customarily the season's first Grand Prix to be held in Europe, generally in March or April – it will be remembered that Mike Hawthorn suffered burns when his Ferrari crashed in this race in April 1954 – and the lap record was held by the late Onofre Marimon in a Maserati in 2 mins 3.8 secs, a speed of 99.36 mph. This year's race was to have been over 80 laps (about 272 miles) starting at 3 pm but was reduced to 70 laps (about 238 miles) and the start put forward to 2.45 pm so that the race could be completed in daylight.

A Driver's Circuit

The circuit is situated just outside Syracuse and is approximately triangular in shape, with two slowish corners at the base of the triangle and an acute hairpin at the apex. But there is no real straight, and the three sides of the triangle are formed by a series of very fast gentle curves of the type which sorts out the very good drivers from the good, and on which Tony really excels. The road is fairly wide and the surface moderately bumpy, though definitely above average by Sicilian standards. Solid-looking concrete walls run on each side of the road for practically the entire length of the 3.4-mile circuit.

The field consisted of 15 cars of which nine were Maseratis and two each of Ferrari, Gordini and Connaught. Modena had sent a very strong works team and of these, the two to be driven by Musso and Villoresi were the latest '1956' type cars with five-speed gearbox. Schell was to drive the streamlined car which Behra drove in the Italian Grand Prix at Monza, and Shelby and Piotti made up the team. Independent Maserati entries were to be handled by Gould (in his ex-works car), Salvadori in the Gilby Engineering machine, Rosier and Volonterio. Gordini had brought with him his new eight-cylinder brainchild with enveloping body and an older 'six' to be driven by Manzon and Pollet; the field was completed by the two independent Ferraris to be driven by Scarlatti and Vidiles and, of course, the two Connaughts.

Friday's practice session ran according to form; Maseratis were obviously confident of an easy race and Musso was fastest with a lap of 2 mins 5 secs, Villoresi being only 2 secs slower. Schell was experiencing brake-fade on the streamlined car but, driving a conventional machine, both he and Shelby were the only other two drivers to get below 2 mins 10 secs. Gordinis were evidently in trouble and although the streamlined car sounded very healthy, it was clearly very slow and came in every few laps with pungent cooking smells emanating from the general direction of the disc brakes.

Dinner time that evening passed and still no sign of the Connaughts, and we began to wonder whether we would have to resort to the Vespas to collect the starting money. However, later in the evening Mike Oliver and one tender arrived; apparently there had been difficulty in obtaining the necessary permits for the vehicles to be driven across France (application is required at least 14 days in advance) and the transporters had been driven more or less continuously for five days, only for one of them to run out of brakes south of Naples. Early Saturday morning the second transporter arrived and it was a very weary team of mechanics who prepared the cars for the somewhat perfunctory ceremony of scrutineering on Saturday morning.

It was obviously desirable to keep practice to a minimum to preserve the cars for the race, consistent with giving the two drivers a chance to learn the circuit and get the feel of the cars; Mike Oliver wisely decided that Tony and Les Leston should not try each car to see which they preferred, but to allocate the 'open' car to Tony and the 'streamliner' to Les. So the last preparations for practice proceeded according to plan until, with about half an hour to go, Leston's car would not start. Trouble was located in the fuel-feed system which took over an hour to put right.

Saturday's practice commenced soon after 3 pm.

Times were rather slower than the previous day's, possibly because the Maseratis were not being really pressed, but more probably because a short stretch of the road had been resurfaced for the race, and had tended to break up during the first training session, making the approach to the last corner before the pits slippery and difficult. Musso's best time was 2 mins 7 secs and Villoresi's fractionally slower. Again Manzon's Gordini was slow, and in trouble; he eventually decided to transfer to the older car which was definitely quicker but he appeared to be having an uncomfortable ride over the bumps.

While everyone was busy with stopwatches clocking Musso, Villoresi and the rest, Tony quietly went out with the Connaught; first of all two or three relatively slow laps to get the feel of things, then 2.13, 2.10, 2.8, 2.7 and finally 2 mins 6 secs before being brought in to digest what he had learned. It had all been so smooth, so apparently lacking in fireworks that few people had any idea how quickly he had been circulating. Then came the announcement:

Reproduced spreads from *Autosport*, 4 November 1955.

'Brooks, No 22 Connaught, fastest lap of the session!' Not a murmur came from the spectators who had applauded each announcement of their idols' times. Someone faster than Musso and Villoresi! – impossible. Mercedes-Benz were not present! Smiles changed to frowns in the Maserati pits where Musso and the others grabbed their cars. This time they all tried very hard indeed, and Musso got down to 2 mins 3.8 secs to equal the lap record and the crowd was happy again. Villoresi turned in 2 mins 4.2 secs, but Tony, during another short spell, was only a second slower – in a strange car on a strange circuit. The Connaught sounded wonderful and looked immaculate and the splendid Connaught mechanics no longer looked weary. This was more like it. Even the local Sicilian Press conceded that the Connaught's excellent practice times gave promise of a good race.

In the meantime, the trouble with Leston's car had been put right but time allowed him only about eight practice laps and he sensibly concentrated on learning the circuit and the car; nonetheless, he got down to a creditable 2 mins 13 secs and was confident that he could take at least 5 secs off that time.

And so to race day: rain fell early in the morning but it soon cleared, the sun came out and the weather was just about perfect for motor racing – warm but not too hot, sunny and with little wind. The crowds began to gather all around the circuit, and the permanent grandstand opposite the pits was soon packed with excited and knowledgeable Sicilians.

The strategy was simple enough: both Tony and Les Leston still needed a little time to settle down, but we hoped that Tony would keep Musso and Villoresi in sight and within striking distance.

As the cars were formed up on the grid, it was as unusual as it was exciting to see a green car on the front row – Musso, Villoresi and Brooks. Behind, Schell and Shelby, then more red cars, with Leston and Salvadori on the fourth row.

The start was a little ragged: the starter stood at one side of the front row, next to Musso's car, and was so surrounded by his friends that hardly anyone saw him drop the flag. Tony in particular had to keep his head turned at right angles to the direction of intended motion and could not watch his rev counter. Furthermore, he had not had an opportunity to practise a start in the car. So whilst Musso and Villoresi rocketed off the line, Tony was rather slow, though Leston got away magnificently. As the noise and smoke drifted away, Gould was left on the line, having stalled his engine, but he was soon on his way, shaking his head and crouching more than usual at the wheel. This, as it turned out, may well have cost him third place.

As expected, Musso led the first time round, followed closely by Villoresi and Schell and then, to our immense excitement, Tony and Leston. After three laps, Tony passed Schell and, driving beautifully with no sign of flurry, set out to catch Villoresi who was only about 3 secs ahead. Towards the end of the fifth lap, Leston spun, denting the near-side front wing of the streamlined car, and dropped several places before getting going again. Roy Salvadori also hit one of those solid concrete walls and came in to change a badly damaged wheel and tyre.

Tony took only two laps to deal with Villoresi and the crowd could hardly believe it as he drew steadily away and closed on Musso. After 10 laps, the position was, Musso; Brooks about 1 sec behind; Villoresi; Schell; Shelby and Manzon. Salvadori came in shortly afterwards with a split fuel tank and his car was pushed away. Rosier's car was another early casualty with what appeared to be damaged rear suspension.

Then came the greatest moment I can remember for a long time in a Grand Prix – a green car was leading; Tony passed the pits with Musso hardly a car's length behind. The crowds were utterly astonished but roared their approval when Musso was back in the lead the next time round. But that was the last time he led the race. The following lap Tony was in front again but he had the unnerving experience of being followed very closely by Musso for several laps during which Tony broke the lap record once and Musso twice. Tony soon noticed that Musso was using his brakes much more than he was and, several times, as they approached the hairpin, Musso passed him on braking. But, using his head, he realised that the discs on the Connaught would out-last Musso's conventional drum brakes and anyhow, as they came out of the hairpin, it was evident that Musso could not use the lowest of his five gears so that Tony could always pass him again. Consequently, Tony realised that he had the measure of his adversary and, keeping well below his permitted rev limit, he proceeded to draw away from Musso. At 30 laps the position was:-

1, Brooks, 1 hr 2 mins 2 secs
2, Musso, 1 hr 2 mins 40 secs
3, Villoresi, 1 hr 4 mins 23 secs
4, Shelby; 5, Schell; 6, Gould

On his 35th tour, Tony lapped at 2 mins 1.5 secs, on his 55th lap, 2 mins 0.8 secs, and his 55th lap at 2 mins 0.2 secs, which now stands as the record. But throughout this time he was lapping consistently between 2 mins 1 sec and 2 mins 3 secs, and, try as he might, Musso could do nothing about it. The green car stayed between 40 and 50 secs in front. On his 38th lap, Tony passed Villoresi and, before the end of the race, he had lapped him for the second time, a fact which did not escape the attention of the crowd who were, by now, thoroughly appreciating his magnificent drive.

All this excitement rather tended to overshadow Leston's effort: at about half distance his car developed magneto trouble and three times he came into the pits for a plug change. Eventually the car sounded its usual self again and he lapped consistently at around 2 mins 8 secs and drove very well indeed. Gould, too, drove outstandingly well and gradually worked his way up to finish close behind Villoresi in fourth position.

So the race drew to a close: careful timekeeping and pit signals gave Tony a clear picture of his position in relation to Musso. At the same time, after Tony had been slowed considerably, Musso did close the gap to 32 secs but as soon as he wanted to, Tony increased the gap and finished 51 secs ahead. The Connaught had gone without falter: a hole had appeared in the exhaust manifold and the noise it made was somewhat alarming, but Tony was unaware of this and had nothing but praise for the car and the way in which it handled.

As he received his garland of victory, Tony was led from the group surrounding the car and 'presented' to the crowd who gave him a wonderful ovation. And, as people swarmed over the track, Tony, who is the most modest and retiring person in the world, quietly slid away to change out of his overalls so that he should not be recognised!

And the car was pushed away for the engine measurements to be checked by the race organisers – they were so astonished by its performance.

It was, indeed, a great occasion and it must give enormous encouragement to everyone at Send. Maseratis have, this year, proved little slower than Mercedes-Benz, so with the latter out of racing next year, who knows?

There is also, surely, an encouraging lesson to be learned from Tony Brooks's great victory; prior to this season he has driven and gained his experience in club meetings, firstly in a Silverstone Healey and then in a Frazer Nash.

John Wyer spotted him and gave him a chance in the Aston Martin team for whom he has driven with great distinction this season. And now, after only a few drives in an obsolescent 2-litre racing car, he has beaten the experienced Maserati team in his first Formula 1 race – a feat indeed. But in spite of the universal acclaim and his now proven brilliance, he is still as quiet, unassuming and charming as ever.

By 1956 Connaught's financial situation was such that the team was restricted to running in races purely to raise money. It had been hoped that the Syracuse success would attract major sponsorship, perhaps from the British motor industry which was then flourishing, but sponsorship never came. Although the fuel and

A brilliant driver despite his physical handicap: Archie Scott-Brown with the B-series Connaught, now with unstreamlined bodywork, that he drove into second place in the 1956 International Trophy at Silverstone. (*T. C. March*)

tyre companies supported motor racing, sponsorship in the modern sense was unknown. During 1956 Archie Scott-Brown (a brilliant driver not in the least handicapped by a malformed right arm, with no proper hand, but a stump of a forearm with partial palm and thumb) finished second in the International Trophy race at Silverstone with a B series car, Fairman took fourth place in the British Grand Prix and Flockhart and Fairman finished third and fifth in the Italian Grand Prix. Despite the formation of a Connaught Supporters Club, the team withdrew from racing after the 1957 Monaco Grand Prix and the cars and equipment were later auctioned. Tony Brooks joined BRM in 1956 and then moved on to Vanwall.

After their disastrous years with the V16 cars, BRM chose the road of simplicity for their new 2500 cc Grand Prix contender and like the Vanwall and Connaught it used a 4-cylinder engine. This was the basic design of freelance engineer Stuart Tresilian, massively oversquare at 102.87×74.93 mm (2497 cc), and used with a 4-speed gearbox, multi-tubular space-frame chassis, magnesium body skin, double wishbone front and de Dion rear suspension with oleo-pneumatic air struts and disc brakes – at the rear chief designer Peter Berthon had opted for the idiosyncratic feature of a single disc brake acting on the transmission.

Peter Collins was contracted to drive for BRM in 1955, but the car was not ready until late in the year. It non-started at Aintree after a practice crash and retired at Oulton Park. For 1956 BRM signed up Mike Hawthorn and Tony Brooks, but a succession of braking problems and valve trouble were followed by Brooks' disastrous crash at the British Grand Prix when the throttle jammed open after a bodged repair in the pits. Roy Salvadori signed up to lead the team in 1957, but withdrew after failing to qualify because of brake problems at Monaco. By the middle of 1957 no self-respecting driver seemed prepared to handle a BRM. However, Jean Behra drove a BRM to victory in the minor 1957 Caen Grand Prix and in the absence

of serious opposition BRMs took the first three places in the International Trophy at Silverstone later that year. Behra and Harry Schell drove for BRM in 1958 and although they did much to restore the morale of this floundering team and scored a few places, including second and third in the Dutch race, it was not until 1959 that BRM scored its first World Championship race victory.

1956

By 1956 racing had reverted to its former status of a duel between Ferrari and Maserati. Ferrari was now racing the Lancia V8 cars in modified form and with a strong team of drivers that included Juan Fangio and Peter Collins won all the year's Championship races, but two – the Monaco and Italian Grands Prix, in both of which Stirling Moss crossed the line first with

Mike Hawthorn testing at Folkingham early in 1956 with the new BRM P25, characterised by its squat, pugnacious lines.
(*T. C. March*)

The season proved disastrous for BRM and culminated in Brooks' horrific crash in the British Grand Prix when the throttle jammed open – the result of a botched repair in the pits. (*T. C. March*)

a Maserati 250F. Fangio won his fourth World Championship for Ferrari.

Since 1955 the Vanwalls had been almost completely redesigned with a new space-frame and suspension by Colin Chapman and remarkably sleek and aerodynamic body with long tapering nose, exhaust manifolding recessed into the body to reduce drag and completely smooth under-surface designed by Frank Costin. Despite continuing mechanical problems, Vanwall was banging on the door and Harry Schell finished fourth in the Belgian Grand Prix on the very fast Spa-Francorchamps circuit.

Because his second driver, Maurice Trintignant, had been released to drive the new and unsuccessful Bugatti in the French Grand Prix at Reims, Vandervell arranged for 1950 World Champion Giuseppe Farina to drive the second car and a third car was entered for Colin Chapman, a brilliant design engineer and head of the Lotus sports car company, who had redesigned the Vanwall for 1956 on a consultancy basis. Farina, however, crashed badly in a sports car race and was unable to drive.

The 1956 French Grand Prix

(from *Vanwall* by Denis Jenkinson and Cyril Posthumus, Patrick Stephens Limited, 1975 and reproduced with that company's kind permission)

Once more the team was back to two drivers. There was no shortage of offers, many from well-known drivers but not with the ability that Tony Vandervell required, but for once luck was on his side. BRM had not entered for the French GP so Mike Hawthorn was unemployed, though he was going to Reims to take part in the 12 hour sports car race with Jaguar. Ever since they had parted company just over 12 months ago, relations between Vandervell and Hawthorn had remained amicable, and it did not take long for Mike to agree to replace the injured Farina. When practice began Tony Vandervell must have begun to wonder just how deep he was going to get in to this Grand Prix racing business. There were three immaculate cars in

The front row of the starting grid at the 1956 British Grand Prix with, from camera, Moss (Maserati), Fangio (Lancia-Ferrari), Hawthorn (BRM) and Collins (Lancia-Ferrari). (*T. C. March*)

front of the pits, representing a face value of 1956 of £30,000, to say nothing of the cost of research and development or overheads. He would never commit himself to an estimate of how much his racing team had cost him and, when newspapers quoted figures like a quarter of a million pounds, he would grunt and say 'What do they know about running a racing team?' When the *Sunday Dispatch* published an article saying Vandervell had spent a million pounds on his racing the Editor, Walter Hayes, now Vice-President of public affairs for Ford of Europe, received such a strong letter from GAV that he was forced to apologise. Hayes, who subsequently instigated the whole Ford-Cosworth Formula 1 engine project, has since done more than his fair share to foster the sport of Grand Prix motor racing!

Although GAV flew to Reims in his de Havilland Dove, he had his personal Bentley taken out in company with the racing transporters as he did not like hire-cars, for they were invariably small and mean. The French GP of 1956 can best be described as a landmark in the history of Britain in Grand Prix racing and a turning point in the history of the Vanwall. From the moment practice started Schell and Hawthorn showed just how quick the cars were. The opposition were hard-pressed to beat the two green cars, and the sun seemed to be shining on Tony Vandervell as well as on the spacious fields of the Marne. Naturally Chapman was not up with the other two, never having driven at speeds like these before, the lap speed being 124 mph. On the second practice day he was having brake trouble on the new car and while running in close company with Hawthorn the rear brakes failed and he hit Mike's car up the back as they slowed for the sharp Thillois hairpin. This set-back left Schell alone in the battle for a good grid position, which he achieved, getting into the second row for the start amidst a sea of red cars. Hawthorn's car was repaired in time for the race, but Chapman's was too badly damaged and his Grand Prix debut ended there and then. Mr Vandervell was not amused, to say the least.

If practice had proved the pace of the Vanwall, the race was truly memorable. Harry Schell's car suffered gearbox maladies and then the engine gave trouble due to overrevving while trying to drive without second gear so he pulled in and took over Hawthorn's car. Mike had been up all the previous night driving in the 12 hour sports car race, and was not feeling very bright, and so tagged along at the back of the field. Harry Schell in contrast was on great form and, once in Hawthorn's car, he began to overhaul the back markers and gain ground on the leading trio of Lancia-Ferraris, whose drivers thought he was a lap behind. Reaching 175 mph down the hill to the Thillois hairpin Schell gained on the red cars at a phenomenal rate and it was not until he was amongst them, taking second place

In the 1956 French Grand Prix at Reims the works Lancia-Ferraris lined up abreast to prevent Harry Schell (Vanwall) from taking the lead.

momentarily, that the Ferrari pit realised he was on the same lap and gave their drivers the panic signal. By now Schell was really wound up tight, his pit were urging him on and the French crowd were standing up cheering the American from Paris, for never before had a British car been seen to challenge the might of Italy like this. Try as they might, the Ferrari men, Fangio, Collins and Castellotti, could not get rid of the tenacious Franco-American driver and his sleek green car. They pulled out all the tricks of team driving to shake him off, deliberately blocking his path, edging him on to the grass verge, baulking him and generally playing it a bit rough, which was more than Harry could cope with. For lap after lap this glorious battle continued, then gradually the green Vanwall dropped back from the red cars, slowed dramatically and headed for the pits. Part of the control rod system to the fuel injection pump was collapsing and though Schell had the throttle pedal down on the stop the mixture control was not opening fully and finally the control linkage broke. A repair was made and Schell rejoined the race, now too far back to do any good and he came home tired and dirty but elated, in next to last position, sure in the knowledge that if the Ferrari team had not used team tactics on him he would have led the French Grand Prix.

Tony Vandervell was in a really belligerent mood after the race, furious at the way the Ferrari team had rough-housed his driver. While quaffing champagne at the bar behind the pits he said to Denis Jenkinson, joint author of his book and Continental Correspondent of *Motor Sport,* who had been rooting for the Vanwall team all along, 'What are we going to do about that bloody Ferrari team? Someone should put in a protest about the way they drove.' The *Motor Sport* man, who had watched that sort of racing with the gloves off between Ferrari and Alfa Romeo, and Ferrari and Maserati, and who really enjoyed Grand Prix racing with no holds barred, said 'Guv'nor, they wouldn't have got away with that if Stirling Moss had been in your car; he'd have found a way by, even if it was over the top'. 'That's no way to go motor racing' roared GAV. 'Oh yes it is', said Jenkinson, 'that really is Grand Prix racing, and what you have got to do is get three drivers like Moss in your cars and do the same to the Ferrari team.' At that the 'old man' gave a snort, drank up his champagne and trundled off to his waiting Bentley.

He did not commiserate with Harry Schell, nor did he pat him on the back for having a good go, but later on when the accounts were being done he sent Harry all the starting money for the French GP, £550 instead of the 50% which his contract stipulated. There was no word of explanation, merely a detailed account of the figures. Schell's reply was so true and sincere. It said 'Thank you for the wonderful gesture of Reims; only you could have done that', and it was written on the back of a menu from a German restaurant!

1957

For 1957 Juan Fangio, after a thoroughly miserable year with Ferrari, rejoined Maserati who were racing a much improved version of the familiar 250F. Ferrari was still racing the Lancia-Ferrari, known now as the Tipo 801, but the team failed to win a single World Championship race. The ever-improving Vanwall team was now led by Stirling Moss and he was partnered by the brilliant Tony Brooks. Later a third car was entered for Stuart Lewis-Evans.

Juan Fangio (Maserati 250F) in the 1957 British Grand Prix. The Argentinian won his fifth World Championship in 1957, Aintree was not one of his better races and he retired because of engine problems. (*T. C. March*)

The Vanwalls

(from *Stirling Moss, My Cars, My Career* by Stirling Moss with Doug Nye, Patrick Stephens Limited, 1987 and reproduced with that company's kind permission)

Like Maserati, Vanwall had been running Pirelli tyres, but Pirelli wanted to withdraw and only reluctantly continued to supply. Meanwhile, Dunlop had made great progress with a new R4 design using nylon cord casing which proved superior to contemporary Pirellis in the wet, and only marginally slower in the dry.

Stirling Moss with the Vanwall at Siracusa in 1957. Tony Vandervell stands by the cockpit. Stirling's father, Alfred, is at the front of the car watching the opposition.

Our first race came on 7 April at Syracuse, Sicily. I qualified my car – 'VW1' – on the front row once we geared it properly, and I took the lead and was able to extend it by a second a lap as the car was running beautifully. After 32 laps my lead was 35 secs, but then the four-cylinder engine's vibration cracked a fuel injector pipe. I lost four laps before rejoining seventh. Tony's car had a water pipe split; it overheated and cracked the cylinder head. I managed to regain two laps on Collins' leading Ferrari and set a new lap record, but could only finish third.

This had been a frustrating début, but the Vanwall's potential was clear. Then Easter Monday Goodwood saw more frustration. My car felt great in practice, pulling 7700 rpm on 6.50 section tyres and holding 7000 rpm out of the long curve at Fordwater. I led for 13 of the 32 laps until its throttle linkage broke on Lavant Straight, while Tony's had already parted after just four laps – though he subsequently rejoined.

Everybody in the Vanwall racing shop, from The Old Man down, displayed enormous determination to succeed, and there was no doubting his dissatisfaction after Syracuse and Goodwood. For Monaco, on our recommendation, they adopted more steering lock, more torque low down for the tight corners and cut-back 'Monaco noses' to avoid damage to the normal long beak. To resist vibration new Palmer Silvoflex injector pipes were used, and the same material was adapted to form a flexible joint in the throttle shaft.

Unfortunately, early in Monaco practice I rammed the chicane, bending 'VW5's' chassis, steering and suspension. I took over Tony's car, 'VW3', with my engine installed and managed a good start from the outside of the front row and led for three laps with Fangio and Collins in my mirrors, then Tony fourth. Approaching the chicane I hit the brake pedal as normal, and I swear there was a system failure. The team said they could find no problem later, but I am adamant the front brakes had gone when I hit that pedal.

The now over-braked rears instantly locked, and my only course was to go straight on, smashing through a pole-and-sandbag barrier, crushing 'VW3's' nose and breaking mine against its steering wheel. Collins and Hawthorn crashed their Ferraris in the general confusion, Fangio – of course – dodged through completely unscathed and went on to win for Maserati, while Tony turned his right hand into something resembling a plate of raw meat on the Vanwall's agricultural gear-change as he drove home into a secure second place, scoring Vanwall's first points of the year.

Unfortunately, Tony then crashed his Aston Martin at Le Mans and was unfit to drive the Vanwall at Rouen and Reims. . . and so was I.

After Le Mans I had gone down to La Napoule near Cannes for a few days' holiday with my fiancée, Katie Molson. I had been water-skiing which I very much enjoyed. I was trying to monoski backwards, but as I turned, the plume of water ripping off the ski blasted straight up my nose. It was very painful, and when we arrived at Rouen next day for the French GP, I went straight to hospital instead, with a terrible sinus infection.

Roy Salvadori and Stuart Lewis-Evans took our places at Rouen and Reims, and Stuart performed so brilliantly he secured a permanent number three position in our team.

I was discharged from the London Clinic just a couple of days before travelling to Aintree for the British GP. Tony was still battered and sore, and in Thursday practice I tried all three cars but Fangio and Behra's Maseratis were faster. Next day both Tony and I qualified on the front row, with Stuart just a second slower.

I managed to lead at the end of the opening lap in 'VW1', and settled down to draw away. Stuart and Tony ran 5-6 by the twenty-lap mark, at which time I had 9 sec lead from Behra. But a lap later my engine fluffed and misfired. I stopped to have an earth wire ripped out and rejoined seventh, but the car was still sick so I stopped again. We had arranged for Tony to hand over his car – 'VW4' – to me if necessary, because he was not fit enough to drive the whole ninety laps. He came straight in and was helped from the cockpit so I could take over. The stop cost 13 sec. Tony took over my original car and soon retired it with magneto trouble, while I had resumed ninth.

By lap thirty, I was seventh. Behra led by over a minute. Four laps later I passed Fangio, and Stuart meanwhile passed Collins into third place. I closed on Musso and passed him on lap forty for fifth place, six laps later taking Collins for fourth. David Yorke signalled me '−55 secs' from Behra. On lap 51 Jean lowered the lap record to 2:00.4, but two laps later I managed 1:59.2 – the first 90 mph lap at Aintree. With 22 laps to go I was 28 sec behind.

On lap 69 I caught and passed Stuart for third, and at that moment Behra's clutch disintegrated and Mike Hawthorn, in second place, ran over some of the pieces and punctured a tyre. This was a fantastic stroke of luck for our team, and it left myself and Stuart running 1-2 in the British Grand Prix in our green Vanwalls, with twenty laps to go.

That was a marvellous moment; one I had dreamed about for years. But it did not last. Two laps later Stuart stopped with his throttle linkage adrift, and now I was leading Musso's Ferrari by over a minute, but feeling terribly alone.

With ten laps to go I stopped for some fuel as a precaution and rejoined with 41 secs still in hand over

A great victory. Stirling Moss after taking the chequered flag at Aintree in 1957 to win in the British Grand Prix. It was the first victory in a Grande Épreuve by a British car since Segrave's win in the 1923 French Grand Prix. (*T. C. March*)

Musso. I took no chances at all in those final laps, and eventually took the flag to win at a record 86.8 mph – Tony and I thus becoming jointly the first British drivers to win a *Grand Épreuve* in a British car since Segrave for Sunbeam at Tours in 1923. . . and also the first all-British winners of a British Grand Prix.

Stuart finished seventh but was disqualified for leaving his car's bonnet out on the course after reconnecting his throttles, which we thought was rather harsh.

Tony Vandervell was delighted and we were absolutely thrilled. It meant an awful lot to me, particularly after having missed two races through my own fault by larking about on a water-ski. That evening I made a brief TV broadcast, then drove off with Ken Gregory and his fiancée to dinner in Chester and bed at 1am in the Kenilworth Motel, ending one of the most satisfying days of my entire career.

But yet again, a high note was followed by a flop.

The Vanwalls' taut suspension was totally unsuitable for the Nürburgring, where they took a fearful hammering, Stuart crashed, I finished a distant fifth and Tony was ninth, having been sick in the cockpit. We were both stiff, sore and worn out but my engine never missed a beat and on the last lap along the hump-back straight in a battle with Behra which I won by one second I saw 7600 rpm in top.

These basically stable understeering cars had to be driven between very precise limits and were never as forgiving, indeed delightful, in their handling characteristics as the essentially oversteering Maserati 250Fs. Sometimes one could lift an inside front wheel and I rarely found another car so sensitive to damper settings and fine tyre differences, but the change from transverse leaf spring to coil spring rear suspension had undoubtedly been a great leap forwards.

Those Goodyear disc brakes were as good as any I had tried to that time, while the problematic flat-spots in the engine power curve would diminish as development progressed. We would be better prepared for Nürburgring the following year, but what never improved was the agricultural nature of that hefty gear-change.

Since the Belgian and Dutch GPs' cancellation, the Italians were allowed to add the Pescara GP to the Championship. Ferrari sent only a single car for Musso because of the hoo-ha following de Portago's Mille Miglia crash, but Maserati fielded four works 250Fs.

In practice there my Vanwall – 'VW5's' – high back-axle ratio and 17-inch rear tyres gave only 6900 rpm instead of the normal 7200-plus. I started from the front row alongside Musso and Fangio.

There were still mechanics on the grid when the flag dropped and Musso made the best start but I was on his tail with Fangio some way behind. Tony had the wretched luck to have his engine fail on the opening lap. Meanwhile, I found a way past Musso on lap two and then held the lead relatively easily to the end. Apart from fluctuating oil pressure, which made me stop to add oil, the Vanwall never missed a beat. Fangio could not make contact and I beat him by over three minutes. Stuart was fifth after tyre problems, but now we had proved that the Vanwall could win on a classical road circuit, and we had at last beaten what Tony Vandervell called 'Those bloody red cars' on their own soil. Another deeply satisfying moment.

The Italian GP itself followed at Monza, where practice went sensationally well for us, with Stuart on pole from myself and Tony so our three British-green Vanwalls lined-up 1-2-3, with Fangio adding just a dash of Italian red on the outside of the front row. Our cars completely outclassed the Ferraris, and the race became a straight fight – Vanwall versus Maserati.

As far as I was concerned, the terrific early slipstreaming battle between outselves and the Maseratis seemed to be resolved on lap thirteen.

My gearbox began to hang-up between gears and I lost ground, but after four laps of worry it somehow cleared. Tony's throttle had begun to stick and he made a pit stop. I led again from Stuart, until his steering tightened and he stopped to investigate, so I was left with five seconds' lead over Fangio and Behra, but again worried about Vanwall reliability.

There was no need. By lap forty I was nearly 18 sec clear of Fangio, and when he changed tyres I moved nearly a full lap ahead. I began to relax, able now to ease off and conserve my car.

With ten laps to go, as at Aintree and Pescara, I made a precautionary pit stop – this time to add some oil and fit fresh rear tyres – and then there was the chequered flag. I had just won Vanwall's third Grand Prix of the season, and at the heart of Italian motor racing. Fangio finished second, Tony seventh. Fangio and I between us had won every World Championship round, and I was thus second to him in the Drivers' table for the third successive year.

If only I had not tried to water-ski backwards at La Napoule I could have run in the French Grand Prix, and who knows what might have been the outcome then?

I demonstrated 'VW5' briefly at the September Goodwood meeting, but its engine blew out a spark plug after only five laps, not having been touched since Monza, which rather left me with egg on my face since the demo had been more my idea than Vanwall's!

Only the non-Championship Moroccan GP remained, at Casablanca, but I developed Asian 'flu during practice and flew home before the race.

Fangio's greatest race – probably the greatest of his long career – was in the 1957 German Grand Prix, a race that saw Vanwall in disarray and victory nearly go to the Lancia-Ferraris of Mike Hawthorn and Peter Collins.

The 1957 German Grand Prix

(from *My Twenty Years of Racing* by Juan Manuel Fangio in collaboration with Marcello Giambertone, Temple Press Limited, 1957)

That race changed the usually staid, even stolid, German spectators into a yelling crowd that could have been taken for South American, judging by its noisy reactions. On the starting grid was a trio of real champions, Collins, Musso and Hawthorn, driving Ferraris, impeccably serviced by factory engineers who had tuned the cars with loving care. It was also known that the three Ferraris could do without tyre changes or refuelling for the duration of the race. In contrast, the Maserati tyres were not certain to last the race, although they would hold the road better. In addition, there was the refuelling problem. Factors like these gave the Ferraris at least one minute's advantage on the Maseratis. During the practice, Fangio set a new lap record. So, as far as speed itself was concerned, there was no problem. But what would happen during the race?

Flagged away, twenty-three cars went off like rockets to cover twenty-two laps, or a total distance of 310 miles. From the third lap, Fangio was in front, trying to build up a good lead on the Ferraris of Hawthorn and Collins, his two most dangerous rivals. Half-way through the race, Juan had a 28-second lead, not enough to let him rest on his laurels as he had to refuel.

The next time round, Fangio stopped at the pit. Refuelling, plus a tyre change, cost him 56 seconds. Meanwhile, Collins and Hawthorn rapidly went out in front. The moment was dramatic. Before Juan took off again, I leaned over and spoke to him.

'Listen . . . Can you take it a bit easy for two laps and not go flat out until Bertocchi gives you a go-ahead signal?'

The old racing fox Juan caught on and was about to smile. I tightened my grip on his arm and whispered, 'Don't smile. Look serious. Shake your head. You're being watched . . .'

Fangio played his part marvellously and behind his goggles his eyes sparkled with joy. He started again, and immediately it was clear to all that things were not going well.

On the next lap his driving made it all too evident that his Maserati was not right. A mechanic in our pit, not in on the game, danced with frustration and let loose a flood of

Italian curses. The stop-watches showed that Collins and Hawthorn, lapping together, were 38.3 seconds ahead of Fangio.

I must admit that I was trembling inside. What if the tactics I had suggested proved too risky? If Fangio lost because of my advice I could never have forgiven myself. Tavoni, one of Enzo Ferrari's best men, was in charge of their team. How could I hope that he would snap at the bait?

Tavoni was hooked. After two laps covered rather slowly by Fangio, no sign or signal went up at the Ferrari pit. Then, as Hawthorn and Collins came by for the third time, I saw a mechanic hold up the blackboard with a signal. I knew what it meant: SLOW UP. KEEP AN EVEN PACE. FANGIO IS LOSING SECONDS.

The two well-disciplined Englishmen obeyed that order, slowing down to spare their engines.

The Nürburgring circuit is 14.2 miles long. To cover it, the cars take between nine and ten minutes. Once a signal is given by a pit, the order cannot be changed until the next time round. In the interval, many things can happen.

Two things happened. Bertocchi made a slight gesture to Fangio the next time he passed. Juan nodded to show he had understood. Just beyond the Ferrari pit, Fangio let loose the most spectacular pursuit of his life. The record was broken on every lap. Meanwhile the two English drivers, convinced they were not threatened, peacefully continued on their way without pushing. During that time, Fangio was making sensational lap times: 9 minutes 25.3 seconds . . . 9 minutes 23.4 seconds . . . finally 9 minutes

17.4 seconds beating the absolute record he himself had established in 1956. Some hundred thousand spectators massed around the circuit roared their encouragement, while at the microphone, one German reporter, Heinz Schaaf, was shaking with excitement.

Finally, the Ferrari pit caught on to the trick and ran up the alarm signal: FLAT. But it was too late. On the lap before the last, Fangio roared up to Hawthorn and Collins, passing them right on the bend. And who could catch Juan again that well-favoured day?

I watched him cross the line in triumph. I was delighted and Andreina, relieved and happy, turned and kissed me. Many drivers congratulated and embraced Juan, still excited by the wave of emotion sweeping over everyone. He was being congratulated, not only for winning the race, but also because he was now virtually world champion for the fifth time. He was the first to achieve it and, since then, no one else has had such spectacular success.

1958

Nineteen fifty-eight was to prove a year of momentous change in Grand Prix racing. The fuel companies wanted cars to run on ordinary pump petrol, as this was obviously better for publicity purposes. This was unacceptable to the racing teams and so a compromise was reached whereby cars would run on 100-130-octane Av-gas (aviation fuel). For several constructors, including Vanwall, this caused major problems because of the difficulty of conversion from running on exotic fuel mixtures to relatively ordinary petrol. In addition race distances were now 300 to 500 km *and* 2 hours. Together these moves encouraged the development of the new breed of lightweight cars, the ancestry of which lay in the introduction of the 1500 cc Formula 2 at the beginning of 1957 (a few races were held in Britain to this formula in 1956). When two drivers shared a car, no Championship points were now awarded.

Maserati had now withdrawn from Formula 1 for financial reasons, although an improved and lighter version of the 250F known as the 'Piccolo' was driven by Juan Fangio in his last race before finally retiring, the 1958 French Grand Prix. Ferrari was now racing the 2417 cc Dino V6 cars, derivatives of the team's Vittorio Jano-designed Formula 2 car first raced in Formula 1 form in late 1957. Facing Maranello was Vanwall with the same team of drivers as in 1957, together with

Juan Fangio in the 1957 German Grand Prix.

BRM, Cooper and Lotus. The 2-litre rear-engined Coventry Climax-powered Cooper, another Formula 2 derivative proved amazingly successful in the early part of the year. With privately owned Rob Walker-entered cars Stirling Moss won in the Argentine (Vanwall had not entered because of their engine conversion problems) and Maurice Trintignant at Monaco after the failure of the Ferrari and Vanwall opposition. Later in the year Salvadori with a works-entered car finished third in the British Grand Prix, second in the German race and fourth in the Italian race at Monza. It was very much a portent for the future.

In the World Championship it was very much a needle battle between Moss (Vanwall) and Hawthorn (Ferrari). Moss won the Dutch Grand Prix (Hawthorn fifth), Hawthorn was second in Belgium (Moss retired) and Hawthorn won the French Grand Prix (Moss second). Collins won from Hawthorn at Silverstone to give a Ferrari 1-2 result. It was however proving a

season of horror for Ferrari, for Luigi Musso, allegedly under pressure from gambling creditors, crashed with fatal results in the French race at Reims and Hawthorn's great friend, 'mon ami mate' Peter Collins was killed in Germany. Somehow poor Hawthorn kept control and after retiring in Germany (where Brooks with a Vanwall was the winner) he finished second in Portugal where Moss won. It was an ironic second place, for Hawthorn was almost disqualified – and Moss helped prevent that disqualification by giving evidence in his support. On his penultimate lap (Moss' last lap) Hawthorn spun off in front of Moss and push-started his stalled car on the pavement against the direction of the race. If Hawthorn had been disqualified Moss would have won the World Championship... Next came the Italian Grand Prix in which Hawthorn finished second to Brooks despite a slipping clutch and Moss retired. There remained one race and the story is best told by Hawthorn himself.

Peter Collins on his way to his last victory, in the 1958 British Grand Prix with the 246 Dino. He crashed with fatal results in his next race, the German Grand Prix. (*T. C. March*)

The 1958 Moroccan Grand Prix

(from *Champion Year* by Mike Hawthorn, reissued by Aston Publications Limited, 1989)

1957 was the first time the Moroccan race had been run and the trip out had not been too good with a cramped and most uncomfortable flight by Air France to Casablanca with no food on board but cheese sandwiches. I had been wondering what to do about getting there this year when David Yorke, the Vanwall team manager telephoned me to say that Tony Vandervell had chartered a Viscount from BEA for the trip and would I like a seat? I jumped at the chance. Such was the interest that the race had caused that there was another charter flight going out on a DC-6, but I thought the Viscount would be more comfortable. Lofty England also came out with me. He had telephoned me a week or two before to tell me that by some strange coincidence he found it necessary to go out to Casablanca and have a look at the Jaguar sales organisation there and found that it coincided with the Grand Prix. I said that it reminded me of that other classic case of coincidence; the football enthusiast whose grandmother used to die regularly every year and was always buried on the day of the Cup Final at Wembley! I was very happy about this because Lofty is one of the greatest team managers in racing and the thought of having him in the pit for this vital race was a most comforting one. Although Tavoni, too, is a very good team manager, it would mean a lot to me to have Lofty standing by.

Rodney Walkerley came out with us as well, forsaking for the first time his usually stately form of progress to and from the Grand Prix. Another friend of mine, Mary Taylor Young, flew out with us, as her parents, Mr and Mrs Martineau, having set out to drive to Casablanca in their 3.4 Jaguar, had had an accident near Barcelona – the car had been damaged quite badly and Rosemary Martineau had had her left arm broken. However, as soon as it was put into plaster she insisted on going on to Casablanca for the race and so Mary came out to look after her mother. We found them already installed in the Maharba Hotel, which was very modern and American in style, like most of the hotels there.

We arrived on the Thursday and were all dining in the hotel that evening when Tavoni came in and gave me the entry list to look at. The sight of it really upset me for I had been given the number 2. Phil Hill had 4 and Gendebien 6. No doubt it was partly due to nerves, but as Peter and Luigi had both been killed with the number 2 on the car I asked Tavoni to have it altered. He soothed me down and said I could have 6, and he would ask the organisers to give Gendebien a number at the other end. However, Olivier Gendebien agreed to take my 2 as he said he wasn't

Mike Hawthorn at Casablanca in 1958. This is a practice photograph, for in the race he wore a tinted visor.

superstitious.

Next morning we went out to our garage to look at the cars. I had my Italian Grand Prix car as before with the Dunlop disc brakes and Phil's car was the lighter Formula 2 chassis with the normal Dino 246 engine and the diagonally finned front brake drums. Gendebien's car was the Monza 500 car, but it was now being tried out with Girling disc brakes. As we went in I could see Phil's car with 4 on it, and Gendebien's with 6, but there was a cover over mine. Oh hell, I thought, number 2 is on it and I just daren't look. Once again Tavoni calmed me down saying it was quite all right because no number had been painted on my car at all. I must admit that I was behaving much more like an Italian than an Englishman, and Tavoni was being the calm, phlegmatic type, soothing his temperamental driver!

Ranged against us for this final and decisive event were three Vanwalls with Tony Brooks and Lewis-Evans backing up Stirling, whilst BRM had no less than four cars, two for Behra and Schell as usual, a third car for Ron Flockhart, now recovered from his accident in Rouen in 1957, and a fourth car for the Swedish driver, Bonnier. In all there were 25 starters as the organisers were running a Formula 2 race in conjunction with the Grand Prix. This helps to make up a good field, but many of the Grand Prix drivers were not too happy about the mixture, and I was one of them. I just do not agree that one can mix fast cars and much slower ones. The line you take on a fast bend is the same for both Formula 1 and 2 cars, but the latter are doing anything up to 30 mph less and it is asking for trouble to come up behind one with such a speed differential.

The Ain-Diab circuit measures 4.7 miles and is a pretty fast circuit. The start and pits, like Portugal, are opposite the Atlantic Ocean; from there one goes round a right-hand corner which winds inland and uphill to another right-hander on to the back straight, which like every straight past the pits, is very fast. This leads on to a vicious right-hander, quite fast and very nasty late in the day as the sun sinks and shines straight into your eyes; then there are a left- and right-hander, both of them fast, bringing you back along the straight parallel with the seashore.

The first day's practice was on Friday afternoon in hot sunshine and I went out fairly quickly to get acclimatized, trying both the disc-braked cars; I preferred my own Dunlops as the Girlings were a little disappointing. They had not got the ratio quite right and the back was tending to lock up quite badly. This was fixed before the race and Gendebien told me that they were very good indeed. Behra set fastest time with the BRM in 2 min 25.2 sec, then Tony was next fastest, then me, then Stirling – nobody was really belting round, but just getting used to things again. The sun was very tricky as also was the sea mist which would suddenly envelope the circuit. It didn't make the circuit dangerous, but it was a little difficult to see at times and the salt tended to stick on my visor. To counteract the glare of the sun we had the Perspex air-intake covers painted a matt black and also the top of the cockpit inside the wrap-round windscreen. I had a dark visor made as well to fight the glare and this worked very well.

Tavoni was delighted to have Lofty in the pit to help. The race was going to need the most accurate timekeeping and signalling so that I could be informed exactly where everyone was. If I was second, I wanted to know how far ahead the first car was and how far back the third; I also wanted to know if anybody was coming up through the field quickly. I was going to drive for second place, which was what I needed to win, whereas Stirling would have to go all out to win and make fastest lap.

Saturday's session once again took place in the afternoon, but a sea mist had reduced visibility enormously, though the dampness was assisting carburation; lap times came down quite a lot and I set fastest time with 2 min 23.1 sec, just a tenth of a second quicker than Stirling. Lewis-Evans was not much slower, but Tony was in the third row, Stirling having taken over his car in preference to the much-lightened machine that had been specially prepared for him. Between the two sessions I had had my axle ratio lowered and this gave me much better acceleration out of the corners; I felt much more confident for the following day.

At one time on the Saturday, Phil and Gendebien had both set better times than me, but I finally got my time down all right. Marie Claire, Olivier Gendebien's wife, who had come over to watch, suggested that I should take the Ferrari mascot out for a lap or two to bring me luck. She had found a chameleon; it was an odd little creature, and had a pair of beady eyes which could look in different directions at once which was a little disconcerting but very useful for watching motor races. It was quite tame and Gendebien had had it in the car with him when he put up his fastest lap. I thought it would be better for the chameleon not to come round with me as he might get car sickness and turn a very peculiar colour.

The night before the race I really meant to go to bed early. Although the past five weeks of waiting had been quite a strain I found it was all gone, instead of getting worse as I had thought it would. I had worried over little things like catching a cold and once I had got a pain in my stomach and thought it might be appendicitis. The night before a big race is always a bit twitch-making; you lie in bed thinking of what might happen, but this night I went straight to sleep with the sound of fog horns blowing. Fortunately by the morning the fog cleared. Thinking back I realise that I could not have got to bed terribly early as it was about 11.30 when, with Mary Taylor Young and Jean Howarth, who had come out on the other charter flight, I returned from a party given for the British contingent by the Ambassador, Sir Charles Duke, and Lady Duke, at the Consul's residence. But I was in bed earlier than some of the drivers who went to another party! The hospitality we were shown was terrific.

The next morning when I awoke I was delighted to see that it was cloudy, but the clouds cleared; by lunchtime the sun was shining and it was very hot. The Moroccan Grand Prix is the main social occasion in the country and, as in the previous year, King Mohammed V and his entourage were present. It was a most colourful sight with the King's bodyguard mounted on white BMW motor-bikes and massed bands and soldiers in bright uniforms. I noticed that the royal cars were German too, nearly all Mercedes. We were all introduced to the King and then he took his place in the Royal Box in the grandstand.

The start was a bit of an anti-climax after all this pageantry. 'Toto' Roche from Reims was the starter, and a quarter of an hour after the appointed time we were still not in our cars. When we were all settled in Roche held things up because one of the Coopers would not start; we were all getting a bit edgy. Then Roche waved the Cooper off the grid and we took this as the starting flag. Everyone moved off leaving Roche to scramble out of the way as best he could. Although I had much stronger clutch linings I took the start easily and Stirling shot away with Phil chasing him;

then came Lewis-Evans, Bonnier and me.

At the end of the first lap Phil was still on Stirling's tail doing his appointed job wonderfully well and I was behind him in third place. On the third lap Phil tried braking with Stirling on the right-hander after the pits, but his drum brakes could not compete with the Vanwall discs and he had to take the escape road; so I moved up to second with Bonnier third. By the sixth lap Phil caught me up again so I waved him through to have another go at Stirling. Round about the 12th lap Tony, who is a rather slow starter, got wound up and after a real ding-dong he took me on the 19th lap. I found that I had the speed on the straights, but out of the corners the Vanwall was quicker. If I passed him all he had to do was to get into my slipstream along the straights and then he would nip past me out of the corners. The Vanwall plan was obviously for Tony to keep me out of second place; if Stirling then won and made fastest lap, he would be Champion.

At one point Tony got a lead of about three seconds, but I got it back and as we swapped places every now and then I noticed there was a little stream of smoke from the engine compartment by the exhausts and occasionally Tony would have to wipe his windshield and his goggles. Well, he's not going to last very long, I thought, nothing to worry about there.

As it turned out I was wrong; it was the breather which was deflecting the fumes on to the exhaust pipe; a little oil would collect there and it was this which was burning and giving off the smoke. I would not have been quite so happy if I had known that at the time. With Tony in the race my title was anything but secure; once he went out there would be no opposition to my plan of finishing second.

By Lap 30 I had gone ahead of Tony again and then the Vanwall blew up, a valve dropped in, broke a piston and the rod came through the side. Oil streamed on to Tony's rear tyre causing him quite a moment before he brought it safely to rest by the side of the road.

Twenty-three laps of the race remained and I was back in third place, with Stirling well out in front with no worries at all, although he had had a little shunt with Seidel's Maserati early on in the race. He had bashed the front, closing up the air-intake a bit, but the water temperature was not affected. Tony's blow-up spilled oil on to the circuit and unfortunately Gendebien spun on it; Picard, who was behind him, could not avoid him. The Cooper went off the road on the left and the Ferrari went off to the right, hitting a rock which completely sliced the back off the car from just behind the seat. There were many conflicting rumours about this accident, too, and Olivier was variously reported to be either perfectly all right, or alternatively seriously hurt with a broken back. The truth of it was that he was suffering from bruises and shock; he was able to go home to

Belgium a couple of days later. It was his wife who returned home in plaster! Poor Marie-Claire slipped on the hotel steps a day or so after the race, fell and fractured her elbow.

Another Cooper also crashed at about this stage in the race; it was driven by Bridger and he too escaped more or less unhurt. Phil now lay second, nearly half a minute behind Stirling who had set the fastest lap in 2 min 22.5 sec, on his 24th circuit. Tavoni signalled Phil to slow down and let me up to second place and I went into this position on lap 39.

In effect the race now became two races; no one opposed Stirling in his efforts to get the maximum of nine points for a win and fastest lap, whilst I had things my own way in my race for the second place and the Championship. The only possible danger to me was Bonnier who was going very well indeed with the BRM in fourth place. Phil tucked in behind me and so we drove on. Although Bonnier picked up on us we were both aware of it and were able to put on speed if he came up too close.

With just about ten laps to go I came along the top straight and I was appalled to see a huge column of black smoke rising up. When I got to the end of the straight and to one of the corners leading down to the sea there was oil on the road and a car buring fiercely on the inside of the circuit. I could just see part of the bonnet hanging from the car with Vanwall written on it. I could see no number on the car.

As I passed the pits I realised that it must have been Lewis-Evans' car, for had it been Moss, Tavoni would have signalled that I was now first. The car had blown up, as Tony's had, but unhappily for Stuart the car had caught fire. He scrambled out, burned and dazed by the shock, and ran clear. But he ran in the opposite direction to the people who could help him, people with fire extinguishers and blankets. It took that much longer to reach him, and poor Stuart was badly burned. He had been lying fifth in the race at the time.

The last laps ran out with Stirling way out in front, neither of us able to do anything about the other. The Ferrari was going well and everything was normal. I realised that, barring a stroke of real misfortune, I was all right, as I was lapping seconds within the capabilities of the car.

Three laps to go and Phil toured gently round behind me, a loyal and brilliant driver, who at both Monza and Casablanca had done his best to help me. Two laps to go. . . one lap. . . and then there it was; the chequered flag. As I passed it *The Autocar* said I gave a great wave; *Autosport* said I gave myself a boxer's salute. I don't know what I did; all I knew was that I had just become the Champion Driver of the World, the first Englishman to achieve the title.

It was an immensely tragic World Championship victory. Poor Lewis-Evans succumbed to his burns a few days later. Hawthorn, thoroughly disenchanted by the death of Peter Collins, by Ferrari politics and by constant travelling round the world soon announced his retirement. It was a brief retirement, for in January 1959 Hawthorn was killed at the wheel of his Jaguar in a road accident on the Guilford By-pass. Vanwall had won the newly instituted Manufacturers' Championship, but Tony Vandervell was distraught at the death of Lewis-Evans, his own health was failing and although some development continued, Vanwall withdrew from racing.

1959

With the withdrawal of Vanwall, racing became a new duel, between Cooper and Ferrari. The front-engined Lotus remained a dismal failure and although Joakim Bonnier won the Dutch Grand Prix for BRM, this British team had little to show for five seasons of effort. Stirling Moss was now driving a Cooper-Climax for Rob Walker at most races, but he also appeared at some races with a BRM painted in the lime green colours of the British Racing Partnership (run by his father Alfred and manager Ken Gregory) and with this he finished second in the British Grand Prix at Aintree. The car was destroyed in the German Grand Prix held at the banked Avus circuit in West Berlin, the result of brake failure while Hans Herrmann was at the wheel.

A new contender in 1959 was Aston Martin, the famous sports car manufacturer and it was the original intention that both Brabham and Salvadori should drive for Aston Martin. Almost inevitably the Aston Martin was a dismal failure. What happened is told by Roy Salvadori in his autobiography published by Patrick Stephens Limited, 1985.

The 1959 Cooper Team

During the latter part of 1958 I learned that Aston Martin would be competing in Formula One the following year with their front-engined car which had existed for a couple of years. Reg Parnell, who was now the Aston team manager, wanted both Jack and I to drive for the team and he was particularly interested in Jack because of his abilities as a test driver.

What happened next is a story that has been incorrectly reported on many occasions. Coventry Climax informed Coopers that for 1959 they were developing a 2495 cc twin-cam engine and if it was successful, the Cooper would have an excellent chance in the 1959 World Championship series. By this stage Jack and I had orally agreed terms with Aston Martin. When John Cooper heard about this, he telephoned Reg Tanner to see whether Tanner could persuade us to change our minds. I already had a substantial personal contract with Esso, but Reg arranged a contract that would provide additional money to persuade Jack to stay with Cooper. Money was not a factor in my choice of team for 1959.

Jack telephoned me and said, 'Roy, I think we have a chance of doing really well with the new Climax engine if we stay with Coopers. I intend telling Reg Parnell that I'm remaining with Coopers. We get on well driving together and I think that we should go on doing so.' I told Jack that I would like to stay with Cooper if I could. I had been driving for Aston Martin since 1953 and I had been happier in that team than any other. I had very close relations with John Wyer and Reg Parnell and I thought that it would be very difficult for me to get out of my agreement with them. I talked to Reg Parnell and made the point that without Jack to test, the chances of success would be much reduced and it would be better if I stayed with Coopers. Reg persuaded me that Aston Martin had a high budget for Formula One and a good development track record. He appealed to my loyalty to the team – after all, they had shown faith in me in my early days and I should have faith in them now. I stayed with Aston Martin and had a rather unsuccessful 1959 season in Formula One.

It is, however, interesting to speculate what would have happened if I had stayed with Coopers. Up until that time I had been the number one Cooper driver, but it is likely that in 1959 Jack and I would have had equal status. If I had stayed the team's efforts would have been divided, even to sharing the first 2.5-litre engine, and Jack would have had much less support. Over the previous couple of years Jack had improved immensely as a driver, but I was still competitive on many circuits. In 1959 he was to win the Driver's Championship by a margin of only four points. I am not suggesting that if I had stayed I would have won the Championship, but inevitably at some races I would have finished higher up the results and I could very well have prevented Jack from winning the Championship. My decision to stay with Astons proved good for both Coopers and Jack and because of my feelings for that team I was not unduly distressed!

In 1959 the rear-engined Cooper with the full 2495 cc Coventry Climax engine was highly competitive, thanks to a good power to weight ratio, superb traction and, compared with the front-engined

Jack Brabham with the Cooper-Climax on his way to a win in the 1959 British Grand Prix. He won that year's World Championship. (*T. C. March*)

Second place in the British race at Aintree went to Stirling Moss with this sickly-coloured pale green British Racing Partnership-entered BRM. Shortly afterwards this car was destroyed when Hans Herrmann crashed because of brake failure in the German Grand Prix at Avus. (*T. C. March*)

cars, excellent handling. Works green and white cars were driven by Jack Brabham, young New Zealander Bruce McLaren and, in some races, by Kansan Masten Gregory. The beautifully finished dark blue and white cars of Rob Walker, meticulously prepared by Stirling Moss' former mechanic, Alf Francis, were handled by Moss and Frenchman Maurice Trintignant, each of whom had won a World Championship race with a Walker Cooper in 1958.

The front-engined Ferraris were still competitive on the fastest circuits and Maranello had a strong team that included Tony Brooks, Frenchman Jean Behra and American Phil Hill. Behra, who had been competing in Grand Prix racing since 1953 with Gordini, Maserati and BRM, was involved in an altercation in the pits at the French Grand Prix with Ferrari team manager Tavoni and struck the Italian. He was sacked from the team and, tragically, was killed at the wheel of a sports Porsche at the Grand Prix meeting on the banked Avus track at Berlin not long afterwards.

Brabham won the first round of the Championship at Monaco, was second to Bonnier's BRM in the Dutch race and had to settle for third place behind the Ferraris of Brooks and Hill in the French Grand Prix on the high-speed Reims circuit. In the British race at Aintree Brabham won again from Moss at the wheel of a BRM. The German Grand Prix was held in two heats on the banked Avus circuit and the Ferraris took the first three places. Moss won with a Walker car in Portugal and in the Italian Grand Prix; the Italian race was on the fast Monza circuit and Moss drove a canny race, running through without the stop for tyres that Ferrari had expected him to make.

The final round of the Championship was the United States Grand Prix, a new addition to the series. The World Championship was still open and could be won by Moss, Brabham or Brooks (but the Ferrari driver would have to both win the race and set fastest lap). Brooks made an early pit stop to check minor bodywork damage, Moss retired with gearbox trouble while leading and Brabham took the lead ahead of team-mate McLaren. For reasons still far from clear Brabham ran out of fuel on the last lap and McLaren won the race with Rob Walker's second entry driven by Trintignant in second place. Brooks finished third and Brabham pushed his car almost a quarter-mile to

finish to take fourth place. It was good enough to clinch the Championship.

1960

From 1960 no point was awarded in the World Championship for fastest lap, but instead there was a single point for sixth place. The most significant development was the new Lotus 18, a rear-engined design by Colin Chapman for his team which had previously raced delicate, sophisticated, but hopelessly unreliable front-engined cars in Formula 1 during 1958-59. Chapman's design was radical and scientific, incorporating a three-bay multi-tubular space-frame, but because of space limitations Chapman abandoned his famous 'strut' rear suspension in favour of a system of reversed lower wishbones and twin radius rods and the model was characterised by its almost box-shape glass-fibre bodywork. In Formula 1 the 18 was powered by the 2495 cc Coventry Climax engine, but the car was also built in Formula 2 and Formula Junior versions. Team Lotus had a remarkable, highly talented squad of young drivers that included Innes Ireland, Alan Stacey, Motorcycle World Champion John Surtees and 'coming man' Jim Clark. In addition once it was realized just how good the Lotus was, Rob Walker bought an example for Stirling Moss to drive. The Walker car was however fitted with a Colotti gearbox made in Italy (instead of the Lotus-made gearbox on the works car) and proved unreliable because of machining errors. This, coupled with Stirling's bad crash early in the year, once again wrecked his chances of winning the World Championship.

While the Lotus was revolutionary, the Cooper remained evolutionary. For 1960 the Surbiton team produced the 'low-line' model, still retaining a simple tubular chassis, but with smaller frontal area and generally lower build. The Cooper's origins lay in the earliest post-war 500 cc cars with rear-mounted motor cycle engine, the Coopers adopted the layout for their first 500 cc cars and retained it for the Coventry Climax-powered sports-racing car that appeared in 1955 and its single-seat successors. Cooper drivers remained unchanged in 1960, World Champion Brabham backed up McLaren and Gregory. Coopers were also raced by private owners and variants included cars with Ferrari and Maserati engines, as well as the usual Climax.

The opposition can be speedily dismissed. BRM now raced rear-engined cars, but these P48s as they were known, driven by Graham Hill, Joakim Bonnier and Dan Gurney achieved little success. Their highlight was when Graham Hill, after stalling on the grid, came through to take the lead in the British Grand Prix, only to spin off because of a locking brake. Ferrari continued to race the front-engined Dinos (although a rear-engined prototype was driven by Ginther at Monaco), Aston Martin struggled on even less successfully than in 1959 before withdrawing after the British Grand Prix and the new front-engined American Scarabs were overweight, underpowered and uncompetitive.

Nineteen Sixty was a truncated season, for the German Grand Prix was held as a Formula 2 race and the Italian Grand Prix held on the banked track at Monza, was boycotted by the British teams on 'safety grounds' which gave Ferrari a walk-over and the Italian team's only Formula 1 victory of the year.

In the first race of the year, the Argentine Grand Prix, the Lotus impressed greatly. Ireland led the race, but fell back to finish sixth. Although Ireland won races at Goodwood and Silverstone and Moss scored a fine victory in the first European race at Monaco, disaster dogged the wheel-tracks of Lotus, as this account of the Belgian Grand Prix by Innes Ireland (from his autobiography, *All Arms And Elbows*, published by Pelham Books Ltd in 1967) reveals:

The 1960 Belgian Grand Prix

The Belgian Grand Prix at Spa in 1960 was a disaster, and for me, a personal tragedy.

Two men were killed, two badly injured – one of them Stirling Moss – and I narrowly missed being added to the casualty list myself. By the end of the meeting, I was absolutely shattered...

But let's start at the beginning.

When we got to Francorchamps I was given a new Lotus. The car that I had first used in Buenos Aires had been sold, under the new policy that Chapman had set, to a very promising young driver named Michael Taylor. He appeared with this prototype for the first time in a Grande Épreuve at Spa.

For Team Lotus, there was myself, Alan Stacey and Jim Clark, who joined the team at the start of the season

Innes Ireland, author of *All Arms and Elbows* and works Lotus driver seen at the wheel of a Lotus 18 at Oulton Park in 1960. *(T.C. March)*

along with John Surtees, who was engaged to ride for Chapman whenever his motor cycle commitments would allow. Alan was new to Monaco and did not put up a very good practice time. As a result he was worried, particularly as he felt that unless he got out and went more quickly, his car might be given to Surtees.

The mental effect of this on a driver, to my way of thinking, is not only appallingly worrying, but downright bloody dangerous.

By the time we got to Spa, Alan was worried about the situation – especially since he did not like the Belgian circuit with its extremely high speeds and highly unnerving surroundings. If you go off the road at speed in Spa, the chances are that you will not get away with it, since all around are trees, houses, ravines and suchlike.

On the first day's practice, there were two pretty bad accidents concerning Lotus cars which were not calculated to jack up our spirits.

The first happened to Stirling Moss. He was taking the very fast curve at Burnenville – a downhill right-hander which one takes at about 135 mph or thereabouts – when his back wheel fell off. It transpired that the hub had sheared off. Anyway, I was one of the first drivers to stop at the scene and I raced across to find Stirling in a pretty bad way. After the ambulance had taken Moss away, I went back to the pits and related what had happened. I had had a look at Moss's car beforehand and I could see that this particular hub had broken. I told Chapman.

'Right,' he said. 'I'll take your car and go and look for myself... in the meantime, none of you are to take your cars out.'

In the pits, morale slumped to zero. When such a terrible accident happens through no fault of the driver, people seem to feel it more. It is one of those times when you realise that a similar thing could happen to you, and it goes quite deep down. For a time, nobody feels like having much of a go.

Almost immediately, amid all the pandemonium of Moss's accident, we heard that Michael Taylor, in my old Lotus, had gone off the road. This too happened on a fast corner, another 130-odd mph affair. Instead of taking the right-hand curve as he meant to do, he just went sailing straight on; how he was not killed, I can't imagine. The car went across a damned great ditch, shot into the air, hit a tree which it completely uprooted and finished up smack into another tree. Somehow or other he came out of it with only a few broken bones, although he had a neck injury which gave him trouble for some months after.

When I visited Michael in hospital shortly after the crash and asked him what had happened, he said: 'The

steering broke. I turned the wheel and nothing happened.'

Indeed, this was the case. The steering column had sheared off, and I must say it gave me a few uncomfortable moments when I realised how long I had been driving that car.

Meanwhile, when the panic of the accidents had died down somewhat, the Lotuses of Stacey, Clark and myself were wheeled off to the circuit garage to have their hubs examined for any fault similar to the one which had developed in Stirling's car.

The results were just terrifying. Clark's was uncracked, Stacey's was cracked halfway round the hub; and mine was all but sheared off! I suppose it was a gauge of how hard the cars were being driven at the time. Moss obviously drove his car harder than any of the rest of us and his hub went first. It is long odds that if he had not, in fact, crashed, I certainly would have done within a very few laps.

Team Lotus: left to right, Innes Ireland, Jim Clark and Alan Stacey who was killed in the 1960 Belgian Grand Prix. *(David Phipps)*

I was, for once, quite speechless.

However, Chapman explained that a fault had been found in one of the machine processes at the works. He had new hubs flown out from England and they were fitted on to our three cars. I can't say, however, that I was filled with confidence when I got to the starting line at this particular meeting.

After all the drama of practice, I was not well placed on the grid, and when the flag went down, I tucked myself in behind Jack Brabham, who took the lead, and then held on tight to him. He had the faster car, the Cooper, on the straight, but I knew that the Lotus's superior roadholding would always get me round and away from corners quicker. I hung on to his slipstream all the way down the straight every time, planning to wait until the last lap, then pull past him on the uphill section after the straight and nip home ahead of him. I was very happy with this situation until, after about six laps, my clutch began to slip badly and I had to go into the pits for an adjustment.

I came out again and got going once more only to find the clutch slipping again, necessitating a further pit stop. Out I trotted for the second time, determined, still, to get back in the race and I really started to press on. Shortly afterwards I passed both Clark and Alan Stacey who were in close company; as I did so I clearly recall thinking: 'Well, old Alan is doing what he said he would, just motoring gently round and not trying to be clever.'

Perhaps I should have been thinking more about myself, though, for shortly afterwards, coming through the double left-hander before La Source hairpin I lost it. I was going at a hell of a rate of knots and the car spun five times through 360 degrees, all the way down the middle of the track. I left great black marks on the road like some gigantic doodle which were still there the following year, I think.

This monumental spin ended with me pointing in the right direction with my engine still running but my right wheels on the grass on the right-hand side of the road. I was quite happy to have got out of it so fortunately and decided that since I and the car appeared to be in good shape, I'd carry on. I put the thing in first gear, worked the revs up, let out the clutch – and I barely moved. My first thought was that the clutch was slipping, but in fact, I had one rear wheel in the dirt and it was spinning like mad while the car was getting nowhere.

Then, suddenly, it gripped. The car shot forward at a fantastic rate, spun through 180 degrees there and then, leapt over the embankment at the side of the road and went crashing down to land on all fours. It all happened so quickly and so unexpectedly that I didn't know whether I was punchbored or countersunk. It was the most extraordinary thing because I just did not know what was going on. Anyway, I climbed out of the car, which was not

badly messed up, absolutely furious with myself. Very dejectedly indeed, I walked back to the pits.

The first thing I learned when I got there was that Chris Bristow was dead. This young driver had been having a tremendous battle with Willy Mairesse during the race and somehow had overcooked it on the same bend where Stirling had crashed. The poor fellow had gone off the road and hit houses, trees and heavens knows what. His car was completely and utterly destroyed and Bristow must have been killed instantly.

Then, very shortly after that, Alan Stacey went missing.

Oddly enough, I did not feel there was anything to worry about even if Alan was late in coming round. There was all sorts of conflicting reports about Stacey being all right, slightly hurt, a stretcher case and so on, but throughout, I did not feel too concerned. Alan, I had always felt, was indestructible. Even after all the appalling tragedy of Spa so far, I couldn't believe that anything could happen to him.

Eventually, Colin Chapman came across to me in the pits and said: 'I think you'd better go and find out exactly what has happened, Innes.'

'Oh, Alan will be all right,' I said, 'but he'll probably cadge a lift with the ambulance. I'll go over and find him.'

So I walked back down to the circuit hospital and saw an ambulance drive in and stop. The doors opened – and a priest got out, shaking his head; at the same instant, I saw Alan lying in the ambulance. He looked just as if he was asleep, the way I'd seen him a hundred times in countless hotel rooms.

I just couldn't believe my eyes. I was completely devastated. I don't think I had ever seen anyone dead before. I simply turned round in absolute horror and ran away. I don't remember where I ran to or what I did, but a little later I went back to the hospital and found they had laid Alan's body out with a winner's laurel wreath resting on him.

I just burst into uncontrollable tears.

I was so completely shattered by this experience that I wept for hours afterwards, unable to control myself properly. Later on that evening I had to get all Alan's kit packed up, and then the police wanted details from his driving licence and so on. I can't tell you how frightful that was.

The real tragedy of the whole thing was that the crash which killed Alan Stacey was one of those million-to-one chances that you would normally never thing about. A bird hit him in the face while he was travelling at, I suppose, something like 140 miles an hour. Of course, Alan must have lost control, the car went in all directions and poor Alan was thrown out and killed – or maybe he had been killed outright by the impact of the bird. I don't know. Whatever happened, it was a terrible tragedy.

Alan Stacey had had to overcome the most difficult physical handicap to get into motor racing at all. He had a tin leg, yet he taught himself to use it and get along with it so well only a handful of people at the time knew of his handicap.

His determination was such that, since he was unable to heel and toe with the brake and throttle while changing gear, he had a motor-cycle type twist-grip throttle built into the gear lever of all his cars so that he could operate the throttle manually when changing gear. I tried it and it was extremely difficult to do, but Alan mastered it.

He got a great deal of fun out of that leg. Many a chambermaid had run from his room at the sight of an apparently dismembered leg hanging over a chair, complete with shoe and sock.

One of his favourite tricks was to take a pencil in his hand while talking, say, after dinner, and slowly and quite unconcernedly thrust it through one of the holes in his leg beneath his flannels. Anyone who did not know his leg was artificial would look aghast at the pencil boring into his leg. I remember once, too, when he lost a bolt out of his ankle and we spent hours searching for the damned thing. Eventually we had to get one out of the workshops.

Also, at some of the Continental meetings when we had to take a medical examination, there were all sorts of diversions created to prevent the doctors from realising that he did not have a proper leg. When they were testing for reflexes, the rest of us had to wait until he had his left leg done, then, as the doctor was about to hit Alan's tin knee with his little hammer somebody had to knock over a chair, or kick the pot under the bed, or fall down or trip up or something.

In the resulting confusion, Alan simply crossed his leg again and sat there waiting to be tapped. It never failed.

Moss was not fit enough to return to Formula 1 until the Portuguese Grand Prix in August, the works Lotus team was plagued by minor problems and so Brabham had a clear run to his second World Championship in a year when the Australian was at peak form with a car of exceptional reliability. With wins in the Belgian, French, British and Portuguese races, Brabham won the Championship from Bruce McLaren by a margin of nine points (43 to 34). Cooper won the Manufacturers' World Championship for the second year running and the marque was at the zenith of its fame. Sadly Cooper

The year 1960 should have been that of the Lotus 18, but for a variety of reasons, the new Lotus failed to achieve at Championship level. This is John Surtees in the 1960 British Grand Prix in which he finished second behind Jack Brabham (Cooper). (*T. C. March*)

fortunes now declined and although the team remained in Formula 1 until the end of the 1968 season, it won only three more Championship Grands Prix (one in 1962, one in 1966 and one in 1967).

The 1960 United States Grand Prix brought the 2500 cc Formula to a close. In that race, won by Moss' Lotus, a Maserati 250F was driven by American Bob Drake, so the Italian car had the distinction of being the only one to run in the first and last races of the Formula. By 1960 the 250F symbolized the past, for it had been an era of substantial change; by 1960 all cars had independent rear suspension and disc brakes (the 250F had drum brakes and a de Dion rear axle) and all successful cars were rear-engined (a year later in 1961, *all* cars were rear-engined); Grand Prix racing had become dominated by British cars and motor racing was to become an important part of British industry; and specialized racing car constructors had replaced the substantial manufacturers who at one time had controlled the sport.

Part 7

AT THE EXPENSE OF
SPEED, 1961-65

1961

For 1961 there came into force a new Grand Prix Formula for unsupercharged cars of 1301-1500 cc, with a minimum dry weight limit of 450 kg. Other requirements were that self-starters were now compulsory, pump fuel had to be used and no oil could be taken on during the race. Minimum race distances were not changed. It was in effect a continuation, with certain changes, of the old Formula 2 of 1957-60.

There were a number of reasons for the decision of the Féderation Internationale de l'Automobile to introduce the new formula, but above all because it was believed that racing was becoming too fast (a perennial excuse for changing the regulations). The British constructors, however, believed that it was a deliberate attempt to stifle British success at the expense of Ferrari and Porsche who were racing the most successful Formula 2 cars and so they bitterly opposed the change. For too long they believed that they would be successful and delayed development of 1500 cc engines. The result was that Ferrari was ready for 1961 (but Porsche was not) and for a single year the British teams were eclipsed. All British entrants, Cooper, Lotus and BRM were obliged to use the 1460 cc 4-cylinder Coventry Climax FPF twin-cam engine, a mildly improved version of the original developed by Climax for Formula 2 in 1957 and subsequently developed into the Championship-winning 2495 cc engine of 1959-60. The new 1500 cc Coventry Climax V8 appeared in Brabham's Cooper at the Nürburgring (the German Grand Prix) and the BRM V8 engine at Monza (the Italian Grand Prix), but neither was raceworthy until 1962.

Ferrari's contribution was the Tipo 156 with V6 engine in 65-degree and, later, 120-degree configurations, featuring a distinctive 'twin-nostril' shark nose and a direct development of the rear-engined Formula 2 car that had raced with success in the latter part of 1960. SEFAC Ferrari, as the team was now known, had a formidable team of drivers that included German Wolfgang von Trips, and Americans Phil Hill and Richie Ginther. The Ferraris were heavy, they had indifferent handling, but compared to the opposition they were substantially more powerful.

That Ferrari dominated the year's racing is fact, but in itself not part of the romanticism and legend of motor racing. The real features of the 1961 season were the remarkable successes of Stirling Moss, successes that have undoubtedly reinforced the Moss legend, the equally remarkable successes of a now obscure Italian driver, Giancarlo Baghetti, and the tragic death of Champion-to-be Wolfgang von Trips.

Still entered by Rob Walker and at the wheel of an outdated 1960 Lotus, Moss drove a brilliant race at Monaco to win the first of the year's Championship Grands Prix and he repeated this victory at the Nürburgring in early August, guessing that it would rain and relying on Dunlop's newly developed and improved rain tyres. In both races the Ferrari drivers fought hard, but were no match for the Great British Racing Genius. Moss delighted in playing the underdog, immensely enjoyed his years with Rob Walker's private team of cars meticulously prepared by his own former mechanic Alf Francis and nothing satisfied him more than 'beating the odds'.

Baghetti's story is less easily explained. His career

Wolfgang von Trips with his 120-degree V6 Ferrari in the 1961 Dutch Grand Prix. He won the race from team-mate Phil Hill and Clark (Lotus). (*David Phipps*)

was that of the shooting star, bursting briefly into prominence and equally rapidly fading from view. For 1961 Ferrari made available an additional car entered in the name of Scuderia Sant', Ambroeus and to be driven by Italy's most successful and promising youngster. The man chosen was Giancarlo Baghetti. His first race was the non-Championship Syracuse Grand Prix and he won in the face of British underpowered opposition and he won again at Naples, another non-Championship race with even weaker opposition. Then came the French Grand Prix, his first

One of Stirling Moss' greatest victories was in the 1961 German Grand Prix. At the wheel of an outdated Lotus he beat the might of Ferrari. (*David Phipps*)

Grande Épreuve which he again won. He never won another race. This is the story of Baghetti's three wins as narrated by Chris Nixon based on interviews with Baghetti (first published in *Classic Cars)* and also relates the swift decline of his racing career.

Giancarlo Baghetti

In 1961 the young Italian, Giancarlo Baghetti, set a record unequalled in the history of motor racing by winning the first three Grands Prix of his life. He recalls those heady days with Chris Nixon.

'Last week, a 26 year-old Italian, Giancarlo Baghetti, arrived in Sicily to drive in his first Grand Prix race, no doubt

bearing in mind the comment of a leading French motoring paper that no one expected a miracle. On the first outing of this young driver, they said, he would be well advised to take his advanced lesson in motor racing very seriously.

'Now, as all the world knows, he took it very seriously indeed. Young Baghetti accomplished the astonishing feat of winning the Syracuse Grand Prix from a field that included Moss, Brabham, Gurney, Bonnier – in fact all the first line drivers with the exception of those of the official Ferrari team, for the fortunes of Ferrari were in his novice hands.

'What so impressed all who saw the Italian's drive to victory at a record speed was the magisterial calmness of the man. His was no wild dash of a tyro driving beyond his skill, but the smooth, calculated progress of a truly great driver. Not for nothing has Baghetti been described in Italy as "the Milanese Brooks", for his intellectual approach to motor racing is indeed reminiscent of Tony Brooks who, by a strange coincidence, also achieved stardom overnight by his 1955 victory in a Connaught on the same Syracuse circuit.'

With those words Philip Turner – Sports Editor of *The Motor* – introduced his astonished readers to Giancarlo Baghetti on 3 May, 1961 and while he was sufficiently impressed by the young man's skills to dub him 'a truly great driver', never in his wildest dreams can Turner have imagined that Baghetti would go on to win his second GP as well, a couple of weeks later. And had he dared to suggest that the Italian would win his third – and a World Championship Grande Épreuve, at that – Turner's colleagues in the Press Box (not to mention his Editor back in London) would surely have concluded that the poor fellow had lost his marbles.

Yet that is precisely what Giancarlo Baghetti achieved, a hat-trick of victories in the first three Grands Prix of his life and although, sadly, he was never to win another, that hat-trick is an achievement that remains unapproached – never mind equalled – almost 30 years on. It is a landmark in motor racing history.

Baghetti was born on Christmas Day, 1933, in Milan. His father was a metallurgist, with no great interest in cars, but when his son was eight years old he built him a little Bugatti lookalike, based on a Fiat Balilla chassis and powered by a 350 cc motorcycle engine. Giancarlo used to drive it around the garden and has it to this day. When he was 13 he took up motorcycle racing, of a sort.

The Greatest Champion never to win the Drivers' World Championship: Stirling Moss, photographed in 1961, when he was at the height of his powers. (*David Phipps*)

'My parents had a summer house in San Remo and there I start racing with a Lambretta. I was too young to do this legally, so I change the date of my birth and got my licence. I won a few races and was asked to ride for Innocenti, but my father hear about this and he says, "Stop – my son is only 13!" That was the end of my motorcycle career.'

It wasn't until 1958 that he took up competition again, this time legally, and with an Alfa Romeo Giulietta 1300, which happened to belong to his father. Baghetti Junior planned his first race with care, but without the knowledge of Baghetti Senior, although the clues were there...

'For weeks before the race (which was at Monza) I spend every night in our garage working on the car,' recalls Giancarlo. 'Every time my father drove it he noticed how much better it was running, but he never suspect what I am doing!'

It would be nice to recall that Baghetti won that very first race, but he didn't. He didn't even finish it. Rather than use his father's car again, he bought an Alfa for himself – a Giulietta SV – and did some more races and some hill climbs in that, with the result that Abarth invited him to drive their cars in the 750 cc saloon car class in 1959. The Formula Junior movement was now well under way in Italy and the following year Giancarlo went racing with a Lancia-engined Dagrada, winning some half-a-dozen races.

At the same time, Scuderia Ferrari was developing its mid-engined car for the new, 1½-litre Grand Prix Formula that was due to come into force in 1961. Greeted with cries of outrage and disbelief when it was announced in 1959, the new Formula was yet another attempt to reduce the ever-increasing speeds of GP racing and in the teeth of fierce opposition, the CSI (as motor racing's governing body was then known) demanded a reduction in engine capacity from 2½ to 1½ litres. Ferrari didn't like the idea any more than the highly vociferous British teams, but instead of complaining and trying to set up a rival, Inter-Continental formula as they did, Enzo got on with the job of designing a car for the new Formula 1.

Ferrari's first mid-engined car made its race début in 2½-litre form at Monaco in 1960, where it was driven by Richie Ginther (also making his GP début). The car retired but Richie pushed it across the line to qualify for sixth place. Its first appearance as a 1½-litre was in the F2 race at Solitude a few weeks later, where it won in the hands of 'Taffy' von Trips, who repeated his victory by winning the F2 class in the Italian GP, which was boycotted by the British teams that year as they refused to race on Monza's banking.

Designated the Dino 156, the new Ferrari was the work of Chief Engineer Carlo Chiti and it was he who gave the car its distinctive, twin-nostril front end. This was not his idea, however – it had been used by coachbuilder Fantuzzi late in 1958 on a team of three 250F Maseratis that had been sold to American entrant Temple Buell for the winter season in New Zealand. When Enzo Ferrari presented his cars for 1961 at his annual Press Conference in February that year, both his Grand Prix and Sports Car models had this twin-nostril treatment and the sleek single-seaters – surely one of the best-looking GP cars of all – became known as the 'shark-nose' Ferraris.

They began life with a 65-degree, V6 engine, which Chiti had developed from the 1½-litre unit originally sketched by Dino Ferrari (who died in 1956) and which was brought forward in 1957/58 by Vittorio Jano. At the Press Conference Ferrari made it clear that the 65-degree unit was only an interim measure and would soon be replaced by a 120-degree unit. He also announced that the prototype which had raced in 1960 would be loaned to FISA – the Federation of Italian Automobile Teams – for certain races in an attempt to discover a home-grown Grand Prix driver or two, following the sad demise of Eugenio Castellotti and Luigi Musso in 1957 and 1958 respectively.

Which is where Giancarlo Baghetti comes in, for he was FISA's choice to race the new Ferrari. This decision caused no little dissent among Italian racing circles, for Baghetti was promoted over the heads of the Formula Junior Champions of 1959 and 1960 – Lele Cammorota and Renato Pirocchi. Also given the thumbs-down was another promising newcomer, Lorenzo Bandini.

After a test drive in the Ferrari at Modena autodrome, Giancarlo arrived in Syracuse to find himself faced with formidable opposition in his first Grand Prix. There were works cars from Porsche (Dan Gurney and Jo Bonnier); BRM (Graham Hill and Tony Brooks); Lotus (Jim Clark and Innes Ireland); Yeoman Credit Coopers (John Surtees and Roy Salvadori); a Rob Walker Lotus for Stirling Moss and a 'private' Cooper for Jack Brabham. The only star drivers missing were Phil Hill and 'Taffy' von Trips from Ferrari.

When practice was over it must have come as a great surprise to one and all to find that the middle of the front row of the grid was occupied by an unknown whose name sounded remarkably like one of Mr Heinz' fifty-seven varieties. Still and all, practice is one thing – the race is very much another and as the cars took up their positions for the start on that Tuesday, 25 April, 1961, surely no-one could possibly have imagined that they were watching history in the making, and that the likes of Stirling Moss, John Surtees, Dan Gurney et al, were about to be convincingly beaten by a young man partaking of his very first Grand Prix.

For his part, said young man found himself about to do battle with many of his great heroes, none of whom he had ever seen in action before, let alone raced against.

'I was very nervous at the start, thinking "After you, Mr Moss; after you Mr Gurney"', but when the flag dropped they became just drivers, men I had to beat'.

That nervousness meant that Giancarlo made a bad start, arrived at the first corner far too fast, braked too hard and for a few terrible moments seemed set to end his Grand Prix career against an unforgiving Syracuse wall. Somehow he gathered it all together, took a deep breath and carried on. At the end of the first lap Surtees led from Gurney and Bonnier and Baghetti was in seventh spot. On the second lap he set up a new 1½-litre lap record, passing Brabham and Hill in the process, while Gurney took the lead from Surtees. At the end of the sixth lap the Italians lining the course went bananas, as their beloved Ferrari came past ahead of all the opposition – Giancarlo Baghetti was leading his very first Grand Prix and, providing he did nothing silly, looked to have the race in the bag.

It wasn't quite as simple as that, though, for Dan Gurney pressed him hard with the Porsche, but the young Italian drove with a maturity beyond his years and went no faster than he had to in order to keep the silver car at bay. Despite a new lap record by Gurney on the final lap, Baghetti took the chequered flag in front of a delirious crowd and after his well-earned lap of honour, was lifted bodily from the Ferrari by the mechanics. A star was born.

Two weeks later FISA entered him for the Naples GP and he won that, too, but Giancarlo shrugs off the victory as one of little consequence. 'It was an easy win because there was no real opposition – all the big names were at Monaco that weekend.'

Nonetheless, a Grand Prix is a Grand Prix and it was his second success on the trot. It was also the only success by Ferrari that day, for in the Monaco GP the 156s of Phil Hill, 'Taffy' von Trips and Richie Ginther were bested by the incredible Stirling Moss in Rob Walker's Lotus-Climax.

Baghetti was not entered for the Dutch or Belgian GPs, so he had to wait until the French Grand Prix in July before he got his hands on the FISA Ferrari again. By this time, all three works cars were equipped with the 120-degree engine, but Giancarlo still had to make do with the older, less powerful unit, which produced a claimed 180 bhp, as opposed to the 190 of the newer one. On the long straights at Reims he found that his car was much slower than the works cars and whereas they filled the front row of the grid after practice, he could only manage 12th-fastest time, nearly six seconds slower than pole-man Phil Hill.

'I was on the fifth row of the grid and I started very quietly, but I got quicker all the time and soon I was having a great battle with the Lotuses of Moss, Ireland and Clark, while the works Ferraris were way out in front.'

This French Grand Prix was Baghetti's first World Championship event and only his third GP of all, yet he drove like a veteran and refused to be overawed by the ultra-fast company he was keeping. First Moss fell out with a fractured brake pipe, then Clark's goggles were shattered by a stone and Ireland dropped back due to the extreme heat of the day (95 degrees in the shade, 126 on the track!). Despite this, there was no respite for the young Italian novice, for no sooner had the British cars fallen away than the Germans were snapping at his heels, as the Porsches of Dan Gurney and Jo Bonnier set about him.

'Then followed a battle reminiscent of the unforgettable Hawthorn-Fangio duel in 1953 on the same circuit,' wrote Gregor Grant in *Autosport*. 'For lap after lap the trio swapped places, often travelling abreast. The more experienced Gurney and Bonnier really went to work, but nothing seemed to shake the cool-headed Italian.'

Giancarlo's eyes light up when he recalls that fantastic battle. 'We touch many times, but it was not dangerous because they were very experienced and they knew that if they touch me too hard we all go off! We were often side-by-side, but I never looked across at them – I just look straight ahead.'

Meanwhile, there was more drama up front, as first von Trips retired with a stone through his radiator, then Hill spun and stalled leaving Ginther in a commanding lead, only to retire out on the circuit with a seized engine. Suddenly, the fortunes of Ferrari were in the hands of

Giancarlo Baghetti, on his way to his win in the 1961 French Grand Prix. (*David Phipps*)

Giancarlo Baghetti, who had the Porsches of Gurney and Bonnier all over him. He stayed remarkably calm, and as the trio of cars fled down the Reims straights, he did some serious thinking.

'When the other Ferraris dropped out I knew I could win, so I thought about tactics. I realised that if I stayed with both the Porsches they could box me in, so I decided to go a little faster in the last few laps and get away from at least one of them. This didn't work because they slipstreamed me down the straights and I couldn't leave them. Then Bonnier fell out with three laps to go, so I had to change my tactics.

'I decided I could win if I arrived at Thillois in second place, which was easy as Gurney always passed me into that bend! So on the last lap I braked even harder than before and he went round Thillois ahead of me. I knew that if I stayed close behind him on the main straight I would not be able to pass – I had to stay a few metres behind in order to take advantage of the Porsche's slipstream and get by. As we left Thillois, Gurney held the middle of the road and I could see him watching me in his mirrors, so I stayed on one side, then dived across to the other and went past him just before the finish line to win by one-tenth of a second!'

It was a famous victory, to say the least, and Giancarlo Baghetti had completed a sensational hat-trick with one of the greatest drives of all time. (That is no overstatement, for although Reims was never regarded as a very difficult circuit it was extremely quick – Baghetti's winning speed was a shade under 120 mph – and throughout the race he had been wheel-to-wheel with some of the fastest, most experienced men in the business. Very few drivers could have withstood such pressure for so long without making a mistake.)

A combination of the extreme heat and a terribly demanding race left Baghetti exhausted afterwards, but he was sufficiently alert to greet Dan Gurney, who sportingly went to the Ferrari pit to congratulate him. The next day, Giancarlo went to Modena where he also received congratulations from Enzo Ferrari. 'Mr Ferrari was happy that I won, but not so happy because all the papers talked about Baghetti, Baghetti, Baghetti – not Ferrari. He say to me, "What car are you driving at Reims, Baghetti?"'

Sadly, that classic win at Reims was to be Giancarlo's last taste of victory (apart from a very minor win at Vallelungha later that year), for the dazzling promise he showed in those first three races was never to be fulfilled. After the euphoria at Reims he was brought down to earth in no mean fashion at Aintree two weeks later. The British GP began in the most appalling conditions with the rain beating down and flooding the track in many places. After splashing around in the middle of the field, Baghetti

tangled with a slower car and then acquaplaned off the track and crashed, damaging the Ferrari, but not himself.

His next race was the final European GP of the year at Monza, where he was at last given a 120-degree engine. Once again the Italian Grand Prix was to be held on the full circuit, which included the banking. The previous year the British drivers had boycotted the race because of said banking, yet in '61 the same drivers were there in force. 'There's nowt so queer as folks', indeed.

Although Ferrari had walked away with the Manufacturers' Championship, the Drivers' title was on a knife edge, between Phil Hill on 29 points and 'Taffy' von Trips on 33. With only the US Grand Prix to come, if Taffy could win at Monza he would be Germany's first World Champion. . .

The two-by-two starting grid was dominated by the five Ferraris of von Trips, Ricardo Rodriquez (19 years old and making his GP début), Ginther, Hill and Baghetti, the first three all lapping in under 2 mins 47 secs. Jim Clark on the Lotus was back on the fourth row and Baghetti recalls that he started with only 30 litres of fuel on board, in an attempt to get among the works Ferraris early on. He did just that and Baghetti had the closest of views of the tragedy that followed.

'On the first lap, Clark passed all the Ferraris in the Parabolica. We got by him on the straight and on the second lap we arrive at the Parabolica: Phil Hill, Rodriguez, Jack Brabham, von Trips, Clark and me. The Ferraris all had full tanks, so Trips brake before Clark, who was just behind, with me beside him. Clark didn't seem to anticipate Trips braking earlier than him and the nose of the Lotus struck the Ferrari's exhaust pipes, which stuck out behind the car. The Ferrari went off the road and up the banking before it fell back on the track. I looked up and saw its empty cockpit because Trips had been thrown out and he broke his neck. Also, 14 spectators were killed.'

Unaware of the tragedy, Phil Hill went on to win the race and the World Championship and it was sad indeed that the first American to win the title should do so in such unfortunate circumstances.

Although not an active member himself, Baghetti has fond memories of the Ferrari team of '61. 'All very nice people. von Trips was a gentleman and Phil, too. I had won three races at once, but there was no envy – they were always ready to give me advice and Phil became a good friend.'

Throughout the year, discontent had been simmering at Ferrari due, it seems, to the continual interference of Enzo's wife, Laura. Ferrari himself never went to races, but that year Laura decided to accompany the team to many events and had a lot to say about a great many things. As a result, at the end of the season, no fewer that nine top personnel left Ferrari in a huff, including Chief Engineer Carlo Chiti and Team Manager Romolo Tavoni. They went to a newly formed company called ATS and set about designing a GP car and a GT car for sale to the public. Phil Hill and Giancarlo only learned about this mass exodus after they had both signed with the Scuderia for 1962. It was not to be a good season...

Although Chiti was replaced from the Ferrari ranks by the brilliant young Mauro Forghieri, there was precious little development of the cars in 1962 and they proved to be slower than in the year before. In practice for the 1961 German GP at the Nürburgring, Phil Hill had produced a stunning lap in 8 mins 55.2 secs – the first man ever to break the nine-minute barrier. In 1962, the best he could do there was a derisory 9 mins 24.7 secs, nearly forty seconds away from Dan Gurney's pole position time in the Porsche!

There were other problems, too. Romolo Tavoni had been replaced by Eugenio Dragoni, a wealthy businessman friend of Enzo Ferrari who took an instant dislike to Phil Hill. Lorenzo Bandini was now on the team and, to his embarrassment, Dragoni began pushing him as Italy's next World Champion. ('He didn't push me because I was Phil's friend,' says Baghetti, without rancour.) Although the Ferraris were clearly much slower than the opposition throughout 1962, Dragoni constantly criticised Hill for his poor performances and claimed that he had been badly affected by von Trips' death and was no longer a driver to be reckoned with. At every opportunity he

belittled Phil's efforts to Enzo Ferrari, while praising Bandini...

It was a very unhappy season and the best Baghetti could do was a fourth place in the Dutch GP and fifth in the Italian. At the end of the year Dragoni told him that if he wanted to stay for 1963 he could only give him a contract for sports and prototype racing, not Formula 1. In the circumstances, Giancarlo signed with Chiti and Tavoni at ATS, as did Phil Hill. Not long after he had signed the contract, Enzo Ferrari called and asked to see him in Maranello. 'He told me, "If you want, you can drive in F1 for us in 1963."

"It is too late," I said. "Dragoni told me no Formula 1." Ferrari was astonished. "But why didn't you come to see me?"'

And so, Hill and Baghetti jumped out of the Ferrari frying pan and into the ATS fire. The new team was a disaster from the start, for despite its supposedly rich patrons – Count Volpi, Giorgio Billi and Jaime Patino – it was drastically under-financed and fell hopelessly behind schedule. The cars were not ready for Monaco in 1963 and when they did appear for the first time, at Spa, they looked like a couple of backyard specials. They went about as well, too. The team stumbled from one disaster to another and disappeared altogether after both cars retired in the US and Mexican GPs.

Their friendship forged in adversity, Phil and Giancarlo stuck together for 1964, joining Mimo Dei's Scuderia

The ATS of Giancarlo Baghetti in the 1963 Belgian Grand Prix. With this ill-prepared and uncompetitive car he drove a slow race until eliminated by gearbox trouble. (*Nigel Snowdon*)

Giancarlo Baghetti, winner of the 1961 French Grand Prix photographed in 1964 when he was driving for Scuderia Centro-Sud.

Centro-Sud team of BRMs. After one race, Hill left to join Cooper, Baghetti soldiered on, but the BRMs were basically the previous year's cars and the best he could do was seventh in the Austrian GP.

And so the career that had begun with one of the greatest achievements in racing history just fizzled out. Giancarlo continued to race sports cars here and there – indeed, he finished second in the 1966 Targa Florio with Guichet, driving a Ferrari Dino – but the great days were gone forever.

He married in 1968 and his wife, Christina, was not at all keen for him to contine racing. Happily, a sculptor friend asked him to photograph some of his work and Giancarlo found a new career. Soon he was photographing beautiful girls for the Italian edition of *Playboy,* which he did for ten years before switching his attention to fashion and cars. He is now a very successful photo-journalist whose work appears regularly in *Corriere delle Sera* and *Auto Oggi,* among other journals. His twenty year-old son, Aaron, is also a photographer and works with him, but wants to become a racing driver – an ambition that has not been well received by his mother!

Today, at 56, Giancarlo Baghetti not only retains all the hair he had 30 years ago, but more, as he now sports a fine moustache. A charming and humourous man, he is completely unfazed by the fact that the career which at first promised him so much, ultimately delivered so little, after that initial explosion of success. 'If you stay for two or three years out of the top rank of Formula 1 teams, it is not possible to get back,' he says with a shrug.

There are those, I've no doubt, who will regard his three Grand Prix wins as just a flash in the pan for a very lucky young man who happened to be in the right car at the right time. However, when you examine the competition he faced at Syracuse and Reims, and the manner of his winning, you have to be convinced that Giancarlo Baghetti was a driver who had greatness at his fingertips, only to see it slip away. Nothing is certain in this world, but I see no reason to doubt that, given a competitive car, in 1962 and '63, he could have gone on to more great things. In the event he did not, but he walked away from a very dangerous game without a scratch and with three Grands Prix to his name, scored in unique fashion.

Giancarlo may not have made World Champion, but he made history, and in some style.

Ferrari won again in the British Grand Prix and in Germany Moss secured his second remarkable victory of the year with his outdated Lotus. At the Italian Grand Prix Ferrari entered four cars and German driver Wolfgang von Trips seemed set to win the Drivers' Championship. Although the race was held on the banked Monza track, this did not deter the British teams as it had in 1960. On the second lap of the race von Trips and Jim Clark (Lotus) collided, the Ferrari plunged into a spectator area and 14 onlookers and von Trips were killed. Phil Hill won the race for Ferrari and gained a tragic World Championship title. Having won both the Drivers' Championship and the Constructors' Cup, Ferrari decided to miss the last round, the United States Grand Prix, and here Innes Ireland scored the first Championship race victory by a works Lotus.

1962

By the start of the 1962 season both BRM and Coventry Climax had their new V8 engines fully sorted, although initially these engines were in short supply. A walk-out of technical staff at Ferrari left Maranello floundering, development stagnated and Phil Hill, backed up by younger, inexperienced drivers, achieved little. British domination reasserted itself and the year devolved into a season-long battle between Graham Hill (BRM) and Jim Clark (Lotus), while both John Surtees with the new Climax V8-powered Lola with Bowmaker finance company backing and Bruce McLaren (Cooper) enjoyed a measure of success. In August Jack Brabham introduced his new Formula 1 car bearing his own name. One great name was missing from the entry lists, for at the Easter Goodwood meeting Stirling Moss, for reasons that remain inexplicable, crashed and brought his racing career to an end.

Alfred Owen, whose Owen Organisation financed BRM, had put the skids under the historically inept team by warning Raymond Mays that unless the BRM was more successful in 1962 their support would be withdrawn. Early in the year Hill won at Goodwood and scored a fantastic victory in the wet at Silverstone when he passed Clark's Lotus sideways at the last corner to win the International Trophy race. Next came the Dutch Grand Prix and BRM's real breakthrough. Hill won the race from the Lotus of Trevor Taylor. In this race Jim Clark drove the monocoque Lotus 25, a form of construction that was soon adopted by other manufacturers.

Dan Gurney scored Porsche's only Championship victory of the year in the 1962 French Grand Prix at Rouen. The new flat-8 car proved no match for the British opposition and Porsche withdrew from Formula 1 at the end of the year.

Graham Hill scored a remarkable victory with the V8 BRM in the International Trophy at Silverstone in 1962, crossing the finishing line sideways to win by a couple of feet. Early in the year the BRMs used a 'stack' exhaust system and it can be seen in this photograph that the car has lost three of the four pipes on the right-hand side. It was the year the BRM made good and Hill went on to win the World Championship. (*T. C. March*)

At Monaco Bruce McLaren won for Cooper, but Jim Clark and the new Lotus won the Belgian Grand Prix, while in the French race at Rouen Dan Gurney scored the sole Championship race victory of the new flat-8 Porsche. Another victory followed for Clark at Aintree, scene of the British race and Hill was the victor in Germany and Italy. Clark won at Watkins Glen (the United States Grand Prix), with Hill second. The result was that the World Championship was still wide open and would be decided by the outcome of the South African Grand Prix at East London on 29 December. Before the race Alan Brinton interviewed both contenders for the title for *Motor Racing* magazine.

Heart to Heart

Graham Hill and Jim Clark Talk It Over

Reigning World Champion Phil Hill at the wheel of his V6 Ferrari at the 1962 British Grand Prix. Only the one Ferrari was entered in this race and the V6 cars were now uncompetitive. (*T. C. March*)

On paper, Hill has the better chance, for Clark *must* win in South Africa to take the championship; nothing less will do. If Clark retires, or comes lower than first, then Hill will automatically take the title, whether he finishes or not.

The new Climax V8-powered Lola showed considerable promise in 1962, although it failed to win a single Championship race. John Surtees is seen in the British race in which he finished second. (*T. C. March*)

This will be the fascinating climax to the second season under the 1½-litre formula. MOTOR RACING's Editor, Alan Brinton, recently talked over the season with the two contenders, discussed their cars, their experiences, their hopes.
This is how it went...

Brinton: At the beginning of the season both of you must have had some inkling of what might happen, or at least a hope or two based on developments at Bourne and Cheshunt. How did you feel about things when you went into the season, Graham?

Hill: Well, I certainly realised that I would have a better chance in 1962 than in the previous four years. But frankly I had no idea at all that it would turn out as it has. There are so many unknowns in motor racing, particularly at the start of a new season. At that time I hadn't seen either Porsche or Ferrari – remember, Porsche were coming out with their flat-eight, and Ferrari were promising a four-valve-per-cylinder job. No, I can't say that I began 1962 feeling that BRM were going to have the successes which they have had. I just thought that we would be there with something of a chance.

Brinton: Stirling's accident must have made something of a difference to your prospects?

Hill: Certainly if Stirling had been on the circuits the situation would have been different for both of us. Don't you agree, Jim?

Clark: I certainly do. Neither of us has any illusions about Stirling's tremendous skill and determination. Of course, a great deal would have depended on what car he would have used for the grandes épreuves, and how well it behaved. But from past experience we know what Stirling can do in a car that is not potentially a race winner – look at Monaco and Nürburgring last year!

Hill: But the fact remains that even after Stirling's shunt at Goodwood it was still too early for either of us to form any opinion about our chances. Porsche hadn't then revealed their Formula 1 car, though we knew that they had two extremely good drivers. Personally, I thought that the Porsche would have done better than it did. Ferrari, too, seemed to have a useful team. Then again, the Lola seemed to be going jolly well, and I formed an early impression that Lotus would be there with a fine chance. I had already seen what a good car the Lotus 24 was, and I didn't know then that Colin Chapman had the 25 up his sleeve.

Brinton: So to you it all looked very open?
Hill: Very open indeed.
Brinton: And you, Jim?
Clark: I thought that our main opposition would come

from Ferrari. My feeling was that they would not have been standing still over the Winter. We kept hearing reports of new things from Maranello, and it looked as though they had, as usual, got new models built while British manufacturers were messing about with bits of tubing and thinking about screwing new cars together. We didn't know then what troubles Ferrari was having behind the scenes. From what I had heard of the Lola up till then, I thought that they could only improve, and that with John Surtees driving it Bowmaker would be something of a thorn in our flesh.

Brinton: Now the BRM, Graham, was first revealed in September of 1961, during practice for the Italian Grand Prix. That must have given you something of a start?

Hill: We thought, in fact, that we were going to have the V8 engine for 1961, but it didn't turn out that way. The car was hanging around for a long time, waiting for bits for the engine. As a matter of fact, I was all in favour of putting a Climax 1½-litre four in the V8 chassis for 1961; it might have taught us something, and helped with development on the handling side. As you say, the V8 eventually turned up at Monza. What few people realised was the terrific effort which was made at Bourne to get them out there at all. We didn't use the V8s in the race, but the journey was valuable, and we put in some more useful testing with the cars after the race.

Brinton: In the light of the Monza trip, and the development carried out over the Winter, you must have had some feeling of confidence when 1962 began?

Hill: Not as much as you might imagine. As I said before, I thought our chances would be better, but frankly I didn't think we'd done enough development during the Winter. I felt, consequently, that we should have been further ahead than we were.

Brinton: What about the Lotus 25, Jim? Why was the decision taken to make the monocoque car? When was it produced, and what was the thought behind it from the driver angle?

Clark: As you know, Colin Chapman is always one for trying new ideas, and he argued that with monocoque construction he could give a more rigid structure for less weight and more compact size. I know that it had been thought about quite a bit towards the end of last season. There was something brewing around the time of the 1961 Motor Show at Earls Court, but Colin Chapman wouldn't tell me then what it was, as I hadn't actually signed up for 1962. All he did say was that he had something radically different that he wanted to try. It wasn't until I got back from the South African races that I became fairly well aware of what was going on. We then had the Lotus 24 in hand, but as yet no V8 Coventry Climax for it. But when I returned from South Africa the initial work started on the 25, with the plumbing and fittings being laid out. At that time it was intended having a steering column gearchange. I couldn't get the pendulum pedals working to my liking, and there were a lot of conferences about that. Colin managed eventually to find enough room for a conventional gearchange, but in fact the whole job took longer than was originally intended, and it was May before the car was ready. When the Lotus 25 was taken to Zandvoort for the first championship race I had done absolutely no testing with it.

Brinton: Were you happy about running the 25 in the Dutch Grand Prix?

Clark: Frankly, I was very doubtful about using the new car. I wanted to run the 24, which was going very well, and the original idea was that Trevor would drive the 25 in the race. In the end it was decided that I should have a bash with the 25 in the race. Not surprisingly, we ran into trouble, but I suppose it taught us a thing or two. One of the problems at first with the 25 was the very reclined seating position, which made visibility difficult, particularly on sharp corners. We made some slight modifications later, and of course I gradually got used to it.

Brinton: There has been considerable argument throughout the season as to which is the quicker car – the BRM or the Lotus. What's your verdict, Graham?

Hill: At Goodwood on Easter Monday I had complained that my car did not seem to be as quick as the Lola or the Lotus. You know, the BRM weighs nearly 1100 pounds without fuel, but with oil and water. It has a slightly bigger frontal area than the Lotus, and indeed it is bigger all round.

Brinton: I gather that you like your BRM set up quite differently from Richie Ginther's. Any reason for that?

Hill: It is just a matter of personal choice. I have my car set up the way I like to drive it – and it is not just a question of fitting harder springs. Also, it depends on the car. If I was driving a Lotus, for example, I might find that I liked it best when set up on the soft side.

Clark: I thought that your BRM – and Richie's, too – really had a lot of steam at Monza.

Hill: And I was pretty certain that you had more than I did at Watkins Glen. It was certainly my impression that your Lotus was quicker in a straight line in the United States Grand Prix.

Clark: That's interesting, because it was my feeling that at Watkins Glen my car was getting out of the corners a trifle quicker than yours, but that by the end of the straight you were beginning to catch me again!

Brinton: Jim, harking back to the French Grand Prix at Rouen, what was the reason for Graham getting away from you at the start? He seemed to walk away from you, though you started from pole position.

Clark: First of all, I didn't really feel up to driving very

Graham Hill, the 1962 World Champion. (*T. C. March*)

brilliantly that day, after the mishap I had during the first practice session, when the steering went wrong. Secondly, I ended up with a brand new car which hadn't been bedded in. It hadn't got the right ratios for Rouen, and I hadn't run the car with a full tank previous to the race. In addition, I found myself having to slip the clutch from time to time; a lot of oil had been dropped on to the circuit; with the result that the corners were even slower. The 25 is not a good car on oil. Then, of course, I had my front suspension go, and my short-lived lead went for a burton.

Hill: Yes, looking back, that was quite a motor race. After I had had my tangle with Jack Lewis' Cooper, and got going again, I thought I could catch you again. Then, when you went out, it seemed that all I had to do was to keep going. Of course, I didn't; the fuel injection linkage packed up and I had to retire. It was a very disappointing day for me, as well as for you.

Clark: But at least Richie gave BRM a third, while we finished up with Trevor's car a nasty mess after he and Trintignant had collided after crossing the line.

Brinton: Let us get back to the question of which car has proved quicker in a straight line.

Hill: There's no doubt in my mind that the most convincing demonstration of straight-line speed during the year didn't come from either BRM or Lotus. I reckon that Surtees' Lola at Reims was the quickest we have seen in 1962.

Clark: Yes, he was going like a bomb that day. When

he decided to go he just dashed away from all of us. And that is a difficult thing to do on a circuit like Reims, because you get a tow effect even when you are a long way behind.

Hill: Yes, I'd say you get help from up to 400 yards behind another car.

Brinton: What about that other ultra-fast circuit, Spa?

Clark: Well, we couldn't form any real assessment from the Belgian Grand Prix, because Graham's BRM was suffering from an intermittent misfire. My car went extremely well at Spa, probably as well as it has ever done. I was particularly pleased with this, because a spare engine had been popped in overnight, and the car was untried. In fact, I had a slight personal problem during that race, which gave me a bit of a fright. Going down the Masta Straight – the quickest section of this very quick circuit – I found that the rush of air was getting under the peak of my helmet and threatening to force it up. I decided that the only thing to do was to throw the peak away, so I caught hold of a strap at the back and gave it a yank. I'd got hold of the wrong strap, though, and pulled my goggles off by mistake! Fortunately, I had another pair round my neck, and managed to get them in place. Then I tugged at the peak and eventually, after a lot of effort, it ripped off. I suppose it has something to do with the air flow round the cockpit of the Lotus 25, but since then I have never worn a peak on my helmet.

Brinton: What sort of rev ranges do you use?

Hill: I don't like to see the BRM rev counter drop below 8000 if I can help it. At the beginning of the year we were using up to 10,000 rpm, and later on this was stepped up to 10,500 rpm – though I have occasionally used higher than that. Later in the season, the useful rev range was somewhat widened, but I still didn't like to see the needle fall below 9000 rpm. It doesn't matter so much in second gear, though, when I don't worry if it is around 8000 rpm.

Clark: You frighten me with all your revs! With the Coventry Climax V8 we started off with an 8500 rpm maximum. Eventually we used 9000 rpm, but never over that. I know that 9200 rpm has either blown up the engine, or appeared about to. In the higher gears the Climax has something quite useful from 7000 to 7500 rpm, but I find it can be used as low down as 6000 rpm.

Brinton: I would like to know something about your cars in relation to different circuits. Tell me, if you could choose a particular circuit on which to run the deciding grand prix for the championship, which one would it be in the light of the season's experience?

Hill: I really haven't got a preference. You know, I firmly believe that if a car is good it will be good on any circuit.

Clark: I think there is a lot in what you say, Graham. To take an example, most people would have said that the

Jim Clark, at the wheel of the Lotus 25, won the 1962 British Grand Prix and it was to prove the first of four successive victories in this race. (*T. C. March*)

Lotus 25 was not the ideal car for Monaco, and yet it went there like a bomb – until it retired. I think I'd like to go back to Zandvoort now, just to see how it compared with my first experience in the Lotus 25.

Hill: There's one thing about East London that concerns me. Apparently it has a couple of hairpins where the BRM could be at a disadvantage compared with the Lotus.

Brinton: Now you, Jim, have raced at East London before, and know it well, while Graham is going there for the first time. Is that going to be an advantage?

Clark: No, I don't think so. To my mind, a grand prix driver should be able to learn a circuit in the time allowed for practice, and I know that Graham will. Of course, I'd be perfectly happy to show him the way round in the race itself!

Brinton: What do you think of the value of the drivers' championship? There are some critics who say that it puts the wrong emphasis on the sport.

Hill: I think that the world championship is very good for motor sport. It results in the personal aspect of motor racing being brought home to everyone. People are more interested in people than in machines. To those in the heart of the game the manufacturers' championship is terribly important, but the general public is not very excited about whether BRM or Lotus win the manufacturers' cup. It's a pity, but there it is.

Brinton: Do you think that the present scoring system is completely fair?

Hill: I think it would be very difficult to improve on it. Naturally, looking back on the 1962 season, it would have suited me better if all the points I had scored could have counted towards the championship, but I do feel that the limitation on the number of qualifying events is just about as fair as it can possibly be, and I haven't any suggestions for improving it.

Brinton: Did you approve of the decision to scrap the point for fastest race lap?

Clark: Oh, yes. There have been several occasions when the fastest lap has been open to doubt, and all in all it was an unsatisfactory system.

Hill: There has been a lot of finger trouble about fastest laps, I agree. We are better without it.

Brinton: Don't you think that the scoring system tends to create some confusion in the public mind, certainly towards the end of the season, when points often have to be thrown away?

Hill: It *is* complicated for anyone not following it very closely, but as I say it is a system which produces the fairest result.

Brinton: Both of you must have one championship race which stands out in your memory above all the others.

Jack Brabham (World Champion in 1959, 1960 and 1966) and Jim Clark (World Champion in 1963 and 1965) were both keen private pilots and used their own aircraft to fly to races. (*Nigel Snowdon*)

You, Graham, must have a vivid memory of winning at Zandvoort, because it was your first victory in a grande épreuve. And Jim, you must have felt the same about your first grand prix win at Spa?

Hill: Yes. the Dutch Grand Prix was terribly important, but I don't think it was my best race. For my money the best dice with you, Jim, was the Monaco GP, even though I retired out on the circuit later in the race.

Clark: I am interested that you pick out Monaco, because that was a race I really enjoyed, too. Everything seemed to be coming to a climax when I was pressing Graham, and I was wondering how to get by; indeed, I was debating whether in fact it would be possible, because unfortunately I had lost fourth gear. I would certainly have liked my race to have gone on at least five more laps, just to see whether I *could* have got into the lead.

Hill: Apart from Monaco, we didn't seem to tangle very much in other races. Except at Watkins Glen, of course, where I thought I was a bit outclassed. You drew out a lead and sat on it. No matter what I did I couldn't get within striking distance. That was one of your outstanding days, and an even finer effort than it appeared at the time, because of losing your clutch.

Clark: I had more worries than that at the Glen. At one

stage the engine gave a cough, and I thought the gearbox was going. I heard a noise from one of the carburettor intakes, and that set me thinking that perhaps a valve had gone. I thrashed on, but though I couldn't get the rev counter above 8000 it didn't seem to make any difference to my lap times. Then towards the end, the synchromesh started tightening up. I was very relieved when the end came.

Brinton: Do either of you find you have an off day?

Clark: This season, I had a definite off day at Rouen, but this was due to a rather special reason − the fright I had in practice. In fact, I think I could have got with it if only I had got going at the start.

Hill: I think I must have off days, but I don't notice them. Perhaps I don't want to!

Brinton: Watching your battles from the sidelines, it seemed to me that the German Grand Prix was one day when both of you, and John Surtees and Dan Gurney as well, all had the bit between your teeth. For me, that was the race of the season.

Clark: It was also my one big mistake of the year, when I forgot to switch on my fuel on the start line, and got away well behind the others. I don't know what would have happened if I had moved off with the others, but at least it would have made things interesting!

Brinton: I imagine you, Graham, were a little relieved when Jimmy had his lapse?

Hill: I didn't realise it at the time. Conditions were pretty bad, of course, and I didn't know where Jimmy was − I was having enough trouble with Surtees and Gurney.

Clark: If you had known how far I was behind you, you would probably have thought it was just the Lotus handling in the wet!

Hill: I realised later on that you were coming up fast, because I got a 15-second signal. Judging by the way you were going there was no problem about a Lotus on a damp track!

Brinton: Just why did you forget to switch on your fuel pump?

Clark: As you know, because of the torrential rain before the race, we had been allowed a warming-up lap to look at the state of the circuit. During that lap my goggles got extremely wet. They were steaming up terribly when the two-minute signal was given. At the start of the Monaco GP I had got away on only seven cylinders, because a plug wetted on the line. So after that I have always started the engine with the pumps off, and switched them on afterwards. I carried out this procedure at Nürburgring. I stopped the engine, and made a quick check to see if the rear mirrors were correctly set. Then I started cleaning my goggles furiously. Because of the conditions there was a danger of them steaming up again, so I held them off my face to prevent this. I was so absorbed in doing this that I completely forgot to switch on the fuel when it was time, and the engine died just as I let the clutch in. I've kicked myself many times since! It was a ghastly error.

Brinton: It certainly made your job a little easier, didn't it, Graham?

Hill: I am sure it would have been an even harder race if Jimmy had been up with us at the start.

Brinton: Graham, was Nürburgring your best race of the season?

Hill: Yes, and it was certainly the hardest.

Brinton: The dice between yourself, Surtees and Gurney was so close that I wonder whether you had anything in hand?

Hill: I had to steel myself to drive fast enough to win, but no faster. The 'Ring is no place for pressing on regardless, particularly when it is damp, and the slightest mistake would have put paid to any hope of winning. So far as having anything in hand is concerned, you really never know quite how much extra you may have. I certainly didn't that day.

Clark: I think that in a situation like that you tend to relax occasionally, but only at points where you know the chaps behind cannot possibly get by.

Hill: That's about it. There was one time, though, when I eased back a little too much where some oil had been dropped, and the other two got right up. That was a bit too close, and I had to concentrate like mad in an effort to draw out three or four seconds on them again.

Brinton: And what in your view was your best grand prix, Jim?

Clark: I have driven harder for longer in some of the races I have not won. Nürburgring still makes me shudder to think of it! I suppose I was reacting from being annoyed with myself, but that day I attempted things with the Lotus I didn't think were possible before. I think my car is probably a little trickier in the damp than some of my rivals, but I think the main reason I had such a go in that race was because I knew there were no puddles on the circuit − owing to the gradients all the puddles drain away pretty quickly.

Brinton: Coming back to the cars, it would be fascinating if you could drive one another's machines. Now while you, Jim have not driven a BRM, Graham has had a go in a Lotus.

Hill: Yes, I drove a Lotus 24 at Karlskoga. I thought it weaved a bit, and seemed to be a bit unstable under braking.

Clark: Now you realise what we have to put up with!

Hill: You seem to manage all right, chum. I thought the traction of the Lotus was very good, though.

Clark: That was probably because you were not used to an underpowered car!

Hill: Anyway, I though it was impressive.

Brinton: We have been talking about your cars and your own experiences. Now what about other drivers. Who, in your view, has been really impressive this season?

Clark: I'd say Dan Gurney.

Hill: And I'd second that. He's driven extremely well all this season.

Clark: I would like to put forward two more names that I think were outstanding – John Surtees and Bruce McLaren. Do you agree, Graham?

Hill: Yes, they are also on my list, but Gurney was the tops. If his Porsche had gone better then he would have been right amonst us all the time.

Brinton: And if Stirling had been in the running this year?

Hill: A great deal would have depended on his having a reliable car. But if he had, then I think he would be in the lead for the championship.

Brinton: Stirling once said that it had taken him ten years to learn to concentrate for the whole three hours of a grand prix. Can you concentrate for that period?

Hill: I think that this is one of the most difficult things in motor racing. I am certainly not entirely satisfied with my performance in concentration. Indeed, I reckon I could improve quite a bit.

Clark: I quite agree. I don't think that even Stirling can concentrate one hundred per cent for the whole of a longish race.

Hill: If anyone thinks we are talking nonsense, I advise them to try to concentrate on something for one brief minute – concentrate absolutely, that is – and see how difficult it is.

Clark: In my view, the average person cannot concentrate completely much longer than that.

Hill: There are a lot of things to think about during a race.

Clark: Such as wondering what is happening to other cars instead of thinking about the next corner. As a matter of fact, I let myself think about other things on the straight bits, because I think it helps me to relax.

Brinton: How do you like to run a race? Do you like to forge ahead and then hold a lead?

Clark: I think my ideal race would be to start at the back of the grid and come right through the field to win – which is what Graham nearly did in the 1960 British Grand Prix. But for comfort I prefer to be out in front right from the start.

Hill: And so do I!

Brinton: Which should make things interesting at East London.

Clark: How right you are!

In the South African race, a new addition to the Championship series, Jim Clark led for 150 miles only to run into minor engine problems and Graham Hill won the race. As a result Hill took the Championship with 42 points to the 30 of Clark and BRM won the Constructors' Cup with 42 points to the 36 of Lotus-Climax. Both BRM, after years of frustration and disappointment, and Lotus has become established as serious and successful entrants. Although BRM was very much to the fore during the next three seasons, the team never again won a World Championship. Team Lotus went on to become the world's most successful racing team, a position it held for many years. During the year Ferrari failed to win a single World Championship race. John Surtees with the Lola finished second in the British and German races. The British V8 teams had established that 1500 cc Grand Prix racing was neither processional nor boring and in fact lap speeds at most circuits were only slightly slower than they had been in the last year of the 2500 cc formula.

1963

Although the works Porsche team withdrew at the end of 1962 and the Lolas were now entered by Reg Parnell's small private team, Grand Prix racing was going from strength to strength. BRM introduced the P61 with central monocoque section, but the drivers, Hill and Ginther, were unhappy with the handling (in tests it was discovered that the structure was insufficiently stiff) and relied on the 1962 P57 cars for most of the year. Hill won the first of what was to prove five victories in the Monaco Grand Prix, and Hill and Ginther finished first and second in the United States, but otherwise it proved a disappointing year. Dan Gurney had joined Jack Brabham in the Brabham team and although it failed to win a single Championship race, Gurney finished third at Spa, Brabham was second in Mexico and Gurney second in South Africa. Ferrari had revived, John Surtees had joined the team and with a much improved V6 car won the German Grand Prix. A new team was ATS, headed by former Ferrari designer Carlo Chiti and team manager Romolo Tavoni with Phil Hill and Baghetti as drivers. The ATS project proved a complete disaster, for the cars were slow, ill-handling and

Dan Gurney on opposite lock with his Brabham in the 1963 British Grand Prix. For much of the race he was in second place behind Clark, but retired because of engine failure. (*David Phipps*)

disgustingly prepared. The year proved to be a Jim Clark and Lotus triumph and this pithy account of their year is from *Grand Prix Cars, 1945-65* by Mike Lawrence, (Aston Publications Limited, 1989).

Jim Clark's Outstanding Season

So far as 1963 is concerned, the story is simply told. Lotus retained Clark and Taylor and the 25, but it was Jimmy's year. The season started with a race at Snetterton, where Clark took pole, but had to settle for second to Hill after a locking brake sent him into a multiple spin. He led from pole to flag at Pau with Taylor second, a tenth behind. It was another pole to flag win in the Imola Grand Prix, with second place going to Jo Siffert's 24-BRM. Siffert then won the Syracuse Grand Prix against a thin field. Clark took pole for the Aintree 200, but his car would not start, and he won the International Trophy at Silverstone with Taylor third.

Thus Clark went to Monaco, the opening round of the

World Championship, with three wins and a second from five races already under his belt. There he sat on pole, was slow away, took the lead on lap 18 and then had his gear selectors break when the race was in the bag. In the Belgian Grand Prix he was on the third row, after gearbox trouble in practice, but was in the lead a mile after the start and won by five minutes with the second half in a deluge.

Dutch Grand Prix: pole to flag win. French Grand Prix: pole to flag win. British Grand Prix: pole, a poor start but another win. German Grand Prix: pole, but the engine was not running cleanly so it was finally second place to Surtees' Ferrari. Italian Grand Prix: relatively slow practice (only fourth on the grid) but another win. United States Grand Prix: second in practice, fuel pump played up throughout, third. Mexican Grand Prix: pole to flag win. South African Grand Prix: pole to flag win.

Where does one find adjectives to describe a season like that? Along the way he also won the Kanonloppet and the International Gold Cup. It was typical of his attitude that when experimental drive-shafts failed him on the line at Solitude he insisted new shafts be fitted so he could join in at about half-distance and give the fans value for money. He did too, and sliced 6.5 seconds off the old lap record.

Let the statistics speak for themselves. In 1963 Clark started in a total of 20 F1 races and took 14 pole positions, 11 fastest laps and 12 wins. In the ten World Championship races it was a case of seven pole positions, six fastest laps, a second and a third. Play with the statistics as you will, it remains the outstanding season in the history of Formula 1. [The final statistic is that Clark won the World Championship with 54 points, the maximum achievable on the basis of the best six performances that counted, to the 29 of Graham Hill. Lotus-Climax likewise scored the maximum number of points in the Constructors' Cup.]

1964

Although BRM, Brabham and Lotus produced improved cars for 1964 (and BRM even experimented with a four-wheel-drive car using the Ferguson system), it was to prove a Ferrari year. The Italian team was racing V8 and flat-12-engined cars, as well as an improved version of the old V6 and John Surtees was to win the Championship by the narrowest of margins.

In the first Championship race of the year, the Monaco Grand Prix, Hill and Ginther took the first two places for BRM, ahead of the Lotus 25s of Arundell and Clark – but Clark had taken pole position in practice and led until the rear anti-roll bar broke. Clark won at Zandvoort from Surtees with the V8 Ferrari and another Clark victory followed in Belgium, but only after Dan Gurney (Brabham) had run out of fuel. Gurney more than made up for this disappointment with a win in the French race at Rouen. Clark again won the British race, ahead of Hill and Surtees. Ferrari had been slow to find form in 1964 and the team's first real success came in the German race at the Nürburgring where Surtees and Bandini took first and third places. In this race the new Honda RA271 V12 made its racing debut.

A second Ferrari victory followed in the Austrian Grand Prix, a new addition to the Championship series, held on the bumpy Zeltweg airfield circuit, but

Jim Clark reigned supreme in 1963. Here he is on his way to his first Championship race victory of the year in the Belgian Grand Prix at Spa-Francorchamps. (*Nigel Snowdon*)

here Bandini was the winner. Surtees won again in Italy and then finished second to Graham Hill in the United States race at Watkins Glen. Because of a dispute between Enzo Ferrari and the Italian Sporting Commission, the Maranello cars were nominally entered by the North American Racing Team and painted United States white and blue racing colours. At Watkins Glen the new Tipo 1512 flat-12 Ferrari, which had appeared at Monza in practice, was raced for the first time by Bandini.

There remained only the Mexican Grand Prix and in a Championship system that counted only the best six performances, Surtees was second with 34 points to the 39 of Graham Hill and Clark was third with 30. Clark steamed into the distance, Hill was delayed in the pits after a collision with Bandini's Ferrari and on the last lap Clark's Lotus expired out on the circuit because of an oil leak. Surtees was waved through by Bandini to take second place behind race winner Gurney (Brabham) and clinched the Championship with 40 points to the 39 of Hill. If Clark had won the race,

then Hill would have been the World Champion.

1965

Once again the year was to be dominated by Jim Clark and Lotus. Clark with the 33 won in South Africa, missed Monaco because he was competing at Indianapolis (which he also won), scored a fourth successive victory at Spa and won the French, British, Dutch and German races. Already Drivers' Championship and Constructors' Cup were in the bag and that he failed to finish in the last three races of the year was almost an irrelevancy. Both Clark and the Brabham team had the use of a new 32-valve Climax engine.

At BRM Graham Hill was now partnered by the young Jackie Stewart in his first year in Formula 1, and although Hill won at Monaco (for the third successive time) and in the United States, Stewart was the real sensation; he was second in France, second in Holland, won the Italian race with Hill second and showed such consistent brilliance that it was clear that he was a really

The 1964 World Champion, John Surtees, on his way to a win in the German Grand Prix with his V8 Ferrari.
(*David Phipps*)

great driver in the making. Hill and Stewart finished second and third in the Drivers' Championship and BRM was second to Lotus in the Constructors' Cup, although amassing a greater total of points overall. Of BRM during this period Mike Lawrence has written, 'In the period 1962-65, BRM not only came good but was sufficiently successful and consistent to bury the unreliable reputation it had gained during the preceding 12 years. Unfortunately it was never to enjoy such success again as first it struggled with a 3-litre H16 engine which was heavy and complex and never gave the power which was hoped for it . . . Eventually BRM once again became something of a joke and when it eventually disappeared in the mid-1970s nobody missed its passing.'

Of the other contenders in 1965, Ferrari had sunk back into mediocrity and failed to win a single race. Likewise Cooper. Likewise Brabham, although Gurney finished second in the United States and Mexico. There was, however, an important newcomer

in Formula 1, Honda whose semi-monocoque car with transversely mounted V12 engine had first been driven by almost unknown American driver Ronnie Bucknum in the later races of 1964. Honda's attitude seemed to be that if the car failed (as it did) much of the blame could be attributed to the driver and in any event Honda wanted publicity focused on the car and not a star driver. In 1965 two cars were entered for Ginther and Bucknum and Ginther won the last race of the 1500 cc formula at Mexico City.

So much of the success of Lotus depended on the close relationship between Clark and Lotus chief Colin Chapman. In 1965 *Motor Racing* magazine published two fascinating interviews by John Blunsden, Clark on Chapman and Chapman on Clark.

Jim On Colin

JB. You have known Colin for almost seven years, and obviously you get on extremely well with him. But have you revised your opinion of him in any way over the years?

Honda made a very serious effort with their much improved RA272 V12 cars in 1965. This is Ginther in the British race. He ran well until eliminated by ignition trouble. (*T. C. March*)

Jim. No, at least, not fundamentally. But Colin has certainly changed. These days he is much more able to accept human fallibility. He is far more tolerant in his dealings with mechanics and with people in general. I think he realised this himself, although he tries to laugh it off by saying 'I'm getting old'.

JB. Has this more tolerant attitude benefitted or been appreciated by the team?

Jim. Certainly it has. Mind you, he is still a hard taskmaster, and still retains that knack of getting people to work near miracles for him. Many a time I've seen him talk mechanics into doing what they genuinely think is impossible. But somehow he fires them with some of his own tremendous enthusiasm, and the job gets done. The thing is, if it's really necessary, he'll always be prepared to roll up his own sleeves and lend a hand, and I think people respect him for that.

When Colin Lets Fly

JB. Would you say he has a temper? And if so, what do you think is most likely to make him lose it?

Jim. I suppose most people have tempers, and occasionally Colin will let fly, but not very often, and when he does it's usually with good cause. He is a perfectionist, with a very neat and tidy mind, and the one thing which really annoys him is incompetence. If Colin finds that someone has done something stupid and admits it, he'll admonish him, and perhaps be pretty angry for a minute or two, but he'll not bear a grudge. But just let that person lie to him to hide his guilt. Then he'll give him the works, and quite right too, because one day that person might try to hide something which affects the safety of the driver.

JB. You, of course, work very closely with Colin, but how does he get on with his drivers generally, and particularly with drivers who are new to the team? (I'm referring to all classes of racing, not just Formula 1.)

Jim. Extremely well. One of the big things about Colin is that he will talk man-to-man with his drivers. There's none of the 'I'm the boss, and you'll do as I say' stuff. As a past driver himself, he knows how important it is for the man in the cockpit to be in the right frame of mind, and he does a very good 'fatherly act' on new drivers to give them confidence. At the same time, he'll make it pretty clear to them, in a nice sort of way, that he expects to have the car back in one piece!

Convincing Talker!

JB. What about drivers fresh to the team wanting all sorts of alterations on their cars? Does he go along with this?

Jim. It depends who the driver happens to be. If he is a very experienced man, then Colin will probably allow the car to be set up in the way he wants it, even though it may not suit other drivers in the team. But if Colin is not convinced that the suggested alterations could work, or that the new driver knows sufficient about the car to know what he wants, he will then do a very skilful job of talking the driver out of the changes, and getting him to adapt his driving to suit the car as it is. He can sound very convincing when he wants to, you know!

JB. Now apart from his obvious talents as a racing car designer, Colin must have that something extra which has made him such a successful businessman. Can you put your finger on it?

Jim. Well, there is no doubt at all that he is an extremely shrewd businessman, and I think someone would have to get up very early in the morning to put one over him! The other thing is that he has such an agile mind, and a tremendous capacity for work. Obviously you have to put in a great deal of personal effort to build up a business the way he has built up Lotus, and his apparent tirelessness has obviously been a very valuable asset during the build-up period.

Outside Interests

JB. Does Colin have many interests outside of racing?

Jim. Yes, and this is one of the surprising things about him. Despite all his business and racing commitments, he somehow manages to find time to keep abreast of everything that's going on in the world. And not only that, but he seems to be well read on any subject you care to mention, and I don't just mean mechanical things. You bring up any subject you like, and I'll guarantee he'll be able to hold a sensible conversation on it, and probably surprise you with the amount he knows about it. It's this agile mind again. He has a genuine passion for finding out about things, and obviously has a very retentive memory. This is one of the reasons why he is such interesting company. My own interests have been greatly widened just through hearing him talk on subjects which before had meant little or nothing to me.

JB. Colin has a passion for flying, and you have done a lot of flying with him. Does he strike you as being a particularly good pilot?

Jim. Yes, I think he is a very good pilot, because it is in his nature to make a good job of anything he touches – the perfectionist coming out again. The more he does, obviously the better he becomes, and he has the right temperament. I can only remember one occasion when things looked a bit dodgy, and that was when we were flying to Monza, and had planned to make a refuelling stop at Nice. But we found we had a strong tail wind, and Colin calculated that we would be able to get through non-stop. But of course when we altered course for Monza we were then more or less flying into the wind, and we started to gobble up the fuel. I became a bit nervous about it all, but Colin was as calm as you like all the way, until eventually we landed, with about a thimbleful left in the tank!

JB. Can Colin switch off and really relax when the opportunity arises?

Jim. Certainly he can. If we hang on for a day after a race, he'll thoroughly enjoy himself on a beach, or just relaxing in an armchair with a few books. He's a great reader when he gets the time – it's this thirst for knowledge he has. The other day, we were waiting between practice runs at a Swiss hill climb and picked up a French magazine. I just skimmed through it, looking mainly at the pictures, but Colin spotted an article which caught his interest, then worked hard to try to translate it because he wanted to know exactly what they were saying.

Colin The Family Man

JB. How would you rate him as a family man?

Jim. Oh, he can be a darned good family man. A really devoted father. Maybe it is because he has less opportunity for doing so that most men, and so when he does get a few days with the family he tries to make up for it. Mind you, I don't know whether he would be able to keep it up indefinitely. I get the feeling that after a few days of complete relaxation with Hazel and the children he's ready to get back to business again.

Jim Clark and Colin Chapman when Team Lotus was dominating the 1500cc Formula 1. Clark and Chapman made one of the greatest partnerships racing has ever seen.

JB. Getting back to racing, does he ever let his striving for perfection get the better of him? In other words, does he tend to interfere with things like car preparation?

Jim. I think Colin's ideal world of motor racing would be one which enabled him to do every single job himself. Of course he can't, and I'm sure he realises this better today than ever before. There was a time when he used to infuriate people by insisting on showing them the way to do things, even things which could be done equally well in more than one way. This sort of thing doesn't happen so much now – he's learnt to delegate. Mind you, I think he sometimes has to make a conscious effort not to interfere, even now!

JB. Do you ever fail to see eye-to-eye with Colin over things concerning pre-race practice, such as what modifications to try, or how many laps you should put in?

Jim. Generally speaking we seem to think along the same lines in these cases; after all, we have the same aim, namely to win the race. If I want to try any experiments on my car, we'll discuss it, and usually Colin will let me try them out. As for the number of laps, I hardly every put in more than five or six practice laps at a go, and so there's never any need to hold out a 'come in' signal. Occasionally he'll get a bit anxious if the opposition starts to go quickly, but then he goes about it in a very subtle way. He'll not come over to me and say, 'Come on now, get your finger out'. He'll just make some remark to someone else like 'Phew, old Graham's going today. He's just done a thirty-nine dead', and he'll rely on the information filtering through to me. When it does, I get the message that he expects me to do something about it!

Information Service

JB. And how about the race itself? Does he try to control you from the pits, or does he leave it to you to run your own race?

Jim. Colin never tries to control me once the race has started. He realises that I know better than anyone else how fast I can drive the car. But he gives me a wonderful pit information service. We have perfected this over the years, and it's now got so that we can almost read each other's thoughts. I've only got to think, 'I wonder where Dan fits into the picture?', and next time round there it is, hung out on the board. But there's one pit signal that Colin will never hang out, and that's the 'Go faster'. He learnt many years ago that a driver can get himself into trouble when he is encouraged to try too hard. Colin is an excellent race tactician, and the Lotus pit organisation is first class.

JB. Colin designs some superb racing cars, but what is he like in helping you to get them fully sorted out!

Jim. I think the results speak for themselves. In Formula 1 we hit a sticky period on the changeover to 13 inch wheels, and it was not until we went back to the Dunlop yellow spots that we got things really sorted out. But the most spectacular improvement has been with the Formula 2 car. Last year, it was a bit of a pig, but this season it has been really terrific. That car is very well sorted indeed now. As for the big sports cars, well, to my mind I'm sure the job of sorting out would have been easier if more time and labour had been available for this project. Unfortunately, Indianapolis meant that something had to suffer, and I'm afraid it's the sports cars which have suffered the most.

JB. You travel around a lot together. You must find Colin good company?

Jim. Very good company. He's a fun-loving person and very affable. He's quite quick to see the chance of a good practical joke, and he'll see the funny side when one is played on him. As I've said before, he's a mine of information, and being a good conversationalist he can be a very interesting person to spend a long journey with.

Something Up His Sleeve?

JB. Colin has already given a great deal to motor racing, but do you think he's got some more big breakthroughs up his sleeve?

Jim. Obviously, although I know one or two of his future plans, there's a lot more he keeps to himself. But personally, I would like to see what he could do if he went to town in the production car field. I'm sure he could be as spectacular in that field as he has been in racing. You know, it's a real education to watch him solving a design problem. He has such a clear and creative mind. I sometimes think, 'Boy, could I do with you up on the farm, to sort out my mechanisation!'. I'll tell you one thing – Colin need never be out of a job: I'll always take him on as a development engineer for my agricultural machinery. And you know, he'd make a damned fine job of it, too!

Colin On Jim

JB. Everyone acknowledges that Jim is a great racing driver, but how do you rate him as a team man?

Colin. Very highly, and for this reason. Jim will always have a real go, and give his very best. In all the time I have known him, I have seen him have remarkably few off days. Now this a tremendous morale booster for the team as a whole. The mechanics will work really hard preparing the cars when they know that the man in the cockpit is going to make the most of what they give him. It means that all the hard work is converted into racewinning potential.

JB. Are there any conditions under which Jim finds it more difficult to produce his best form?

Colin. Yes, when he is right on top. I think he feels the strain more when he's expected to win, and he's sitting up there ready to be shot at. I thought this would happen when he won his first world championship, in 1963, and sure enough, he had a most difficult time early in 1964. I have the feeling that he might have to go through another tricky period now that he has won the title again. Everyone will be expecting him to win, just when he has lost the target to attack, namely the championship. Now that the title is his, he's going to miss the fight for it.

JB. Do you think he's reached the point where he's stopped learning?

Colin. Definitely not, he's getting better all the time. When he won his first title, people were hailing him as one of the 'greats', but I felt then, 'Just you wait. He's only 27 years old, and he's going to get better all the time.' He's proved it already during the last two years, and believe me, he's going to go on getting better, too.

JB. He feels that he is not a particularly good test driver. Would you agree with this?

Colin. Not really. In some respects I think he is very good. For example, he is a very good trouble-shooter. He can tell me exactly what is wrong, and can get the optimum mechanical performance out of carburation, brakes, gearbox, and so on. If he has a fault as a test driver, it is that he is too inclined to adapt his driving to suit the imperfect characteristics of his car. Then, he brings into use his great natural skill, and perhaps in the end he can get the car round faster than he might have expected even if the car had been ideally set up. This ability to 'live with' a racing car is a wonderful talent in the race, but it can be a bit of a nuisance at times during a session of chassis testing.

JB. How does Jim get on with the mechanics?

Colin. I would say better than most drivers. He has a good personal relationship with them, and even when things go badly wrong he's far more likely to let me have it rather than moan to the mechanics!

JB. Naturally, every driver likes to win, but would you say that Jim sometimes finds it a bit difficult to accept defeat?

Colin. Naturally, any driver must feel a certain disappointment if he has been beaten, but in Jim's case it depends upon why he was beaten. If he feels that he has been let down by the car or by a component of it, and that this has robbed him of a victory, he'll feel a little low for a few minutes – say, ten at the most. By that time he'll have shrugged it off, and will be back to his usual cheerful self.

JB. Now what about the minutes before a race? Does he get a bit of a twitch on?

Colin. Oh yes, but he is extremely good at disguising it. Don't be misled by that very calm looking expression on the starting grid. Deep down he's pretty tensed up. If he wasn't, he probably wouldn't make such meteoric starts!

JB. How is it that Jim can put in four or five fantastically quick ones right from the fall of the flag?

Colin. This, of course, is one of the big things about Jim. He has tremendous powers of concentration, and he can make a supreme effort right from the word 'Go'. But for the rest of the race he is for the most part driving with a little bit in hand. I can honestly say that I have rarely seen Jim drive flat-out for more than about five laps at a time in a GP. The fact that he can do so right at the start is, of course, a big advantage, because it takes him clear of the drivers who take a little time to settle down.

JB. This theory that Jim dislikes driving in traffic – fact or myth?

Colin. Complete myth. The thing is he rarely has to. Either he has the ability to get out in front right away, or soon work his way up there, or else his car is not competitive, in which case there is little point in dicing it. For example, if two cars prove to be very evenly matched you can dice it out all through the race, first one leading and towing the other, and then the other taking over and doing the towing. But at the end of it all, the same two cars are in the same relative positions. In other words, all the dicing and scrapping has achieved absolutely nothing (except

Jim Clark storms to victory with the Lotus 33-Climax in the 1965 British Grand Prix. Once again he scored maximum points in the World Championship. (*T. C. March*)

perhaps given the crowd something to shout about). In a case like that, Jim will do the sensible thing, and sit on the other chap's tail and worry him. Sooner or later he'll probably make a mistake under pressure, and Jim will be past, or else, if the car is still there at the end, Jim will save his overtaking manoeuvre until the final lap. It's as simple as that.

JB. And what about Jim in the rain?

Colin. Well, need you ask? This is what really shows him up against the others. His extreme sensitivity comes out when conditions are bad, and he has put up some brilliant performances in the wet, and not all of them have been appreciated. For example, you may remember that day at Nürburgring, in 1962, when he inadvertently switched off his fuel on the start line, and got away last. A thing was made of the tremendous dice between Graham Hill, John Surtees and Dan Gurney for the lead, but do you know Jim was taking 6 seconds a lap off them and working his way past the slower cars? In the end, even he frightened himself, and rather than risk crunching the car he decided to ease up and settle for his fourth place. But had he maintained his earlier pace, and if he had been able to get past them, he would have won the race, after setting off last. That, to my mind, was a really great drive, which didn't get the credit it deserved.

JB. Jim seems to do a great deal of racing. Do you sometimes send him to meetings he would prefer not to attend?

Colin. He does a lot of racing, yes, but this is because he wants to. Mind you, he is inclined to alter his mind quite a lot, and you may find that he will be racing somewhere when, a few months before, he had said that he definitely wasn't interested. For example, right now he says that he doesn't want to do the Tasman series, and if he sticks to this, then we'll not encourage him, but send someone else. But I wouldn't be a bit surprised to hear that he had changed his mind!

JB. Do you ever find yourself talking him into going anywhere?

Colin. I suppose sometimes I do, in so far as occasionally I can detect that he hasn't a lot of enthusiasm for a particular race. Then, I'll probably waken up his interest in it until in the end he's all for it. But if he still prefers not to go, then he doesn't go. But as I said, Jim likes his racing, and usually he doesn't need much talking into it!

JB. Jim says you have a wonderful understanding with him during the race with regard to pit signals, but do you get any sort of return messages from him?

Colin. No. A long time ago we gave up giving signals from the car to the pits, because you're telling the opposition as much as you're telling your own pit, and that's crazy. After all, what's the point in signalling 'I'm

An informal
photograph taken
during the Tasman
series, with left to
right, Australian
driver Frank Gardner,
Jack Brabham and, in
shorts, Jim Clark.
(Nigel Snowdon)

running out of brakes' when there's nothing we can do about it in the pits, and the only reaction will be a signal to the chap behind from his pit saying, 'Clark brakes', which will spur him on to a bigger effort. But though I get no signals from him, I can usually sense when Jim is in some sort of trouble; it's something about the way he sits in the cockpit, I think, but whatever it is, I can normally tell when something's up.

JB. Do you try to influence his race in any way from the pits?

Colin. Influence, perhaps. Dictate, never. I make a point of providing him with some information on every lap so that he has the clearest possible picture of the race as a whole. Then it's up to him to make the decisions. For example, if his lap times were falling for no apparent reason. I wouldn't dream of asking him to speed up, but I might just give him a lap time, which he can then interpret as he thinks best. Maybe the figure is satisfactory for the condition of the car, or on the other hand this may tell him

that he's taking it just a little bit too easy. But it is Jim who makes the decision whether or not he should alter his speed, not me.

JB. Now how about timekeeping of the other sort? Would you say Jim is a reliable sort of chap from the point of view of punctuality?

Colin. Reliable, yes, in so far as I always know that he will present himself on time for a test session, or in good time for practice or the race. If he happens to be late, there will be a very good reason for it. But I would not go so far as to say that he is obsessed with the need for punctuality, and he does tend sometimes to be a bit late arriving when he has to meet top brass at social functions. I think that this is because deep down he just doesn't enjoy these affairs, and he likes to put off the evil hour to the last possible moment!

JB. But he is a lot less shy than he used to be, surely?

Colin. Yes, I think he probably is, although I don't think he'll ever really enjoy the spotlight of publicity for its own sake. At the same time, he behaves extremely well at social functions, and even at a dreary affair he will make a point of going around shaking hands with all his hosts before leaving, whereas I must admit my own inclination will be to sidle out quietly without being noticed! This is Jim's natural politeness coming out.

JB. You spend a lot of time together. Do you find Jim a good companion?

Colin. Yes, we are good friends, and we get on well together. I think he is a nervous passenger on the road, but I don't know that I frighten him, and in any case these days he seems to be doing most of the driving (which doesn't make me nervous!) while I do the chauffeuring when we're flying. I wouldn't say that Jim actually creates much humour − you could hardly call him a ball of fire − but he can certainly keep his end up in repartee and has a good sense of humour.

JB. Would you say he finds it easy to relax?

Colin. Certainly I would, and I think at times that he would like a bit more opportunity for doing so. Recently we spent an enjoyable three days' holiday down in Spain, and I think we managed to get through without discussing motor racing once!

JB. Everyone has his faults or weaknesses. Have you noticed any applicable to Jim?

Colin. Well, he bites his nails, if that's what you mean! And he has one rather surprising tendency for someone who is called upon to make split-second decisions. In his private life he just can't make up his mind about things. I don't mean necessarily really big decsions, but the little everyday things, like what to choose from a menu, or whether or not to buy something.

Anti-press!

JB. Finally, would you say that Jim has any pet hates?

Colin. Yes, he has. He has a complete and utter distaste for the Press! This may sound surprising, but in fact it isn't really. In the first place, Jim races because he loves it. Naturally, he likes making a lot of money out of it, too, but to him it is a sport, not a business. And this means that he couldn't care less about publicity. If he had his way, at the end of a meeting he would creep away into obscurity until it was time for the next race. He's not interested in the glamour or the frills. Secondly, there's been a terrible amount of rubbish written about him by the Press, and he resents this, especially as the worst stuff seems to be churned out by those who invade his private life the most. You've no idea how he gets hounded. He used to complain because so many inaccuracies were printed about his racing, and so he made a real effort to talk to the Press and give them the facts. But still the distortions appear, and frankly he holds the Press generally in pretty low regard. In a way I can understand his feelings. I'll tell you one thing. If you want to see Jim explode, just listen to a so-called professional journalist asking him a completely asinine and irrelevant question, and wait for the reaction. It can be quite impressive! Oh, by the way, I think MOTOR RACING and some of your contemporaries are exempted from Jim's list of 'undesirable fiction'!

Despite the general unhappiness about the introduction of the 1500 cc formula, it had proved a great success. The achievements of Lotus, Coventry Climax and BRM had consolidated Britain's position as the foremost racing nation. The racing had been close and fast. And it marked the end of an era, an era during which racing was contested by comparatively small enthusiastic teams without, in the majority of cases, significant financial backing. The high costs of the 3-litre formula that followed and the introduction of sponsorship would change all that. The role of Coventry Climax cannot be underestimated. Progressive development of the FWM V8 engine had kept Lotus at the forefront of racing and it was sad that their very advanced flat-16 1500 cc engine was never raced. The company had been acquired by Jaguar and, apart from supplying a few engines while teams awaited their new 3-litre units in 1966 and the early part of 1967, disappeared from the racing scene.

1966

For 1966 there came into force the new 3000 cc Grand Prix formula which had been decided upon as long before as 1963. There was an alternative of 1500 cc supercharged (for it was possible that a team would want to supercharge an engine from the preceding 1500 cc formula), but the real – and unintended – significance of this alternative would not emerge until the appearance of the first turbocharged Renault Formula 1 car in 1977. For 1966 a minimum dry weight of 500kg was imposed and race distances were changed to between 300 and 400 km.

No one was quite sure what engine would be needed for the new formula – and, initially, engines were to prove the real problem – and, after it was all over, John Cooper of Cooper Cars wrote, 'The new 3-litre Grand Prix Formula was starting in 1966 and we believed that it would be immensely expensive with all the cars having four-wheel-drive and 24-cylinder engines!'

An alternative view was that despite their many failures over the years Ferrari would have the financial and technical power to dominate. To quote David Phipps (*Autocourse, 1966-1967*), 'Early in May 1966, in an article headed BRABHAM FOR WORLD CHAMPION? I asked "What is there to prevent a Ferrari walkover in Formula One racing this year?" In reply I said, "It may be a long shot, but I have a sneaking feeling that the Brabham-Repco, with about 320 bhp, 7 mpg and a well-tried chassis, will be the best all-round car for most of the season. The more powerful cars will be bigger and heavier and will use more fuel, and their peaky torque curves will make

them more difficult to drive than the Brabham!"'

'At the time several people ridiculed the article, and one or two editors refused to publish it. But looking back over the Grand Prix year it seems that most of the points I made were valid. Brabham never had much more than 320 bhp, yet he won races on circuits of all types. Even when he did not finish he was usually well placed when forced to retire, and Dennis Hulme backed him up magnificently with a string of second and third places.'

Jack Brabham at the wheel of the very simple space-frame Brabhams designed by Ron Tauranac and with Australian Repco V8 engines with a single overhead camshaft per bank of cylinders won the French, British, Dutch and German races and took the Drivers' Championship.

Of the other marques raced in 1966, Ferrari produced both a 2.4-litre V6 raced in certain events early in the year and a new V12 3-litre which John Surtees drove to victory at Spa before falling out with Ferrari at Le Mans and switching to the Cooper team. Surtees had crashed badly with a Lola in the Can-Am series, in North America in the Autumn of 1965, made an almost miraculous recovery and the final straw in a disintegrating relationship with Ferrari had been team manager Eugenio Dragoni's suggestion that Surtees was not fit enough to take a full share of the driving burden in the 24 Hours race. BRM raced V8 cars with the engine enlarged to 2 litres while they waited for the overweight and over-complex H16 to become raceworthy (but Stewart won the Monaco Grand Prix, the first Championship race of the new formula, with a 2-litre car); Lotus struggled with 2-litre

Brabham scored his first win with his new Repco-powered Formula 1 car in the 1966 International Trophy at Silverstone. At this stage in the season the team had only one of the new cars ready to race and a second did not appear until the French Grand Prix at Reims nearly two months later. The car that raced at Silverstone was the BT19 built to take the 1965 16-cylinder 1500 cc Coventry Climax engine that never became available. (*T. C. March*)

Climax and BRM-powered cars, but also used the H16 BRM and Clark scored a remarkable victory with a 43-H16 in the United States Grand Prix; Cooper opted for the V12 Maserati engine (a much developed derivative of the engine raced by the Maserati works in 1957). Rindt finished second at Spa after leading for much of the wet race, was second again at Watkins Glen and Surtees was second in Germany and won the last race of the year at Mexico City. Neither the new McLaren team (using both Ford and Serenissima V8 engines, nor Dan Gurney's Eagle Team (using the 2.7-litre Climax 4-cylinder unit until the V12 Weslake became available) scored anything worthy of mention. Likewise the new V12 Honda driven by Ginther was unsuccessful. Brabham won the 1966 Drivers' Championship with 42 points to the 28 of Surtees.

The 1966 World Champion, Jack Brabham, and the only man to win the Championship with a car bearing his own name. (*Nigel Snowdon*)

1967

Simplicity was to be the keynote of the successful cars of the 3000 cc Formula for many years and Brabham continued to dominate Formula 1 in 1967. Hulme won the Monaco and German Grand Prix, took seconds in Germany and Canada and thirds at Zandvoort (the Dutch race), Watkins Glen and Mexico City to win the Championship. Jack Brabham won in Canada and finished second in Holland, Germany, Italy and Mexico, good enough for second place. The car that led to the rationalisation of racing was to be the Lotus 49. Persuaded by Colin Chapman, Ford invested £100,000 into the development of the twin-cam V8 Cosworth engine which was, ultimately, to monopolise Formula 1 starting grids for many years. Lotus had the exclusive use of the Cosworth engine in 1967, but it was to be available to other teams from the following year.

Although Jim Clark with the Lotus 49 won the Dutch Grand Prix on the model's début – a remarkable feat in itself – the cars suffered teething troubles during the year. The other Lotus wins in 1967 were by Clark in the British, United States and Mexican Grands Prix. Clark took third place in the Drivers' Championship with 41 points to the 57 of Hulme and 46 of Brabham.

Ferrari failed to win a single Championship Grand Prix in 1967 and suffered a tragic blow with the fatal crash of Lorenzo Bandini at Monaco, but other users of V12 engines enjoyed a measure of success. Pedro Rodriguez scored an unexpected victory for Cooper in the South African Grand Prix at the beginning of the year when Hulme (Brabham) made a late pit stop for brake fluid; Dan Gurney with the Eagle won the Belgian race (the zenith of the Weslake-powered Eagle's career which ended in 1968); and Surtees took an impressive victory in the Italian Grand Prix with the new RA300 Honda. BRM's best performance with the H16 was a second place by Stewart in Belgium.

One of the Brabham team's finest victories in 1967 was at Monaco where Hulme scored the first of two Championship race victories that year. Hulme was still using a 1966 chassis and the 1966 engine with Oldsmobile-based cylinder block. (*Nigel Snowdon*)

Denis Hulme won the World Championship in 1967, with Brabham in second place, and it was a win based on consistent performances rather than any other factors. (*Nigel Snowdon*)

The Lotus 49 with Cosworth-Ford V8 engine was the sensation of 1967 and the engine was to dominate racing for many years. Here Clark is seen on his way to a win in the 1967 British Grand Prix, one of four Championship wins that he scored during the year. (*Nigel Snowdon*)

1968

By 1968 the Cosworth engine was also being used by McLaren (who had 'toyed' with a V12 BRM-powered car in 1967) and the Matra entered by Ken Tyrrell for Jackie Stewart. Brabham used a four overhead camshaft Repco engine that proved hopelessly unreliable and BRM, having abandoned the H16, raced new V12 cars. Cooper, in their last season of racing, used BRM V12 engines, Beltoise drove a works Matra with the team's own V12 which had been raced extensively in sports cars and Honda raced both the improved V12 RA301 and introduced, with disastrous results, the air-cooled V8 RA302. Ferrari too adhered to the V12 and Chris Amon had been joined in the team by the young Belgian, Jacky Ickx.

Jim Clark with the Lotus 49 won the South African Grand Prix. This was the last occasion on which Lotus ran in their traditional green and yellow colours, for as from the beginning of the European season the cars were decked out in the red, white and gold colours of 'Gold Leaf Team Lotus', the first real outside sponsorship in Formula 1. Before the first European Grand Prix in Spain, the Grand Prix scene had been shaken by tragedy. Jim Clark was killed in a Formula 2 race at Hockenheim and over 20 years later it remains almost unbelievable that one of the greatest drivers of all time and undoubtedly the greatest of his day should be killed in such a trivial race and when he still had so much potential unfulfilled. Shortly afterwards BRM driver Mike Spence was killed while testing a Lotus at Indianapolis.

In addition Jackie Stewart injured a wrist in a practice crash for the Formula 2 Madrid Grand Prix at the end of April, missed the Spanish and Monaco Grands Prix and was in pain for much of the year. Without Clark (whose place in the Lotus team was taken by young Jackie Oliver) and without Stewart, missing from the first two European races, Graham Hill, perhaps the most hard working of all Formula 1 drivers of the post-war years, had a much enhanced chance of winning his second World Championship with the improved Lotus 49B. Hill won in Spain and Monaco, McLaren won the Belgian Grand Prix with his new Cosworth-powered McLaren M7A (Stewart ran out of fuel whilst leading). The Dutch Grand Prix was run in the wet and Stewart scored a brilliant victory with Beltoise at the wheel of the V12 Matra in second place. Stewart was third in the French race, again held in the wet, at Rouen, and Ickx scored Ferrari's only win of the year. The race was marred by the fatal crash of the inexperienced Jo Schlesser driving the air-cooled V8 Honda on its race début. On the approach to the Nouveau Monde hairpin he lost control and hit the bank, the car overturned and caught fire and within moments the fire had spread across the road.

In the British race at Brands Hatch Hill retired and Stewart, slowed by his painful wrist, finished a poor sixth. The winner was Jo Siffert, with the new Lotus 49B of the Rob Walker/Jack Durlacker team and this was the last World Championship race victory scored by a private entrant. Bad weather was only too frequent a phenomenon at European Grands Prix in 1968 and the German race at the Nürburgring was run

The 1976 season was marred by dissension, disqualification and by Niki Lauda's near-fatal accident. James Hunt won the World Championship by the margin of one point from Lauda. 'Master James' is seen with his McLaren M26 in the Dutch Grand Prix which he won. (*Nigel Snowdon*)

James Hunt, World Champion in 1976 and the last British Champion, despite Nigel Mansell's gallant efforts. (*Nigel Snowdon*)

The remarkable P34 six-wheel Tyrrell which was always a front runner in 1976. This is Patrick Depailler in the Swedish Grand Prix in which he finished second behind Jody Scheckter with a similar car. (*Nigel Snowdon*)

Although 1977 was largely dominated by Niki Lauda and Ferrari once more, the strongest 'second' contender was Jody Scheckter with the Harvey Postlethwaite-designed Wolf. Scheckter is seen at Monaco where he beat Lauda into second place. (*Nigel Snowdon*)

The turbocharged Renault first appeared in 1977 and gradually became more reliable and competitive. The team's first victory came in the 1979 French Grand Prix at Dijon where Jean-Pierre Jabouille won with this RS11 car. (*Nigel Snowdon*)

Ferrari remained very much to the forefront during 1978 and 1979. Above is Carlos Reutemann who finished third in Canada in 1978 with his 312T3 behind team-mate Villeneuve and Scheckter (Wolf). The photograph was taken during Friday practice in the wet. Below is Gilles Villeneuve on his way to a win with the 312T4 in the 1979 South African Grand Prix. (*Nigel Snowdon*)

Ferrari raced cars with the flat-12 engine during 11 consecutive seasons, but by 1980 the cars were proving unreliable and outpaced by the opposition. Here in the Dutch race at Zandvoort Villeneuve (Ferrari 312T5) leads Bruno Giacomelli (Alfa Romeo 179), Carlos Reutemann (Williams FW07B), Mario Andretti (Lotus 81) and John Watson (McLaren M29C). (*Nigel Snowdon*)

Below: In 1980 Frank Williams, who had reformed his team following the take-over by Canadian Walter Wolf, began to enjoy substantial success and Alan Jones was World Champion at the wheel of Williams FW07B cars. Here Jones is seen in the Canadian race which he won from team-mate Carlos Reutemann. (*Nigel Snowdon*)

Left: Nelson Piquet, the Brazilian driver who forged such close links with the Brabham team and won the World Championship in 1981 and 1983. He won again in 1987 with a Williams-Honda. (*Nigel Snowdon*)

Below: Ayrton Senna must now rank as one of the greatest drivers of all time. This photograph was taken in 1986 when he was a member of the JPS Lotus team. (*Nigel Snowdon*)

One of the most exciting drivers of all time, almost a cult figure: Gilles Villeneuve who crashed with fatal results in practice for the 1982 Belgian Grand Prix at Zolder. (*Nigel Snowdon*)

Above: In 1987 the McLaren team – for just the one year – was toppled from its dominating role in Formula 1 and Alain Prost, seen here at Monaco, won 'only' the Brazilian, Belgian and Portuguese Grands Prix and finished fourth in the World Championship. (*Nigel Snowdon*)

At the wheel of the Lotus 99T, now with 'active' suspension, Honda turbocharged engine and Camel sponsorship, Ayrton Senna was a force to be reckoned with throughout 1977 Senna, who took third place in the World Championship, is seen on his way to winning the Monaco Grand Prix. (*Nigel Snowdon*)

Opposite page: Nigel Mansell with his Williams-Honda in the 1987 Brazilian Grand Prix. Mansell finished second that year in the World Championship to team-mate Piquet. (*Nigel Snowdon*)

For 1989 Nigel Mansell left Williams to drive for Ferrari and scored an unexpected win in the first race of the season in Brazil after Senna (McLaren) and Berger (Ferrari) had collided at the first bend and Patrese's leading Williams blew up its Renault engine. (*Nigel Snowdon*)

In the 1968 German Grand Prix run in mist and rain Jackie Stewart with Ken Tyrrell's blue Matra MS10 scored what was probably the finest victory of his career and won by a margin of just over four minutes. (*Nigel Snowdon*)

in torrential rain and thick mist. The proceedings were enlivened by American servicemen who threw empty bottles on the track, one of which punctured a tyre on Gurney's Eagle. Stewart drove what was probably the finest race of his career to win by just over four minutes from Hill. The next two races were to prove a McLaren benefit, for Hulme won in Italy and Canada. Stewart scored his third victory of the year in the United States race at Watkins Glen and, as in 1964, the Championship was still wide open and could be won by Hill, Stewart or Hulme. For much of the last race at Mexico City Hill led with Stewart in his wheel-tracks, but Stewart fell back because of an engine misfire. Hill went on to take the Championship with 48 points to the 36 of Stewart. Of the year's 12 races, 11 had been won by cars with Cosworth engines.

Graham Hill, World Champion for the second time in 1968, at the wheel of the Lotus 49B. His hard work, his good humour and immense tolerance made him one of the most popular of drivers. (*Nigel Snowdon*)

193

The Saga of the Wings

The first use of a high-mounted aerofoil can be traced back to the Porsche 550 *Spyder* entered in the Supercortemaggiore 1000 kms race in June 1956. Of this Denis Jenkinson wrote in *Motor Sport*, 'An experiment that could have a future is the upside-down aerofoil controlled by the driver of the Porsche *Spyder* to apply increased loading on the tyres when cornering. It has a range of −3 degrees to +17 degrees and acts through the centre of gravity of the car. Although made with typical Swiss engineering ability, it was rejected by the scrutineers, and the cousins May, from Zurich, were unable to test their theories under racing conditions.' One of these cousins was Michael May, later responsible for the 'HE' cylinder head development for the Jaguar V12 engine.

In 1966 Jim Hall's Chaparral team, based near Midland in Texas, very experienced in Can-Am sports car racing and backed by General Motors, had produced their 2E Can-Am car with a large aerofoil mounted above body turbulence on tall struts bolted to the suspension uprights. The aerofoil was connected hydraulically to a foot pedal in such a way that pressure of the driver's left foot would pivot it nearly flat for minimum drag on the straights, but release of pressure would flip it into maximum-downforce position. This aerofoil was next adopted on the 1967 2F sports Prototype which took on Ferrari and Ford in the Prototype World Championship.

Of this car Peter Lyons wrote (*The Chaparral 2, 2D and 2F*, Profile Publications Ltd, 1972), 'To watch a good driver's artistry with the wing pedal was enthralling. Jim Hall once remarked that his whole clutchless Chaparral concept "gives me more combinations." It sounds like talking about punches, but he was talking about the different ways to deal with corners and traffic. [The Chaparral was also fitted with GM 3-speed 'automatic' transmission.]

'An important factor about the wing, as Phil Hill pointed out, was that (providing it didn't fall off completely), it was "fail safe". Should anything go wrong in the feathering mechanism, or should the driver suddenly need his left foot on the brakes, the wing instantly went into its full-drag, full downforce, maximum understeer mode.

'Another point was that the whole car was a single integrated engineering whole; the two most prominent features, the transmission and the flipper, complemented each other − in fact the one led to the other.' During 1967 the 2Fs ran in eight races and Phil Hill/Mike Spence won the last, the BOAC 500 Miles race at Brands Hatch.

Wings were adopted by the Grand Prix teams in 1968, but unlike that on the Chaparral, they were not an integrated part of the design. At the Belgian race at Spa in 1968 one of the Ferraris featured an aerofoil mounted high above the gearbox behind the cockpit and Brabham also adopted fixed wings mounted on struts above the gearbox. By the Dutch race Ferrari had moved the aerofoil forward over the engine. McLaren and Lotus had adopted rear wings by the French Grand Prix and on the Lotus they were not only tall, spindly affairs, but the downward thrust operated directly on the rear suspension uprights. During practice for the French race Oliver crashed badly when the aerofoil failed and the causes and implication of the accident were discussed by Bill Garvin in *Speedworld International* of 13 July, 1968.

They started small. The rear wing on Chris Amon's Ferrari at the 1968 Belgian Grand Prix. Amon is leading Surtees (Honda). (*Nigel Snowdon*)

Now that Formula 1 racing cars are beginning to look like aeroplanes, there's one aspect of the transition that seems to have gone unnoticed. Racing drivers are simultaneously taking on the role of test pilots: they are delving into the unknown. Jackie Oliver was reflecting very seriously about this aspect of his job after his crash during practice for the French Grand Prix at Rouen last Friday.

'I can't really say why it happened because I honestly don't know,' says Jackie. 'I was catching Attwood and Siffert through the very fast right-hander before the pits then slipstreamed up on them. Some 300 yards beyond the corner I was in Attwood's slipstream and some 20 ft behind him when the car seemed to wander across the road. The next thing I knew it had swapped ends and it was going backwards. I had got on the brakes to slow it as soon as it started to spin, but then I declutched to get the thing going forwards again which I succeeded in doing. The trouble was, I wasn't going straight down the circuit then. I was going off at an angle of about 30 degrees. I got on the dirt, saw the brick wall coming up, but just couldn't get the car back off the dirt. Luckily enough I hit the wall with a glancing blow which reduced the impact somewhat, bounced off the wall, and come to a standstill. I jumped out and put as much distance between myself and the car as I could in the shortest possible time. Obviously something happened for the car to dive off the road when running in a straight line – now what that was I just don't know. We checked the engine and the gearbox and they hadn't seized; there weren't any marks on the road or anything found on the post mortem of the car to suggest that anything broke. The only other possibility is the new thing we're trying, the aerodynamics (the *aerodoomanics* as Graham Hill calls them), which one would tend to pick on, it being a new thing, but this by no means conclusively proves that this was the cause.'

When Colin Chapman saw that it was one of his cars that had crashed he ran up the track where he saw the Lotus 49B lying in two pieces – in the crash the bell-housing had broken and the radius rods were torn out, so that rear wheels, gearbox and aerofoil lay some distance from the rest of the car. 'Did you hit anything?' he asked the dazed Oliver: 'No,' replied Jackie, who was already thinking in terms of what had sparked off the incident.

Colin turned around and rushed down to the pits to tell Graham not to go out because Jackie's car had broken in two. But on returning to the scene he realised that, in fact, Jackie had hit something very, very hard, and his survival proved the strength rather that the fragility of the Lotus. Unfortunately Colin had already told a number of people that it appeared the bell-housing had broken and this was announced over the public address system and later reported in some newspapers.

Then they started to break. Oliver's Lotus 49B in the pits at Rouen in 1968. The aerofoil broke during practice. Oliver crashed heavily and the car broke in two. (*Nigel Snowdon*)

The effects of the aerofoils now fitted to the front and rear of almost every Formula 1 car is the creation of a downward pressure. In the case of the Lotus this is quite a considerable force – it is calculated that at a speed of 150 mph the front aerofoils on the 49B create a downward force described technically as negative lift, of 200 lb and the rear wing a force of 400 lb. As Colin Chapman explained, 'This had proved to be a very real advantage in fast corners where the downward forces press the car harder into the road to give better adhesion and consequently a higher cornering speed – it's a real bonus because it's equivalent to that much extra weight giving the car better adhesion but you don't have the problems of accelerating it or cornering it as you would have if it were simply added to the mass of the car itself.'

These forces are calculated for the car when it is travelling alone – the exact effect that the turbulence created by another car or cars has on the aerofoils has not yet been determined. Jackie Oliver explained, 'It's not difficult to see that if you get a freak condition, you could get a 400 lb up-load at the back and 200 lb at the front. But if you got this effect adversely, that is, say up on the front wing at the left-hand side of the car and downwards on the right, you're going to get the thing going across the road. You're going to get one light wheel and one heavy wheel, together with the possibility of the turbulence then affecting the back wing and making it light – then, there it goes.' But Jackie was careful to point out that both he and Colin, who proposed this theory, were only guessing, and that it was only a theory.

Jackie personally ruled out the possibility of driver error. 'Someone said I got a wheel on the dirt to start with. Now, I'm sure I didn't get a wheel on the dirt but even if I did, a car doesn't spin if you get a wheel on the dirt when it is travelling in a straight line and there are no side forces at all. I've had all four wheels out in the dirt many times in a straight line and nothing happens.'

Whatever happened last Friday afternoon at Rouen is a mystery and remains so. But it does seem that racing drivers are exploring the unknown at today's very high speeds. Recently Air Commodore Widdows remarked when Bobbin' Robin told him he had driven Ulf Norinder's Lola T70 at 195 mph at the Nürburgring, 'Good heavens, boy, I used to test aeroplanes that couldn't go that fast!'

This accident did not deter the teams and at the British Grand Prix at Brands Hatch rear wings were fitted to 11 of the 20-car entry. Matra had joined the 'Wing' car ranks, BRM and Honda soon followed and the following cartoon by A. F. Litherland published in *Speedworld International* in August 1968 summed up the way developments were going. At the Italian Grand Prix at Monza Jack Brabham drove in practice

one of his BT26 cars fitted with high-mounted aerofoils front and rear and they were used in the race at Watkins Glen. *Autosport* commented, 'The Repco Brabham BT26s of Jack Brabham and Jochen Rindt were still bi-planes and Jack started out with his rear wing manually adjustable, as in practice at Monza, but soon decided that he was quite busy enough just driving and changing gear.'

So-called bi-plane wings proliferated in the 'Temporada' series of Formula 2 races held in the Argentine in late 1968, in Tasman races (held in Australia and New Zealand for cars of up to 2.5 litres) and early season Formula 1 races. From time to time aerofoils broke, as on Surtees' Honda in the 1968 British race and on Ickx' Brabham in South Africa at the beginning of March 1969. Then came the Spanish Grand Prix on the tortuous Montjuich Park circuit in Barcelona. Newcomer to the Lotus team Jochen Rindt was leading the race and Graham Hill had moved up to third. As Hill crested the two bumps before the hairpin bend, the Lotus went into a spin, hit the guard rail on both sides of the road and came to rest, a shattered wreck. Uninjured, Hill made his way back to the pits, convinced that the rear wing on his Lotus had failed (tall rear wings only were fitted to the Lotus 49Bs). Before the pits could signal a warning to Rindt, the wing collapsed on the Austrian's car, he lost control at almost the identical place to Hill, the Lotus hit the inside guard rail, shed two wheels as it slithered across the road into the outside guard rail, careered off the wreck of Hill's car and came to rest upside down. Rindt was trapped in the car in a pool of petrol and he was lucky indeed to escape with facial cuts and a broken nose and cheekbone.

The Commission Sportive Internationale was slow to react and nothing happened until the Monaco Grand Prix, as related by Patrick McNally in *Autosport*: 'The controversy surrounding wings, which was brought to the boil at Barcelona when collapsed aerofoils were blamed for the accident that befell the Lotus team, came to a head at Monaco... The organisers of the race, the Automobile Club de Monaco, had spoken to every entrant individually before practice had begun asking them whether they would agree to run without aerofoils. Every entrant consented (although some with great reluctance), with

Mercedes' new racing car?

But they still proliferated. Jack Brabham drove a car with 'bi-plane' (front and rear wings) late in 1968. This is Ickx with the Ford-powered Brabham BT26A in biplane form in the 1969 Spanish Grand Prix. Following is Bruce McLaren. (*Nigel Snowdon*)

Then disaster struck. After Hill and Rindt had both crashed in Spain, 'wings' were banned at Monaco. This is Hill in the second practice session at Monaco with his hastily modified Lotus 49B. (*Nigel Snowdon*)

the exception of Ken Tyrrell, representing Matra International. Quite rightly, he pointed out that the Club was not in a position to enforce their decision . . . and if they did he could lodge a formal protest to the FIA (Féderation Internationale de l'Automobile) which would inevitably result in the Monaco Grand Prix losing its Championship status.

'Realising that they had reached an *impasse*, the Club let the first practice session commence with the cars still equipped with their wings, but at the same time they were busy contacting various members of the CSI who were present, so that the ruling body might sit in judgement later that evening. Five representatives of the CSI (which significantly did not include the British delegate) voted on the subject; and they decided to invoke the safety clause which permits them to alter the rules immediately without any stay of execution and put a ban on wings which was to continue until after the Dutch Grand Prix, when they could have a full meeting.

'Understandably Tyrrell was furious, for he was running the only car designed since the advent of the wing – the Matra MS80 – and therefore stood to lose more than the rest of them. Team Lotus were the others to suffer more for, although the 49 was not designed around aerofoils as was the MS80, Chapman had been using them to a very distinct advantage. There is little doubt that, had Chapman been present and Tyrrell and he been allied, the situation might have been very different (he was present on race day).

'As always seems the case, the CSI had made another good decision, but at the wrong place and the wrong time.'

On 22 June, the day after the Dutch race, the CSI and the constructors met and regulations for aerofoils in much reduced and modest form were agreed.

But what had caused the wing folly? Mainly the fact that all the cars of the period were closely matched in performance and each designer was either seeking that extra 'edge' or felt compelled to follow the fashion. Already four-wheel-drive development was advanced and once that had proved a blind alley, more serious attention was devoted to the study of aerodynamics and eventually led to the ground-effect cars of the late 1970s.

1969

For this year minimum weight was increased to 530 kg to permit the inclusion of fire extinguishers, approved roll-over bars and safety fuel tanks. Honda and Eagle had withdrawn, Ferrari fielded only a single car, the BRM V12s were pathetic and the season devolved into a straight fight between Matra and Lotus, with McLaren a good also-ran. Ken Tyrrell had closed a deal with the French Matra company whereby they withdrew from Formula 1 and supplied their new MS80 cars for Tyrrell to run for Stewart and Beltoise with substantial funding from the French Elf petrol company. Lotus had now signed up Jochen Rindt to partner Graham Hill and while the British driver's career was sadly waning, Rindt was charging far too hard and making too many mistakes. That doyen of motor racing journalists, Denis Jenkinson, famed for his erudition and his long gnome-like beard, had pledged that he would shave off his beard if Rindt won a Championship Grand Prix. For much of the year 'Jenks' seemed safe from the razor . . .

Stewart won the South African Grand Prix (with the 1968 Matra), the Spanish race with the new MS80 characterised by bulbous side tanks and Hill won for Lotus at Monaco after the retirement of both Matras. Rindt was missing at this race following his bad crash in Spain. More victories followed for Stewart in Holland, France and Britain. Jacky Ickx scored the first of his two Brabham wins of the year at the Nürburgring (with Stewart second). Stewart won at Monza by the narrowest of margins from Rindt and clinched the World Championship with Ickx in second place. The results of the rest of the year were academic. Ickx won the Canadian race from the 'boss', Jack Brabham, after a collision with Stewart which put the Scotsman out of the race. Rindt's long awaited victory came at Watkins Glen and the final race of the year was won by Hulme (McLaren). In the United States Hill was eliminated in a serious accident. Late in the race he spun on oil and push-started his Lotus. He was unable to do up his seat belts on his own and when the car spun and overturned two laps later because of a deflating tyre, Hill was thrown out and suffered two broken legs. Hill was now 40 and it was well time that he retired from this arduous sport, but instead he struggled to make a come-back, something which

Jackie Stewart and the Tyrrell-entered Matra
MS80 dominated the 1969 season. Here they are
seen in the French Grand Prix held that year on
the picturesque Circuit des Charades at Clermont-
Ferrand. It was the scene of yet another
Stewart/Tyrrell victory. (*Nigel Snowdon*)

neither his *amour propre* nor his finances necessitated.

The Ford-Cosworth engine dominated the year
and powered every Championship race-winning car.
As early as their 21 March issue *Autosport* had
commented, 'All those who are concerned at the
increasing Ford domination of Grand Prix racing will
be rooting for John Surtees, who is a driver of
unsurpassed determination and experience and could
provide some surprises with the 48-valve BRM, or for
Chis Amon, who will be driving a fully-aerofoiled and
more powerful Ferrari this year.'

This elicited a reply from Walter Hayes, Vice-
President, Public Affairs of Ford of Europe who had
been so instrumental in persuading the company to
fund the engine:

'In your editorial last week you talked about "all
those who are concerned at the increasing Ford
domination of Grand Prix racing". The previous week
our good friend and customer Bruce McLaren wrote
about 'King-sized Formula Ford'.

'Well now. . . it wasn't so long ago that "all

those" were expressing great unhappiness about the
withdrawal of Coventry Climax leaving Britain with
only one GP engine shop: BRM (and they also ran
their own cars).

'Worried constructors, concerned about the
shortage of power units and the future of Formula 1
itself, actually went to the SMMT (Society of Motor
Manufacturers and Traders) with a proposal for a
British Motor Industry Grand Prix engine. One
constructor tried to interest the Government, and a
distinguished SMMT personality did his best to
involve the Minister of Technology. The fact that a
number of oil, petrol and tyre companies packed their
tents at the same time wasn't encouraging.

'Ford of Britain, therefore, decided to fill the gap
because:
1. It believes that motor sport is the one form of
international activity in which Britain is supreme, and
would like things to stay that way.
2. You can judge any school by the quality of its sixth
form, and if the sixth form is in trouble so is the
school.
3. Ford enjoys motor racing; some of our best friends
are racing drivers.
4. It gave a genius called Duckworth a chance to do
what he'd always wanted to do.
5. The programme also produced a Formula 2 and a
16-valve road engine.

'In the first season all available engines went to
Lotus. Some people started to say, halfway through the
season that it was not fair for Lotus to receive privileged
treatment, although Ford thought they owed Colin
Chapman a thing or two; they had been living together
for a long time.

'Nevertheless, in the second year of the engine's
life it was made available, which means sold, to many
other teams, and since then we have encountered many
things which have at least gladdened us and, we would
have thought, one or two other spectators. For
example: Rob Walker's face when Jo Siffert won the
British Grand Prix last year and a great privateer had
a great day; Graham Hill in a sombrero after Mexico;
Jack Brabham's grin when he landed pole position at
Kyalami this year after a miserable 1968 season; Jackie
Stewart water-skiing at Nürburgring [the 1968
German Grand Prix]; Bruce McLaren after last year's
Race

of Champions and Denny Hulme too, come to think of it.

'Meanwhile if "all those's" concern increases too much, why don't they persuade somebody else to have a go?'

The Ford-Cosworth V8 engine was to dominate Grand Prix racing for many years to come.

The Four-Wheel-Drive Cars

One of the phenomena of the 1969 racing season was the strong interest in four-wheel-drive cars and four were built for the 1969 season.

Although 4wd became an accepted part of the Grand Prix scene in 1969, there was certainly nothing new about the basic idea and the objectives it was intended to achieve. Designers have always felt that it is inherently wrong for cars to be driven through two wheels only and that a 4wd system would achieve greater stability, better adhesion and more power to the road.

One of the first companies to build a 4wd car was the Dutch Spyker concern, both Maserati in Italy and Bugatti in France experimented – of Ettore's two Type 53 4wd 4.9-litre cars, his son Jean crashed one at Shelsley Walsh in 1932. In the States Gulf Oil sponsored Harry Miller's project. Then there were the British specials, Robert Waddy's 'Fuzzi' of 1937-38 with two JAP 500 cc Speedway engines and Archie Butterworth's air-cooled Steyr-powered AJB based on a jeep chassis which ran in British hill climbs in 1950-51. Another fascinating 4wd car was the flat-eight Anderson Special sports car built in Scotland in the late 1930s.

The first really serious attempt at building a 4wd Grand Prix car was the early post-war Cisitalia. This was designed by the Porsche team and in many respects was an extension of pre-war Auto Union practice. This 1½-litre flat-12 supercharged car, now at the Porsche museum, was the most promising of early post-war Grand Prix designs and featured four-wheel-drive that was engageable or disengageable at the driver's will – it was intended mainly to provide good acceleration at the start and out of corners. Money, however, ran out before the car was raced. The next major development was also German, the Mercedes' project to run their 1954-55 W196 Grand Prix car with 4wd, but the team withdrew from racing before the 4wd system reached fruition.

The real pioneer of four-wheel-drive was Harry Ferguson, the tractor king, who formed Ferguson Research Ltd with the specific purpose of furthering the system. When Ferguson died, he left funds for research to continue under the directorship of former Aston Martin designer

Claude Hill and ex-racing driver Major Tony Rolt.

The essence of the Ferguson system was that not only should there be the differentials between the front wheels and the rear wheels as on most previous 4wd systems, but an additional differential between the pairs of wheels with a system whereby the torque was divided automatically between front and rear so that no single wheel could spin – either it was all four or none.

Ferguson proved the value of this sytem with their own front-engined P99 Grand Prix car which was raced in Rob Walker's colours and name in 1961. Jack Fairman retired the P99 in the Inter-Continental Formula British Empire Trophy at Silverstone, where it ran with a 2½-litre Climax engine. The following week the P99 ran in the British Grand Prix at Aintree, but it was disqualified after receiving a push-start and after Moss had relieved Fairman at the wheel. After these two failures – which were not attributable to the Ferguson transmission system – the car vindicated itself with a victory by Moss in the Oulton Park Gold Cup. It was also driven in the 1962 Tasman series by Graham Hill and Innes Ireland. As the result of tests at Indianapolis in 1963 Andy Granatelli ran the Studebaker/STP car with Ferguson transmission and 2.8-litre Novi engine there the following year; the STP car was eliminated in a crash, but a direct result of the experience with this car was the STP 4wd Turbocar which Parnelli Jones drove into sixth place in 1967 (the car broke near the finish but was still classified). The old, original Ferguson had not reached the end of its working life, for, in 1964, Peter Westbury used it to win the RAC Hill Climb Championship. Later Westbury built a small number of cars using the Ferguson system, including BRM-powered sports cars, under the name Felday.

Despite the very considerable promise which the Ferguson P99 had displayed – especially in the wet – no Grand Prix constructor but BRM was interested or had the facilities to build a Grand Prix car on similar lines. The BRM team used a 1963 Grand Prix chassis with the usual 1½-litre V8 engine turned back-to-front in the frame so that the flywheel and clutch were immediately behind the driver's seat. The drive was taken through a drive-train to the left of the cockpit via a 6-speed BRM gearbox mounted to the left of the driver's knees. The central Ferguson differential was attached to the gearbox with a gear-train to front and rear prop-shafts. To drive the new car in 1964 BRM signed up Dickie Attwood, but the P67 was never raced. In 1967 this BRM was sold to David Goode and it was subsequently driven, with a 2.1-litre engine, to victory in the 1968 RAC Hill Climb Championship by Peter Lawson.

In 1969, after a period in which it seemed that the Ferguson system was not going to be fully exploited, three different constructors raced 4wd Grand Prix cars. The first of the teams to plunge into 4wd was Lotus and Colin Chapman was probably the one technician with complete faith in the system. In 1966 Lotus had sketched out plans for a 4wd car powered by the BRM H16 engine, but the appearance the following year of the Cosworth-Ford engine brought an end to these plans. Lotus switched their 4wd ideas to Indianapolis and raced there in 1968 wedge-shaped 4wd cars with Pratt & Whitney engines and sponsored by STP. Mike Spence was killed at the wheel of one of these cars during qualifying trials, and in the race all three retired. Eric Broadley also built a 4wd Lola with Hewland transmission for the 1968 '500' race and one of these cars, typed the T150 and powered by the Ford turbocharged engine, was driven by Al Unser, but crashed.

In 1969 Chapman still persevered with 4wd cars in the shape of the Lotus 64s with turbocharged Ford engines and huge rear spoilers and these were to be driven by Hill, Rindt and Andretti. Three days before final qualifying Andretti had a rear hub fail on his Lotus as he entered the final turn during practice, the car smashed into the wall at 150 mph, disintegrated and caught fire. Chapman was unable to get new hubs made in time for the race and so the 64s non-started. Also at this race were the 1968 turbine Lotus 56 wedges now fitted with turbocharged Offenhauser engines and three of the latest Lola T152 4wd cars – that of 1968 winner Bobby Unser took third place.

Despite his dislike of four-wheel drive, Jochen Rindt was persuaded to drive a Lotus 63 in the poorly supported Gold Cup race at Oulton Park in 1969 and finished second. (*Nigel Snowdon*)

And it was Colin Chapman who was one of the first to have a 4wd Grand Prix car ready to race in 1969. The transmission of the new 63 was designed by Lotus, largely made by ZF in Germany and was based on the 1961 Ferguson P99 system. Basis of the 63 was a stressed-skin monocoque with the Cosworth V8 engine mounted back-to-front so that the clutch and flywheel faced forwards. The 5-speed gearbox, transfer gears and torque control unit were mounted between the driver's seat and the engine. The fore-and-aft drive-shafts were on the left of the car, as the system was derived from the Lotus Indianapolis cars on which there was a left-hand weight basis to suit the Indy curves. These drive-shafts ran in enclosed tubes to the two cross-shafts mounted on either end of the chassis and with differential units offset to the left. The disc brakes were mounted inboard on the cross-shafts and this counteracted the extra unsprung weight of the outer universal joints, and the brake calipers were hung below the discs. There were short drive-shafts to all four wheels and the hubs were in deep recesses in the wheels.

To achieve a satisfactory 50/50 weight distribution the driver was seated well forward and as a result the pedals were in front of the front axle cross-shaft. Because of this layout there was no room for a normal steering mechanism. Vertical pillars at the corners of the chassis carried pivoting arms of triangular shape. Joining the inner corners of the slave arms was a transverse track rod and links ran rearwards at an angle of about 45 degrees to the steering arms on the hubs. A rack-and-pinion unit was mounted on the front of the chassis and the left-hand end of the rack was fitted to the chassis so that the free end also acted as a push-pull arm and this was attached to the right-hand triangular swinging member.

Another completely new feature of the 63 was the suspension and this represented a complete breakaway from normal Grand Prix practice. At front and rear there were fabricated rocker arms operating inboard-mounted coil spring/damper units. Fuel bag tanks were mounted on both sides of the monocoque and in the rear cross-member. The 63 had a sleek wedge-shape with a long, pointed nose and looked most unusual by conventional Grand Prix standards. The Lotus 63 was intended to eventually replace the existing 49B 2wd model, but while it was being developed Chapman arranged for the 63s to be driven by John Miles, who had no previous Formula 1 experience and therefore no preconceived ideas and, whenever he was available, Mario Andretti, who on the strength of his Indianapolis experience was a great 4wd enthusiast. In 1969 the 63 was plagued by torque-split ratio problems and in later races in the season it ran with by far the greater proportion to the rear wheels, which seemed to negate the idea behind the design.

Although it looked like a conventional Grand Prix car, the Matra, in contrast to its Lotus rival, was a purely experimental 4wd car. It was typed MS84, which meant Matra Sports 8-cylinder, four-wheel-drive. The MS84 had a transmission system designed and built by Harry Ferguson Research Ltd. Because it was purely experimental it had a tubular space-frame chassis which was far easier to modify as development progressed than a monocoque. Furthermore, it featured conventional Grand Prix suspension. As on the Lotus, the engine was turned back-to-front so that the clutch and flywheel faced forwards. Enclosed in a single casing behind the driver's seat were the 5-speed gearbox, central differential and control unit and the stepped take-off drive. The basis of the gearbox was the usual Hewland and from the Ferguson unit enclosed drive-shafts ran fore and aft along the left-hand side of the driver's cockpit and at approximately the height of his elbow. The gearbox had a right-hand change. The shafts running fore-and-aft led to the offset differential housings which had fully enclosed, short transverse shafts. These were rigidly attached to the chassis and on their ends were mounted the disc brakes with the calipers

hanging below. The power was transmitted to the wheel hubs by very short universally jointed drive-shafts. As the car was so experimental, great things were not to be expected of it.

The Lotus 63 and the Matra first appeared in practice at Zandvoort, the Lotus was raced at Clermont-Ferrand, the Matra at Silverstone and at the latter circuit the third of the new cars appeared for the first time. There was the McLaren M9A designed by Jo Marquart which differed substantially from both of its contemporaries. The Cosworth V8 engine was the sole stressed member behind the bulkhead – just like the 2wd Lotus 49B and Matra MS80 – and the remainder of the car was a monocoque structure riveted up from light alloy panels. The monocoque consisted of two tubes containing the fuel tanks joined by the floor or panel and the steel-reinforced bulkheads. As would be expected, the engine was reversed in the frame; the crankcase and cylinder heads were attached to the rear bulkhead and the transmission housing was inside the body ahead of the bulkhead. At the end of the engine (what was in fact the normal front) a fabricated box-section member was bolted to the cylinder heads and crankcase

At Silverstone, scene of the British Grand Prix in 1969, Jean-Pierre Beltoise drove the space-frame, four-wheel-drive Matra MS84, but the car was slow and he finished ninth. (*Nigel Snowdon*)

Only appearance of the four-wheel-drive McLaren M9A was in the 1969 British Grand Prix, in which it was handled by Derek Bell. It was an early victim of suspension problems. The car is seen before official practice. (*Nigel Snowdon*)

ran to the rear bulkhead of the monocoque. The bodywork was neat and simple without any engine cover. The McLaren was driven at Silverstone by Derek Bell, but it retired early in the race with suspension trouble. It was not again raced during 1969, but there is no reason to suppose that it would have recorded better lap times than any other 4wd car.

Another 4wd car, practised but not raced in 1969, was the Cosworth designed by Robin Herd. It was scheduled to run in the British Grand Prix with Brian Redman at the wheel, but failed to appear because of technical problems. The Cosworth had exceedingly odd but aerodynamically very efficient lines and, although it was still very much of an unknown quantity in 1969, it had the best brains in the business behind it and could well have proved the most successful of all the 4wd designs.

Very wide tyres proved that a 4wd car had not only to be as mechanically efficient as its 2wd rivals, but more so. Not only were 4wd cars slower in the dry, but they were slower in the wet practice session for the United States Grand Prix. No 4wd cars were raced after the end of the 1969 season – with one noteable exception. The Lotus 56B, raced experimentally in 1971, featured both a Pratt & Whitney gas-turbine engine and four-wheel-drive. The only success was a second place in a Formula 5000 race at Hockenheim.

to carry the rear suspension. The driver sat well to the front of the car with one half-shaft enclosed in a tubular extension passing over his legs.

The transmission housing was a McLaren design and the only items of outside manufacture were the ten pinions of the Hewland DG300 5-speed gearbox. The gearbox had a hollow primary shaft with a shaft from the twin-plate clutch passing through it to the front where the two were splined together. A pinion on the layshaft drove though an idler pinion to a straight-cut gear on the central differential. This central unit was of McLaren design, but of Ferguson type. From the central differential, two shafts led to the spiral bevel drives front and rear, each of which incorporated its own differential. There were exposed drive-shafts with constant velocity joints. Again, the disc brakes, with hollow discs for turbo-cooling, were mounted inboard. As on the Lotus 63, there were 13-in wheels, these being the centre-lock, peg-drive type. The suspension uprights, shorter than those on 2wd cars, were buried within the wheels.

Suspension was by double wishbones and torsional anti-roll bars front and rear, the upper wishbones operating coil spring/damper units. Long, lower radius rods at the rear

The much tested, but never raced Cosworth four-wheel-drive car designed by Robin Herd. In reality it was probably the most promising of an uninspiring quartet. Mike Costin is at the wheel during testing at Silverstone. (*Cosworth Engineering Limited*)

1970

The 1970 season was all about the brilliance of Jochen Rindt with the new Lotus 72 and was overshadowed by Rindt's horrific death in practice for the Italian Grand Prix. Rindt with the old 49 won at Monaco when Brabham, apparently set for a certain victory with his latest Cosworth-powered car, slid into the straw bales at the Gasworks hairpin. By the Dutch Grand Prix, Gold Leaf Team Lotus had the new 72 raceworthy following an unsuccessful appearance in Spain. The 72, designed by Maurice Phillippe was as dramatically innovative as its predecessor and featured torsion bar suspension, inboard brakes, a very low 'shovel' nose and large and distinctive nose fins. Although it was powered by the same engine as most of the opposition, it was distinctly faster, and Rindt won in Holland, France, Britain and Germany. He retired in the Austrian race and then at Monza he swerved under braking for the Parabolica curves and hit the guard rail. The nose of the Lotus passed under the rail and struck a supporting post. Rindt received terrible injuries and was killed outright in the crash. Lotus withdrew from the race, but subsequently 'novice' driver Emerson Fittipaldi with a 72 won the United States Grand Prix. Rindt has been the only posthumous World Champion.

For much of the year Rindt's closest challenger was Jacky Ickx with the new 312B Ferrari, featuring a flat-12 engine. In the early part of the season Ferrari fielded only the one car and it was some races before Maranello found its form. Ickx was second in Germany, won in Austria (Regazzoni with another 312B was second), Regazzoni won the Italian race and Ickx won in both Canada and Mexico (with Regazzoni

Jochen Rindt at Brands Hatch with the Lotus 72. In the British race he scored his fourth Championship win of the year. He was killed in practice at Monza, but won the Championship posthumously. (*Nigel Snowdon*)

second in both races). Although Ferrari had come good again in 1970, it was soon to slip back into mediocrity.

At the end of 1969 Tyrrell and Matra had parted company because neither Ken Tyrrell nor Jackie Stewart would accept Matra's insistence that they use the Matra V12 engine. There was however a new team, March, formed by Robin Herd, Max Mosley, Alan Reece and Graham Coaker. How Tyrrell decided to race the new March 701 and how it was seen that Tyrrell had no other choice is recounted in this extract from *The Story of March* by Mike Lawrence (Aston Publications, 1989).

'Stewart was not keen on an untried engine, and he had tested it in secret, but felt he had to have a Cosworth, yet despite his [World Championship] title his options were limited. He would not drive a Lotus because he felt that the cars were not built with proper regard to safety (his one drive in a Lotus had been in the 1964 Rand GP) and buying a car from Brabham or McLaren was out for both were contracted to Goodyear while Tyrrell was with Dunlop. Ken Tyrrell approached BRM with the idea of buying a chassis which would be fitted with a Cosworth, but was rejected on the grounds that it wouldn't do, Old Boy, to fit a British Racing Motor car with an American-financed engine even if it was designed by a Lancastrian and built in Northampton. If Jackie went to Ferrari it would mean cutting out Ken who had given him his big break and had just helped him to the Championship, so his only realistic option was March.

'Alan Rees could see this and he persuaded his partners that sooner or later Tyrrell would come knocking on their door. "I'd been in racing since 1958, much longer than the others. I'd always liked to work out questions in the sport and I could see there was nowhere else he could get a car from." This was beyond their wildest dreams, but Alan took them through the logic of Tyrrell's dilemma and they pencilled in Stewart as a March driver, while crossing their fingers.'

Tyrrell duly ordered two cars (which were paid for by Ford) and a spare which he paid for himself. There was nothing remarkable about the new car except that there were five on the grid at the first race of the year in South Africa: Tyrrell cars for Stewart and Servoz-Gavin, the works cars for Amon and Siffert and a car

entered by the STP Corporation for Andretti. Stewart won in Spain, was second in Holland and Italy, but by the end of the year was driving the new Derek Gardner-designed Tyrrell 001 which was in 1971 to prove itself a great car. In addition Amon took two seconds with a works car. Brabham had won the South African race and BRM scored a remarkable victory in Belgium with the new Yardley-sponsored BRM P153. Graham Hill had recovered from his accident and drove a Lotus for the Brooke Bond Oxo/Rob Walker team without success. Cosworth-powered newcomers were John Surtees' Surtees TS7 and the De Tomaso 505 run by the Frank Williams team. Piers Courage was killed at the wheel of a De Tomaso in the Dutch Grand Prix at Zandvoort and yet another tragedy had seen the death of Bruce McLaren during testing with a Can-Am car at Goodwood. Overall not a year of monopoly by Cosworth.

1971

For 1971 maximum race distance was changed to 325 Kms. With four victories by Ferrari and one by BRM in 1970 the challenge to the Cosworth V8 was mounting. The Cosworth had suffered many failures in 1970 and towards the end of the year the pressure of work at Cosworth had contributed to a lack of reliability. Now Cosworth allowed outside concerns to overhaul the 1969 and 1970 engines, while they concentrated on building – and maintaining – an improved 440 bhp version, the '11-series' of which only 15 were built. High on the list for the new engines were Team Lotus and the newly named ELF-Team Tyrrell.

Team Tyrrell

Throughout 1970 the new Tyrrell 001 had been a well-kept secret and designer Derek Gardner (previously with Ferguson Research and working on four-wheel-drive transmissions) drew up the car in a converted bedroom at his house in Leamington Spa in Warwickshire and the 'mock-up' was built in his garage. The new car first appeared in the Gold Cup race at Oulton Park in 1970 and it was driven by Stewart in the last three Championship races of the year. Although he took pole position in Canada and was second fastest in Mexico, the car retired in all three races – twice because of minor and easily cured mechanical problems and in Mexico because he hit a stray dog.

To quote Doug Nye (*The Grand Prix Tyrrells*, Macmillan, 1975): 'For 1971, Ken formed ELF-Team Tyrrell with backing from the French oil company and transformed the Ockham woodyard [Ken Tyrrell was in the timber business] into a serious Grand Prix car manufacturing facility.

'Tyrrell himself was a rather reluctant débutant. He said: "There is no reason for me to build my own cars other than the need to become independent of outside manufacturers. If anything delayed them we could find ourselves without a car. Racing is our business, and we can't allow that to happen. It's certainly not saving any money to build your own cars, 001 cost us £22,500, and I bought the Marches for £9000 each."

The Tyrrell workshops at Ockham in 1971. Hanging on the wall are two of the early season nose-cones used by the team. To the right is a full width nose of the type adopted by Tyrrell during 1971. (*Nigel Snowdon*)

Derek Gardner and Ken Tyrrell (right) with the car in its later 1971 form with engine air-box and full-width nose. (*Nigel Snowdon*)

In 1973 Jackie Stewart won his third World Championship at the wheel of Tyrrell-entered cars. When he retired at the end of the year, he had won a record 27 World Championship Grands Prix. (*Nigel Snowdon*)

'He insisted that he was not going to become a "constructor" in the sense that cars would be sold to outside customers. He wanted nothing of that. He just wanted to run a self-supporting Grand Prix Team, which would win races.

'During the winter Derek Gardner joined the team full-time, taking residence in one of a pair of Portakabins erected in the yard, alongside the wooden workshops and rambling age-old office building which had served the team for years.

'Works Manager Neil Davis resided in the other Portakabin, while the rest of Tyrrell's nineteen strong team populated the assembly works and newly established machine and glass-fibre shops...

'Ken's wife Norah (motor racing's most attractive grandmother) was company secretary in addition to her race-track duties as time-keeper and lap-scorer, while Eric Baker was the team's vital accountant.

'In this way ELF-Team Tyrrell became a tight, self-contained unit, capable of making virtually everything they required short of castings.'

The Tyrrell was basically a simple design with open-topped 'bath-tub' monocoque, the Cosworth engine rigidly mounted against the rear bulkhead to form a fully stressed part of the chassis, Hewland FG400 transmission, double wishbone front suspension and rear suspension by twin parallel lower links and single top links. Because of the ELF connection, the cars were painted a French blue. They were better built than most of the opposition, they were superbly prepared and Tyrrell of course had the major advantage of Stewart, the best driver of the time, and well backed up by young Frenchman Francois Cevert.

Although the first car, 001, was withdrawn from racing early in 1971, three more cars were built and they were progressively developed during the year; an early change was the abandonment of the low flat nose with twin wings in favour of a full-width aerodynamic nose.

Stewart's year was almost comparable to that of Clark in 1963: South African GP: pole position and second place to Andretti's Ferrari; Spanish GP: a start from the second row on the grid and a win from Ickx' Ferrari; Monaco GP: pole position and led from start to chequered flag; Dutch GP: third place on the grid, brake problems and 11th at the finish; French GP: pole position and led from the start to chequered flag (and Cevert finished second); British GP: second fastest in practice, took the lead on the fourth lap and led for the remainder of the race; German GP: pole position, led from the first corner to the flag (and Cevert finished second); Austrian GP: second fastest in practice and retired because of a broken stub axle; Italian GP: transmission problems in practice and an early retirement because of engine failure; Canadian GP: pole position and won after a battle with Peterson's March. If Stewart won at Watkins Glen he would have matched Clark's 1963 total. After starting again from pole, he fell back because of tyre trouble and Cevert scored his first Grand Prix victory. Stewart won the World Championship with 62 points to the 33 of Ronnie Peterson (March) and 26 of Cevert.

The second most successful team in 1971 had been the BRMs running in their familiar white, brown and black colours – Pedro Rodriguez finished second in Holland, Siffert won in Austria and Peter Gethin won the hard fought Italian Grand Prix at a remarkable 150.754 mph. It was also a tragic year for the Bourne team. Pedro Rodriguez was killed in a sports car race in July and Jo Siffert died in the last Formula 1 race of the year, the Rothmans World Championships Victory race at Brands Hatch, organised after the cancellation of the Mexican Grand Prix. Despite new models from Brabham (now owned by Ron Tauranac following Jack Brabham's retirement from racing) and McLaren, none of the other teams achieved much. One of the more innovative efforts of the year was the gas-turbine four-wheel-drive Lotus 56B, closely related to the team's Indianapolis cars, which ran in a few races without success.

1972

Minimum weight was now increased to 550 kg because of a new rule that prescribed a minimum thickness of 1.5mm for the outer skin of monocoque chassis. Although Tyrrell remained very much to the fore in 1972, the new Champion was to be Emerson Fittipaldi, the youngest ever at the age of 25, at the wheel of the improved but dated Lotus 72Ds now finished in black and gold colours and known as John Player Specials. Fittipaldi won in Spain, Belgium, Great Britain, Austria and Italy to amass a total of 61 points. For much of the year at the wheel of the new Tyrrell 005 with square-section, flatter monocoque and with totally enclosed engine, Stewart battled hard, but Tyrrell was plagued by a myriad of minor problems and had lost its edge. With wins in the Argentine, newly added to the Championship series, France, Canada and the United States he took second place in the Championship. Denis Hulme (with his McLaren in South Africa), Jean-Pierre Beltoise (BRM at Monaco) and Jacky Ickx (Ferrari in Germany) won a race each. Brabham had been bought by Bernard 'Bernie' Ecclestone and their plain white finish revealed only too clearly the lack of sponsorship - to be accompanied by a lack of results.

The BRM victory was perhaps the most remarkable. 'Big Lou' Stanley, now *supremo* of the BRM, gained substantial Marlboro sponsorship to replace the Yardley sponsorship which had now gone to McLaren and planned to run a six-car team. With the new P180 V12 never fully developed, the team's resources and manpower hopelessly overstretched and all the personnel becoming more and more despondent, it proved, with two exceptions, a complete shambles of a year. Race day at Monaco had dawned bright and sunny, but despite a delayed start the race was run in torrential rain. At the fall of the flag Beltoise with the P160 made a lightning start, took the lead on the inside of the first corner, St. Devote, and with a clear road ahead of him and a wall of spray behind proved totally uncatchable, even by that superb wet-weather driver Jacky Ickx who finished second with his

At Monaco in 1972 Jean-Pierre Beltoise scored a remarkable victory with the BRM P160B, now painted in Marlboro colours. The race was run in torrential rain and Beltoise accelerated through from the second row of the grid to snatch a lead that he never lost. (*Nigel Snowdon*)

Ferrari. The race average of 63.849 mph was slower than that in 1955. At the end of the year Beltoise also scored the P180's only win in the unimportant and poorly supported John Player Trophy at Brands Hatch. The year marked the beginning of the end for BRM, the team lost its Marlboro sponsorship at the end of 1973, it was taken over personally by Stanley from the Rubery Owen organization at the end of 1974 and finally disappeared in 1978.

Alan Henry wrote this profile of the new Brazilian 1972 World Champion which was first published in *Autocourse* and is reproduced with the kind permission of Hazelton Publishing.

EMERSON FITTIPALDI
World Champion

WORLD CHAMPION: two words that mean more to motor racing people than to the followers of any other sport. For no other sport has such a rigorous, such an exacting and demanding method of selecting its champions. To win a Grand Prix World Championship a driver must choose the right car, and be able to develop it so that it remains competitive through a whole season, while he himself must maintain top physical and mental form for a period of at least nine months, and meanwhile win more races, or amass more championship points than any one of a score of powerful rivals.

In theory, nobody who is not worthy of the title should win it, and in practice there have been no exceptions. Yet some champions have suffered for winning their titles in eras dominated by another driver. Jack Brabham won two titles in an era dominated by Stirling Moss, himself never a World Champion, then a third title more than half a decade later when Jimmy Clark was the dominant figure in the sport. So Brabham's name is invariably absent from those spurious lists which name the 'all-time greats,' yet only Fangio won the World Championship more often than this man. The championship doesn't measure the fastest driver, indeed the system is so selective that some of the very fastest drivers, like Chris Amon and Ronnie Peterson today, have never won a single Grand Prix. It doesn't even measure the most successful driver in a season if by most success you mean winning more races than anybody else. By such a simple criterion Moss would have been World Champion in 1958 and Clark again champion in both 1964 and 1967. But there's something very endearing about a system which rewards qualities additional to sheer speed, and honours the doggedness and determination of men like Denny Hulme and John Surtees, and the sport is unquestionably enriched by having such men as World Champions. To be motor racing's World Champion, it's not enough to be the best driver in the world–you have to be a little better than that.

Thus Emerson Fittipaldi became the 1972 World Champion (with a record of five victories, two seconds and a third) to head Jackie Stewart (with four wins, one second and a fourth). Yet the new World Champion, at 25 years the youngest ever, must live in the shadow of Jackie Stewart, the most publicised racing driver of all time. How does Emerson feel about this? 'For myself, it doesn't matter. I don't care. But for motor racing, I think it's important that the World Champion is somebody the public knows and recognises, and somebody that has a good public image. It's not good for racing if the World Champion is somebody who wants to remain hidden, who doesn't want to talk to the press or appear on television. Now I think Jackie [Stewart] has done a fantastic job – maybe he was doing it partly for himself, but the fact is he has made racing more widely known, more popular, to a point where I think Grand Prix racing is stronger than it ever has been. And we have to thank Jackie for that. I also feel I have a duty to myself, and to my family, to make as much money from racing as possible, and if that means a lot of public appearances, then I must make them. Already I have had to face a lot of exposure in Brazil, so I know what it's like. First of all you can forget about having any "private" life at all; there's always some function to attend, or some interview to give. Now I am used to it in Brazil, but here it is a little more difficult because I don't understand the language so well; most difficult here in England, I find it easier in Spain, and Italy, and France where I understand the languages a little better.'

I interviewed him on opening day of the Earl's Court Motor Show and if he was finding it difficult making numerous appearances at various stands, conversing constantly in a foreign language, it certainly didn't show. He conducted himself in a very relaxed manner – a little shy perhaps, lacking Jackie Stewart's self-confidence, and having to consult Lotus Team Manager Peter Warr about the commercial implications of being photographed with this car or that. But he did his duty effectively and one can't help attributing to Emerson a Clark-like sagacity in his attitude to publicity, for it can easily create a great image while destroying a great athlete. I think for a while that Fittipaldi the public figure will happily endure Jackie Stewart's stealing a large area of limelight.

But Fittipaldi the driver thinks differently. 'Of course I want people to regard me as the best driver in the world, and of course I want to be better than Jackie.' He modestly concedes that he must still regard Stewart as his better, but is by no means reticent in expressing his aim of being able to beat Stewart. 'It's not going to be easy, particularly because Jackie has the experience, five or six years more than me. I find I am learning all the time, every testing session, every practice, every race. Every lap I try to learn something. I watch every other driver, not just Jackie, and if I see them doing something different to me I must try it on the next lap. Maybe they are braking at a different point, or changing gear at a different place. I listen very hard to where Jackie is changing gear – I know he is much

cleverer than I am in selecting gear ratios because he has been racing on these circuits much longer than me, so I watch very carefully what he is doing. We all like to think we find the perfect line through a corner very quickly, but whenever I see a driver using a different line to mine I must try it, and sometimes it is quicker, my line was not the best one. These tiny differences mean a lot; I don't think many people understand just how competitive Formula 1 really is. To find that last half second which puts you ahead of the rest of the field is really very difficult, and to go half a second per lap slower than your best time is easy. But it's a tremendous effort to find that last half second. It's not enough any more simply to arrive at a circuit and say "is my car ready?" then climb into it and go off and practise, and get on the front row. Now it requires fantastic concentration right through all the practice sessions, and not just at the track, in the hotel afterwards and over dinner you must be thinking about what can be done to improve the car.'

Emerson takes his wife Marie-Helena with him everywhere and gives his reasons. 'I want my wife to understand exactly what I am doing, and to do this she must come to the races and watch and see what is involved. I am away so much that if she didn't come to the races we would have very little life together. If I were to leave my wife at home I would say "why be married?" Now I know some people may have good reasons for not bringing their wives to races, but I want mine to be with me.' His sense of family is very strong, and the relationship with his brother Wilson is much closer than it appears in public at races where each is getting on with his own job. The brothers Fittipaldi and their wives share not only their 'racing' home at Lausanne in Switzerland, but also their home in Brazil. 'We are very close,' says Emerson. 'We discuss everything we do, every decision one of us makes.'

I asked him specifically if he discussed with Wilson Colin Chapman's invitation to Ronnie Peterson to join John Player Team Lotus. 'For sure, yes. We discuss everything like that.' They regard their futures as being joined and they will return to Brazil at the end of their racing careers, and their intention ultimately to build racing cars there was the base for the rumour that they were to build their own Formula 1 cars. He lists Wilson among the four 'new' drivers to emerge during 1972 as the most promising. The other three are Carlos Reutemann, Carlos Pace and Jody Scheckter. 'Wilson drove a very good race at Watkins Glen. He's very fast, and now his attitude is changing I am sure he will be a very good driver. It takes him a while to see things clearly but once he understands he will do things properly. I wouldn't say I am cleverer than Wilson – at school perhaps I appeared cleverer, but that was simply because Wilson was not at all interested in school'.

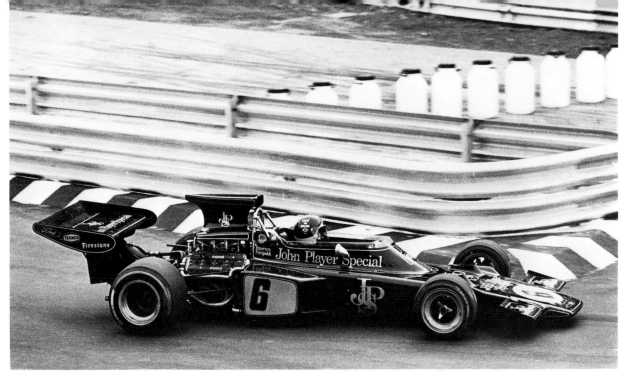

In 1972 only a single car was entered by John Player Special Team Lotus in the Italian Grand Prix at Monza and Fittipaldi scored a fine win, one of five wins in Championship races that year. *(Nigel Snowdon)*

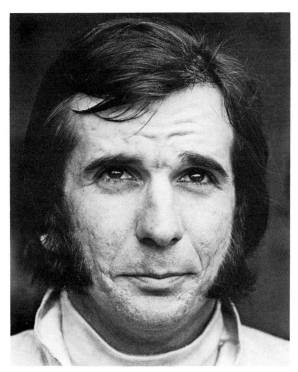

Brazilian driver Emerson Fittipaldi, who won his first World Championship in 1972 at the wheel of Lotus 72 cars. He won again for McLaren in 1974, but in 1976 joined his brother, Wilson's, own unsuccessful Formula 1 team. *(Nigel Snowdon)*

Emerson's own mind is the thing I find most impressive about him. Confronted with the intrusion of a driver of Ronnie Peterson's calibre into what has become 'his' team might have thrown a lesser man. But Emerson has it well rationalised. 'I have to race against Ronnie anyhow, and I would much rather be racing against him as a member of the same team. Ronnie and I are very good friends and we have had long talks about how things should be next year. We have both agreed to share whatever we learn about the cars. If Ronnie finds something that makes his car a little faster, then he shall tell me about it. And if I make some improvement to my car, then Ronnie's car shall have it straight away. This way we should be able to develop our cars almost twice as quickly and with two top drivers on the team we should be able to keep our cars ahead. Also Colin Chapman has agreed to spend much more time on the racing programme from now on, and we will have a brand new design of car in April, so I think we should have a very good year.'

His loyalty to Chapman and Lotus is unquestioned and he proudly points out that he hasn't driven any other sort of single-seater for over three years. To date, Lotus have never sustained their winning effort in the year following any of their four previous World Championships, but now their team is led by a young man who, despite a very relaxed bearing and modest disposition, is probably the most dedicated and fiercest competitor of them all.

1973

Yet again the regulations were changed with a rise in the minimum weight to 575 kg because of the requirement for deformable monocoque structures. Cosworth continued to hold sway and the Tyrrell team regained supremacy in what was to be Jackie Stewart's last season. The team continued to use the existing 005 and 006 chassis, but a new car, 006/2 appeared early in the year. Cevert and Stewart were second and third to Fittipaldi's John Player Special in the Argentine, Fittipaldi won again in Brazil, but then Stewart domination asserted itself in South Africa. Fittipaldi won again with the old 72D in Spain but Stewart won in Belgium (with Cevert second) and at Monaco (Fittipaldi second) and Denny Hulme won for McLaren in Sweden and Ronnie Peterson for JPS in France. Another McLaren victory, by Peter Revson, followed in the British race at Silverstone, a race restarted after Jody Scheckter with the third McLaren had spun off, coming to rest in the middle of the track, and brought the race to a halt in near complete chaos. At long last the Tyrrells got back into their stride again. Stewart and Cevert took the first two places in the Dutch Grand Prix, a tragic race in which Roger Williamson lost his life when he crashed his March, perhaps because of tyre failure; the car overturned and caught fire and he died in the inferno. Another Stewart-Cevert one-two followed in the German race at the Nürburgring and Stewart was second to Peterson in the Austrian race. Peterson won again from Fittipaldi in Italy and Stewart's fourth place was good enough to clinch the World Championship.

There remained the two North American races. In Canada Jody Scheckter (McLaren) and Cevert collided, the two cars spun into the guard rails and although neither driver was badly injured two ambulances were dispatched to the scene. This resulted in the new pace car system coming into operation and this took up station ahead of fourth-place driver Ganley (Williams). The race had started in the wet and there had been many stops for new tyres as the circuit dried out. When the pace car pulled off, there was very real confusion as to who was leading. Most believed it to be Emerson Fittipaldi (JPS), but the chequered flag was eventually shown to Revson's McLaren and Fittipaldi was officially second ahead of Jackie Oliver

with the new Shadow.

In practice for the United States race Cevert hit the guard rail in the Esses at high speed, the Tyrrell was ricocheted into the guard rail on the other side of the road with tremendous force, and Cevert was killed instantly. Tyrrell withdrew his cars and so Jackie Stewart, who had already decided to retire at the end of the year, missed what would have been his 100th World Championship race. Even so the great Scotsman had achieved three World Championships and a record 27 Championship victories.

Stewart has remained a great ambassador for the sport and has done much to help improve safety circuit. The death of Cevert was a dreadful blow to Tyrrell and the team entered 1974 with the need for two new drivers. Although Tyrrell was very much in contention in 1974, the Ockham team's fortunes slipped into a gradual decline, a decline from which they still have not recovered.

1974

It was to prove very much a McLaren and Ferrari year. In 1973 McLaren had introduced the Gordon Coppuck-designed M23, it was to prove one of the most successful of all McLaren designs and was to sustain the team through to the end of 1976. McLaren now had Marlboro sponsorship and veteran Denis Hulme had been joined by Emerson Fittipaldi, the 1972 World Champion who was weary of lack of development progress at Lotus. A third McLaren for Mike Hailwood was run with Yardley sponsorship.

After a year of disastrous failure in 1973, the Maranello team's 312B3 had been completely revised by designer Mauro Forghieri and the 1974 cars driven by Clay (Gianclaudio) Regazzoni and Niki Lauda proved the fastest Grand Prix cars of the year. To quote Pete Lyons (*Autocourse, 1974-75*, Haymarket Publishing Ltd), 'Just what it was that the 312B3 had over its suddenly doubtful competitors became the chief study of the Formula 1 circus. There were many theories, many interpretations of the various elements. Certainly the car itself had fundamental good qualities. Its engine, to most rival designers' way of thinking, was the chief thing. It did use rather more fuel than the British V8 [the Cosworth] – although some of the winter's work had reduced its consumption by about

5% – and therefore went to the starting grid a bit overweight (because of the extra fuel carried), but by his Kyalami start Lauda forever erased in a smear of molten rubber the comforting dictum that Ferraris were poor starters. The engine had more top end power than the Cosworth, perhaps 30 bhp more (495 claimed), which did not show up in higher terminal velocity so much as in the ability of the car to carry more aerodynamic cornering and without losing on the straights from drag . . .'

Apart from McLaren, a vast number of teams used the Cosworth-engined cars. Amon (racing driver Chris Amon's abortive venture), Brabham, Ensign, Hesketh, Iso Marlboro (the latest venture of the ever-persistent Frank Williams), JPS/Lotus (still racing the old 72 after the latest 76 had proved a failure), Lola (raced by Graham Hill's Embassy cigarette-sponsored team). Lyncar, Maki (a rare Japanese contender), March, Parnelli, Penske, Shadow, Surtees, Token, Trojan and, of course, Tyrrell. Of these aspirants, so very few were even to sniff success.

By the last round of the Championship, the United States Grand Prix at Watkins Glen, Fittipaldi and Regazzoni had both scored 52 points in the World Championship: Fittipaldi had won for McLaren in Brazil, Belgium and Canada and taken second places at Brands Hatch and at Monza (and Denny Hulme had also won the first of the season's races in the Argentine). Ferrari missed out in the Championship stakes because both Regazzoni and Lauda were charging hard for victory. Regazzoni had won only in Germany, but had finished second in Brazil, Spain, Holland and Canada. Lauda had won in Spain and Holland and finished second in the Argentine, Belgium and France.

Lauda's season cannot, however, be recounted without mentioning his misfortunes in the British Grand Prix. The Austrian was leading in the closing stages of the race when a tyre started to deflate. Lauda kept going until the tyre disintegrated completely and on his penultimate lap pulled into the pits for a wheel-change. When he accelerated down the pits road to rejoin the race, an official with a red flag stopped him. Already spectators had crossed the road to watch the finish and a course car was blocking the pit road. On appeal Lauda was reinstated into fifth place, where he would have finished if he had been allowed to rejoin the race.

Fittipaldi with the M26 in the 1974 French Grand Prix. In this race he was out of luck and retired because of engine problems. (*Diana Burnett*)

Ferrari began a renaissance in 1974 with the much improved 312B3 cars driven by Clay Regazzoni and Niki Lauda. Lauda is seen in the British Grand Prix at Brands Hatch, a race which he lost because of a deflating tyre. After a late pit stop he was not allowed to rejoin the race, but was eventually on appeal classified fifth. (*Nigel Snowdon*)

Brabham had won two races (Reutemann in South Africa and Austria), Jody Scheckter with the Tyrrell 007 had won in Sweden (with team-mate Patrick Depailler in second place) and at Brands Hatch as a result of Lauda's problems. Even the John Player Special team with the outdated Lotus 72 enjoyed a measure of success and Ronnie Peterson won for them at Monaco and Monza.

For Regazzoni luck ran out at Watkins Glen; plagued by handling problems, necessitating pit stops, he finished at the tail of the field. Fittipaldi took fourth place behind the Brabhams of Reutemann and Pace and Hunt's Hesketh – good enough to win the World Championship by a margin of three points.

1975

For 1975 Ferrari had developed the 312T car, still with the ever-improving flat-12 engine, but with a new transverse gearbox. With generous financial backing from Fiat, superb engineering by Mauro Forghieri, team 'liaison' by young lawyer Luca Montezemola and Clay Regazzoni and Niki Lauda as drivers, Ferrari reigned supreme and only when Ferrari faltered, did the opposition seem quick. The new cars did not appear until the South African race and the team took a little while to find its form. Lauda scored his first win at Monaco, won again in Belgium and Sweden and lost a hard-fought battle in Holland to finish second to James Hunt's Hesketh. Lauda finished first ahead of

Although 1975 was to prove a Ferrari and Lauda year, and the young Austrian won the World Championship, the Dutch Grand Prix threw up a surprise result. The winner was James Hunt with the Hesketh 308, seen here leading Lauda. (*Nigel Snowdon*)

Hunt in the French race at the Paul Ricard circuit, was out of the leading positions in the rain that marred the later stages of the British Grand Prix, finished third in Germany, was again out of the results in Austria, was third in Italy (Regazzoni won) and won the United States race. Lauda had taken the World Championship by a margin of 19½ points.

Three races in 1975 require special mention. The Spanish race was marred by arguments over the security of the safety barriers and much of practice was boycotted by the drivers. Emerson Fittipaldi refused to compete in the race. Rolf Stommelen was leading the race with his Embassy Hill when the rear wing failed, the car went out of control and was launched over Pace's Brabham and the barriers to kill four spectators. The race was stopped after 29 laps and Jochen Mass (McLaren), who was leading at the time was declared the winner. Only half points were awarded in the Championship. It was a race that should never have taken place.

The British race was marred by heavy rain that resulted in a total of 16 drivers crashing, innumerable pit stops and only six cars still running when the race was abandoned 11 laps before its scheduled finish. After a great deal of wrangling Fittipaldi was declared the winner and the McLaren driver also won the Argentine race and with second places in Brazil, at Monaco, in Italy and the United States finished second in the Championship with 45 points. Heavy rain also meant that the Austrian Grand Prix was stopped short; leading when the race was stopped was Vittorio Brambilla (March) who managed to crash on his slowing-down lap. Half-points were again awarded, but this was the first Championship race victory by a works-entered March.

Of the other teams, the most successful was Brabham. Carlos Pace won for the team in Brazil and Reutemann with a succession of good places remained a Championship contender for much of the year. Hunt scored that fine victory with the Hesketh in Holland and took some good places. Scheckter won the South African Grand Prix and Laffite with his Williams finished second in Germany. The once so successful Lotus/JPS team failed to win a single race. American Mark Donohue died of injuries suffered when his March crashed because of tyre failure in Austria.

1976

Despite Ferrari's successes, the Cosworth-Ford engine continued to dominate racing in numbers and was once again to power the World Champion's car. There was, however, a new contender with 'non-Cosworth' power, the Ligier JS5 with the Matra V12 engine. Although Ligier has achieved very little success over the years, the team still competes in 1991.

Inevitably Lauda won in Brazil (from Depailler's Tyrrell) and South Africa (from James Hunt, now with the McLaren team). Regazzoni and Lauda took the first two places in the street race at Long Beach (from Depailler's Tyrrell again) and Hunt won the Spanish race at Jarama from Lauda. It was in Spain that the first of a series of disputes that marred the year first began. Hunt was disqualified because his McLaren was 1.8 cm too wide, breaching the maximum width rule of 215 cm introduced on 1 May 1976, the result of tyre bulge. On appeal the disqualification was rescinded and a fine of $3000 substituted. It was the appeal decision that caused the furore, and it was a widely held view – and not only at Ferrari – that the disqualification should be upheld . . . after all, said many, there is little point in rules if they are not enforced.

In Spain Tyrrell had revealed the radical P34 six-wheel car, designed by Derek Gardner and intended to exploit the advantages of reduced frontal area, greater front-end adhesion, increased tyre tread contact and greater brake surface area. Lauda and Regazzoni took the first two places in Belgium and Laffite brought the Ligier across the line in third place to achieve a 1-2-3 finish for 12-cylinder cars. As one commentator suggested, if Matra had pursued development of their V12 engine with vigour, it could have changed the face of Grand Prix racing. Although Lauda won at Monaco, Scheckter and Depailler brought their six-wheeled Tyrrells across the line in second and third places. And the Tyrrells followed this up by taking first and second places in Sweden, with Lauda in third place. Lauda led the opening laps of the French Grand Prix, but was soon eliminated by engine trouble and Hunt was the winner, with another second place for Depailler with the Tyrrell.

James Hunt took the chequered flag at Brands Hatch to take what was to prove a short-lived victory. At Paddock Bend on the opening lap Regazzoni tried to snatch the lead from Lauda. Regazzoni spun, Hunt's McLaren was launched into the air by the Ferrari's rear wheel and Laffite crashed his Ligier into the bank. Hunt continued slowly round the circuit with one front wheel at a drunken angle. The race was stopped and Hunt, as he later said, pulled off on Bottom Straight once he realized that the race was stopped. According to the rules, no driver could restart if he had failed to complete the lap on which the red flag was shown. This would have eliminated Hunt, Regazzoni and Laffite, but after a great deal of debate and argument all three restarted, Regazzoni and Laffite at the wheel of their training cars. All three were disqualified on appeal and the real victory went to Lauda who had finished second on the road in the restarted race.

Near-disaster followed in the German Grand Prix in which Lauda crashed his Ferrari at *Bergwerk*, a 150 mph section of the course and as well as suffering severe burns, inhaled toxic fumes from the burning bodywork of the Ferrari. The causes of the accident remain a mystery. Lauda was expected to die, mainly because of breathing difficulties, but he made a near-miraculous recovery to return to racing at the Italian Grand Prix to defend his World Championship. The German race was stopped and restarted and Hunt won from Scheckter with a six-wheel Tyrrell. In Austria John Watson scored a brilliant one-off victory for the Penske team that was to withdraw at the end of the year, ahead of Laffite with the Matra and Hunt in fourth place, while Hunt won the Dutch race at Zandvoort after a wheel-to-wheel duel with Watson whose gearbox broke.

At Monza Hunt started from the back of the grid. Fuel samples taken before the Saturday's practice revealed that the McLaren's fuel octane rating was 101.6 (slightly above the permitted limit of 101). Friday's practice had been wet, the Saturday time was disallowed and Hunt scraped on to the grid because the three slowest competitors withdrew. Hunt went off the track early in the race when he missed his braking point at Chicane Two. Ronnie Peterson led almost throughout to score a brilliant victory for the underfinanced, 'shoe-string' March team ahead of Regazzoni, Laffite (Ligier) and Lauda.

Lauda still led the World Championship with 64

points to the 47 of Hunt. Hunt won both the Canadian and United States races, Lauda was out of the points in Canada and finished third at Watkins Glen, so he still led the Championship with 68 points to the 65 of Hunt. In the final race of the year, the Japanese Grand Prix held in the wet at Fuji, Andretti nursed his tyres to score the only JPS victory of the year from Depailler (Tyrrell) and Hunt. The British driver led for most of the race, but made a late stop for tyres, rejoined in fifth place and in the remaining five laps snatched back two places. Lauda made the brave decision to pull out of the race after two laps because of the very bad conditions. Hunt won the Championship by 69 points to the 68 of Lauda. 'Master James' had driven magnificently all year, but in the history books his Championship is marred by a season of dissension in motor racing and is overshadowed by Lauda's accident and recovery.

The 1976 season proved a duel between Lauda and Hunt (McLaren), marred by protests during the year and Lauda's horrific crash in Germany from which he bounced back to race again in Italy. Hunt kept his Championship hopes alive by fine wins in Canada and the United States and clinched the Championship by finishing third in the wet Japanese Grand Prix (seen here), while Lauda withdrew because of the conditions. (*Nigel Snowdon*)

For 1976 Derek Gardner produced the totally innovative six-wheel P34 Tyrrell for which Goodyear produced special 10-inch tyres for the front wheels. The aims were greater front-end adhesion and a smaller frontal area. It almost succeeded. Note the perspex panels in the front scuttle through which the driver could monitor the state of his tyres – and spectators could see the driver at work. In 1976 the P34 won in Sweden, seen here and driven by Scheckter, and Depailler finished second. The P34 was a front runner for most of the year, but failed to win a single race in 1977. (*Nigel Snowdon*)

1977

Despite a loss of confidence in Niki Lauda at Ferrari, caused partly by Lauda's withdrawal from the Japanese race the previous year and partly by Ferrari internal politics which could be relied on to destroy relationships with most of their drivers sooner or later, Lauda won the World Championship for the second time. Lauda won in South Africa, was second at Long Beach, Monaco, Zolder (the Belgian race) and Silverstone, won at Hockenheim (to which the German Grand Prix was transferred because the Nürburgring was now considered too dangerous), was second again in Austria and won in Holland. By this stage it was public knowledge that Lauda would be leaving Ferrari at the end of the year to drive for Brabham and there was a hostile reaction in Italy. The Austrian arrived at Monza surrounded by bodyguards and took second place. He needed only a single point to clinch the World Championship and settled the outcome by finishing fourth in the wet at Watkins Glen. At this point Lauda withdrew from Ferrari and his place was taken by young French-Canadian Gilles Villeneuve. Although Carlos Reutemann had also won the Brazilian Grand Prix early in the season, Lauda's Championship was largely attributable to a combination of Ferrari consistency and Lauda's determination, for the 312T2 was by no means the best car of the year and it had been a fiercely competitive season.

The first race of the year, the Argentine Grand Prix, had been won by Jody Scheckter, at the wheel of the Wolf WR1 on its race début. The Wolf, financed by Canadian oil millionaire Walter Wolf was a development by Dr Harvey Postlethwaite of his design for the Hesketh 308C. Wolf had put together a fine team based round the Williams organization which he had bought in 1976, and the new team included racing manager, Peter Warr, formerly of Lotus. Scheckter's superb season continued with a second place in South Africa, third at Long Beach and in Spain, a win at Monaco, second place in Germany, third in Holland and at Watkins Glen and a win in Canada – good enough to give him second place in the Championship with 55 points to the 72 of Lauda.

The most significant cars were not to show their true form in 1977 and in the case of one its great days were to be way in the future. Lotus had developed the first 'wing' car, the 78 and this gained immensely improved cornering grip, making it the fastest car under braking or accelerating from a low speed, but because of increased wind resistance at the expense of straight-line speed. Lotus also suffered more than their fair share of engine failures during the year. Nevertheless the team won five races (Mario Andretti at Long Beach, Jarama in Spain, Dijon and Monza and Gunnar Nilsson in Belgium) and Andretti took third place in the World Championship.

At the British Grand Prix the Renault RS01, the first turbocharged Formula 1 car, made its first appearance driven by Jean-Pierre Jabouille. The Renault was remarkably quick, although suffering from 'turbo lag' under acceleration, but very unreliable and it was to be a year before a Renault finished a Grand Prix. Renault was also the first team to use the new Michelin radial racing tyres and in due course both Goodyear and Pirelli (when they re-entered Formula 1) adopted radial tyres. The 1977 German Grand Prix, won by Lauda, was Goodyear's 100th Grand Prix win (the first had been by Ginther and the Honda at Mexico City in 1965).

When Jacques Laffite won the 1977 Swedish Grand Prix, it was the first all-French win in a Championship race since the inception of the series in 1950 – French driver, French car (Ligier JS7) and French engine (Matra MS76 V12). (*Nigel Snowdon*)

A month later the turbocharged Renault made its début in the British Grand Prix at Silverstone. Many sceptics doubted whether it would be quick enough to qualify, but European Formula 2 Champion Jean-Pierre Jabouille qualified comfortably and ran well until the turbocharger failed. Although few realized it at the time, it was the beginning of a revolution. (*Nigel Snowdon*)

The cake was shared by several other teams in 1977. Laffite with the Matra-powered Ligier scored the first all-French Formula 1 win in Sweden, but only after Andretti was forced to stop to take on more fuel. Fuel caused the downfall of Watson and the Brabham-Alfa Romeo at Dijon and the Irish driver was leading when he ran out of petrol. After their Champion year in 1976 James Hunt and McLaren slipped badly and the McLaren team went in to a long decline. The new M26 was largely a failure, but Hunt won both at Silverstone after Watson with his Brabham-Alfa Romeo retired with fuel pressure trouble and again at both Watkins Glen and Fuji. In Austria Alan Jones scored a one-off victory for the Shadow team, a fine performance by a less than well financed team.

It was another year of tragedy. In the South African race Welsh driver Tom Pryce was killed in one of the most stupid, futile of all racing accidents. His team-mate Renzo Zorzi had stopped at the side of the track because of mechanical problems with his Shadow. A young and inexperienced marshal ran across the track with a fire extinguisher, was hit and killed by Pryce's Shadow, the extinguisher hit Pryce's head and he was also killed instantly; Pryce's car continued out of control until it collided with Laffite's Ligier. Pryce was one of the most promising of young drivers. In March Brabham driver, Brazilian Carlos Reutemann, was killed in a light aircraft crash. In the final race of the year in Japan Villeneuve (Ferrari) collided with Peterson (Tyrrell), the Ferrari was launched into the air and two spectators standing in a prohibited area were killed.

Niki Lauda, Twice Champion of the World
by Alan Henry
(first published in *Autocourse*, 1977-78, Hazleton with whose kind consent it is reproduced)

Not only is Niki Lauda a motor racing hero — everybody knows that — but he's also developing into a master of the art of surprise. To start with he surprised us with the speed of his recovery and return to the cockpit in September 1976. He followed up that with a surprising withdrawal from the Japanese Grand Prix. He surprised many people by hanging on to the team leadership at Ferrari in the face of an early burst from Carlos Reutemann and then decided to quit the team at the end of 1977. His final surprise was more of a shock. Following interminable wrangling, Niki Lauda withdrew from the Ferrari team for the last two races of the season following a fourth place championship-clincher at Watkins Glen.

That he became World Champion racing driver for the second time, however, suprised very few. His determination had become an example to everybody else in the sport; his single-mindedness was amazing, almost disarming; and his self-confidence at its highest point ever. What's more, Niki Lauda revealed an unusually critical ability of self-appraisal, something many racing drivers feign but few actually possess. But why, oh why, should he decide to sacrifice that legendary Ferrari reliability, finance and resources for a move to Bernie Ecclestone's Parmalat Brabham organisation?

Niki Lauda, World Champion for the second time in 1977. After clinching the Championship in the United States, Lauda withdrew from the Ferrari team. For 1978 he signed up with Bernie Ecclestone's Brabham team. *(Nigel Snowdon)*

Sitting at Watkins Glen two days before he clinched his World Championship title, Lauda's clipped English gave way to a softly spoken, almost emotional, but very calculated response.

'One morning I just found myself not feeling about Ferrari as I'd felt in the past. Like painters, we racing drivers have an artistic inclination and are individualists. Our task is to have a free head, come to the race and do more than normal people can manage. But it became like being married to a bad woman. If you're in that situation then you haven't got a clear head, you can't give of your best. I worked there for four years, some good, some bad. But I suddenly realised that I hadn't got the same feeling towards the team as a whole that I had in the past.'

Lauda emphasised that he is rather a difficult person to work with, to work for, setting high standards for his own performances. 'And I expect other people around me to try to attain those sorts of standards. I worked hard this year with the team. I had always been prepared to give 110 per cent to Ferrari but, to do that, you've got to be in a very happy situation. You might work all night, for example, for an employer whom you like and get on with well. If you do a normal job, without this special relationship, you simply take the attitude 'well, it's five past five, time to go home.' You need so much to have a good relationship with the person you're driving for in this business.

'As far as Enzo Ferrari was concerned, things began to change this year. Political problems, aggravation, Italian press. In the past I'd have done anything he wanted me to do. Suddenly my freedom had gone and I felt I didn't want to do more than normal. But only to do that would mean not to win; I knew that I had to work hard to be successful. So I realised that if I didn't do what I did in the past then we wouldn't be successful.

'I don't know a special point in time when it happened, but our relationship went all wrong.'

Lauda cited the example of Ferrari's planned entry to the cancelled Imola Formula 1 race as an indication of what went wrong in 1977. He condemned the idea of entering Cheever in this event as unprofessional when they were on the verge of clinching their world titles. The fact that he was almost unbeatable at the time didn't enter into it as far as Niki was concerned. It was their attitude, the principle of the whole business.

'I knew this was never going to work; it was stupid. You have four years with everybody saying 'don't do this, let's do that, we've got to be professional to win,' so then they go and do this. And it would be at my expense. After some time they don't see things clearly.

'All they said was, "you're well ahead, what are you worrying about? You're almost there. We'll run three cars in Canada and Japan, Mr Villeneuve in the third car. What is there to worry about your championship now?'' But think for a moment. What would have happened if I was one point behind Scheckter because of some bad luck and the whole business was very critical. Do you think they'd have changed their mind and been ''all professional'' again? No way, they wouldn't have done it!'

Bearing all these problems in mind, did Lauda think that he had become a difficult driver to work with? 'No. Not difficult for a professional team. I drive for Bernie now, so there's no problem at all. He wants the same thing as I do. He wants to win, we both do. But I would have a problem if I stayed with a team like Ferrari because it's a fight.'

But why, with the world apparently at his feet, did Lauda choose Brabham? Think of all the other teams that might have been available. Why has he decided to go to a team with a complicated racing car, an engine that's proved very fast, but an overall combination that hasn't proved very reliable?

'Because, after four years ar Ferrari, I need a sympathetic climate. Look around, what do you see? Teddy Mayer, professional no doubt. Walter Wolf, professional no doubt. There are very few truly professional teams.

'Secondly, I want a fresh challenge. To go to McLaren, easy. A winning team, everything organised, James a nice guy. Sure, it would be very nice to drive for them. But I look for more. I want to be in big problems to come out from them, I don't know why. So, Wolf, Scheckter, a one-car team. Not so easy. So, for me, Bernie is the right thing. Different engine, Italian people. I understand them, I speak the language. But there's something harder to come.

'It's a brand new car. One day I went to England to negotiate with Bernie. We spent an afternoon talking. Talking about how we'd get the money together, about my contract. Then he said, "Come out to the back, I've got something to show you." And there it was. The BT46, complete and ready to go. I was so excited I knew that I just had to drive that car. If Bernie had said, "Look, you give me £10 and you can drive that car," I'd have said, "Here's the £10!" ''I had to think, "Easy, be sensible, draw back.'' But it was terrific. That's when I realised that I wanted, so much, to drive it.

'So I think logically about Gordon Murray. All his cars have been fast from the word go. The BT42, BT44, BT44B and the BT45. He's not just good, he's fantastic. Each car has been an excellent machine. Normally a new car is difficult and you've got lots of work to do. I reckon the BT46 must be as good as it looks. So then you say, "It's not reliable''. But what is reliability? It's the easiest thing in the world. Just run the car. Get the thing working, look at it logically. Take for example, the brake pedal is getting soft. There's no point in just accepting it. Get it working properly. It shouldn't be soft, so make ducting that works. Then,

when you come to a place like Zolder — which is hard on brakes — it might get a little bit soft, but it still brakes well. And if it's only all right at Zolder you know it will be fantastic everywhere else.'

But isn't the car too complicated? Lauda's voice rose slightly. 'Yes, that's the point. Exactly. I like it. The more complicated it is, the more I like it. The more digital stuff, jacks, brakes; I love it. There's more for me to play around with, more to experiment with, more to make work. Take flying. You give me a single-engined plane. Well, I'll take it up for a circuit. Nice, but no challenge. You give me a Jumbo with four engines, 5000 things that might go wrong. Fantastic. A challenge, let's get on and try to fly it!'

Lauda's intense fascination with flying (he has the use of a private jet which he flies himself) reflected the meticulous and calculating approach which he brings to bear on his motor racing. But didn't he think that, on the face of it, the qualities required for flying safely were not the same as those required to be a top racing driver?

He thought carefully for a moment, 'Listen,' he replied with an almost conspiratorial whisper, 'I tell you the difference between flying and driving. In driving a racing car you have to get the best compromise out of a chaotic situation. You have to compromise all the time. You come into a corner, lose control, bounce it up the kerb, fight the car to get back control. Every bloody lap you face a different chaotic situation and it's your business as a driver to find a way out of it. In a plane it's different. If you get into a chaotic situation then you're a stupid fool. You have to follow rules. They're all written down and you have to know them by heart'.

So where is the challenge, the stimulus, in flying? 'To be ready I know all the rules off by heart. If 6000 things go wrong, you've got to be ready. If a red light comes on you think "air duct overheat, right, do this" The next light comes on you think "ah yes, oil pressure down, do this". But if you don't know for the first time and you have to think for 10 seconds and in that 10 seconds the gear doesn't come out when you select it and you don't notice it because you're still thinking about the oil pressure, then you crash. The challenge is to be ready for the unexpected. My nerves are better than most. From my racing experience I'm ready for an emergency. All right, so a wing falls off. What does the book say about a wing falling off. Nothing. OK, then we compromise. . .!'

Far from being a fatalist, Lauda believes that he should be as calm as possible all the time, looking for every way of avoiding a difficult situation and, if he finds himself in one, finding the best way out of it. For that reason he doesn't panic. As he knows well, it's the easiest thing in the world to do something as simple as getting killed.

The cool approach conveys a false impression to

many people. They look on Lauda as a computer, almost super-human from the way in which he recovered from his injuries. But such suggestions seem to make Niki genuinely nervous. He doesn't approve of them – or agree with them.

'People believe sometimes that I'm a great driver, that I know all the answers. This is total rubbish because I don't know everything; it's stupid. But you've got to know yourself. Take for example when you crash a car. Eighty per cent of the time you know immediately why you've crashed. but for the first 10 seconds after the shunt you think "What can I do to make things look better? Let's look for an excuse." You look at the tyres; they're flat. But the rim is broken, so you can't say it's a puncture. Damn. After a moment you have to shake yourself mentally and say "Listen, you idiot, what are you doing? You made a mistake, think about it." Then it's quite hard to be realistic, forget it and go home admitting to yourself that you made a mistake.

'This takes some training. Honestly. So now, when I have a crash that's my fault, I know. Take Monza, when I crashed in practice. I got out of the car and said "I messed it up." Then a journalist comes up and says "What happened?" I say "I messed it up." He says "puncture?" "Look, no puncture. I messed it up." "Oil on the track?" "Look, listen. No oil on the track, I just messed it up." They can't believe that you make a mistake. More interestingly, they won't believe that you can make a mistake and admit it!'

So that applies to Japan as well? 'Yes, if I make a mistake then I stand for it. All right, so I don't race in Japan and lose the championship. All right, well I'm here. Look in my eyes. You don't believe me, OK, then that's up to you. If you do, OK, fine you're with me. Through the years you develop this sort of sense.'

Predictably, Lauda stands by the decision that cost him the World Championship in 1976. 'Look, at the time, I reckon I was right. I still do. You know very well that you thought we were all mad during the first few laps. All right, everything dried and James was World Champion. But people forget how the conditions were. All right, nothing happened. Hunt was champion and Lauda the idiot pulled out. But think for a moment. If something had happened, if something had gone wrong with James' pit stop and he'd have lost a few more seconds. If, say, somebody had been killed. If I'd been champion. Then they'd have all been dancing round saying, "Lauda, he's a genius, he's fantastic, what a tactician . . .!" But this would have been nonsense because I'm not; it's just not reality to think like that.'

Lauda's approach to racing hasn't changed since his accident, but he insisted that the risk element is not what

Niki Lauda and his Ferrari 312 T2 at the United States Grand Prix at Watkins Glen. He finished fourth, good enough to clinch his second World Championship. Lauda had agreed to drive for Brabham in 1978 and was now so disenchanted with Ferrari that he withdrew from the remaining two races of the season. (*Nigel Snowdon*)

stimulates him, simply the satisfaction of pitting his skill against a car on a circuit and coming out on top. 'All right, so I don't doubt that motor racing is dangerous. But it's the technique of racing that I find stimulating. I don't feel the risk factor is so important and I don't get excited by it. I don't honestly think that this makes me unusual as a racing driver. Take a fast lap, for example. I'm satisfied when I manage one really quick lap because I've performed well, got it all together. It's this, not the risk that I like. To know that you've got on top of the car despite banging the guard rail, getting sideways, going on the grass. It's the satisfaction that I find stimulating, not the danger.'

Putting a label to Lauda's most satisfying race of the year was difficult. He tended to shy away from the question, admitting that, yes, he did good drives at Hockenheim, Kyalami and Zandvoort. He also said that he made mistakes at Anderstorp and rated that the worst race of the season. Sometimes he's happier with a fifth place than a first, basing that satisfaction simply on the basis of how he feels he has performed on the day in question.

What of Austria, the race he might have won but didn't? Did he feel that he had eased up too much in the opening, damp stages of the race? His reaction was firm, bordering on the annoyed.

'Ease up? I didn't bloody ease up. I drove balls out all the time at the start. The car nearly flew off the road five times, it didn't handle. I'd got dry settings on and the car was oversteering like mad. People said he eased off, tactics, he didn't take any risks. Just nonsense, pure nonsense. Then they say "Ah, he's caught up. He's pushed the throttle." But I pushed the bloody throttle all the way. I eased up ever so slightly towards the end when it was obvious I wasn't going to catch Jones but, otherwise, flat out all the time.'

But, despite the problems and the politics, Niki Lauda became the 1977 World Champion racing driver. The smooth style, the toothy grin, the dry humour, the slight build. All these aspects go to make up the little Austrian driver who has now won a total of 15 World Championship Grand Prix races in four seasons. A man either liked wholeheartedly or disregarded as some sort of freakish automaton. A man who encapsulates both total independence on the one hand and a warm, endearing personality on the other.

Niki Lauda lets people take him as they find him, worrying little about the barbed remarks from his critics and only smiling with a subdued satisfaction over the praise from his fans. A master of Formula 1 technicalities, the twice World Champion rounded off this interview on an almost cautionary note.

'There is one thing I would like everyone to realise. That is, a driver is nothing without a good car. Reliance on good machinery affects a driver's fortunes so much nowadays that it's hardly possible to talk categorically about "good drivers" and "bad drivers?" I have had good machinery and I feel I make the most of what I've got. Perhaps the time will come when I don't get the chance to get my hands on such machinery, although by that time I won't be competitive and I may not be enjoying myself. If that happens, then it will be time for me to say goodbye. . .'

1978

It was to prove the year of the 'Wing Car' and Lotus with the 78 and 79 cars dominated. Imitators were many, including ATS, McLaren and, later, Tyrrell and Williams (Frank Williams had reformed his own team), but none could match the speed and grip of the Lotus and Andretti and Ronnie Peterson (who had moved from Tyrrell to Lotus) scored a record number of wins. Andretti won the first race of the year in the Argentine, finished fourth because of gearbox problems in Brazil, Peterson won in South Africa, Andretti took second at Long Beach and both cars failed at Monaco. Here Patrick Depailler won with the new Maurice Phillippe-designed Tyrrell 008, scoring the team's only victory of the year (both the six-wheel P34 and its designer Derek Gardner had been abandoned).

All these Lotus/JPS successes were with the 1977-78 and the new 79 did not appear until the Belgian Grand Prix where Andretti (79) and Peterson (78) took the first two places. The same 1-2 followed in Spain, but Peterson was now at the wheel of a 79. Niki Lauda won the Swedish Grand Prix with his Brabham-Alfa Romeo, a remarkable victory made possible by designer Gordon Murray's innovative rear-mounted fan that literally 'sucked' the Brabham to the track (and threw dirt up at following drivers). This device was immediately protested by the other teams, and it was held that, whilst the result in Sweden would stand, the 'sucker' was banned. It was the first Grand Prix victory by an Alfa Romeo *engine* since 1951.

By the French Grand Prix the Lotus steamroller had re-asserted itself and Andretti and Peterson again took the first two places. Earlier in the year the hard working and determined Carlos Reutemann had won in Brazil and at Long Beach and he scored a third win with the Ferrari 312T3 at Brands Hatch from the Brabhams of Lauda and Watson – but only after both 79s had retired. When Andretti won the German Grand Prix from Scheckter's Wolf WR5, he had an 18-point lead in the World Championship. Peterson won for Lotus in Austria, ahead of Depailler's Tyrrell and another 1-2 for Andretti and Peterson followed in the Dutch race at Zandvoort.

Then followed Monza. Shortly after the start there was an accident involving ten cars. Mainly

Although 1978 was to prove a Lotus year, one of the sensations was the Brabham 'sucker' car with rear-mounted fan that Lauda drove to victory in Sweden. The victory was allowed to stand, but the device was banned. It had been a clever answer to the 'wing' cars.

because the starting signal had been given before the cars on the back half of the grid had lined up, these were still moving at the signal, while the front rows were stationary; the cars bunched, Patrese's Arrows contacted Hunt's McLaren which struck Peterson's Lotus; the 79 hit the armco, bounced back into Regazzoni's Shadow and burst into flames in the middle of the road. Peterson suffered broken legs and severe concussion and it seemed that all would probably be well and that he would make a good recovery. On the Monday morning one of the most popular and able drivers died because of blood clots, caused by marrow from the broken bones entering the blood stream.

It was almost dusk before the race, now shortened, was restarted, and although Andretti and Villeneuve finished first and second on the road both were penalized for jumping the flag and the Brabham-Alfa

'Wing' car took on a new meaning with the ground-effect Lotus 78 that the team raced in 1977-78. Mario Andretti described it as 'it feels like it's painted to the road'. Andretti won the United States GP West, in Spain, France and Italy, whilst his team-mate Gunnar Nilsson won in Belgium. Here Andretti leads Lauda (Ferrari) at Long Beach. (*Nigel Snowdon*)

Romeos of Lauda and Watson were classified first and second. The last two races of the year went to Ferrari, Reutemann at Watkins Glen and Villeneuve at Montreal. Andretti won the World Championship with 64 points to the posthumous 51 of second-place man Peterson.

Ronnie Peterson, An Appreciation

by Alan Henry

(first published in *Autocourse 1978-79*, Hazleton with whose kind permission it is reproduced)

His Grand Prix racing career spanned the best part of a decade and, unrealistically, we though that Ronnie had become one of the 'untouchables'. The tall, blond-haired Swede with the perpetual coy grin and the self-effacing temperament had become an enduring pillar among the Grand Prix fraternity. His career started before Rindt had won his World (sadly posthumous) Championship, continued through the best days of the Jackie Stewart era and then into the days of Fittipaldi, Lauda and Hunt. Drivers came and drivers went but still Ronnie was there, more than ever this year justifying his affectionate nickname 'Super Swede'. Respectfully playing second-fiddle to Mario Andretti, 1978 was the season in which Ronnie had gambled 'taking one step backward to take two steps forward.' The gamble seemed to be reaping rich dividends: when he arrived at Monza, few people regarded him as anything but the first-class-top-liner he truly was. Second in the championship perhaps, but without doubt facing his best chance of winning the title in 1979.

Monza, 1978, could well have been one of the greatest days in Colin Chapman's life. It should have been a time of joy and happiness, celebrating Mario Andretti's World Championship, but it will be remembered simply as a bleak misery. Monza, the circuit which had rewarded Chapman's endeavours so cruelly in the past, was to become the back-drop for yet another Lotus tragedy. The tragedy that resulted in the death of Ronnie Peterson.

The bland facts of the matter are that Peterson's Lotus 78 was helped into a guard-rail not 300 yards from the start of the Italian Grand Prix thanks to the imprudence of another driver. The car erupted into a horrifying fireball from which Peterson was dragged, suffering badly broken legs, through the bravery of James Hunt and Clay Regazzoni. The fact that Ronnie was badly injured – for the first time in his career – was bad enough. But complications set in after a five-hour operation to set his shattered legs and he lapsed into a coma. In the early hours of Monday morning he died.

The accident shocked the Grand Prix world to the core; even the most hardened and experienced aces trembled. But this appreciation isn't intended to be an examination of the controversial sequence of events that led to Ronnie's death: it is intended to keep fresh the memory of the man generally regarded as the fastest Grand Prix driver of his era.

Bengt-Ronnie Peterson was a graduate from the cut-and-thrust world of kart racing from which, in the mid 1960s, he made his way into the hotly contested arena provided by the 1-litre Formula 3. In 1969, probably the most competitive year of all, Ronnie was the man to beat in Formula 3. His achievements were outstanding, his credentials substantially endorsed when he won the prestigious Monaco Grand Prix-supporting race in his works-backed Italian Tecno. From then on he never looked back.

Ronnie Peterson, one of the most popular drivers of the 1970s, initially with March, later with Lotus before rejoining March in 1976. He returned to Lotus in 1977 and stayed with them until his horrific crash at Monza in 1978. Peterson never won the World Championship, but he was highly competitive throughout his career and was a posthumous second in the Championship in 1978. *(Nigel Snowdon)*

When Max Mosley, Alan Rees and Robin Herd were laying the foundations for March Engineering, they needed a young driver to 'grow up' with them. Their choice, unsurprisingly, fell on Ronnie. For the best part of four years he was one of the Bicester family: he was tutored by the diligent Rees, disciplined occasionally by Mosley and learnt to work with the easy-going Herd. He won them the 1971 European Formula 2 Championship and, the same year, finished second in the World Championship at the wheel of the March 711. Colin Chapman offered him a drive, but March wouldn't let him go. He stayed with March throughout 1972 where, thanks to the abortive and unsuccessful 721X, his career took a step backwards. Nevertheless, Chapman still wanted him and he was signed to join Emerson Fittipaldi at the start of 1973.

From that point onwards, Ronnie proved devastatingly quick. Fittipaldi was reigning World Champion but, in Lotus 72s set up by the brilliant Brazilian, Ronnie was always faster. He won the 1973 French, Austrian, Italian and United States Grands Prix. Fittipaldi, unwilling to continue this sort of relationship, moved on to McLaren and another Championship in 1974. Ronnie stayed with Lotus, but proved unable to sort out the new 76. Nevertheless, he won the Monaco, French and Italian Grands Prix in the old 72.

The next three years were to provide a great deal of disappointment. In 1975 the Lotus 72 was desperately in need of replacement and only a fifth place, in the streaming rain at Österreichring, stood out to underline Ronnie's driving talent. In 1976, after one race in the Lotus 77, Ronnie quit Lotus by mutual agreement with Chapman and moved back to March to drive the straightforward 761. It was a different relationship, however, and although Ronnie won the Italian Grand Prix there was not enough finance to run the team as everybody would have liked. The 1977 season was an even bigger disaster with the six-wheeled Elf Tyrrell P34, a car which Ronnie realised wasn't going to do the job after only two races in it!

Then came the big gamble: with sponsorship from Polar Caravans and the Italian Count Zanon, Ronnie was installed as number two alongside Mario Andretti at Team Lotus. It was a controversial deal and one which sparked off a great deal of press speculation as to just how the two aces would work with each other. Andretti, if he was wary, concealed his feelings almost completely; Peterson, for his part, played his agreed supporting role to perfection. And, as a bonus, he stepped in to win at both Kyalami and Österreichring when his boss faltered.

Their final 'double act' was at Zandvoort, two weeks before the Monza crash. The two Lotus 79s ran nose-to-tail for the entire race distance, Ronnie occasionally coming alongside Mario 'to have a quick word' as the American used to joke about their regular close-running tactics. The

ultimate cachet to be bestowed on the Mario and Ronnie Show came from their team chief Colin Chapman who told me that 'Without doubt they were the most outstanding combination I ever had.'

But that was his racing. Beneath the blue helmet with its yellow peak was a very human individual, a family man with modest tastes and a simple charm that endeared him to everybody. Even in the hard-bitten world of Formula 1 you would have been hard-pressed to find anyone who didn't like Ronnie Peterson. Doubtless because he was prepared to race saloon and sports cars as well as Grand Prix machines, the fans loved him and the fact that he seldom drove anything with less than his maximum effort made them love him all the more. Truly, with Peterson it was a case of 'flat out all the way.'

It goes without saying that our sympathy is extended to his lovely wife Barbro and their little daughter Nina. The loss of any Grand Prix driver is an occasion for sadness, but particularly so in the case of this warm-hearted and thoroughly straightforward individual. Those who knew him and loved him will always recall his life and times with deep affection and genuine respect.

Alan Henry also wrote this superb profile of the 1978 World Champion, Mario Andretti, which is again reproduced with the kind permission of Hazleton Publishing.

Mario Andretti
by Alan Henry

STATISTICS can be notoriously misleading barometers of fact, but before saying anything else it is worth recording that Mario Gabriele Andretti, at 38 years of age, became World Champion racing driver in only his second full season of Formula 1 driving. Of his 12 Grand Prix triumphs to date, Mario has won 11 of them at the wheel of Colin Chapman's Lotus cars. When he became team Lotus's number one at the start of 1976, Mario and Chapman had little to offer each other except mutual regard. That they jointly turned each other's Formula 1 fortunes through 360 degrees in less than three seasons is a tribute to their total commitment and sense of purpose.

Mario, America's second World Champion following Phil Hill, has been racing 21 seasons and 'has always made a dollar. Even when I began, I got paid for my racing.' Now, after blazing triumphant trails through the specialised worlds of USAC and NASCAR, Mario has achieved one of his most burning ambitions, to become Champion of the World. 'That's something even my little daughter can understand,' beams Andretti.

Ground effect was a difficult concept and as Wolf designer Harvey Postlethwaite commented, 'If you're slightly out on your calculations, then you are completely wrong.' Mario Andretti won the 1978 World Championship driving both the 1977 car and the new Lotus 79, but the 'edge' that Lotus possessed was to wane as the season progressed. Here the 79 is seen in the pits on its Championship race début in the Belgian race at Zolder. Colin Chapman stands at the right front wheel. (*Nigel Snowdon*)

Before Mario took the decision to concentrate solely on Formula 1, he had amassed some pretty impressive racing credentials on the other side of the Atlantic. The Italian emigré who, as a little boy of 15, had cycled from his home in Lucca to watch Moss and Jenkinson flash through Firenza in their Mille Miglia-winning Mercedes-Benz and been fired with his original enthusiasm for racing by Alberto Ascari, had come a long way from his humble origins. Eleven years ago he won the NASCAR classic Daytona 500; he took a Ford prototype to victory at Sebring the same year and won his Indianapolis 500 victory two years later. That last-mentioned achievement resulted in the street where he lives in Nazareth, Pennsylvania, being renamed 'Victory Lane.' By 1971 he had won his first Grand Prix, the South African, in a Ferrari. But still he was not ready to concentrate on Formula 1, so he stayed predominantly in the world of the USAC ovals until the lure of fresh achievement threw him and Chapman together in 1976.

They had been together in the past. In 1968 Andretti

had been invited to drive a Lotus 49B at Watkins Glen. It was his first Grand Prix and he started from pole position, although he admits 'the car made it easy for me'. He failed to finish, but he remained on Team Lotus' strength as a 'third driver' the following year, driving both 49Bs and the abortive four-wheel-drive 63, the latter involving him in a spectacular accident during the German Grand Prix at Nürburgring.

In 1970, with backing from Andy Granatelli's STP organisation, Mario drove several races in a March 701. 'A pretty awful car,' he admits, 'I didn't talk to it and it didn't talk back to me. But I was new to the game and so were they. It wasn't a very satisfactory relationship at all. Then I had some time with Ferrari and he kept pressing me to live in Europe, which I wasn't prepared to do, and then I dropped out to concentrate on USAC.' It was a difficult decision for Mario, but he really didn't see the point of pursuing a Formula 1 career unless he was to do it well.

His return to the Grand Prix arena came at the end of

1974 when he turned up again as driver of the Maurice Phillippe-designed Vel's Parnelli car. A promising début in Canada was followed with a superb third place on the grid two weeks later at Watkins Glen, but this soon evaporated into one of Mario's biggest disappointments. The car had ignition trouble on the warm-up lap and started the race late. For the American driver, who had won the Watkins Glen 6-hours in a Ferrari 312P since his Grand Prix début there six years earlier, it was a massive opportunity missed. It hit Andretti particularly hard and he freely admits it.

The Parnelli effort went downhill in 1975, one major contributory factor being the non-availability of the Firestone racing rubber round which the car was designed. Mario's transatlantic commuting was even blamed by Phillippe for his apparent lack of racing form that season, but Andretti denies it had any effect on him. By the end of the season it seemed unlikely that the Vel's Parnelli team would continue far into 1976. They didn't.

But Colin Chapman was still watching. 'I'd always felt that if Mario were prepared to concentrate on European racing then he'd make World Champion,' he insists, 'but it took me the best part of 10 years trying to persuade him to do it. He went to March, to Ferrari, he even pinched a bunch of my guys to start his own operation *(Parnelli-Ed)*, *bu*t eventually decided to come home to us, and it's paid off...'

World Champion in 1978 Mario Andretti (left) with that great Champion of an earlier age, Stirling Moss, at that year's Spanish Grand Prix. *(Nigel Snowdon)*

On the subject of the transatlantic commuting, which Mario still keeps up despite his reduced commitment on the USAC front, Chapman makes it clear that he does not dictate any terms to Mario. Apart from joking 'think how much better he would be if he *didn't* do that commuting,' Chapman makes it clear that he does not influence Mario at all on such matters. 'We try to give him as much help as we can,' Chapman adds. The relationship between the two is very much man-to-man, the 38-year-old American standing out as a mature beacon in a world of transient young superstars. One gets the feeling that a sense of mutual respect prevents both Mario and Colin from pushing each other too far.

As Chapman's careful development of the ground-effect car principle has rendered conventional Grand Prix machines largely uncompetitive in little over 12 months, so Mario's painstaking development, testing and setting up of these machines has ensured the best has been realised from both the Lotus 78 and 79.

'The 79 has been a fantastic car this year,' Mario explains, 'but it's so critical to set up. If it's right, it's tremendous. But if you get a mix-up on the settings then I reckon "start again". I had to do that in France (as well as Canada) and then the car began talking to me again...'

Although some of Andretti's rivals maintain that his super-sensitive USAC approach − half a turn on the roll-bar, critical corner weighting and suchlike − is not really as necessary as Mario thinks, the balance of evidence is certainly in the new champion's favour. And Chapman backs this up quite firmly.

'We've learned one hell of a lot from Mario and we work very well together as a team,' says the Lotus chief. 'Formula 1 chassis adjustment is a very much more delicate and refined business than it used to be and I think Mario is a master of it. I think it's probably derived from his USAC experience and bringing that approach to bear on Formula 1 has made a great deal of difference.

'I feel only now are some of the other teams realising what it takes in this respect. Things like tyre stagger, corner weighting, small adjustments to ride heights and spring rates are so crucial now. I think that it's always been possible to get the cars balanced, but in the past it hasn't been as easy. Now, with such wide tyres generating such cornering forces and with tremendous downloads from wings, it's becoming increasingly important to make those minute adjustments to get the best from the cars and I believe that Mario is setting the standard in this respect.'

Did Mario's perfectionism ever drive Chapman to distraction? The Lotus chief laughs brightly. 'No, I can't say it has. When Mario thinks about something I think about it and 99.9 per cent of the times he's right. I don't think we've ever had a fight when he's wanted to do one thing and I've wanted to do something else. It just hasn't happened.'

This past year Mario concentrated on Formula 1 like never before, giving up all realistic chance to score his second victory at Indianapolis because the Belgian Grand Prix clashed with the first weekend's qualifying at the Brickyard. The sacrifice was worthwhile, of course, for he led the Zolder race from start to finish in the first-time-out Lotus 79. As a result of missing Indy qualification he relegated himself to starting the Memorial Day classic from 33rd position. Plans to commute backwards and forwards between Zolder and Indy by means of chartered Concordes, tantalising as they were, never came off.

But the new World Champion is adamant that he will not try anything like that again in 1980. In fact, Mario will be much more selective about the events he competes in from this point onwards.

'I'm increasingly finding the need to keep my time as free as possible,' Andretti explains. 'Not just from the point of view of the team but from the standpoint of looking forward to the next race. That was why I had to give up the Ontario 500 this year. For the first time I found myself not looking forward to the race. Now, when I go to a race I go to give 100 per cent and not just collect the starting money; that's too easy. I go there to work my ass off and give 100 per cent effort. But next year I'll revise my schedule to give myself a little extra free time.

'In the past I've gone through the schedule and thought, "look, there's a free weekend there," so I'd accept a race somewhere until I used to think "Oh God, no". It became claustrophobic, I felt I had no place to go. At the moment I'm doing what I really love, Formula 1, and because we need to do so much pre-race testing to keep on top of the tyre war I think I have enough for now.

'Next year Indy is a definite conflict. It clashes with Monaco, so it's definitely out for me. I'm not rushing backwards and forwards and I'm certainly not starting from 33rd place again. If I start from 33rd place it's because that's all I can qualify at. I'm not doing it because of mere circumstance. I'm going to leave my door open for some races, but there will be considerably fewer than this year. I'm just going to work real hard at Formula 1 and see how I feel. I'm past the stage where I need to do every race that I'm offered. I can get my satisfaction from doing what I'm doing now, and doing it to the best of my ability.'

A burning sense of competitive purpose attracted Andretti into Formula 1, although the American admits he could have languished in USAC trying to build up an all-time record of achievement. It was the sort of fresh challenge that he thrived on. But did his Formula 1 ambitions extend any further? Did he ever want to have his own cars or his own team?

No way. Mario is categoric and very much to the point

Lotus conference at the 1978 Spanish Grand Prix. Lotus supremo Colin Chapman is on the left, next to him is Ronnie Peterson, number two Lotus driver in 1978, World Champion-to-be Mario Andretti has his back to the camera. Peterson died following a crash at the start of that year's Italian Grand Prix, but was a posthumous second in the World Championship. (*Nigel Snowdon*)

on this matter. 'I suppose the original idea was to try to win the championship with an American car *(Parnelli-Ed)*. That looks good on paper, for sure, but Dan Gurney proved to be his own worst enemy for that very reason. Those sort of thoughts were very important to him. But I'm just a driver and that's all I ever wanted to be. I never wanted an Andretti car or any bullshit like that. I just haven't got those goals or ambitions, it's as simple as that. I'd like to see two or three American teams in Formula 1, simply from the point of view of increasing the interest in the sport, but that's it. As I say, I think if Gurney had been a little more objective about his racing he'd have been World Champion more than once, and I think Colin would back me up on that one. The public didn't know who Weslake was and he'd have had a lot more success if he'd fitted his Eagle chassis with a Cosworth engine.'

So Mario stayed as the pure 'driver only' and succeeded where Gurney, undeniably a brilliant competitor, failed. Aided perhaps by the fact that Mario is getting on towards 40 years old, that championship success and triumph is every bit as good as he expected.

'It really feels fantastic, better even than I thought it would. No let down. Only I know how much winning it means to me. We used to talk about it, Colin and I, and I realised just how many people had won titles in his cars. I didn't want to be the one who didn't. It was like at Indy when I went there in '64 with Clint Brawner. He said "stick with me and I'll get you to win at this joint." I thought "well, that's nice," but secretly wondering whether the old boy was blowin' off a bit of steam. Then it all worked out in 1969. I like that. I like people who think big and it's good when that sort of approach is rewarded.

'It's tremendous to have won the championship, but the character building part of the whole business is when you're close and haven't quite done it. The character-builders come when the engine blows up four laps from the end. It's a real test to see whether you can deal with that sort of situation. Last year we lost four races through unreliability, two when we were undisputably in the lead. But that's the sort of thing you have to face, and when you're not 21 any more it hurts. Before you're 35 you go like hell and think 'well, there's always another year, another year, another year...! But suddenly you think it's almost got to be now or never.'

As far as the future is concerned, Andretti plans to race for several more years yet. He has firmed up a continuing commitment to Colin Chapman's organisation and, although he has business interests ouside the sport, they have to run themselves. Until, that is, he has finished his career as a driver. And when he does that, he is adamant that he will come to motor racing only as a spectator.

'I've always said that I'm only involved in racing as a driver, a participant. I don't want to be a team manager or have my organisation. When I quit, I quit and only come back as a spectator. I've got a number of business involvements, but they've got to look after themselves although I'll want to expand them when I retire and get more involved. All right, by racing standards you're an old man in your early 40s. But by other standards you're still young with plenty of living still to do!'

After the particular brands of individuality radiated by both Niki Lauda and James Hunt, Mario's character provides a marked contrast. He is not as dispassionate about the buisness as Niki would have us believe he is, neither has he the convention-defying sense of outlandish fun demonstrated by James. He is a family man who would rather jet back across the Atlantic to spend three days with wife Dee Ann and children Mike, Geoff and Barbara-Dee instead of burning the midnight oil in a nightclub. For Americans he is a national hero, for motor racing he provides a stabilising influence, less volatile and impulsive

perhaps than his younger, immediate predecessors. In fact, he is another example of the fact that there is no 'standard image' racing driver. Like people in any other walk of life, they are varied as much in character and temperament as they are in nationality.

Nineteen-seventy-eight saw Mario Andretti achieve his most burning ambition, to become World Champion racing driver. But as he reflects over memories of black-and-gold domination at the wheel of Chapman's sensational Lotus 79, there is one major thing that mars his pleasure. Of course, that is the tragic loss of his team-mate and friend Ronnie Peterson, the man who fell dutifully into line behind and followed him across the finishing line on four separate occasions.

The loss of Ronnie hit Mario particularly hard. Although he started out being wary of the Swede's presence in the team, the two men quickly struck up a strong personal friendship and sense of trust. Ronnie abided totally by his role as number two and supported Andretti admirably.

'The association that Ronnie and I had was only really starting, particularly as we had some problems when he joined up last year. Looking back, it seems as though we both knew better. But those things either work out or they don't. You either slide right in next to the guy or not. I'd known him for so long and he was the sort of guy who I appreciated having around. I respected his ability and I enjoyed racing against him. He leaves a big gap. We grew together so much this year and spent our off-track time together, we always ate together, and you just can't imagine how much I was looking forward to racing him next year in that new McLaren and then sitting down and having a beer with him afterwards...

'That's the sort of thing that's so special about this business, particularly when you strike up the sort of relationship I'd got with Ronnie.'

1979

The pendulum swung yet again in 1979 and the dominant marque proved to be Ferrari with their new ground-effect 312T4; this possessed the combination of a very powerful engine, a superb gearbox and efficient Michelin tyres, a combination more than sufficient to overcome the ground-effect design shortcomings faced with the wide flat-12 engine. In contrast the latest Lotus 80 proved a disaster, mainly because the design produced too much downforce and made the car very difficult to control. For most of the year reigning World Champion Mario Andretti, partnered by Carlos Reutemann, was forced to race the previous year's 79 cars and Lotus failed to win a single Grand Prix.

Early in the year, however, the most successful marque proved to be Ligier, now using the Cosworth engine and the JS11, with aerodynamic work by the French company SERA and with engineering controlled by Gérard Ducarouge, formerly of Matra, proved a highly effective 'ground-effect' package. Laffite won for Ligier in the Argentine and Brazil (with the other Ligier of Depailler second) and Depailler again won for the team in Spain, but that was the sum total of the team's wins as Ferrari so rapidly grew in strength and reliability.

While Jody Scheckter, who had joined the team from Wolf, drove strategically, almost calculatedly planning his Championship victory, his team-mate Gilles Villeneuve drove with immense fire, determination, guts and sometimes lack of judgement. Villeneuve won from Scheckter in South Africa and an identical result followed at Long Beach. At Zolder Scheckter snatched the lead from Laffite to win his first race of the year and he scored another win at Monaco. It was after Monaco that James Hunt, now with the Wolf team, retired from racing. Hunt had said that 1979 would be his last season, but the Wolf had proved uncompetitive and so he made his surprise decision in mid-season. While the other drivers were at Dijon for the French Grand Prix, Hunt was spectating at Wimbledon. At Zolder Alfa Romeo made a return to Grand Prix racing after an interval of 28 years, but little success was to come the team's way.

The French race witnessed a comfortable win by Jabouille (Renault) and a fantastic duel between the Ferrari of Villeneuve and the Renault of Arnoux for second place. To quote *Autocourse*, 'While Jabouille [Renault] cruised serenely on, there was a battle behind of an intensity not seen for many moons. No one – not even Gilles [Villeneuve] or René [Arnoux] – knew how many times the Ferrari and Renault passed and repassed. It was lurid and exhilarating to watch; and later the two drivers said it had been fun!' Jabouille won by a margin of close to 15 seconds, but less than three-tenths separated second-place man Villeneuve from Arnoux at the chequered flag. This first Renault victory with a much improved car was to prove the real

boost for other teams to develop turbocharged cars.

All year the Williams FW07 cars, 'a Lotus 79 with just a few differences', as designer Patrick Head described them himself, had been improving and they probably had the best chassis of the year. Everything that Frank Williams had worked so hard for over many years came good at Silverstone where Alan Jones took pole position for the team and Regazzoni won with his Williams from the Renault of Arnoux. Jones later won at Hockenheim, from Regazzoni, at Holland and in Austria.

But Ferrari bounced back and when Scheckter and Villeneuve took the first two places at Monza the South African had clinched the World Championship. Alan Jones won again for Williams in Canada with Villeneuve in second place and Villeneuve won the last race of the year at Watkins Glen. Villeneuve, described by one Grand Prix commentator as 'perhaps the most tenacious fighter we have seen in racing for years' took second place in the Championship with 47 points to the 51 of Scheckter.

This is Alan Henry's profile of World Champion Scheckter, first published in *Autocourse, 1979-80* and reproduced with kind consent of the publishers, Hazleton Publishing.

Jody Scheckter
Champion at 11–1

'I suppose the first time I really appreciated that I'd won the World Championship was when I got home to Monaco a few days after Monza. I found that my laundry was returned in two days rather than four!' That calm grin crept across Jody Scheckter's face as he recounted his feelings during the first few days after his Championship clincher at Monza. We were talking over lunch in Montreal's Meridien Hotel the day before he was due to get out on the Île Notre Dame circuit to start practice for the Canadian Grand Prix, the first major race since he became Champion.

'Oh yes, and another thing. Somebody told me that I'd be running number one next year when I was chatting at Imola and, do you know, that really pleased me. Just peel off a number one from my Ferrari (Jody had ran number 11 throughout 1979) and I suddenly appreciated that was one of the things I'd really wanted all the time but I'd never really thought about it...'

So, at the age of 29 years, Jody Scheckter became the 1979 World Champion racing driver, a feat achieved by winning three of the season's fifteen qualifying rounds and achieving steady finishes in the top half dozen in many others, consistent with the revised points scoring system that was introduced in 1979. At the end of the day Alan Jones had won four races and Scheckter's team mate Gilles Villeneuve had equalled the South African's tally of three triumphs. But Scheckter had worked the system to his best advantage; he was Champion by the rules that prevailed at the time. And it's worth pointing out that he would have achieved the same result under the old, superseded, points scoring system.

Scheckter is a very different individual now as compared to the bouncy 23 year old who muscled his way into a third McLaren M19A at Watkins Glen in 1972 and turned the heads of the establishment by running fourth first time out in a Grand Prix. His progress in F1 seemed meteoric at the time. On his first F1 outing at Kyalami, for the 1973 South African GP, he planted his M19A on the outside of the front row − his second Grand Prix drive! Then he led the French GP at Ricard with the new M23,

South African Jody Scheckter who won the World Championship with the Ferrari 312T4 in 1979. He retired from racing at the end of the following year. (*Nigel Snowdon*)

frustrating the efforts of his more experienced fellows to such an extent that the normally ice-cool Emerson Fittipaldi got into a flap and drove his Lotus 72 into the back of Jody's machine, eliminating them both. Two weeks later his efforts stopped the British Grand Prix at Silverstone after he ran wide on the exit of Woodcote at the end of the first lap, triggering off a multi-car pile-up of horrendous proportions. . .

Jody used to be aggressive and punchy in the extreme. 'I remember when I was racing in the States in '73 I used to turn up barefoot to press conferences. I was King of the World, I was going to be the youngest Champion ever and win the title six times. Only when you get wiser do you realise it's probably best to be the oldest World Champion around. . .'

Since those heady McLaren days, Jody's career has progressed through Tyrrell and Wolf to Ferrari. On the way he collected the almost affectionate nickname 'Fletcher,' after the baby seagull in the book Jonathan Livingstone Seagull who kept trying to fly before he was ready to and continually collided with the cliff face as a result. Ironically, it almost seemed that Jody's career started to run out of steam towards the end of his Tyrrell period and that the initial sparkling promise might not be maintained. . .

It's particularly interesting to note that Jody's F1 debut came indirectly, as the result of Lotus offering him a drive in the 1972 Austrian Grand Prix. He declined, but made it plain to McLaren that, bearing his refusal in mind, they'd really have to give him a chance. That gave rise to Watkins Glen '72 and the part-time F1 programme with the Colnbrook team in 1973. Then came the full-time offers for 1974.

'I'd grown up amongst McLaren people as far as F1 was concerned,' explains Jody, 'and I suppose, almost unconsciously, I'd been drilled against driving for Lotus. A bit like parents unconsciously put prejudices in their childrens' minds. Anyway, Lotus came along with a ten page contract which rather frightened me and a list of "can't do this, can't do that." 'I didn't want to be bound by that sort of thing at such an early stage in my career. Then Luca Montezemolo rang up with an offer of a Ferrari drive. He said "do you want to live in Italy?" I told him that I'd live anywhere. He said "fine; we'll pay you so much and we want to know tomorrow." You see, I just wasn't ready for this kind of treatment so early on'.

With McLaren attempting to set up a Yardley backed team alongside their newly contracted Marlboro cars, it seemed clear to Jody that they wouldn't be able to keep Hulme, Revson and him happy. In the event Fittipaldi and Hulme drove the Marlboro cars, Revson went off to Shadow and Hailwood was contracted for the Yardley car. Scheckter went to Tyrrell alongside Patrick Depailler.

'Tyrrell was right for me at the time,' stresses Jody, 'but I stayed there too long. By the end of my second year I was ready to go. The first year was fine and I won a couple of Grands Prix, but by the end of 1976 I was ready to go. To some extent I think Patrick got some number one treatment towards the end of my stay at Tyrrell, but that was because he seemed to agree with everything, particularly about that six wheeler. I didn't see that it was a worthwhile improvement and I'm afraid I made myself rather unpopular by saying so. A lot of people had their lifelines hanging on that car, so I wasn't exactly loved for saying that . . .'

His relationship with Walter Wolf seems almost a hard-headed business affair by comparison with his other links. Cordial and pretty successful during their first year together, Scheckter progressively seemed to fall out of sympathy with Wolf throughout 1978. They almost won the Championship in 1977, but dropped away badly the following year when Harvey Postlethwaite's new ground effect machine took to the tracks. There was a good deal of bad feeling at the end of the contract when Wolf is believed to have been reluctant to let him test a Ferrari before the end of the season, but it was all tidied up by the time the '79 season began. Even so, one gets the impression that there's still a sour taste in the mouth here. . .

Then came Ferrari. Throughout the motor racing world shudders of horror vibrated from supposedly informed heights (including journalists such as the writer and, I recall, the editor of this authoritative annual!) Scheckter; at Ferrari. Heaven forbid! That stroppy South African upsetting all those volatile Italians: there's no way in this world . . .

Jody knew that life at Ferrari might be difficult, but equally he was drawn to them by their enviable performance record over the past few seasons. Like Lotus, they're a team that you can't keep down. But the season didn't exactly start on the most optimistic note. After being punted off the road in the first corner pile-up at Buenos Aires, the circuit doctor didn't allow him to take part in the restarted Argentine GP. They thought Jody's wrist was injured. In Brazil, he trailed Villeneuve home sixth in the old T3 and then spent the next two races finishing second to his team mate in the new 312T4.

Was Jody optimistic after the two South American races? 'Look, I had made the decision to join Ferrari and that was that. Now it may sound funny, but I don't care whether a car is good or bad once I've signed a contract. If it is bad, then I just consider myself unlucky and I've made a bad decision. But I've got to live with that. The time to worry is when you're negotiating contracts at the start of the season. Meanwhile, you've just got to do the best you can.

Scheckter in practice for the 1979 Monaco Grand Prix with his Ferrari 312T4. He retired from the race because of handling problems. (*Nigel Snowdon*)

'But Ferrari has been good. I thought things would be difficult, but I didn't find it anywhere near as difficult as I'd been told. I've enjoyed myself this year, even though I felt, if I hadn't been enjoying things, I'd have still got myself into one of the best cars with the best teams in the business. But as it's turned out, I have enjoyed myself!'

On the subject of Gilles Villeneuve, Jody reacts with an almost paternal degree of interest. 'I'd have probably won the Championship much earlier if I'd not got such a fast team-mate,' he smiles, 'but he has made some mistakes, mistakes which have probably cost him a chance of the Championship. I just wanted to do things my way. Do what I had to do and try my best. And it all turned out alright. I didn't get flustered under pressure and try too hard and start crashing which, on the face of it, I might well have done with Gilles going so quickly. Here I was, the established driver, apparently getting blown off by Gilles. . .

'Gilles is good, very good, but I see things in his driving that I used to do when I was younger. He regularly drops wheels into the dirt, but I try to keep the car off the kerbs. Sure, he kept up the pressure, but I was always confident'.

Apart from the normal Ferrari practice that if one driver is ahead, then the other one shouldn't pass him when running in 1-2 formation, Scheckter is adamant that 'no team orders came into effect this year. . .'

So what does the Championship mean to Scheckter? He's no great traditionalist, although he says he likes traditional circuits like Monza, adding the overall rider that safety is the paramount consideration. 'It can be an even greater sport if it's safer. There's room for more professionalism here.' On the political side of Formula 1 racing, however, Scheckter maintains an almost royal 'we have no opinion' silence.

Remarkably, perhaps, Jody feels that the whole business is too frantic, too intense and too competitive to be enjoyable. 'Very occasionally you get a certain feeling when you string together a really fast lap at Monaco; that's fabulous. But usually I find that I'm so far stretched all the time that I'm past the enjoyment stage'.

But Scheckter tries hard, admitting almost ruefully that he went to the Imola race a week after Monza with the intention of simply cruising round. Once he got onto the circuit he gave it everything he'd got. 'I can't enjoy doing things badly. I've got to give it everything or nothing at all. It's particularly important, for example, when you're trying to get the mechanics roused up to really work with you. . .'

So how long does Jody Scheckter see himself continuing in Grand Prix racing? 'I really don't know. I will continue with Ferrari at least until the end of next year, but beyond that I really don't know. I'd like to do it for as long as I gain self-satisfaction from participating, but I won't hang on too long once I've stopped enjoying things. It's too dangerous and professional not ro require a 100 per cent effort. . .'

1980

In 1980 Alan Jones and the Williams team achieved almost complete domination. The latest Ferrari 312T5 represented a superior 'ground effect' package than its predecessor, but lacked reliability and speed. Brabham and Ligier showed power and promise and Renault was still growing in strength, but Lotus, McLaren, Tyrrell, together with other less famous contenders, remained in the doldrums and the Wolf team had withdrawn.

The season started in the way it was to continue, with a win by Jones in the Argentine. René Arnoux won the Brazilian Grand Prix for Renault, but although the French team was to stay in racing until the end of the 1985 season it failed to achieve a complete breakthrough. A second victory for Arnoux and Renault followed in South Africa, with the Ligiers of Laffite and Pironi in second and third places. At Long Beach Piquet with his Brabham BT49 took pole position, snatched the lead at the start and led throughout to win from Patrese (Arrows) in a remarkable second place. Pironi and the Ligier JS11 won the Belgian race at Zolder, but Jones and Reutemann took second and third places with their Williams FWO7Bs. The Williams strength came to the fore again at Monaco where Reutemann won from the Ligier of Laffite and the Brabham of Brazilian Nelson Piquet whose greatness still lay in the future.

Alan Jones won the Spanish Grand Prix for Williams, despite overheating and after a series of retirements amongst the leaders. The race was however overshadowed by politics and the struggle for power between FOCA (the Formula One Constructors Association) and FISA (the Fédération Internationale de Sport Automobile, the governing body of motor racing). The prolonged wranglings between those who did (the Constructors) and those who organised (FISA) came to a head when the organisers of the Spanish race supported FOCA and rejected (and ejected) FISA. Alfa Romeo, Ferrari and Renault all supported FISA (the Cosworth users, the 'kit-car' constructors, supported FOCA) and withdrew from the race. It was eventually decided that the Spanish race did not count for World Championship points.

Jones followed up with another win at the French race, ahead of the Ligiers of Pironi and Laffite, won

Australian Alan Jones (left), the 1980 World Champion, and team boss Frank Williams who enjoyed well deserved success after so many years of effort. (*Nigel Snowdon*)

again at Brands Hatch from Piquet, but the roles were reversed in Germany and at Hockenheim Laffite with the Ligier won from the Williams entries of Reutemann and Jones. By this stage in the season Jones led the World Championship with 41 points to the 34 of Piquet whose position was the result of consistency. Jabouille won for Renault in Austria, but, again, Williams was not overshadowed and Jones and Reutemann took second and third places. At Zandvoort Piquet won and closed within two points of Jones in the Championship table.

A portent for the future at Imola was the appearance – but in practice only – of Gilles Villeneuve with the new turbocharged Ferrari. Piquet won the Italian race from Jones and Reutemann and now led the Championship by a single point. Although Piquet took pole in Canada, and Pironi with his Ligier led initially, the Brazilian retired his Brabham, and the Frenchman went ahead again to lead Jones across the line by a margin of 16 seconds. Pironi was however disqualified for jumping the start and the race was awarded to Jones – second on the road – and this clinched his World Championship. A final victory of the year followed for Jones at Watkins Glen and his final Championship score was 67 points to the 54 of Piquet and 42 of team-mate Reutemann. It was a more than well deserved victory, but the real shock of the season had been the complete failure of the Ferrari team. It had been a terrible year for Jody Scheckter, the 1979 World Champion, who retired at the end of this – for Ferrari – disastrous year. To quote, once more, *Autocourse*, 'Champagne has rarely been given to the man who finished 11th but the Ferrari mechanics sprayed Jody as he stepped out of the cockpit and walked down the nose and onto the front wing – which promptly bent under the strain. As Scheckter ended his career in a light-hearted but dignified manner, it was fitting that his successor should be receiving the applause for a drive that was worthy of a World Champion!'

Although drivers with Cosworth-Ford-powered cars won the World Championship in both 1981 and 1982, Grand Prix racing had reached a turning point. From 1981 onwards the turbocharged cars played an ever more dominating role.

Part 9: THE TURBOCHARGED ERA, 1981-88

1981

With Ferrari's switch to turbocharged power every team – substantial or insignificant – began to think in terms of developing or buying a turbocharged engine. The great disadvantage of the 'conventional' supercharger of former years was that with a supercharger a considerable amount of the engine power was absorbed in driving it. The turbocharger, however, is driven by back-pressure in the exhaust manifold.

A turbocharger consists of a small centrifugal compressor with a radial-inflow turbine mounted on a common axial shaft and driven by the exhaust gases. Both the compressor and the radial inflow turbine are mounted within their own casings. The radial-inflow drive turbine works in a temperature of at least 1000 degrees C in the exhaust gas flow. The exhaust gas speed in relation to the compressor is controlled by the turbine entry nozzle. A diaphragm valve, known as the wastegate, permits excess boost to be blown away to the atmosphere and maintain constant optimum pressure in the induction system.

The designer will endeavour to match the turbocharger to the wastegate so the desired boost level is maintained as constantly as possible. At corners where the throttle is lifted so that there is insufficient exhaust gas energy to keep the turbine spinning fast, opening the throttle will not immediately speed up the turbine because of the inertia of the rotor assembly. This throttle lag has always been one of the biggest problems with turbocharged engines. It was partly solved by reducing the turbocharger mass to a minimum, by lightening so far as possible the turbine

wheels and providing extra fuel flow when the throttle was first opened.

Throughout 1981 the Renault team, the pioneers in turbocharging, grew more and more competitive, while Ferrari, new at the game, scored two victories early in the season, but spent most of the time struggling, partly because of continuing mechanical problems and because the chassis of the 126CK was not up to handling the immense power of the turbocharged engine. During the year the ranks of the turbocharged cars were joined by Brabham whose BMW-powered BT50 appeared in practice at the British Grand Prix, but was not raced that year, and the Toleman with Hart 4-cylinder engine that was first entered at the San Marino Grand Prix at Imola in May, but did not qualify as a starter until the Italian Grand Prix in September.

There were other innovations in 1981. Lotus introduced the 88, incorporating carbon-Kevlar construction, and a unique twin-chassis concept. The aim was to solve many of the drawbacks of 'ground-effect' cars, particularly the very stiff suspension and the problems of car control and driver discomfort and physical stress that it created. The aerodynamic download created by the bodywork compressed directly on to the wheel uprights, while the secondary structure which carried the driver, fuel and engine was comparatively softly sprung. It was a concept of immense potential, but sadly it was held to be in breach of the regulations and after protests and counter-protests Colin Chapman had no alternative but to abandon the concept.

McLaren had been revitalised by new

management headed by Ron Dennis (soon to take complete control) and with John Barnard as chief designer. Barnard evolved for 1981 the MP4/1 car with a moulded monocoque using carbon composite. Within the limitations of Cosworth power it was an immediate success and McLaren still uses the same basic concept for the latest cars.

For 1981 FISA had banned sliding skirts, an important feature of 'ground-effect' cars. For months there had been conflict between FISA and FOCA and so FOCA decided to run their own race, the South African Grand Prix, in which sliding skirts were permitted, but of course this did not form part of the Championship series. This race was won by Carlos Reutemann (Williams) from Piquet (Brabham). The so-called 'grandee' teams, Alfa Romeo, Ferrari and Renault did not take part. In March agreement was reached between the parties and the so-called Concorde agreement, a *modus vivendi* between the two factions, was finalised. Six-wheel cars and four-wheel-drive were banned and only fixed skirts at least 60 mm above the track surface were permitted. As this resulted in a substantial loss of downforce, designers sought methods to lower the sidepods of the cars, thereby regaining some of the downforce. Gordon Murray of Brabham was the first to evolve an hydraulic system which raised the car to the required minimum height when it is stationery, but lowered it when it was moving so that the ground clearance was almost nil. Other designers soon followed Murray, there were the usual protests, but the system was held to be legal.

The Championship season started at Long Beach where Jones and Reutemann took the first two places with their Williams FW07Cs, a result repeated in Brazil save that Reutemann led Jones across the line. By the third race at Buenos Aires Piquet and Brabham had found their form and won from Reutemann and Prost (Renault). Piquet won his second race in succession at Imola, but Reutemann won again at Zolder from Laffite whose Ligier was once more Matra V12-powered.

So far in the season Ferrari – and Renault – had been overshadowed. Briefly, albeit, the pendulum swung once again and Villeneuve scored two remarkable victories for the Maranello team. At Monaco Villeneuve was second fastest in practice.

It was not until 1981 that a second turbocharged car was raced, the Ferrari 126CK, but the turbocharged revolution was now under way. Villeneuve scored two remarkable victories, at Monaco and in Spain. At Jarama by using the power of the Ferrari along the straight and holding off a howling pack of opposition through the corners, Villeneuve won by two-tenths of a second, but less than a second covered the first three cars. (*Nigel Snowdon*)

Although Piquet led much of the race until, under pressure from Alan Jones, he misjudged *Tabac* corner and hit the barriers. Jones assumed the lead, but an engine misfire developed and when he made a frantic stop for extra fuel, Villeneuve took the lead and won.

A second victory for Villeneuve followed at Jarama, but it was a victory of a very different kind. Although Laffite with the Ligier was fastest in practice, initially Jones with the Williams led until Villeneuve powered ahead when Jones made a rare mistake on lap 14 and ploughed into the sand. For the remainder of this 80-lap race the Canadian drove brilliantly, exploiting the power of the Ferrari on the straights and avoiding mistakes at the turns, while a hounding pack pursued him. At the flag just over a second covered the leading four cars – Villeneuve – Laffite – Watson (McLaren) and Reutemann (Williams). But the Ferrari bolt was well and truly shot and the remainder of the season was largely a Cosworth and Renault benefit.

Prost won for Renault in France, Watson won for McLaren at Silverstone (the team's first win since 1977), Piquet for Brabham at Hockenheim and Laffite with the Ligier V12 in Austria. Another Renault victory – Alain Prost at the wheel – followed in Holland. Thanks to good places Piquet (second in Holland) still jointly led the Championship with Reutemann. At Monza Prost led the Williams duo of Jones and Reutemann across the line and another Laffite (and Ligier) victory followed in Canada. Alan Jones won the last race of the year, the unattractive Caesars Palace Grand Prix, held on a tortuous configuration of that hotel's car park at Las Vegas, but Piquet finished fifth, enough to snatch the World Championship by a single point from Carlos Reutemann. Alan Jones finished third in the Championship and retired from racing, although he made occasional, later racing appearances. It had been a season of mixed fortunes, disappointing in many respects and the turbocharged cars still had to show their true potential.

1982

The 1981 season was totally overshadowed by Ferrari – not by the fact that Ferrari won the Constructors' Cup – but by the breakdown in relations between drivers Gilles Villeneuve and Didier Pironi, by Villeneuve's terrible death at Zolder, Pironi's later horrific crash and Patrick Tambay's subsequent fine performances. The World Championship was won by Finnish driver Keke Rosberg at the wheel of the Williams FW07C and the new FW08, but it is a

Nelson Piquet with the Brabham B49C in the pits at the 1981 German Grand Prix at Hockenheim. With wins in the Argentine, at San Marino and Hockenheim Piquet took his first World Championship. (*Nigel Snowdon*)

victory that is now almost completely forgotten. Brabham raced turbocharged BMW-powered cars in South Africa, switched back to Cosworth power and returned to BMW engines under pressure from the German company. Of the 17 teams competing in 1982, 11 still relied exclusively on Cosworth power and both Ligier (Matra-powered) and Alfa Romeo were still using normally aspirated engines.

At the first race of the year, the South African

By 1981 the turbocharged Renaults were beginning to achieve real success and Prost scored three wins for the team that year. Here Prost is on his way to a win in the Dutch Grand Prix at Zandvoort. (*Nigel Snowdon*)

Another new turbocharged car to appear in 1981 was the Toleman with 4-cylinder Hart engine. After struggling throughout the European season the team eventually achieved a finish at Monza where Brian Henton took tenth and last place. (*Nigel Snowdon*)

Jacques Laffite with the Matra-powered Ligier JS17 scored two victories in 1981, the second in the rain-soaked Canadian Grand Prix on the Circuit Île Notre-Dame at Montreal. Laffite took fourth place in that year's Championship.

Grand Prix, the drivers went on strike and refused to take part in the first day's practice because of a dispute over the wording of the super-licence contract which enabled them to compete in Grand Prix racing. Only after protracted negotiations did the race go ahead. Kyalami proved a Renault race and Prost and Arnoux took first and third places.

More problems followed in Brazil where Piquet (Brabham) and Rosberg (Williams) were first and second on the road, but disqualified, giving victory to third-place man Alain Prost. Because the British users of the Cosworth engine were worried about the ever-increasing power of the turbocharged Ferrari and Renault engines, they had been building cars of sophisticated and expensive lightweight materials which fell short of the 580 kg minimum weight limit. They circumvented this problem by using a water-cooled braking system with a large water tank. When the tank was full the car was above the limit, but after the start the water was quickly dispersed, bringing the cars well below the weight limit. The Cosworth users claimed that the regulations permitted them to refill the tanks before post-race scrutineering. In Brazil this was protested by Ferrari and Renault and on appeal the protests were upheld.

Next came Long Beach won by Niki Lauda (McLaren) from Rosberg and then it was the fateful San Marino Grand Prix at Imola. Ten of the 'FOCA' teams boycotted the race as a protest against the disqualification of the two cars in Brazil and so the runners were reduced to Ferrari, Renault, Alfa Romeo, together with Tyrrell (running because they had sponsorship from the Italian Candy washing machine company), the German ATS and Italian Osella teams and Toleman. Let Gerald Donaldson, with these extracts from his brilliant biography, *Gilles Villeneuve* (Motor Racing Publications Limited, 1989) take up the story.

The 1982 San Marino Grand Prix

Despite having the full weight of the crowd behind them, the Ferraris couldn't match the qualifying pace of the Renaults. Arnoux was on pole with a time of 1 minute, 29.765 seconds and Prost was beside him half a second slower. Gilles's time of 1 minute, 30.717 seconds got him third on the grid – and that final grid position of his life is now commemorated by a Canadian flag, re-painted on the pavement on the third starting spot at Imola each year.

Pironi's time of 1 minute, 32.020 seconds was fourth fastest, and in trying to achieve it he had a big accident. The number 28 Ferrari went off the road and backwards into a barrier at very high speed, and he didn't know why. 'The car suddenly snapped out of control. Maybe it was suspension failure, maybe a tyre. I'm not sure.'

Arnoux powered away in the lead at the start with Prost in tow, but the Ferraris overtook the second Renault before the first lap was finished. Prost retired with piston failure on lap seven and the San Marino Grand Prix became a three-car race. The Renault-Ferrari-Ferrari trio roared round in that order until lap 27, when Gilles overtook René and stayed there for four laps. The Renault regained the lead again and on lap 35 Didier overtook Gilles and stayed in front of him for half a dozen laps, then Gilles regained second place. The three front runners were separated by less than a second until lap 44, when the French machine spewed out smoke and then flame going past the pits, and the Italian cars took over the race.

The hordes on the hillsides around the Autodromo Dino Ferrari erupted in a roar of approval as Maranello's finest circulated nose-to-tail – with their idol in the number 27 car surely on his way to another Grand Prix win. Then the number 28 usurped the lead on lap 46 and three laps later it was 27 in front again, despite having been rudely chopped by 28 on the entry to the corner at Tosa. The fans loved it – the home team was obviously putting on a show just for their entertainment.

The crew in the Ferrari pit was without Mauro Forghieri, who was unable to be there because of a family problem. The Ferrari pit board 'SLOW' sign was shown to Villeneuve and he promptly eased off, slowing down by two seconds per lap to save the cars from unnecessary punishment and particularly to save fuel, which testing had shown would be marginal over the length of the race.

But on lap 53 Pironi was in the lead again, having speeded up surprisingly. Four laps later Villeneuve scrabbled sideways through the Acque Minerali chicane and seemed to be pressing after Pironi rather hard. On lap 58 he moved alongside Pironi under braking at Tosa and was again cut off in no uncertain terms and the crowd began to sense that the Ferrari manoeuvres were not being made lightheartedly.

Lap 59, one to go, and Villeneuve drove into Tosa ahead of Pironi and that appeared to be that. Number 27 immediately slowed down again as they went past the pits on their final lap. Then, as the matching set of red cars sped toward Tosa at 180 mph – through the right-hander that today carries the name Curva Villeneuve – number 28 pulled out of the slipstream of number 27 and chopped

While Didier Pironi celebrated his win in the 1982 San Marino Grand Prix at Imola, second-place man Gilles Villeneuve looks grim. Villeneuve believed that Pironi had won dishonourably and against team orders, and declared that he would never again speak to the Frenchman. He never did and within a fortnight Villeneuve was dead, killed in a practice accident at Zolder. Pironi was critically injured in a practice accident at the Hockenheim circuit and did not race again. Nevertheless Ferrari won the 1982 Constructors' Cup. (*Nigel Snowdon*)

in front in a brutally aggressive move that left the crowd gasping. There was neither room nor time left for a response and the cars crossed the finish line with Pironi in the lead.

On the victory podium Pironi waved to the crowd in triumph. Michele Alboreto was all smiles at having finished third in his Tyrrell. But the second-place man on the rostrum was there under protest. He wouldn't speak to Marco Piccinini and the team manager had to get Joann [Villeneuve's wife] to persuade Gilles to join his teammate in front of the Imola crowd. Gilles wore an expression of mingled fury and despair that was frightening in its intensity. It was very obvious to even those who didn't know him that something was desperately wrong.

Joann certainly knew exactly what was wrong because during the race her timing analysis showed the Ferraris were running up to three seconds slower when Gilles was leading. It became obvious to her that Didier

was intent on pursuing his own interests, not those of the team. Immediately after the awards ceremony, without having exchanged a word with Pironi, Gilles stalked off the podium, walked straight to his helicopter, and flew away to Monaco.

Didier Pironi joked about his victory being the perfect wedding present but his jubilation was conspicuously muted. Realising all was not well with his teammate, he made a defence of his result. 'Even Gilles knows that the "Slow" sign means only to use your head. It has to be interpreted as keeping your eye on your brakes, your tyres, your fuel, and so on. It certainly doesn't mean you, if you think you can win, don't do it. I do hope Gilles won't bear me any rancour. Time heals all wounds.' But time, the thirteen days of it remaining in Gilles Villeneuve's life, did not heal his wounds.

It was Marco Piccinini's task [Piccinini was Ferrari team manager] to try to smoothe the troubled waters after

241

Imola, and he remains reluctant to apportion blame. 'I have never said who was right or who was wrong and it would certainly not be productive at this stage. And also, the two people involved are not alive any more and it would not be loyal and not correct.

'I have a clear view of what I think happened and was sorry about what happened afterwards. Maybe it was because of the reduced pressure they had, with only fourteen cars racing and both Renaults stopping. Maybe that led them to forget they were in the same family. That's what I think happened.

'Pironi was very sorry for the situation which was generated and the two drivers met with Mr Ferrari, his son, and myself after the race in Mr Ferrari's office at Fiorano. We discussed the situation and I think at the end of the day something was also linked to the environment – the press, their friends, etc. – of each driver which maybe generated a certain degree of misunderstanding.'

Though Gilles vowed never to speak to Pironi again, he momentarily forgot himself that day at Fiorano. After Gilles landed in his Agusta, Pironi walked by and said, 'Salut, Gilles.' Giles nodded his head and replied, 'Salut' then immediately cursed himself privately. While he couldn't comprehend what he viewed as Pironi's act of treachery, because he would never have considered it himself, hatred did not come easily to Gilles. His mind was in a turmoil of conflicting emotions.

Thirteen days later Villeneuve was dead, fatally injured in a practice crash at Zolder, scene of the Belgian Grand Prix. Throughout practice there was a taut atmosphere in the Ferrari pit as Villeneuve implemented his vow not to speak to Pironi. Neither driver had been as fast in practice as had been hoped. Pironi was slightly faster on the Saturday and this spurred Villeneuve to greater efforts. Shortly before the end of practice, on what would have been his last lap, Villeneuve moved to the right to pass Jochen Mass (March), just as Mass moved across to let the Ferrari through. The cars touched, the Ferrari cartwheeled across the track, the nose dug into the sand. Villeneuve, his neck already broken, was flung out of the cockpit as the Ferrari flew on. The severity of the accident was only too obvious, and the Ferrari team packed up to return to Maranello. Villeneuve died that evening.

Many tributes have been written to Villeneuve, perhaps the finest was written by his friend, journalist Nigel Roebuck, published in *Autosport* for 13 May, 1982. If suffices here to quote from Roebuck's

appreciation published in *Autocourse, 1982-83*: 'Gilles has gone, and with him the light of genius in Grand Prix racing. In time, of course, another star will emerge to brighten the stage. For me, though, it will never twinkle with the same intensity again. We are back to normality once more. The impossible cannot happen.'

The Belgian race was won by John Watson (McLaren) from Rosberg. Only a single Ferrari was entered at Monaco and Pironi would have won but for electrical trouble on the last lap; he finished second to

McLaren was the most successful of the Cosworth users in 1982 and raced with great success the John Barnard-designed MP4B of carbon-fibre construction first pioneered on the cars raced by the team in 1981. Niki Lauda is seen in the British Grand Prix which he won. (*Nigel Snowdon*)

The 1982 Drivers' Championship was however won by Finnish driver Keke Rosberg with another Cosworth-powered car, the Williams FW08. Rosberg is seen on his way to a win in a new addition to the Championship series, the Swiss Grand Prix held in fact on the French Dijon-Prenois circuit. *(Nigel Snowdon)*

Patrese's Brabham. The Grand Prix circus moved on to Detroit where Watson (McLaren) won from Cheever (Ligier-Matra). Next came the Canadian Grand Prix, marred by a starting grid crash when young Italian driver Riccardo Paletti ran into the back of Pironi's stalled Ferrari and suffered massive internal injuries which resulted in his death a few hours later. When the race was restarted, the Brabhams of Piquet and Patrese took the first two places. By the Dutch race three weeks later, Frenchman Patrick Tambay had joined Ferrari and Pironi scored his first win for Maranello. The British race was won by Lauda (McLaren), but Pironi and Tambay took second and third places for Ferrari. In practice for the French Grand Prix Tambay was timed on the Mistral straight at the Paul Ricard circuit at 215 mph. The Renaults of Arnoux and Prost won the first two places, but the Ferraris were third and fourth.

Ferrari's second great disaster of the year followed at the Hockenheim Motodrome. It was another freak accident and it occurred in gloomy, wet conditions during the practice session on the Saturday afternoon. One of the problems with ground-effect cars in the wet was that the spray was forced under the sidepods and emerged as a fine, almost fog-like mist. In these conditions Pironi closed up on Daly's Williams and when Daly moved to the right to pass Prost's Renault, Pironi assumed that he had done so to allow the Ferrari through; Pironi's Ferrari hit the right rear wheel of the Renault, was launched into the air, landed on its nose and ploughed into a crash barrier which tore off the front section of the chassis. Pironi suffered terrible leg injuries and although Enzo Ferrari promised to keep a place open in team for him, the Frenchman never raced again. He was killed in a powerboat racing accident in 1987.

Tambay now carried a heavy mantle of responsibility as the sole Ferrari representative, but he took the lead and won the race after Piquet had collided with Salazar's ATS. In Austria Elio de Angelis won by the narrowest of margins from Rosberg's Williams and it was the first Lotus win since the 1978 Dutch Grand Prix. Tambay finished fourth after a pit stop to replace a punctured rear tyre. For the first time since 1975 there was a Swiss Grand Prix held on the French Dijon circuit and Rosberg (Williams) won from Prost. Italian-born American Mario Andretti joined Ferrari for the Italian Grand Prix and Tambay and he took second and third places behind Arnoux's Renault. The last race of the year was the Caesars Palace Grand

Prix at Las Vegas and young Michele Alboreto scored a rare win for the Tyrrell team. Although Rosberg won the World Championship (with 44 points to the 39 of Pironi) and Ferrari won the Constructors Cup, the spoils were remarkably divided:-

Brabham	3 wins
Ferrari	3 wins
Lotus	1 win
McLaren	4 wins
Renault	3 wins
Tyrrell	1 win
Williams	1 win

Yet another tragedy in 1982 was the death of Colin Chapman, one of the most talented and able of designers, who had built Lotus into a substantial public company, only to see it totter under the combined threats of recession and the de Lorean scandal, a project in which Chapman had been closely involved.

1983

In late 1982 FISA announced that 'ground-effect' cars would be banned and that all cars must feature a flat underbody within the wheelbase. The year was the last in which refuelling stops, innovated by Brabham at Brand Hatch in 1982, were permitted. Although these had come to form an exciting and tactical part of Grand Prix racing, the risk of a major conflagration in the pits was only too obvious. The ranks of the turbocharged cars were now joined by Lotus with the Renault-powered 93T (unsuccessful and replaced during the season by the improved 94T), Alfa Romeo, ATS with BMW power, and Spirit with the new Honda engine. Later in the year the TAG-powered McLaren was to appear.

It was to be another Piquet and Brabham year, by the narrowest of margins from Prost and the Renault, and they started the season with a win in Brazil, a race from which second-place man Rosberg was disqualified because his Williams had received a push-start in the pits. Watson and Lauda took the first two places with their McLarens at Long Beach, while Prost won the French Grand Prix for Renault with Piquet in second place. Patrese drove a brilliant race for Brabham at Imola, but lost the lead through a misjudged pit stop – Tambay won for Ferrari and Patrese crashed. At Monaco the Williams team gambled that a wet track

By 1983 the Brabham team was in their second season with the BMW turbocharged engine and raced the BT52B. With Piquet still as number one driver Brabham provided a formidable combination. Piquet snatched his second World Championship by a margin of two points, mainly through consistent performances during the year. He is seen in the Italian Grand Prix which he won. (*Nigel Snowdon*)

Andrea de Cesaris has had a long, hot-headed career as a Formula 1 driver but, now with the Jordon team, is still exceptionally fast. Seen here in the 1983 South African Grand Prix, he scored a remarkable second place with the turbocharged Alfa Romeo 183T. (*Nigel Snowdon*)

would dry out and Rosberg started the race on slicks; he took the lead on the second lap and went on to win, despite an engine misfire and badly blistered hands, from Piquet's Brabham. The Belgian Grand Prix returned in 1983 to the magnificent Circuit National de Spa-Francorchamps, shortened but not emasculated, and here Prost won from Tambay (Ferrari) and his new Renault team-mate Eddie Cheever. The first half of the season was completed at Detroit and Alboreto scored another remarkable victory for the Tyrrell team with Rosberg in second place.

In Canada it was Arnoux (Ferrari) – Cheever (Renault) – Tambay (Ferrari) and Prost won the British race from Piquet. Another Arnoux and Ferrari victory followed in Germany and Prost won the Austrian race (Arnoux second). Arnoux and Tambay took the first two places in Holland and Prost's lead in the World Championship was steadily being whittled away. Alain Prost appeared at the Italian Grand Prix at Monza, flanked by bodyguards, for had not during testing the *tifosi* (as the Ferrari supporters are known) dropped stones in front of the Renault and abused the Frenchman with animal noises. It was to no avail, for Prost was never in contention and retired with turbocharger trouble, while Piquet snatched an early lead and completely dominated the race. A new addition to the Championship series was the European Grand Prix at Brand Hatch. Piquet drove another storming race to win from de Angelis (Lotus) and close within two points of Prost in the World Championship. In 1983 the South African Grand Prix was the last race in the Championship. It was completely dominated by Piquet who led throughout, changing to hard tyres during the race and strolling home. The Brazilian won the World Championship, his second, with 59 points to the 57 of Prost and he was the first to win at the wheel of a turbocharged car.

1984

By the start of the 1984 season the turbocharged engine reigned supreme. With the Williams FW09 powered by Honda, Ligier by Renault and even the minnows of Formula 1 with turbocharged engines, only the Tyrrell team used the Cosworth-Ford engine.

After tentative appearances with their TAG-powered cars the previous year, McLaren International emerged in 1984 as by far the most successful team and one of the best organised that has ever competed in Grand Prix racing. Designer John Barnard, following a policy of careful and thoughtful evolution, had redesigned the monocoque of the 1983 car to accommodate the 6-cylinder TAG engine, which was shorter than its Cosworth predecessor, and to take account of the fact that there was a 220-litre fuel limit in 1984, as well as a ban on refuelling.

By 1984 the specification of the TAG PO1 engine had been finalised and the power output on race boost was now 750 bhp at 11,500 rpm, comparable with that of Renault, but rather less powerful than the BMW engine used in the Brabham. Problems with the early engines had included shortcomings of the Bosch Motronic engine management system and alternator failures, but these had been resolved by the start of 1984 and the ultimate efficiency of the Motronic system was to play a major role in the success of the TAG engine. Porsche were able to comply with McLaren's requirements for 15 race engines together with five extra sets of components by June 1984.

The one weak area of the 1984 McLaren was the transmission which was still a McLaren-evolved gearbox with mainly Hewland internals and not really up to coping with the power of the TAG engine.

Of the 16 Championship races held in 1984, McLaren won 12, with Prost, who had joined the team from Renault, winning seven, Lauda five and the drivers finishing 1-2 in two races. Prost and Lauda took first and second places in the World Championship and McLaren won the Constructors' Cup with the record total of 143½ points.

It is worth more to look at the races that McLaren did not win. In the Belgian Grand Prix at Zolder both McLarens retired, but the race was led throughout by Alboreto with the new 126C4 Ferrari, merely an updated version of the car raced by Maranello in 1983. Warwick took second place with his Renault, and the French marque was in decline. Piquet was at peak form with the Brabham in Canada and not only took pole position, but led throughout, and Lauda and Prost finished second and third. In a restarted race at Detroit following a multi-car crash Piquet, who had again taken pole, led throughout and Martin Brundle with the underpowered Tyrrell-Cosworth took a fine second place. Prost fell back to finish fifth and Lauda was eliminated by electronic problems.

The Detroit success was to lead to the Tyrrell team, for reasons that were totally ill-founded, being accused in effect of using fuel additives on the basis of traces of hydrocarbons in the water tank. The team was also found guilty of carrying unsecured mobile ballast (small lead balls in the fuel tank) and because there were drainage holes in the flat bottom of the car, a technical, but insignificant breach of the rules. Tyrrell

lost their Championship points and were barred from taking part in the remainder of the year's races, that is from the Italian Grand Prix onwards.

The only other McLaren failure of the year was at Dallas where both Lauda and Prost crashed and Rosberg won with his Williams – Honda. Undoubtedly the fastest driver of the year was Piquet who took pole position at nine of the year's 16 races. At the time McLaren's domination seemed something of a 'flash in the pan' and few would have believed that the team would be able to maintain supremacy for so many years.

McLaren Turbocharged Portfolio

For 1983 Ron Dennis of McLaren had arranged exclusive use of the Porsche-built TAG 6-cylinder turbocharged engine. The interim MP41/E car was first raced by Niki Lauda in the 1983 Dutch Grand Prix in which the Austrian retired because of brake problems. (*Nigel Snowdon*)

By 1984 the McLaren-TAG was supreme and won 11 of the year's 16 races, Lauda and Prost took the first two places in the World Championship and McLaren won the Constructors' Cup. In the last race of the year, the Portuguese Grand Prix, Prost and Lauda took the first two places. Here in practice at Estoril Lauda leads Arnoux (Ferrari) and Prost. (*Nigel Snowdon*)

In 1985 Prost won the World Championship for McLaren with the MP4/2B and McLaren again won the Constructors' Cup. At Monaco Prost won after other teams ran into problems. (*Nigel Snowdon*)

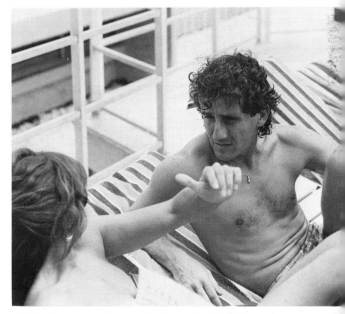

Alain Prost, seen here relaxing at the Brazilian Grand Prix, won the World Championship for the second year in succession in 1986. (*Nigel Snowdon*)

Alain Prost with the McLaren MP42/C on his way to a win in the 1986 San Marino Grand Prix. Following Lauda's retirement Prost was partnered by Keke Rosberg, but the Finn achieved little success. (*Nigel Snowdon*)

Racing in 1987 was largely dominated by Williams and Renault and Prost, by his standards, finished a poor fourth in the World Championship. The Portuguese race at Estoril was one of three won that year by Prost with the MP4/3. (*Nigel Snowdon*)

For 1988 the McLaren team was joined by Ayrton Senna. McLaren was now racing the Honda-powered MP4/4 cars and won 15 of the 16 races that year. Senna is seen here on his way to his second place in the Australian Grand Prix at Adelaide. (*Nigel Snowdon*)

1985

Despite Tyrrell's problems, for 1985 he was able to arrange to use Renault turbocharged engines and, with the new Zakspeed, driven by Jonathan Palmer, there was later in the season an all-turbocharged field. McLaren repeated their Drivers' World Championship and Constructors' Cup wins, but by a much narrower margin. Although the opposition was not strong enough to defeat McLaren it was strong enough to achieve a fair measure of success and the young Brazilian driver Ayrton Senna, formerly of Toleman and now of Lotus, de Angelis (Lotus), Alboreto (Ferrari), Rosberg (Williams), Piquet (Brabham) and Mansell (Williams) all won races – Senna, Alboreto, Mansell and Rosberg two each.

Throughout the year the McLarens were consistent – their consistency was their strongest card – while Ferrari promise, with wins by Alboreto in Canada and Germany soon faded; the Renault-powered Lotus was fast, but also unreliable, the Brabhams were also fast but unreliable (when Piquet won the French Grand Prix it was the first Brabham win in over a year and it was the first on Pirelli tyres since 1957); as for Williams, despite three wins, their greatest years in turbocharged racing were still to come.

Although Prost won the World Championship by a margin of 20 points from Ferrari's Alboreto, his team-mate Lauda, in his last season, had a thoroughly miserable year, failing to win a single race and crashing in his last appearance at Adelaide. The Austrian took a miserable tenth place in the Championship with 14 points.

Throughout the years of the turbocharged cars Ferrari was a consistent second, for the promise of 1981-82 was never fulfilled and the cars proved no match for either McLaren or Williams. In 1984 Maranello's only win was in the Belgian race at Zolder where Michele Alboreto (seen here) and René Arnoux took first and third places. The 1984 car was the 126C4, an updated version of the car raced in 1983. (*Nigel Snowdon*)

When Nelson Piquet won the 1985 French Grand Prix with the BT54 it was the first Brabham win for over a year, the team's only victory that season and the first win on Pirelli tyres since 1957.

1986

For 1986 FISA implemented a fuel capacity of 195 litres; it was hoped that by limiting fuel consumption, speeds would fall, but even more restrictive changes would be needed to contain the power of the turbocharged cars. Now that Niki Lauda had retired from racing, Prost was joined in the McLaren team by former Williams driver Keke Rosberg.

The year was one of mixed fortunes, the racing was close and there was a year-long battle between McLaren and Williams, with Ferrari and Lotus as good also-rans. Keke Rosberg's powers had faded, he was never fully at home at McLaren and to all intents and purposes McLaren was a one-driver team. Likewise at Lotus Senna lacked any real support, while Williams had the exceptionally strong two-driver team of Nelson Piquet and Nigel Mansell. At Brabham, Riccardo Patrese had been joined by Elio de Angelis from Lotus,

and the team was racing the new BT55 with BMW engine canted on to its side and 7-speed gearbox. The cars proved uncompetitive and the team's morale crumbled when de Angelis was fatally injured in a testing accident at the Paul Ricard circuit in May.

Piquet won in Brazil from Senna with the Ligiers of Laffite and Arnoux third and fourth, Senna scored a fine victory from Mansell in Spain and it was not until the San Marino Grand Prix at Imola that Prost scored his first win of the year. Another victory for Prost followed at Monaco, with Rosberg in second place. Mansell won the next two races, in Belgium (with Senna second) and Canada (with Prost second). Senna won at Detroit from Laffite (Ligier), while Mansell won at the Paul Ricard circuit and at Brands Hatch.

This Williams domination continued at Hockenheim and the Hungaroring (the scene of the new Hungarian Grand Prix) and Piquet won both races. Prost won again in Austria, Piquet and Mansell took the first two places for Williams in Italy and Mansell won again in Portugal. When Gerhard Berger won the Mexican Grand Prix with his BMW-powered Benetton ahead of Prost and Senna, the French McLaren driver had closed within six points of Championship leader Mansell's total. There remained but one race, the Australian Grand Prix, and Mansell, holding third place at Adelaide, seemed assured of the World Championship until the left-hand rear tyre burst while the Williams was travelling at close to 180 mph. Prost won the race and took the Championship by the narrow margin of 72 points, to the 70 of Mansell, 69 of Piquet and 55 of Senna. Clearly the days of the TAG-powered McLaren were numbered.

1987

For 1987 FISA required that all turbocharged engines be fitted with provision for a pop-off valve which opened if a pressure of 4-boost was exceeded. These valves were distributed at races by FISA on a random basis. It was yet another attempt to limit the power of turbocharged engines. For this year onwards there was an alternative category of 3500 cc for normally aspirated cars, the formula that was to replace turbocharged cars in 1989, and amongst the contenders in this category were the Tyrrells, the

Nigel Mansell came so very close to winning the World Championship in 1986, but a rear tyre failure at over 180 mph in the Australian Grand Prix put him out of contention for the race and the Championship. Mansell made a superb start in Australia, leading away from Senna (Lotus) and team-mate Piquet. (*Nigel Snowdon*)

In 1987 the Williams FW11B cars powered by Honda engines dominated and Piquet and Mansell took the first two places in the World Championship. Gerhard Berger however won the last two races of the year for Ferrari with the much improved F1/87 turbocharged car. Here Berger is seen on his way to his second victory in the Australian race. (*Nigel Snowdon*)

Larrousse Calmels team of Lolas and the Marches.

John Barnard had left McLaren in August 1986 to set up the Guildford Technical Office for Ferrari with the aim of developing a completely new car and his place at McLaren had been taken by Steve Nichols. McLaren continued to race the TAG engine, fitted to the improved MP4/3, but the team was to have the Honda V6 engine in 1988. Already Lotus had the use of the Honda unit and the 99T with computer-controlled 'Active' suspension and Senna at the wheel was to prove formidable competition for McLaren. Ferrari raced the new F1/87 car driven by Michele Alboreto and Gerhard Berger and Berger was to score two fine wins late in the year. The strongest team, however, was Williams and the Honda-powered FW11B cars, still driven by Piquet and Mansell, were to dominate the year.

Prost made a good start to the season by winning in Brazil from Piquet, but then Mansell won at Imola from Senna, Prost and Johansson took the first places for McLaren at Spa and Senna won from Piquet at both Monaco and Detroit. It was at the point in the season that the Williams' superiority asserted itself and the team won the next six races in succession: 1st (Mansell), 2nd (Piquet), French Grand Prix; 1st (Mansell), 2nd (Piquet), British Grand Prix; 1st (Piquet), German Grand Prix; 1st (Piquet), Hungarian Grand Prix; 1st (Mansell), 2nd (Piquet), Austrian Grand Prix; and 1st (Piquet), Italian Grand Prix. When Prost broke this run of success by winning at Estoril in Portugal it was his 28th Grand Prix win – and he had also broken the existing record held since 1973 by Jackie Stewart. Mansell won again in Spain, and Mansell and Piquet were first and second at Mexico City. Mansell non-started in Japan after a practice crash, and Berger won for a revitalized Ferrari team. A second victory for Berger (with Alboreto in second place) rounded the season off in Australia. Senna had finished second for the fifth time in 1987 at Adelaide, but was disqualified at post-race scrutineering because the Lotus was found to have oversize brake ducts. Although Piquet and Mansell took the first two places in the World Championship and Williams won the Constructors' Cup, it was too late to stop Honda from withdrawing the use of their V6 turbocharged engines.

For 1986 Elio de Angelis, stalwart of Team Lotus for many years, left to drive for Brabham (and was tragically killed in a testing accident at the Paul Ricard circuit in May). Senna was partnered by Johnny Dumfries. Senna won only two races during the year with the 98T (still powered by the Renault engine) and finished fourth in the World Championship. Although Senna disliked the Detroit street circuit, it was there that he won from Laffite's Ligier. Here at Detroit Senna leads the other Ligier driven by René Arnoux. (*Nigel Snowdon*)

1988

In a further attempt to curb the power of the turbocharged cars FISA imposed a turbocharger boost limit of 2.5 bars and fuel tank capacity to 150 litres.

For 1988 Ayrton Senna joined Alain Prost at McLaren and the Honda-powered McLaren MP4/4 won 15 of the year's 16 races. Of these Senna won eight, Prost seven and the team finished 1-2 in ten races. The team's ambition to win all the races was not to be, for in the Italian race Prost retired and Senna was eliminated when he collided with the Williams of Jean-Louis Schlesser which he was lapping. This one race was won for Ferrari by Gerhard Berger with Alboreto second.

Of the other teams there is very little that could be said. More and more teams were running 3500 cc cars, including Williams which, following the loss of Honda, had adopted the Judd engine. As the best of the also-rans, Ferrari took second places in Brazil (Berger) and Monaco (Berger), while Mansell finished second for Williams in the British race and Portugal and Capelli was second for March in Spain. So absolute was McLaren's success that there was little room for the others.

When the turbocharged era came to an end at Adelaide in 1988, it brought down the curtain on one of the most exciting eras in the history of Grand Prix racing.

Part 10: THE 3.5 AND 3-LITRE ERA, 1989-98

1989

When the turbocharged cars finally disappeared and the 3500 cc formula became universal in 1989, McLaren continued to be the most successful team with their latest MP4/5 cars powered by the Honda RA109E V10 engine. Of the year's 16 races, Ayrton Senna won six and Alain Prost four, as well as finishing second four times. But the year was not without conflict for the Woking-based team. In the Portuguese GP at Estoril, Mansell (Ferrari) and Senna collided after Mansell had been shown (but had not seen) the black flag, disqualifying him for having illegally reversed his car in the pit road. Also, throughout the season relations between Senna and Prost had become ever more strained as each strove to win another World Championship, their rivalry culminating in their cars colliding at the chicane towards the end of the Japanese GP. Although Senna was able to restart and finished in the lead, he was subsequently disqualified for having received a push-start and then bypassed the chicane in rejoining the track. This handed the title to Prost.

Of the other teams, Ferrari showed the greatest promise, but the John Barnard-designed V12 Tipo 640, with semi-automatic 7-speed gearbox, was unreliable. Mansell, a newcomer to the team, scored a surprise victory in his first race in Brazil, but thereafter retirement followed retirement. Meanwhile, team-mate Gerhard Berger survived an horrific high-speed crash at Imola with light burns, and Mansell's entry for the Spanish GP was suspended as a penalty for the incident in Portugal.

However, Ferrari and Mansell scored second places in France and Britain and thirds in Germany and Belgium, and with Berger taking a long-awaited win in Portugal and second places in Italy and Spain, Ferrari was certainly the best of the rest.

Boutsen and Patrese finished first and second in their Renault-powered Williams in Canada, and Boutsen went on to win the rain-soaked Australian race, while Patrese took second place in the United States GP at Phoenix, and again in Mexico. Benetton, meanwhile, made substantial progress with their Ford-powered B189 cars, Alessandro Nannini emerging a delighted winner of the Japanese race after Senna's disqualification. Of the other teams, Stefan Johansson's third place in Portugal with an Onyx was highly creditable, but the Leyton House March team, which had shown so much promise in 1988, disappointed, and the once great Team Lotus achieved virtually nothing, their lowest point of a miserable season being the Belgian GP, for which neither driver was able to qualify his car.

1990

Prost and Berger changed places, Prost joining Mansell at Ferrari and Berger becoming Senna's driving partner in the McLaren team, which again dominated the season to reach a level of supremacy unprecedented in Grand Prix racing. Driving the MP4/5B, Senna won six races and again emerged World Champion, despite being pressed hard all year by Prost in his Ferrari. But Berger found it hard to compete with Senna's brilliance, his best

In 1990 McLaren remained dominant, but the spoils were more evenly divided. Belgian driver Thierry Boutsen scored a fine victory with his Renault-powered Williams FW13B in the Hungarian Grand Prix. Riccardo Patrese also won the Monaco Grand Prix for the Williams team. (*Nigel Snowdon*)

World Champion Ayrton Senna scored six victories with his V10 Honda-powered McLaren MP4/5B in 1990, including the Belgian Grand Prix at Spa. He also took pole position in practice at ten races. (*Nigel Snowdon*)

In the Japanese Grand Prix at Suzuka Nelson Piquet was the winner with his V8 Ford-powered Benetton B190 and his team-mate Roberto Moreno took second place. (*Nigel Snowdon*)

Nelson Piquet (left) and Roberto Moreno on the victory rostrum at Suzuka in 1990. (*Nigel Snowdon*)

results being seconds in Brazil and Imola and third places in Monaco, Mexico, Germany, Belgium and Italy.

The Ferrari Tipo 641 was a much-improved car and Prost drove it magnificently all year. His first victory came in Brazil – the second race of the year – and he followed it with further wins in Mexico, France, Britain and Spain (where he was followed home by Mansell). By also claiming second places in Belgium and Italy, he was only 7 points behind Senna at the end of the year. Mansell, for his part, won in Portugal and was second in Australia.

Of the others, Riccardo Patrese scored a fine win for Williams in the San Marino GP, while Boutsen was second in the British race at Silverstone, but the Renault-powered cars lacked the staying power to sustain their challenge all season. The Benetton team was now under the engineering direction of John Barnard, and Nelson Piquet scored wins in Japan and Australia, having

earlier taken second place in Canada. Team-mate Alessandro Nannini also finished second in Germany, but his Grand Prix career ended tragically later in the year when an arm was severed in a helicopter accident, although brilliant surgery later enabled him to race touring cars. His place at Benetton was taken by Roberto Moreno, who finished second to Piquet in Japan. The other terrible accident of 1990 occurred at Jerez during practice for the Spanish GP, when Martin Donnelly's Lotus crashed after a suspension failure, his critical injuries ending a promising F1 career; Donnelly has since been operating his own team in the lesser single-seater formulae.

A sensation this year was the pace of Jean Alesi in his second season with Tyrrell, for whom he led the United States GP at Phoenix for a while and eventually finished second behind Senna. He was second again at Monaco, which led to an offer from Ferrari for the 1991 season, but where he was destined not to shine. Meanwhile, the Leyton House team (the March part of the name had now been dropped) made something of a comeback, Ivan Capelli claiming second place in France, while Aguri Suzuka kept his home crowd happy by finishing third in Japan for the Larrousse Lola team.

1991

When Ayrton Senna won the first four races of the new season with the latest V12 Honda-powered McLaren, while Ferrari looked dismal and other teams just mediocre, another year of total McLaren supremacy seemed in prospect. But the pendulum then swung the other way, and Nelson Piquet won for Benetton in Canada after Nigel Mansell's Williams-Rernault had stopped on the last lap, and then the two Williams of Patrese and Mansell finished first and second in Mexico. The new-found strength of the Williams team was soon much in evidence, and Mansell won the next three races in France, Britain and Germany, severely demoralizing McLaren and seemingly upsetting Senna's World Championship prospects.

But then Senna fought back, holding Mansell back in second place in Hungary before winning ahead of team-mate Berger in Belgium. Mansell took the chequered flag again in Italy, where Senna finished second, fractionally ahead of Prost and his Ferrari, and a Williams finished first again in Portugal, only this time it was Patrese at the wheel, Mansell having been black-flagged for receiving assistance away from his pit area after he had lost a wheel in the pit road as he accelerated back towards the track. By finishing second in this race Senna had regained the initiative, and although Mansell won again in Spain it was too late.

The McLarens dominated in Japan, and with his title secure Senna conceded the lead to his team-mate Berger before the end of the race as a gesture of thanks for the support he had received from him all year. The two had developed quite a bond, and later Berger, a notorious prankster, would remark: 'He taught me a lot about how to win, and I taught him how to laugh.'

With the World Championship already decided, the Australian GP was likely to bring the season to an end in an anti-climax, but in the event it ended in chaos, the race having to be abandoned after just 14 of its scheduled 81 laps when torrential rain had reduced visibility and adhesion so much

that car after car had crashed out of the race. The order at the front was Senna, Mansell and Berger when the flag was brought out to bring it all to a halt.

This year there had been a bright new team in the paddock, and Eddie Jordan could look back on his inaugural season as an F1 entrant with some satisfaction, both Andrea de Cesaris and Bertrand Gachot having scored points to earn him fifth place in the Constructors' Championship. Jordan's only disappointment was that he thought he had secured the services of one Michael Schumacher, until almost within hours of having done so – or so he thought – Benetton proved he hadn't. It was to be quite a loss.

1992

Nigel Mansell waited a long time to win the World Championship, a contest in which he had been runner-up three times, the first being way back in 1986, but when the time came he did it in decisive style. In the Williams-Renault FW14B he had the best car in the field, and in Riccardo Patrese he had a team-mate who, though fast in his own right, had no illusions about beating his British

The German Grand Prix provided one of the highlights of Jean Alesi's debut season with Ferrari, earning him a place on the podium alongside Williams drivers Nigel Mansell and Riccardo Patrese. Alesi also finished third in Monaco and Portugal. (Pioneer)

Martin Brundle did a sterling job for Benetton as Michael Schumacher's team-mate in 1992, scoring points in 11 of the season's 16 races and finishing on the podium five times, including here at Silverstone. Below, the colourful Benetton-Ford exposed. *(Ford)*

CAMEL BENETTON FORD B192

Riccardo Patrese was Nigel Mansell's favourite team-mate. At Silverstone the two Williams-Renault drivers finished 1-2 for the sixth time during Mansell's 1992 World Championship season, to the delight of his banner-waving followers. *(Rainer Schlegelmilch)*

driving partner on a consistent basis. It was not entirely surprising, therefore, that Mansell's car was the first across the finishing line in the first five races, for the Williams' speed was matched by commendable reliability, and in four of those races Patrese finished in second place.

By the time Mansell set off for Hungary and the 11th of the season's 16 races he had put three more wins into his personal record book, and although he had to give best to Ayrton Senna and his McLaren-Honda on this occasion, a comfortable second place ahead of Berger's McLaren was sufficient to put his points total beyond reach with five races still to go. Three of those he failed to finish (prior to that he had only retired once during the season), but in the other 12 races he won nine and was second in the other three. It was quite a swansong, for having failed to negotiate a new contract with Frank Williams he was off to America to write more headlines in IndyCar racing.

In the end it was Michael Schumacher who finished closest to runner-up Patrese in the points

Mark Blundell began his 1993 season well by driving his Ligier-Renault JS39 into third place behind Alain Prost and Ayrton Senna in the South African Grand Prix. *(Gitanes)*

table, his second place in the final race in Adelaide elevating him past the two McLaren drivers. Although he won only one race – the Belgian GP – his speed and consistency earned him points 11 times, an achievement matched by his Benetton team-mate Martin Brundle after his disappoiinting start to the season, which had brought him four straight retirements.

With Luca di Montezemolo back in charge at Ferrari there was hope that some order would be brought to the Italian team, which had failed to win a single race in 1991, but this dubious record was to be repeated, both Jean Alesi and Ivan Capelli suffering 10 retirements during a season which demonstrated that much repair work still needed to be done before the team could once again be considered serious contenders for victory.

1993

Although Mansell had moved on, the competitiveness of the Williams-Renaults had tempted Alain Prost out of retirement for one more season, much to the annoyance of Ayrton Senna, who also coveted what he saw as the best seat in Formula 1. So while Senna had one more season with McLaren, now having to make do with Ford V8 engines following the withdrawal of Honda, Prost was joined by Damon Hill, promoted from being the team's talented test driver. Senna also had a new team-mate in Michael Andretti, but Mario's son found Formula 1 quite a struggle and before season's end he had returned to the USA and Mika

Hakkinen, hitherto the team's test driver, had taken his place.

Prost, meanwhile, for whom seven more race wins would take his career total to a record 51, was able to cruise to his fourth World Championship, notwithstanding that Senna's virtuosity managed to earn him five victories, including an emotional one in Australia, where he took his leave of the team after six seasons. Hill scored his maiden win for his team in Hungary, then went on to claim the next two races in Belgium and Italy, but as in 1992, when he took his first GP win in Belgium, Schumacher had to be content with a solitary win, this time in Portugal. But significantly, throughout the year he had never finished outside the top three with the Benetton-Ford.

Jean Alesi had been joined by Gerhard Berger at Ferrari, where things were beginning to improve, albeit against a complicated background with John Barnard operating the team's advanced research facility in England and Harvey Postlethwaite handling the production and development side at Maranello. It was an arrangement which could not last. Nevertheless, Alesi's second place in Italy and third at Monaco, and Berger's third in Hungary, were confirmation of the team's growing potential.

Meanwhile, time was running out for Lotus, despite the best efforts of Johnny Herbert, who

Race-winner Prost, joining in the applause for Blundell on the podium at Kyalami, was heading for his fourth World Championship in his final season as a driver. *(Gitanes)*

managed to score points in four races, and Alessandro Zanardi, who did so once prior to surviving a terrifying accident in Belgium, which ended his season abruptly. Lotus would share sixth place in the Constructors' Championship with the new Sauber team, but although they would struggle on for one more season, their points-winning days were now at an end. It had also been a difficult year for another veteran team – Tyrrell – who failed to score all season, but at least they would soldier on for another five years.

1994

One weekend in Italy continues to dominate all recollections of the 1994 Grand Prix season. The miraculous escape of Rubens Barrichello from a terrifying accident during practice for the San Marino GP, followed the next day by the fatal accident to Roland Ratzenberger during qualifying

A pause during his tragically short time as leader of the Williams team as Ayrton Senna looks concernedly at the timing monitor during a pre-race practice session. (ICN UK Bureau)

David Coulthard beats Williams team-mate Damon Hill into the first corner at the 1994 Canadian Grand Prix. Michael Schumacher's Benetton-Ford and the Ferraris of Jean Alesi and Gerhard Berger are ahead of them, but Hill would come through to finish second to Schumacher. (ICN UK Bureau)

for the race. Then the startline accident when crash debris badly injured spectators, and the tragic aftermath leading to the death of Ayrton Senna almost immediately after the race had resumed. Echoes of Imola reverberated throughout the world in the days and weeks thereafter, and they led to a massive effort to improve circuit safety standards everywhere.

Against this sombre background, Damon Hill found himself suddenly elevated to team leadership at Williams, and he came close to winning what would have been a highly emotional World Championship until his car was crippled by a collision with Michael Schumacher's Benetton-Renault during the final race at Adelaide, which handed the title to the German by a solitary point.

Schumacher had been the pacemaker earlier in the year, winning the first four races, and he would score four more wins during a controversial season in which he earned two disqualifications, one for a driving misdemeanour and the other for a technical infringement. Hill, for his part, amassed six wins, the other two races going to Gerhard Berger, who in Germany scored Ferrari's first GP win since 1990, and Nigel Mansell, who guest-drove four

Rubens Barrichello and his Jordan-Hart beat the rain in qualifying to claim an unexpected pole position for the 1994 Belgian Grand Prix, which meant he led Schumacher and Hill on the formation lap. *(ICN UK Bureau)*

Nigel Mansell returned to Formula 1 for four 'guest' appearances with the Williams team and led the Australian Grand Prix after Hill and Schumacher collided while contesting the World Championship. It was Mansell's last GP victory. *(ICN UK Bureau)*

Copybook start. Schumacher is already clear of the field as his Benetton-Renault exits the first double corner of the 1995 Spanish Grand Prix ahead of Alesi, Hill and Berger. *(ICN UK Bureau)*

False start. Two weeks later at Monaco, Coulthard spins to a stop after being squeezed by the Ferraris of Alesi and Berger at Ste Devote corner. Out came the red flags for a stop and restart. *(ICN UK Bureau)*

races for Williams – which meant that Hill's regular partner David Coulthard had to step aside – and scored a somewhat fortuitous win in the season's finale in Australia following the Schumacher-Hill incident.

At McLaren, Martin Brundle had joined Mika Hakkinen as the team switched to Peugeot engines, but the technical arrangement proved less than satisfactory and would only last the one season. The closest Hakkinen came to victory was a second place in Belgium, but he finished third on five occasions, while Brundle was the runner-up in Monaco and was on the podium again in Australia. Meanwhile, Jordan, who had struggled for the previous two seasons, were back up to fifth place in the Constructors' Championship, where they had been

at the end of their first season. It was proving tougher than expected to reach the top.

1995

Although there had been some controversy over the manner in which the 1994 World Championship had gone Michael Schumacher's way, there was no dispute over the decisive way in which he won the 1995 contest, his points margin of his Benetton – now powered by a Renault engine under new 3-litre rules – over Damon Hill's similarly powered Williams this year being an emphatic 33. Nine of the 17 races ended with Schumacher spraying and swigging the victor's champagne, something which Hill was able to do four times.

Their two team-mates also climbed onto the

After his fourth victory of the 1995 season, Michael Schumacher shared the podium at Magny-Cours with Williams drivers Damon Hill and David Coulthard, all of them having used Renault Sport's new 3-litre V10 engine. *(ICN UK Bureau)*

Three-wheeling to victory at Monza. For the second time in 1995, Johnny Herbert was on hand to scoop up a win when Hill and Schumacher clashed while contesting the lead of a Grand Prix. The previous time was at Silverstone. *(ICN UK Bureau)*

top step of the victory podium for the first time. Johnny Herbert had found that being in the same team as Schumacher was a frustrating experience, for the team had been moulded very much around the German's demands, but at least he was handily placed to pick up an emotional victory at Silverstone after Schumacher and Hill had collided, and he did so again at Monza, where the two leading Championship contenders again clashed on the track. In the next race, in Portugal, David Coulthard, who had been challenging Herbert for the lead at Silverstone before being forced to make an unscheduled pit stop, took his first victory since joining Hill at Williams.

But the most emotional win of the year was in Canada, where Jean Alesi finally brought his Ferrari first across the finishing line at the end of his 91st Grand Prix and after so many earlier disappointments. He was joined on the podium by both Rubens Barrichello and Eddie Irvine, who had also made it the best day yet for Eddie Jordan since he had entered Formula 1.

Mark Blundell had joined Mika Hakkinen at McLaren for their first season with Mercedes engines, but this technical association, like the previous one with Peugeot, would have a difficult beginning and Hakkinen in particular was plagued with too many retirements. However, his second places in Italy and Japan indicated the team's potential before a high-speed accident in practice for the final race in Australia almost cost the Finn his life, which was only saved by the brilliant response of the medical team at the scene. After careful nursing he made a complete recovery and was able to demonstrate that his greatest racing days were still ahead of him.

1996

Damon Hill found himself with a new driving partner at Williams, who had recruited IndyCar Champion Jacques Villeneuve to replace David Coulthard, who in turn was to replace Mark Blundell at McLaren. But if Damon thought the Canadian – the son of the legendary Gilles – would

Eddie Irvine made a fine debut as a Ferrari driver, taking third place in the 1996 Australian Grand Prix at Melbourne. Here he leads narrowly from Jean Alesi, whose later attempt to pass the Ferrari driver ended with the Benetton off the circuit. *(ICN UK Bureau)*

A typical modern pit garage – clinically clean, heavily staffed and full of electronic aids. Rubens Barrichello's Jordan-Peugeot 196 with tyre-heating blankets in place before embarking on another test run. *(Jordan)*

pose limited opposition in his first season of F1 racing, the Australian race which opened the new season quickly dispelled the notion. Villeneuve not only started from pole position, but looked like winning the race until falling oil pressure forced him to ease up and follow Hill home.

Mission accomplished. Olivier Panis proved you can overtake on a wet track at Monaco. He started the 1996 race 14th on the grid, was 12th on the first lap and led from lap 60 onwards in his Ligier-Mugen Honda. *(ICN UK Bureau)*

However, three wins from the first three races gave Hill a good start to his World Championship year, and although Villeneuve won the fourth race, three more wins for Hill from the next five GPs suggested that he was well in control of the situation. They included a win in Canada, where understandably Villeneuve had very much wanted to win, but he turned the tables on Hill at Silverstone, where he claimed his second victory. Thereafter, Villeneuve became stronger by the race, two more wins in Hungary and Portugal ensuring that the Championship would not be decided until the final round in Japan. There, the wheel fell off his challenge – literally – sending his Williams off course, and Hill, who had been in command of the race from the start, went on to the 21st GP victory of his F1 career and a well-earned World Championship.

Michael Schumacher was now a Ferrari driver, the final and most expensive ingredient of the Italian team's continuing quest for Grand Prix glory. With Eddie Irvine a fully supportive number-two, Schumacher did well to score three wins against the odds in Spain, Belgium and Italy and he

Although Michael Schumacher's Ferrari was ahead in the opening seconds of the 1996 San Marino Grand Prix, David Coulthard's McLaren-Mercedes was soon past and led until Damon Hill took over and scored his fourth win in five races. Below, Monaco was wet again in 1997, and Schumacher was dominant from start to finish. *(ICN UK Bureau)*

earned a place on the podium in five other races, his driving skill, especially in the wet, doing much to overcome the inadequacies of his car. Highly paid he may have been, but he was proving his worth of every last lira that was coming his way

Jean Alesi and Gerhard Berger had moved in the opposite direction – from Ferrari to Benetton – but victory eluded them both, although Alesi collected points from 11 races and he finished on the podium eight times. Mika Hakkinen, meanwhile, did well to score points for McLaren from the first two races while still not fully free of the after-effects of his major accident, and his challenge, like his fitness, grew steadily as the season progressed, earning him three third places from the last four races. But David Coulthard came closest to scoring a victory for McLaren, finishing a close second behind the Ligier-Mugen Honda of Olivier Panis, who was the surprise winner of the Monaco GP, a rain-marred race from which five cars, including Schumacher's Ferrari, crashed out on the first lap and only four of the 21 starters survived to the finish, although a further three had covered a sufficient distance to be classified.

1997

Having run Damon Hill so close for the 1996 title, it was perhaps not surprising that the

THE 3.5 AND 3-LITRE ERA 1989-98

following year the World Championship should go to Jacques Villeneuve, although the way it did so was bizarre indeed. Heinz-Harald Frentzen had been preferred to Hill by the Williams team, but the former Sauber driver found it difficult to adjust to his new environment and he managed just a solitary victory at Imola, whereas Villeneuve's score was seven.

His chief opponent, therefore, became Michael Schumacher, who was finally driving a car more worthy of his talent and benefiting from excellent race management in the Ferrari pit by Jean Todt and Ross Brawn. Five victories and three second places had kept his challenge alive during a year when Villeneuve's free spirit had brought him into conflict with the authorities and earned him various penalties, culminating in his disqualification from the results of the penultimate race in Japan, where he had crossed the line in fifth place.

This meant that Schumacher led him by one point going into the final race in Jerez, Spain, which in turn meant that the Ferrari driver only had to finish ahead of him to take the title. For much of the race he did so, but when Villeneuve closed in and was poised to overtake at the beginning of the 48th of the 69 laps, Schumacher did the unthinkable and drove into the side of the Williams, only to come off

Giancarlo Fisichella's Jordan-Peugeot being chased by Jean Alesi's Benetton-Renault in Canada in 1997. They finished nose-to-tail, but in reverse order, close behind Michael Schumacher's winning Ferrari. Below, the overtaking moment of the year: Damon Hill takes his Arrows-Yamaha past Schumacher's Ferrari into the lead of the Hungarian Grand Prix. (ICN UK Bureau)

Heinz-Harald Frentzen's Williams-Renault and Rubens Barrichello's Stewart-Ford. Both drivers would have a difficult 1997 season, though relieved by Frentzen's victory at Imola and Barrichello's second place at Monaco. *(ICN UK Bureau)*

second-best as he slid off the track into instant retirement.

With Villeneuve's title now assured, he was able to drive his scarred car cautiously, allowing the McLarens of David Coulthard and Mika Hakkinen to close in and, after they had exchanged places under orders from their pit, overtake the slowing Williams on the last lap. Hakkinen had been handed his long-overdue first GP victory on a plate, but in the year ahead he would prove decisively his worthiness of it.

A second Schumacher was now brightening the F1 scene, younger brother Ralf having joined another young tiger, Giancarlo Fisichella, in a rejuvenated Jordan team. Both demonstrated great potential, but though Schumacher was first to gain a place on the podium, he proved accident-prone

The Williams team dress up for 'Blondie'.
Jacques Villeneuve's unpredictable hair
colouring was a feature of 1997. It was not
Schumacher's lunge at him in Spain which had
turned his hair white, but it *had* made him
World Champion. *(ICN UK Bureau)*

and his Italian team-mate produced the more
consistent results, including a second place in
Belgium. But at the end of the year he was off to
Benetton to join another youngster of great
promise, Alexander Wurz, who had stood in for
fellow Austrian Gerhard Berger – unwell with sinus
trouble – for three races and driven so well that he
finished third at Silverstone. With Berger
announcing his retirement at the end of the year,
Wurz was his logical successor.

1998

New technical regulations, resulting in
narrower cars and the introduction of grooved dry-
weather tyres, dominated pre-season testing, which
indicated clearly that the McLaren-Mercedes,
running in new livery, would be the cars to beat.

Gentlemen racers. So dominant were the McLaren-Mercedes before the 1998 Australian Grand Prix
that Mika Hakkinen and David Coulthard agreed that whoever left the first corner in the lead (it was
Hakkinen) would go on to win. So after a pit mix-up had put Coulthard ahead, he eased up to let his
team-mate back in front. The Finn was duly grateful, but the betting fraternity were furious. *(ICN
Bureau France)*

New name, new colours. In 1998 the Williams team promoted the Winfield tobacco brand. Here, World Champion Villeneuve leads Eddie Irvine's Ferrari at Imola. The unsightly side wings visible on the Ferrari were soon to be banned. Below, in 1998 more overtaking took place in the pits than on the track. Jarno Trulli's Prost-Peugeot having a quick wheel change at Imola. *(Prost)*

Ready for take-off. Alexander Wurz's Benetton-Renault about to be launched over Jean Alesi's Sauber-Petronas and Heinz-Harald Frentzen's Williams-Mecachrome into a multiple roll which would halt the 1998 Canadian Grand Prix. *(ICN Bureau France)*

With Hakkinen and Coulthard aboard they would stake almost permanent claim to the front row of the grid, their aerodynamic excellence widely attributed to the input of Adrian Newey, formerly Williams' aerodynamics expert and now McLaren's technical director.

But as the season developed, Ferrari also made significant progress, aided considerably by tyre supplier Goodyear, who made up all the ground lost earlier in the year to Bridgestone – McLaren's supplier – and taken the initiative, notwithstanding the American company's declared intention that 1998 was to be their last season in Formula 1, which they had supported so well since 1965.

Hakkinen had led the World Championship

points table all year, but Michael Schumacher had almost closed the gap and was poised go top of the table at the Belgian GP when, blinded by wheel spray, he ploughed into the back of Coulthard's slowing McLaren, running a lap behind, the Ferrari losing its right front wheel. This cruel twist of fortune, which resulted in a heated exchange in the pit road afterwards, was not the last of a whole chapter of disasters which, provoked by the capriciousness of the Belgian weather, caused this to be the most costly, damaging and potentially dangerous Grand Prix seen for many years, although happily no-one was seriously hurt. Carnage after the initial start resulted in 13 of the 22 cars being damaged, followed by a further 10 of

the 18 which – thanks to the availability of spare cars – took part in the restart.

But the day brought great joy to Eddie Jordan, who watched Damon Hill and Ralf Schumacher avoid the carnage and bring their cars across the line in a 1-2 photo-finish. For Hill, it was his 22nd GP success, but the other 21 had been at the wheel of a Williams, the car widely assessed at the time to be the best available, even though its 1998 successor had been found somewhat wanting.

Since winning the 1996 title Hill had spent a season in the wilderness with Arrows, relieved admittedly by the near-miss of a victory in Hungary when his car, losing hydraulic pressure, was overtaken on the last lap. Then, for 1998 he had joined Jordan with a specific mission – to bring them that elusive victory. That the mission was accomplished in such appalling conditions made the victory all the sweeter.

Grand Prix racing had come a long way in the 20th century. The days of amateurism were long past and it had become an activity fed by huge financial sponsorship which, thanks to television, played before a global audience counted in billions. Not all of the changes had been for the better – they rarely are – but the fact that countries are literally queueing up for the privilege of staging a World Championship Formula 1 race is the best possible testimony of its health and prosperity.

Wet weather again played into Michael Schumacher's hands at Silverstone, where he won the British Grand Prix against all the odds. But poor visibility would be his undoing in Belgium a month later, when he ran into the back of Coulthard's McLaren and emerged with a three-wheeled Ferrari. A delighted Damon Hill was on hand to pick up the victory, the Jordan team's first and his own 22nd.
(Zooom Photographic)